金砖国家可持续发展报告

创新金砖国家投融资机制，促进务实合作互利共赢

国家开发银行
对外经济贸易大学 著

Report on BRICS Sustainable Development (2018)

Innovating Investment and Financing Mechanism of BRICS Countries
Promoting Pragmatic Cooperation and Mutual Benefits

2018

中国社会科学出版社

图书在版编目（CIP）数据

金砖国家可持续发展报告：创新金砖国家投融资机制，促进务实合作互利共赢.2018/国家开发银行，对外经济贸易大学著.—北京：中国社会科学出版社，2019.4

ISBN 978 – 7 – 5203 – 4455 – 5

Ⅰ.①金… Ⅱ.①国…②对… Ⅲ.①世界经济—可持续性发展—研究报告—中国—2018 Ⅳ.①F113.4

中国版本图书馆 CIP 数据核字（2019）第 094440 号

出 版 人　赵剑英
责任编辑　卢小生
责任校对　周晓东
责任印制　王　超

出　　版　中国社会科学出版社
社　　址　北京鼓楼西大街甲 158 号
邮　　编　100720
网　　址　http：//www.csspw.cn
发 行 部　010 – 84083685
门 市 部　010 – 84029450
经　　销　新华书店及其他书店

印　　刷　北京明恒达印务有限公司
装　　订　廊坊市广阳区广增装订厂
版　　次　2019 年 4 月第 1 版
印　　次　2019 年 4 月第 1 次印刷

开　　本　710×1000　1/16
印　　张　28.75
插　　页　2
字　　数　467 千字
定　　价　150.00 元

凡购买中国社会科学出版社图书，如有质量问题请与本社营销中心联系调换
电话：010 – 84083683

序言一

2018 年是金砖合作第二个"金色十年"的开局之年，也是金砖国家领导人会晤十周年。在过去十年中，作为新兴市场国家的领头羊，金砖国家合作成绩斐然：取得设立金砖新开发银行、应急储备安排、工商理事会、智库理事会等一系列开创性、标志性成果；金砖合作机制逐渐成为南南合作的重要平台；金砖国家在世界贸易格局中的地位不断提升；金融合作成果显著，并且正在发挥广泛而深刻的影响；金砖国家人文交流合作覆盖的领域正在不断扩展。

国家开发银行是中国最大的对外投融资合作银行，是金砖国家银行合作机制的发起行和成员行，也是金砖国家智库中方理事会副理事长单位，在研究规划、中长期投融资、综合金融服务、风险防控等方面有着独特的优势，长期以来，以"融资＋智库"推动金砖国家务实合作，取得了良好的成效。截至 2018 年 9 月末，国家开发银行资产总额已突破 16 万亿人民币，国际业务贷款余额超过 3200 亿美元，覆盖 100 多个国家和地区，继续保持境内机构外汇贷款余额第一位。国家开发银行在金砖国家累计发放贷款超过 1000 亿美元，贷款余额近 550 亿美元，为促进经贸往来和经济可持续发展做出了积极的贡献。

在经济金融全球化时代，投融资合作对于经济社会的驱动作用日益显著。近年来，金砖国家在推动务实合作的过程中，已把投融资视为促进金砖国家经济发展、参与国际经济金融合作和治理的重要突破口。在刚刚结束的 2018 年南非约翰内斯堡金砖国家第十次领导人会晤上，中国国家主席习近平指出：当今世界正处在大发展大变革大调整时期，未来 10 年是"世界经济新旧动能转换的关键 10 年"，是"国际格局和力量对比加速演变的 10 年"，也是"全球治理体系深刻重塑的 10 年"，这给金砖国家务实合作带来了新的挑战，提出了更高的要求。国家开发银行作为国家高端智库培育单位，联合对外经济贸易大学共同编写了《金砖国家可持续发展报告（2018）》，以"创新金砖国家投融资机制，促进务实合作互利共赢"为切入点，全面梳理了金砖国家经济发展和投融资总体情况，阐述深化投融资合作的意义和目标，通过对金砖国家发展规划、重点产业以及外商投资情况的研究，提出金砖各国投融资的重点领域与产业，指出营商环境、法律风险、汇率风险，以及经济结构转型与产业革命对接面临的挑战四个方面是现阶段困扰金砖国家投融资合作的现实问题，并提出了针对性、前瞻性的建议，包括探索构建金砖国家多边评级机制，推动发展金砖债券市场，深化本币结算和货币互换，建设金砖国家多边投融资模式、"智库＋金融"合作模式，建设金砖国家框架内可持续投融资模式，探索数字经济（区块链等）在投融资领域的应用。

我们深信，在第二个"金色十年"，金砖国家将进一步巩固和拓展经贸财金、政治安全、人文交流等领域的合作，启动并推进金砖国家新工业革命伙伴关系，继续对世界经济增长贡献力量，为构建人类命运共同体而奋斗。一方面，金砖国家互相借鉴、携手合作，以投融资创新作为经济发展、务实合作、互利共赢的重要抓手，积极推动基础设施建设，提升城市化、工业化、信息化水平，不断培育新的经济增长点，增强国家核心竞争力，建立绿色可持续发展经济。另一方面，金砖国家坚定不移地推动、参与自由贸易和全球化进程，充分发挥各自在制造业、能源矿产、软件技术、金融、农业等领域的优势，扩大参与全球价值链的广度和深度，更好地实现与产业革命的对接。

希望本书能为金砖国家务实合作提供切实可行的政策建议和智力支持。未来我们将继续深化金砖国家在政治、经济、金融、贸易、社会、人文等领域的多层次、全方位合作，为推动金砖合作第二个"金色十年"从愿景变为现实，促进金砖国家共同繁荣发展贡献力量！

国家开发银行副行长

2018 年 12 月 14 日

Foreword I

2018 is the first year of the BRICS' second 'Golden Decade' for cooperation and the tenth anniversary of the BRICS leaders' meeting. In the past decade, as the bellwethers in the emerging market countries, the BRICS countries have achieved remarkable results in cooperation: a series of groundbreaking and landmark achievements such as establishment of BRICS New Development Bank, the arrangement of emergency reserve, the Business Council and the Think Tank Council. BRICS cooperation mechanism has gradually become an important platform for the South-South cooperation. The status of the BRICS countries in the world trade structure has been continuously uplifted. The financial cooperation has achieved remarkable results and is exerting extensive and profound influence. Humanities communication and cooperation scope in the BRICS countries are expanding.

China Development Bank (CDB) is China's largest foreign investment and financial cooperative bank, the sponsoring and membership bank under the BRICS banks cooperation mechanism and the unit of the Chinese Council vice chairman of the BRICS Think Tank. It has unique advantages in research planning, medium and long-term investment and financing, integrated financial services, risk prevention and control, etc. For a long period, it has been promoting the pragmatic cooperation of the BRICS countries with 'financing + Think Tank' mode and achieved good results. As of the end of September 2018, the total assets of CDB had exceeded RMB 16 trillion and the balance of international business loans had exceeded USD 320 billion, covering more than 100 countries and regions, continuously maintaining the first place regarding loan balance in foreign exchanges among domestic institutions. CDB has issued more than USD 100 billion loan facilities to the BRICS countries and the balance is up to USD 55 billion. It has made positive contributions to promoting economic and trade exchanges and sustainable economic development.

In the era of economic and financial globalization, investment and financing cooperation is playing an increasingly important role of driving the economy and society. In the recent years, in the process of promoting pragmatic cooperation, the BRICS countries have recognized financial investment as an important breakthrough to accelerate their economic development and participate in the international economic and financial cooperation and governance. In the just-concluded the 10th Summit meeting 2018 of the BRICS countries in Johannesburg, South Africa, Chinese President Xi Jinping pointed out that the world today is in great development, great change and great adjustment. The next 10 years are ' *the key to the transformation of the old and new kinetic energy of the world economy* ', ' *the key to accelerated evolution of the international pattern and strength comparison* ' and ' *the key to profound reshaping of the global governance system.* ' This has brought new challenges to the pragmatic cooperation of the BRICS countries and put forward higher claim. As a national high-end think tank nurturing unit, CDB jointly drafts *the BRICS Sustainable Development Report* (2018) Shorten as *the Report* with the University of International Business and Economics. With the goal of ' innovating the BRICS investment and financing mechanism and promoting pragmatic cooperation and mutual benefit ', it comprehensively reviews the overall situation of the economic development and investment and financing of the BRICS countries, and elaborates the significance and objectives of deepening investment and financing cooperation. Through research on BRICS development plans, key industries and foreign investment, it proposes key areas and industries for investment and financing of BRICS countries; it points out that the business environment, legal risks, exchange rate risks, and challenge for economic restructuring and industrial revolution are the practical problems that plague the investment and financing cooperation of the BRICS countries at current stage; the Report proposes targeted and forward-looking suggestions, including exploring and constructing a multilateral rating mechanism for BRICS countries, promoting the development of the BRICS bond market, deepening local currency settlement and currency swap, building a multilateral investment and financing model, a 'Think-Tank + financing' cooperation model, and a sustainable investment and financing model within the BRICS framework, exploring the application of digital economy (block chain, etc.) in investment and financing.

We are convinced that in the second 'Golden Decade', the BRICS countries will further consolidate and expand cooperation in economic, trade and finance, political security, humanities exchanges, etc., and initiate and promote the BRICS new industrial revolution partnership, continue to contribute to world economic growth and fight for building a community of common destiny. On one hand, the BRICS countries learn from each other and work hand in hand, make investment and financing innovation an important driving force for economic development, pragmatic cooperation and mutual benefits, actively promote infrastructure construction, upgrading urbanization, industrialization and informatization, constantly cultivate new economic growth points, strengthen nation's core competitiveness, and establish a green sustainable development economy. On the other hand, the BRICS countries unswervingly promote and participate in the process of free trade and globalization, fully use their respective advantages in manufacturing, energy and minerals, software technology, finance, agriculture, etc., expand the breadth and depth of participation in global value chains, and better implement the connecting to the industrial revolution.

I hope this book can provide practical policy advices and intellectual support for the pragmatic cooperation of the BRICS countries. In the future, we will continue to deepen the multi-level and comprehensive cooperation of the BRICS countries in politics, economy, finance, trade, society and humanities, promote the second 'Golden Decade' of BRICS cooperation from vision to reality, and contribute to the common prosperity and development of the BRICS countries!

Ma Xin

Vice President of China Development Bank

序言二

　　金砖国家合作是发展中大国合作的典范，旨在引领发展中国家共同发展，引领世界经济发展，引领新型国际发展。自 2009 年金砖国家领导人举行首届会晤起，金砖合作已经走过了十个年头。金砖国家在过去的十年中取得了卓越成就，其经济总量在世界经济中的占比从 12% 上升到 23%，几乎翻了一倍。在不久前在南非举行的金砖国家领导人第十次会晤上，习近平主席指出，当前世界经济深层次、结构性问题和地缘政治冲突、保护主义、单边主义直接影响到新兴市场国家和发展中国家发展的外部环境。金砖国家要把握历史大势，深化战略伙伴关系，巩固"三轮驱动"合作架构，让第二个"金色十年"的美好愿景变为现实。

　　对外经济贸易大学是教育部直属的全国重点大学，首批"211 工程"和首批"双一流"建设高校，在国际贸易、金融和法律等学科领域的研究位居前列。学校相关学院和下属的研究中心一直以来都在大力支持和推进有关金砖国家的研究和智库建设，旨在为深化金砖伙伴关系、促进新型国际发展合作、提升新时代中国开放经济发展的水平做出应有贡献。

　　2018 年 5 月，在由金砖国家智库合作中方理事会主办、对外经贸大学承办的"2018 金砖国家智库国际研讨会暨第十七届万寿论坛"上，来自全球多个国家的专家就未来金砖合作的全球性意义、合作新路径等问题展开了讨论。

　　此次对外经济贸易大学有幸与国家开发银行合作，联合编写了《金砖国家可持续发展报告（2018）》，对金砖国家的投融资机制所面临的挑战和如何创新进行了较为全面和深入的研究。报告对金砖国家经济发展和投融资的总体情况进行了概括和阐述，指出金砖国家的投融资合作发展潜力巨大，也是推动和深化金砖合作的重要基础。金砖国家投融资合作的目标包括完善全球金融治理体系、帮助各国实现经济结构改革、促进金砖国家基础设施建设及产业合作，以及深化金砖国家经贸往来等。

通过对金砖各国的投融资重点领域与产业和外商投资情况的研究，从营商环境、法律风险、汇率风险，以及经济结构转型与产业革命对接等方面提出金砖国家投融资合作所面临的挑战和亟待解决的问题。最后，报告针对创新投融资机制提出建设性思路与政策建议，包括探索构建金砖国家多边评级机制，推动发展金砖债券市场，深化本币结算和货币互换，建设金砖国家多边投融资模式、"智库＋金融"合作模式，建立金砖国家框架内可持续投融资模式，以及探索数字经济（区块链等）在投融资领域的应用。

希望此报告能为金砖国家未来的合作和发展提供多方位的视角与切实可行的经验借鉴。毫无疑问，金砖国家应不断深化合作，共同参与、维护、贡献全球经济治理，改革发达国家主导全球治理的局面，致力于维护公平正义的世界经济秩序，反对一切形式的贸易投资保护主义，通过主动开放和提高投资贸易的自由化与便利化推动全球化进程的发展，打造"金砖国家智库共同体"，实现金砖国家智库合作机制化、常态化，努力实现第二个"金色十年"，共同发展，共同繁荣！

对外经济贸易大学校长

Foreword II

BRICS cooperation is a model for cooperation among large developing countries, aiming at promoting developing countries to develop together, and leading the world economy and new types of international development. Since the first BRICS leaders' meeting in 2009, the BRICS cooperation has gone through ten years. The BRICS countries have achieved remarkable success in the past decade, and their economic aggregates have risen from 12% to 23% in the world economy, almost doubling. At the tenth meeting of the BRICS leaders held in South Africa lately, China's President Xi Jinping pointed out that the deep structural and geopolitical conflicts of current world economy, together with protectionism and unilateralism, directly affect the external environment for the development of emerging market countries and developing countries. The BRICS countries must grasp the historical trend, deepen the strategic partnership, consolidate the 'three-wheel drive' cooperation structure, in order to turn the beautiful vision of the second 'Golden Decade' into reality.

The University of International Business and Economics (UIBE) is a national key university under the direct administration of the Chinese Ministry of Education. As one of the first universities entering the '211 Projects' and 'Double Tops' Construction, UIBE has been ranked among the top in the fields of international trade, finance, and law. Relevant schools and affiliated research centers of UIBE have been supporting and promoting research and think tank construction related to the BRICS countries, aiming at making contributions on deepening the BRICS partnership, promoting new international development cooperation, and raising the level of China's open economic development in the new era.

In May 2018, hosted by the China Council of the BRICS Think Tank

Cooperation, the '2018 BRICS International Think Tank International Symposium and the 17th Annual Wanshou Forum' was organized and held at UIBE. Experts from many countries around the world discussed the global significance of the future BRICS cooperation and the new path of cooperation.

Now this time UIBE has the honor to cooperate with China's National Development Bank to jointly prepare the BRICS Sustainable Development Report (2018), which is a comprehensive and in-depth investigation on the challenges and innovations of the BRICS investment and financing mechanism. The report summarizes and elaborates on the overall situation of BRICS economic development and investment and financing. It points out that the development potential of investment and financing cooperation in BRICS countries is huge, which is also an important basis for promoting and deepening BRICS cooperation. The objectives of the BRICS investment and financing cooperation include improving the global financial governance system, helping countries to achieve economic restructuring, promoting infrastructure construction and industrial cooperation in BRICS countries, and deepening economic and trade interactions among BRICS countries. By investigating on the key areas of investment and financing of the BRICS countries, as well as their industry and foreign investment situations, the report proposes challenges and issues that need to be addressed in aspects such as the business environment, legal risks, exchange rate risks, economic restructuring and industrial revolution docking, etc. Finally, the report proposes constructive ideas and policy recommendations for innovative investment and financing mechanisms, including exploring and constructing a multilateral rating mechanism for BRICS countries, promoting the development of the BRICS bond market, deepening local currency settlement and currency swaps, building a multilateral investment and financing model and 'think tank + finance' cooperation model for BRICS countries, establishing a sustainable investment and financing model within the framework of the BRICS, and exploring the application of the digital economy (Block chain, etc.) in the field of investment and financing.

I hope this report will provide a multi-faceted perspective and practical experience for future cooperation and development of the BRICS countries. There is no doubt that the BRICS countries should continue to deepen cooperation, jointly participate in, maintain and contribute to global economic governance, reform the situation in which developed countries dominate global governance, commit themselves to maintaining a fair and just world economic order, oppose all forms of trade and investment protectionism, promote the development of the globalization process by proactively opening up and improving the liberalization and facilitation of investment trade, and create a 'BRICS think tank community' to realize the institutionalization and normalization of the BRICS think tank cooperation and strive to achieve the second 'Golden Decade' and common development and prosperity!

Wang Jiaqiong

President of UIBE

Abbreviation

ABS	Application in asset securitization
AIIB	Asian Infrastructure Investment Bank
ASEAN	Association of Southeast Asian Nations
BVI	British Virgin Islands
CDB	China Development Bank
CHIPS	Clearing House Inter-bank Payment System
CIS	Commonwealth of Independent States
CPTPP	Comprehensive Progressive Trans-Pacific Partnership
CPI	Consumer Price Index
CRA	Contingent Reserve Arrangement
DVP	Delivery Versus Payment
EIB	European Investment Bank
EIF	European Investment Fund
FDI	Foreign Direct Investment
FTA	Free Trade Agreement
GDP	Gross Domestic Products
IT	Information Technology
IBRD	International Bank for Reconstruction and Development
IDA	International Development Association
IMF	International Monetary Fund
KYC	Know Your Customer
LNG	Liquefied Natural Gas
NDB	New Development Bank
OECD	Organization for Economic Cooperation and Development
ODI	Outward Direct Investment

PPI	Producer Price Index
PISA	Program for International Student Assessment
PPP	Public-private Partnership Project
R&D	Research and development
SWIFT	Society for Worldwide Inter-bank Financial Telecommunication
SELIC	Special Clearance and Escrow System
UIBE	University of International Business and Economics
WTO	World Trade Organization

目　录

中文报告

English Report

Конспект

RESUMO

中文报告

第一章 开启金砖合作金色新十年，深化金砖国家投融资合作

一 2017 年新兴市场国家经济发展概况

（一）金砖国家引领新兴市场国家经济发展

进入 21 世纪以来，新兴市场国家①逐渐崛起，成为不可逆转的时代潮流。新兴市场国家普遍具有市场经济体制逐步完善、经济发展速度较高、市场发展潜力较大的特征。近几年来，随着世界经济向好及国际贸易和投资回升，新兴市场国家对世界经济增长的贡献率逐步增加。根据国际货币基金组织（IMF）的统计数据，2017 年，全球 GDP 总量为792809 亿美元。其中，新兴市场国家 GDP 总量达到271702 亿美元，占全球 GDP 的比重从 2006 年的 22% 上升至 2017 年的 34%，成为推动世界经济发展当之无愧的主引擎（见图 1 - 1）。

金砖国家作为新兴市场国家的"领头羊"，表现得更为亮眼。IMF 报告指出，在过去十余年中，金砖国家对世界经济的贡献率超过 50%。2017 年，金砖国家经济发展态势向好。从经济总量来看，金砖国家 GDP为 185574 亿美元，占新兴市场国家 GDP 的 68%；从国际贸易来看，金砖国家国际贸易总额为 32390 亿美元，占世界国际贸易总额的比重从 2006年的 11% 上升到 2017 年的 15%（见图 1 - 2）；从投资情况来看，金砖国家外商直接投资从 2006 年的 1389 亿美元上升到 2017 年的 2781 亿美元，

---

① 根据 IMF、MSCI、道琼斯等目前较为公认的机构列出的新兴市场国家列表，本书中说的新兴市场国家包括巴西、智利、中国、哥伦比亚、捷克、埃及、希腊、匈牙利、印度、印度尼西亚、马来西亚、墨西哥、巴基斯坦、秘鲁、菲律宾、俄罗斯、南非、泰国、土耳其、阿拉伯联合酋长国、朝鲜、波兰和卡塔尔。

境外直接投资从 2006 年的 1028 亿美元上升到 2017 年的 1654 亿美元（见图 1 – 3）。

（10亿美元）

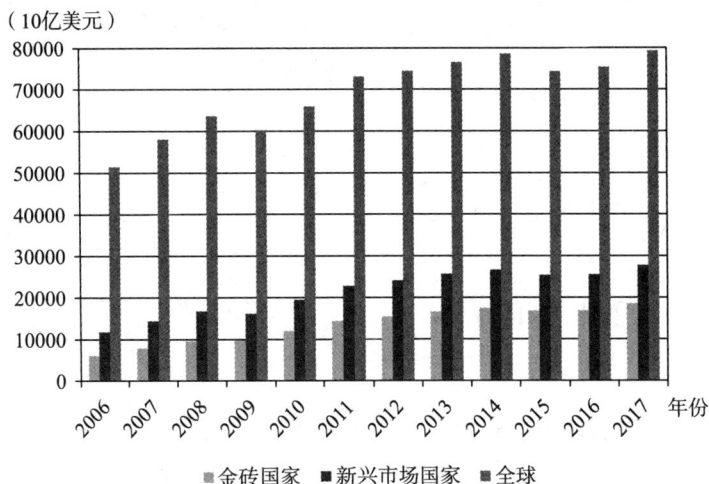

图 1 – 1　2006—2017 年金砖国家、新兴市场国家和全球 GDP 对比情况

资料来源：国际货币基金组织。

（百万美元）

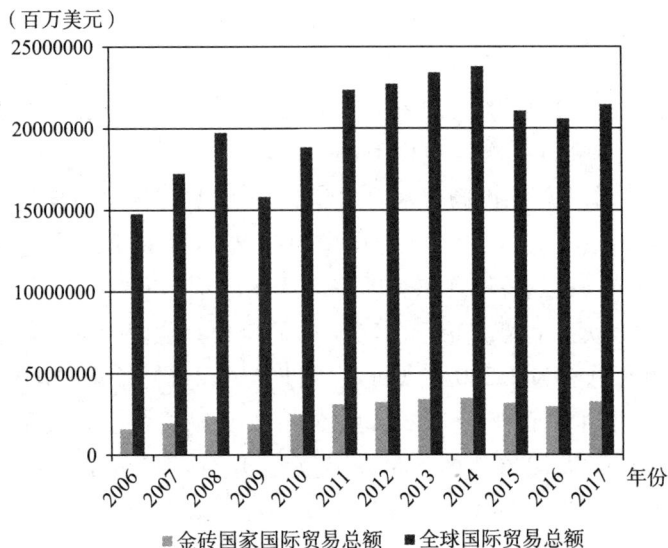

图 1 – 2　2006—2017 年金砖国家和全球国际贸易总额对比情况

资料来源：UNCTAD 和国际货币基金组织。

（百万美元）

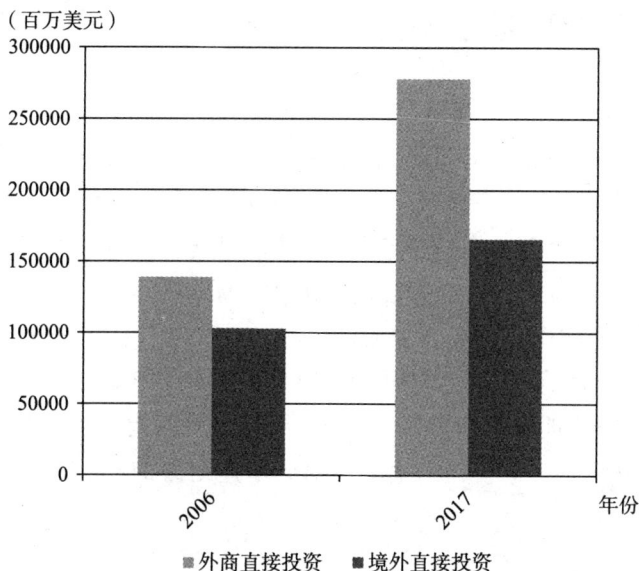

**图 1-3　2006 年和 2017 年金砖国家外商直接投资和
境外直接投资对比情况**

资料来源：CEIC。

　　从金砖国家之间的比较来看，2017 年，在 GDP 增长率方面，中国与印度的 GDP 增长率较快，超过 6%，巴西、俄罗斯和南非均在 1% 左右；在人均 GDP 方面，巴西、中国、俄罗斯和南非均步入中高收入国家行列，而印度人均 GDP 虽较 2016 年有所增长，但仍属于中低收入国家。[①] 在汇率方面，中国人民币、印度卢比兑美元的汇率窄幅波动，波动率保持在正负 2% 以内，巴西雷亚尔、俄罗斯卢布兑美元的汇率在正负 4% 的范围内波动，南非兰特兑美元的汇率波动幅度最大，最高达 6% 左右。

　　金砖国家一直致力于建立更为平衡、包容的经济伙伴关系。在合作起步阶段，面对国际金融危机的巨大冲击，各成员国携手共进，共渡难关。2017 年，随着全球经济的稳步向好，金砖国家在巩固和深化务实合

---

　　① 根据世界银行公布的数据，2017 年按人均 GDP 水平划分，国别的分组标准为：高于 12235 美元为高收入国家，在 3956—12235 美元的为中高收入国家，在 1006—3955 美元的为中低收入国家，低于 1005 美元的为低收入国家。

作的同时，也各自实现了国内经济的复苏与发展。

1. 巴西

自2011年起，由于劳动力匮乏、工业生产力低下以及国际需求疲软，巴西经济增长趋缓，甚至有衰退的迹象。自2017年以来，为了摆脱衰退并刺激经济复苏，巴西政府加大结构性改革力度，初见成效。巴西实体经济有所发展，消费者信心稳定，劳工市场状况也逐渐改善。总的来说，巴西仍然为一个综合发展潜力较强的新兴市场国家。

（1）GDP及GDP增长率

得益于世界经济环境的整体改善和政府的改革新政，2017年，巴西经济复苏较为明显，实现了自2014年以来的首次增长。2017年，巴西GDP回升至2万亿美元的水平，GDP增速约为1%（见图1-4）。

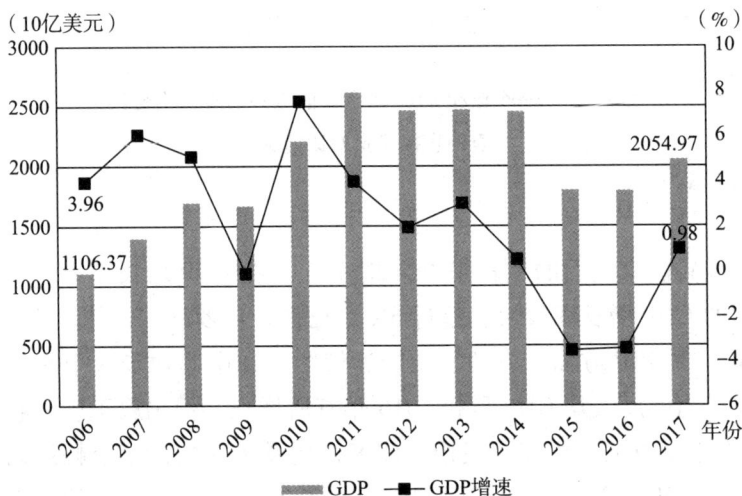

图1-4　2006—2017年巴西GDP及GDP增速变化情况

资料来源：国际货币基金组织。

（2）人均GDP

2017年，巴西人均GDP小幅增长，接近1万美元的关口，较2006年增长约70%，但是，较2011年的高点下降约25%（见图1-5）。

（美元）

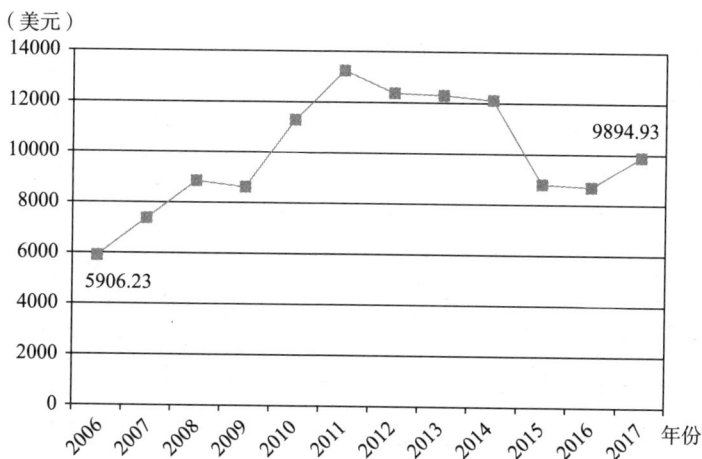

图 1-5　2006—2017 年巴西人均 GDP 变化情况

资料来源：国际货币基金组织。

（3）居民消费价格指数（CPI）和生产价格指数（PPI）

自 2006 年以来，巴西的通货膨胀率增长缓慢，最高达到 9%，而且生产价格指数常年波动较大。2017 年，巴西的通货膨胀得到有效控制，降至 3.4%，创下 19 年以来的新低，生产价格指数增长率也下降至 -2.5%（见图1-6）。这主要得益于当年巴西粮食产量的增长，抑制了大部分食品价格的上涨。

（4）失业率

2017 年，巴西就业市场持续恶化，失业人数大幅增加，失业率上升至 12.8%。巴西虽然经济态势向好，但是，国内失业率自 2014 年持续增加，就业形势依旧严峻（见图 1-7）。未来，巴西政府加大政府投资力度，进行基础设施建设，巴西劳动力市场将会得到改善。

（5）商品服务进出口增长率

随着全球经济的持续复苏及大宗商品价格的回升，巴西对外贸易增速明显回升，成为推动经济增长的主要动力。2017 年，巴西对外贸易出口和进口分别增长 10.9% 和 3.8%，外贸顺差达 670 亿美元，创 29 年以来最好成绩（见图 1-8）。

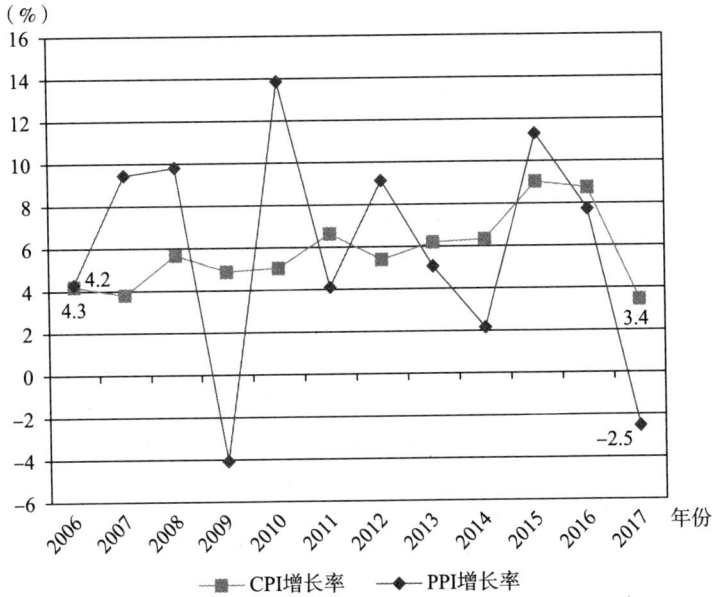

图 1-6 2006—2017 年巴西 CPI 增长率和 PPI 增长率变化情况

资料来源：国际货币基金组织。

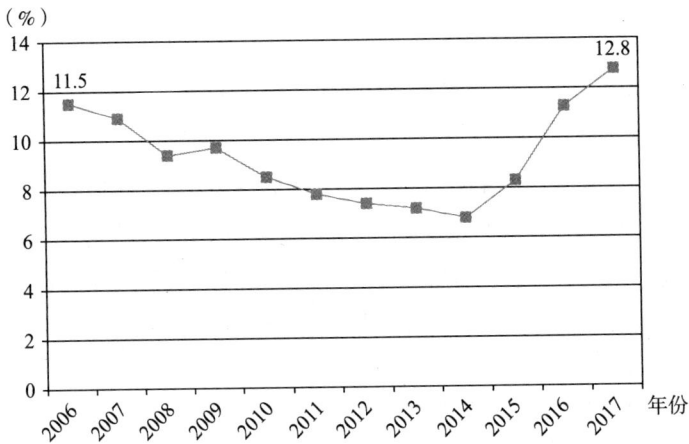

图 1-7 2006—2017 年巴西失业率变化情况

资料来源：联合国统计局。

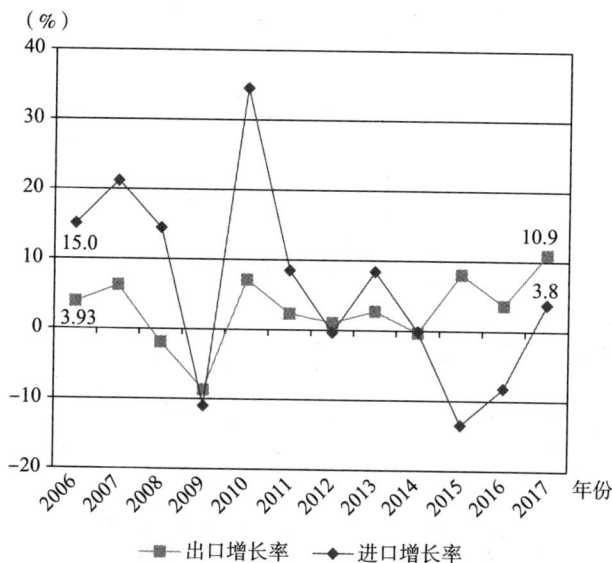

图 1-8　2006—2017 年巴西商品服务进出口增长率变化情况

资料来源：国际货币基金组织。

（6）外商直接投资（FDI）和对外直接投资（ODI）

2017 年，巴西的外商直接投资和直接对外投资都出现了小幅下降，分别为 703.3 亿美元和 62.7 亿美元。2008 年国际金融危机后，巴西的外商直接投资连续两年大幅增长，随后开始逐年下降。尽管在 2014 年实现了增长，但是，由于国内经济及政治出现了危机，外商直接投资整体上呈下降趋势。但是，在新兴市场国家中，巴西对外资仍保持着吸引力。

2008 年的国际金融危机对巴西的对外投资政策影响较大，对外直接投资额在 2009 年降至负数。2017 年，巴西的对外直接投资延续了自 2014 年开始的下降趋势，较 2016 年下降约 50%（见图 1-9）。

（7）汇率

2006—2011 年，巴西雷亚尔兑美元汇率一直处于较低的水平并缓慢升值。自 2012 年起，雷亚尔逐年贬值，并在 2016 年达至最高点。经济疲软、美联储升息以及大宗商品价格大幅下调等是造成雷亚尔贬值的主要原因。随着 2017 年经济形势的改善，巴西雷亚尔兑美元汇率较 2016 年实现了小幅升值（见图 1-10）。

（亿美元）

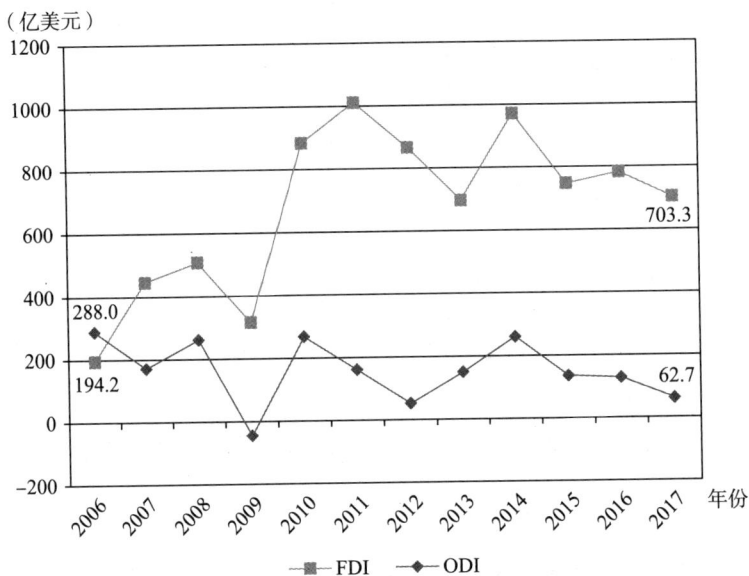

图 1 - 9 2006—2017 年巴西 FDI 与 ODI 变化情况

资料来源：CEIC。

（雷亚尔）

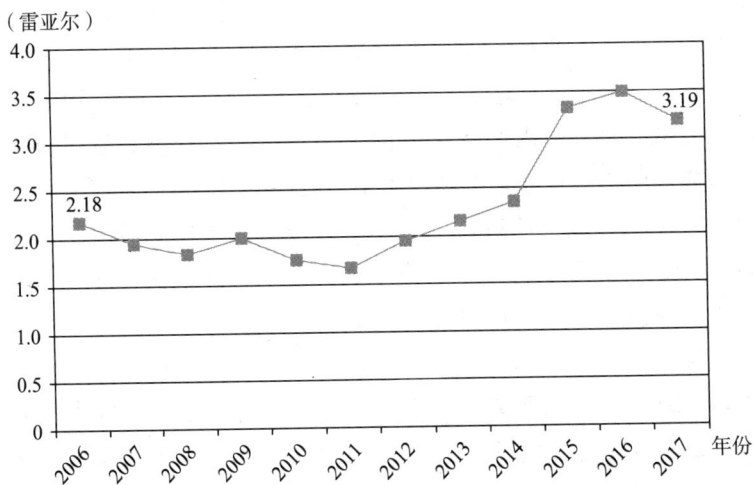

图 1 - 10 2006—2017 年巴西雷亚尔兑美元汇率变化情况

资料来源：联合国统计局。

2. 俄罗斯

在经过 2015 年西方国家制裁和油价下跌的双重打击后，俄罗斯政府调整产业结构和刺激经济的各项政策开始发挥作用，2017 年，俄罗斯经济在低迷状态中缓慢复苏，逐渐好转。回升的矿产业、油价和个人消费成为俄罗斯 GDP 的主要增长点，但建筑业、服务业下滑较为明显。预计俄罗斯经济未来几年将呈现弱反弹态势，增强抗风险能力仍然是经济政策的主导思想。

（1）国内生产总值（GDP）及 GDP 增长率

2017 年，俄罗斯经济增长好于预期，GDP 增长率从 2015 年的 −2.5% 回升至 1.55%，GDP 总量较 2016 年小幅增长至 15275 亿美元，但是，与 2013 年顶峰时期相比，仍有较大差距（见图 1−11）。整体来看，俄罗斯经济受 2008 年国际金融危机影响较大，虽然经济迅速反弹，但增速减缓，其主要原因是西方国家的制裁以及国际原油市场价格的大幅下跌。

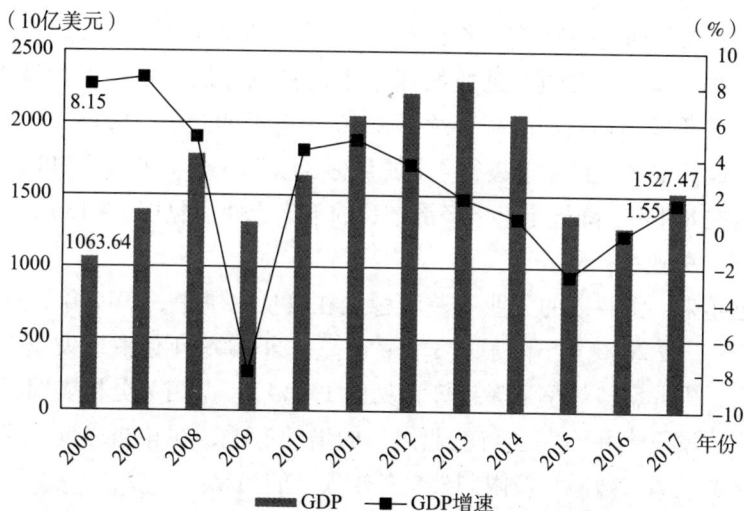

图 1−11 2006—2017 年俄罗斯 GDP 及 GDP 增速变化情况

资料来源：国际货币基金组织。

（2）人均 GDP

2017 年，俄罗斯人均 GDP 实现了自 2013 年以来的首次增长，达到 10608 美元，在金砖国家中排名最高（见图 1−12）。

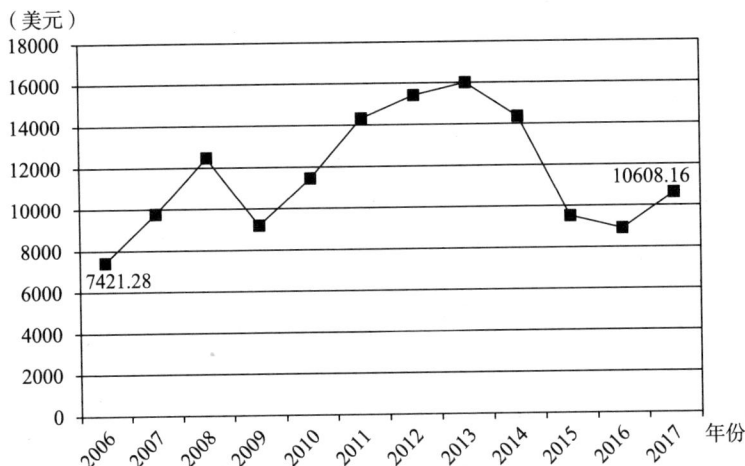

图 1 – 12　2006—2017 年俄罗斯人均 GDP 变化情况

资料来源：国际货币基金组织。

（3）居民消费价格指数（CPI）和生产价格指数（PPI）

俄罗斯长期受高通货膨胀困扰，2015 年，通货膨胀率接近 16%。此后，俄罗斯政府高度重视通货膨胀水平的控制，加之卢布的持续升值，2017 年，俄罗斯通货膨胀率延续了 2016 年下滑的趋势，降至 3.7%，达到历史最低水平，且低于央行 4% 的目标通货膨胀率。此外，PPI 增长率也稳定在 8.4%，降低了未来经济增长的不确定性（见图 1 – 13）。

（4）失业率

近年来，俄罗斯的失业率一直稳定在较低水平上，2017 年，失业率为 5.2%，较 2016 年下降了 0.3 个百分点。自 2009 年俄罗斯失业率创下新高后，失业率整体呈下降趋势（见图 1 – 14）。据相关分析表明，俄罗斯的失业率下降并不完全与就业岗位的增加有关，在相当程度来说，是其适龄劳动力人数减少及限制外籍务工人员的结果。

（5）商品服务进出口增长率

在国际贸易方面，俄罗斯原材料市场的良好表现促进了出口型产业的快速发展，国内民众消费能力提升以及进口替代政策的有效实施也拉动了进口贸易。2017 年，俄罗斯的商品与服务进出口均有较大的发展，出口增长率为 9.1%，进口增长率为 20.3%（见图 1 – 15）。

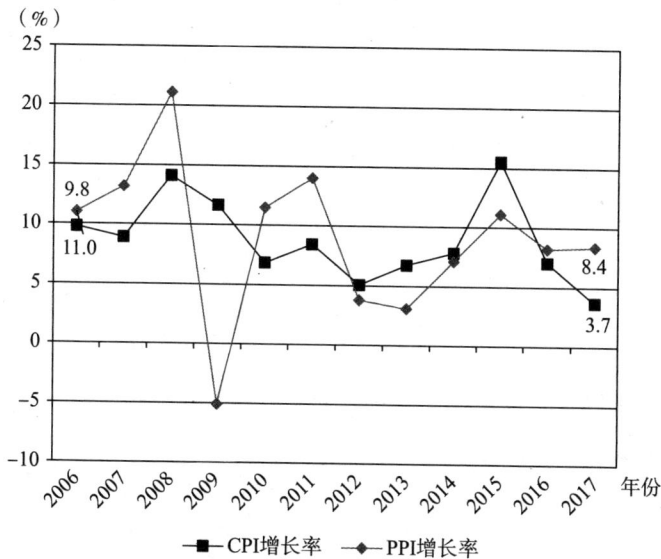

图 1 - 13　2006—2017 年俄罗斯通货膨胀率（CPI 增长率）及 PPI 增长率变化情况

资料来源：美国联邦储备银行。

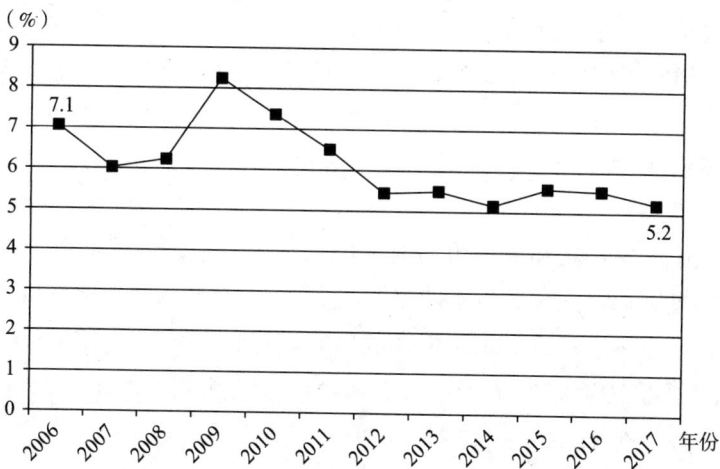

图 1 - 14　2006—2017 年俄罗斯失业率变化情况

资料来源：Haver Analytic。

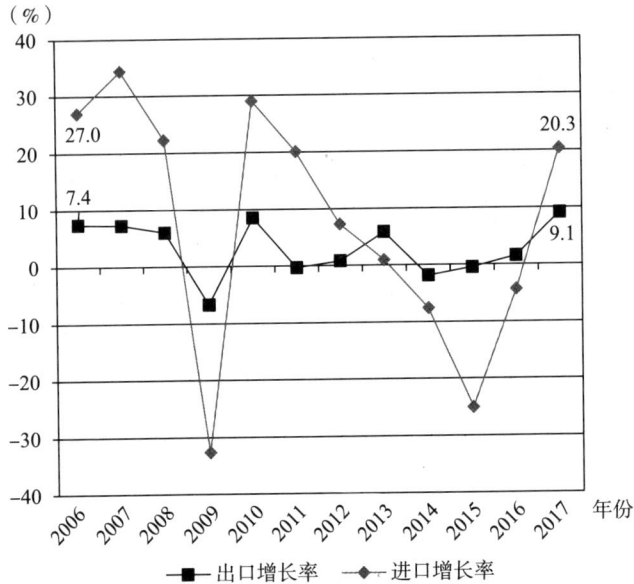

图 1 - 15　2006—2017 年俄罗斯商品服务进出口增长率变化情况

资料来源：国际货币基金组织。

（6）外商直接投资和对外直接投资

总体来看，俄罗斯的 FDI 与 ODI 相关性较高，发展态势上整体趋同，在经历 2015 年的低潮后，2017 年，俄罗斯的 FDI 和 ODI 分别增长到278.9 亿美元和386.3 亿美元（见图 1 - 16）。尽管如此，俄罗斯的 FDI仅占其 GDP 的 2%。

（7）汇率

在欧美国家制裁和原油价格大跌的双重压力下，俄罗斯卢布自 2013年后大幅度贬值。此外，由于俄罗斯在 2014 年为控制通货膨胀问题而采取自由浮动汇率制度，导致了汇率危机的爆发，致使 2016 年汇率较 2014年卢布贬值近 50%。2017 年，由于俄经济回暖和大宗商品价格的回升，卢布汇率得以小幅升值（见图 1 - 17）。

3. 印度

2017 年是印度经济深化转型的一年，也是艰难的一年。即使如此，得益于印度稳步扩张的私人消费和产业开放政策，印度经济增速始终保持高速增长。但是，国有银行不良资产庞大，大宗商品价格上涨引发的通货膨胀，以及长期存在的"无就业发展"问题仍在制约印度经济的增长。印度政府的"废钞令"和税改政策对经济发展产生了一定的负面影响。

（亿美元）

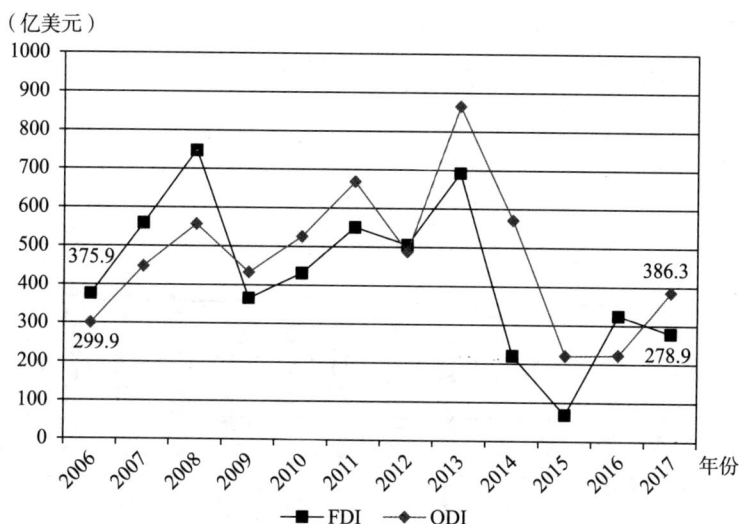

图 1-16　2006—2017 年俄罗斯 FDI 与 ODI 变化情况

资料来源：CEIC。

（卢布）

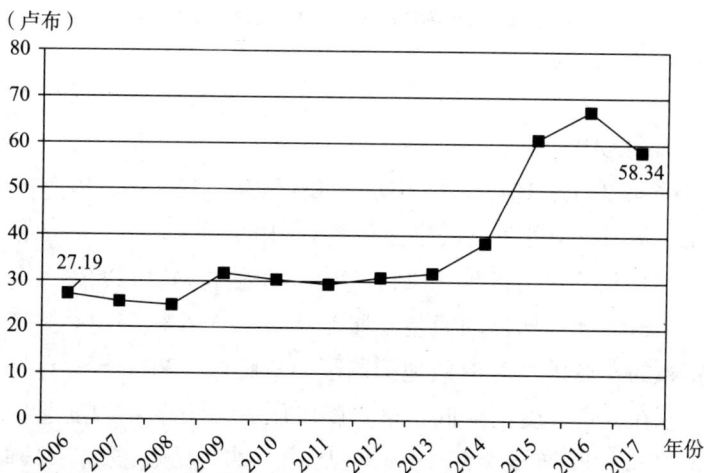

图 1-17　2006—2017 年俄罗斯卢布兑美元汇率变化情况

资料来源：联合国统计局。

（1）国内生产总值（GDP）及 GDP 增长率

自 2006 年以来，印度的国内生产总值保持稳步上升的趋势。2017年，印度 GDP 为 26110 亿美元，是 2006 年的近 3 倍。在 GDP 增长率方面，尽管印度总统莫迪大胆推进改革政策，实施结构性改革以助推印度经济增长，但是，在 2017 年，印度 GDP 增速放缓，仅为 6.74%，三年来首次低于中国的经济增速（见图 1 - 18）。

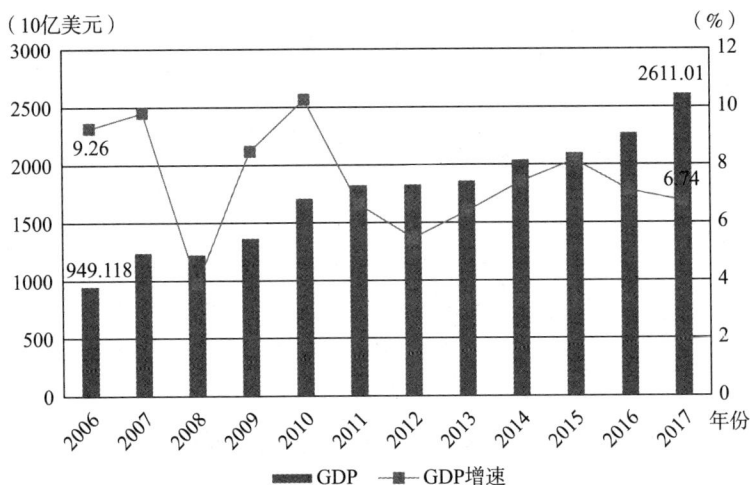

图 1 - 18 2006—2017 年印度 GDP 及 GDP 增速变化情况

资料来源：国际货币基金组织。

（2）人均 GDP

自 2006 年以来，印度人均 GDP 平稳缓慢上升，2017 年达到 1982.7美元，在金砖国家中处于最低位（见图 1 - 19）。

（3）居民消费价格指数（CPI）和生产价格指数（PPI）

2006—2014 年，印度的通货膨胀率一直高于 6%。2016 年年末，印度政府宣布的“废钞令”有效地抑制了通货膨胀，2017 年，食品价格的快速下行也在一定程度上降低了通货膨胀压力，2017 年印度通货膨胀率下降到 3.3%，PPI 增长率为 3.6%（见图 1 - 20）。预计未来一段时间内，通货膨胀水平将趋于平稳，但不断上涨的能源价格依旧是通胀压力的主要来源。

（美元）

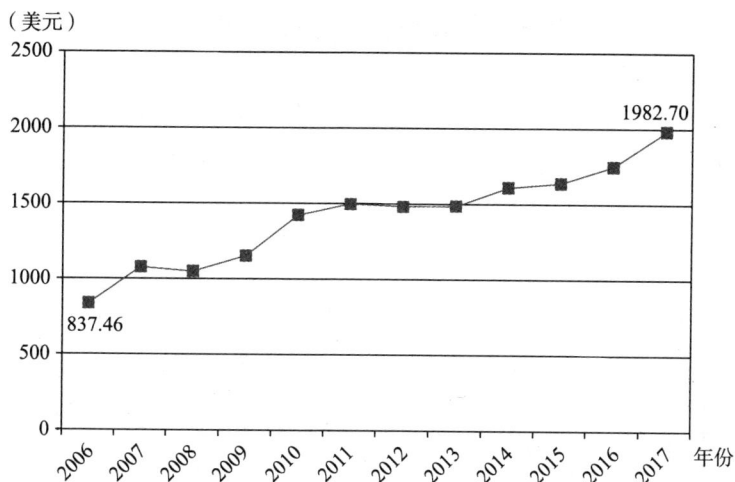

图 1－19　2006—2017 年印度人均 GDP 变化情况

资料来源：国际货币基金组织。

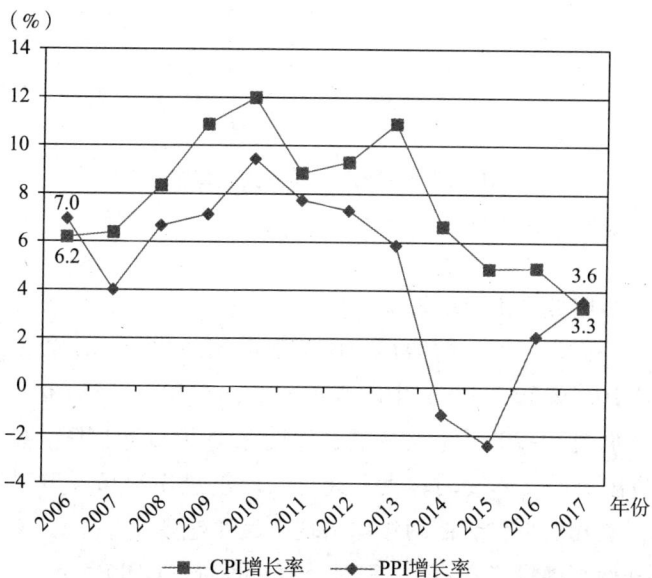

图 1－20　2006—2017 年印度通货膨胀率（CPI 增长率）及 PPI 增长率变化情况

资料来源：国际货币基金组织。

（4）失业率

长期来看，印度的失业率一直稳定在较低的水平上。2017 年，印度失业率为3.5%，比2016年略微增长（见图1-21）。2014年，莫迪上台前曾许诺每年创造1000万个就业岗位，但是，三年来仅新增23万个就业岗位。此外，其推出的"印度制造"计划，真正投入到实体经济的资金很少，对解决就业的实际效果有限。这些都为印度未来的就业市场埋下了隐患。

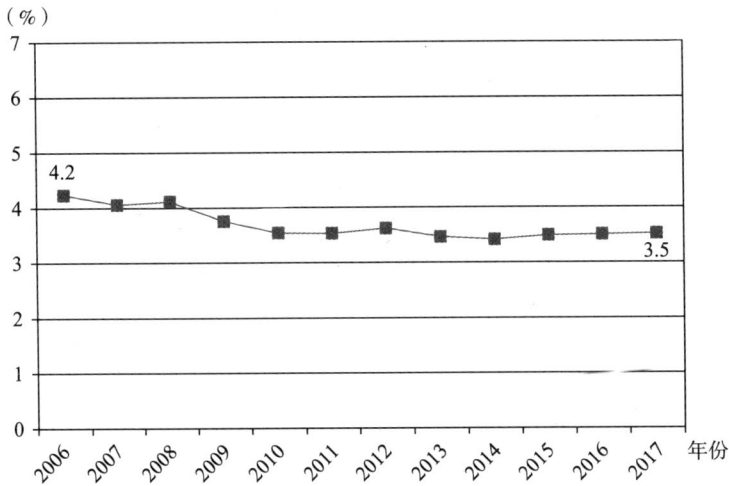

图1-21　2006—2017年印度失业率变化情况

资料来源：Modeled ILO Estimate。

（5）商品服务进出口增长率

2017年，矿产品贸易的增加使印度商品服务进出口增长率均有所上升，分别达10.6%和7.2%，中印双边贸易总额也升至844亿美元，创下最高纪录（见图1-22）。总的来看，印度深受2008年国际金融危机的影响，印度进出口增长率波动较大。此外，印度进出口贸易联动明显，从2015年的增长相对低位，后两年均出现了反弹趋势。

（6）外商直接投资（FDI）和对外直接投资（ODI）

2006—2009年，印度的外商直接投资增长迅猛，增幅是2006年的4.7倍，但随后有所下降。印度政府在2014年开始的"印度制造"计划大幅降低了外商投资的约束，FDI在2016年达到高峰。2017年，印度FDI为422.1亿美元，较2016年出现小幅下跌。印度的对外直接投资自

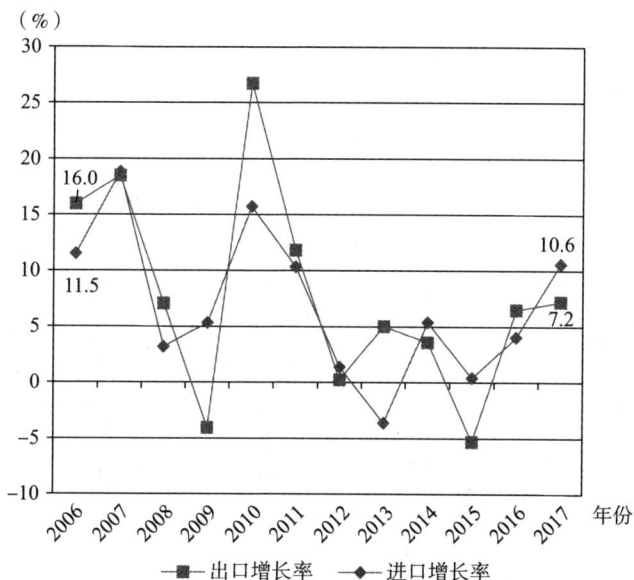

图 1 - 22　2006—2017 年印度商品服务进出口增长率变化情况

资料来源：国际货币基金组织。

2008 年起逐年减少，在 2013 年触底后反弹，2017 年涨幅较大，增长至
112.6 亿美元（见图 1 - 23）。

（7）汇率

2006—2016 年，印度卢比兑美元汇率长期处于贬值状态，其间经历
了印度经济增长速度放缓、国际金融危机导致的国际需求下降和美国加
息等一系列事件。商品服务税法改革，外资信心增强，使 2017 年印度汇
率较 2016 年出现小幅升值，并开始走强（见图 1 - 24）。

4. 中国

2017 年，中国经济实现超预期发展。在经过国际金融后危机时期下
行调整后，2014 年，中国国家主席习近平指出，中国经济呈现出新常态，
经济增速表现为从高速增长转为中高速增长。2016—2017 年，中国经济
增速企稳并小幅回升，体现了中国宏观经济的基本面优势条件与增长韧
性。其突出的发展主要由于供给侧结构性改革持续深化、工业生产稳中
向好、结构转型不断优化、消费增长快于投资增长速度等推动。

（亿美元）

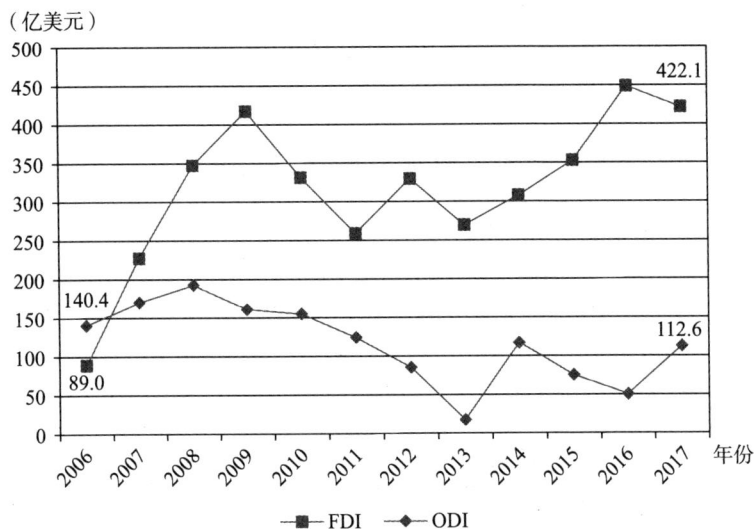

图1－23　2006—2017年印度FDI与ODI变化情况

资料来源：CEIC。

（卢比）

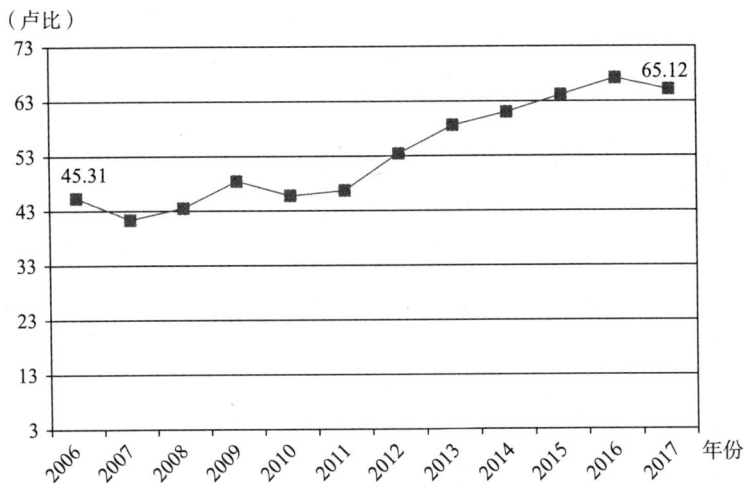

图1－24　2006—2017年印度卢比兑美元汇率变化情况

资料来源：联合国统计局。

（1）国内生产总值（GDP）与 GDP 增长率

从国内生产总值看，自 2006 年以来，中国 GDP 逐年快速增长，于 2017 年突破 12 万亿美元，是 2006 年的 4.3 倍。从 GDP 增长率看，2017 年，中国经济增长高于预期，但增速较十年前明显放缓。2017 年，中国 GDP 增速较 2016 年小幅提升至 6.9%，实现了自 2011 年以来的首次增长提速，领先于其他金砖国家（见图 1 - 25）。

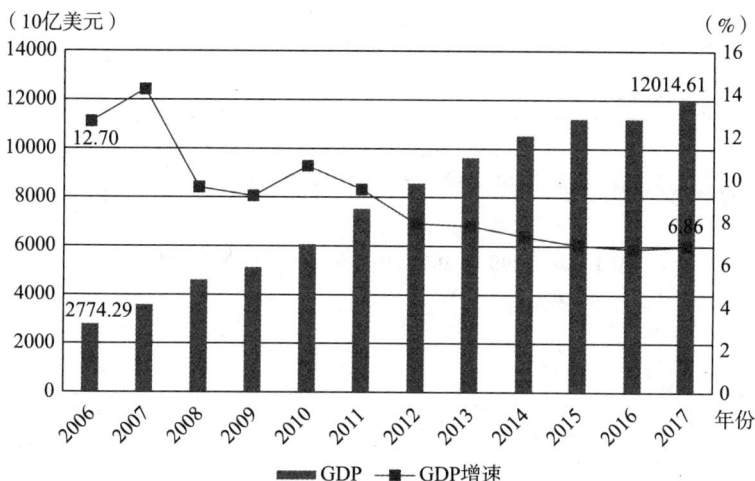

图 1 - 25　2006—2017 年中国 GDP 与 GDP 增速变化情况

资料来源：国际货币基金组织。

（2）人均 GDP

2017 年，中国人均 GDP 延续了一贯的增长趋势，达到 8643 美元，较 2006 年涨幅超过 4 倍（见图 1 - 26）。

（3）居民消费价格指数（CPI）和生产价格指数（PPI）

自 2012 年以后，中国对通货膨胀率控制较好，稳定在 2% 左右。尽管经济加速增长，消费价格通货膨胀率仍低于预期目标。2017 年，中国 CPI 增长率小幅下降至 1.6%，PPI 增长率同样的小幅下降至 4.9%（见图 1 - 27）。其中，食品价格下降是 CPI 涨幅回落的主要原因。

（4）失业率

2017 年，中国的失业率自 2006 年以来首次低于 4%，这得益于中国

（美元）

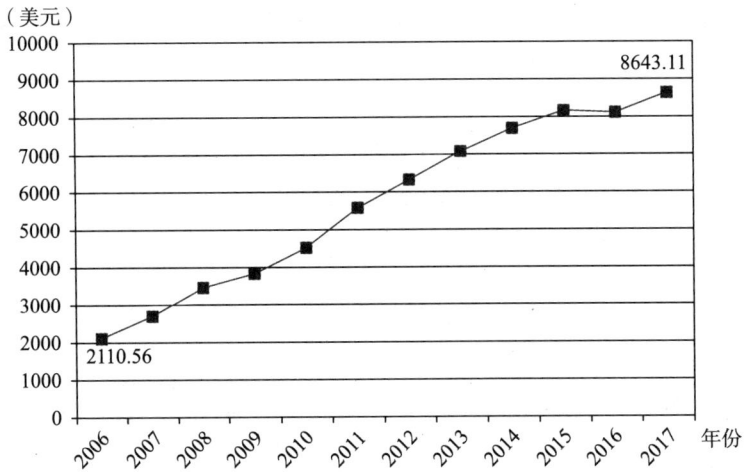

图 1 – 26 2006—2017 年中国人均 GDP 变化情况

资料来源：国际货币基金组织。

（%）

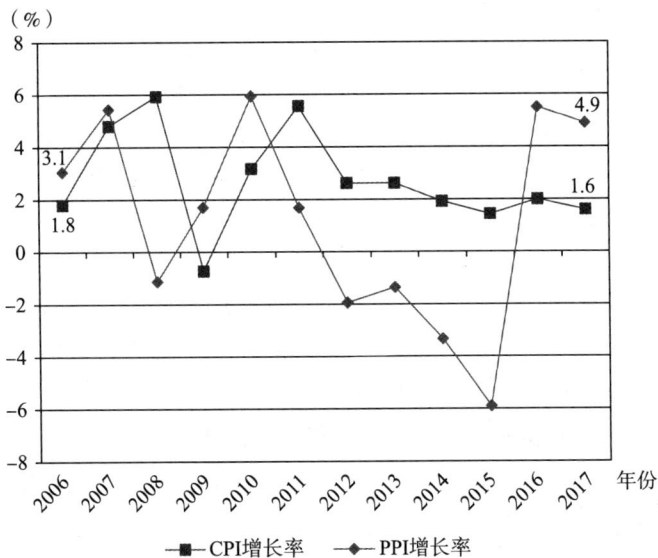

图 1 – 27 2006—2017 年中国通货膨胀率（CPI 增长率）及 PPI 增长率变化情况

资料来源：国际货币基金组织。

的经济复苏，企业效益增长明显，以及各行业增加值均保持了增长态势（见图 1 - 28）。

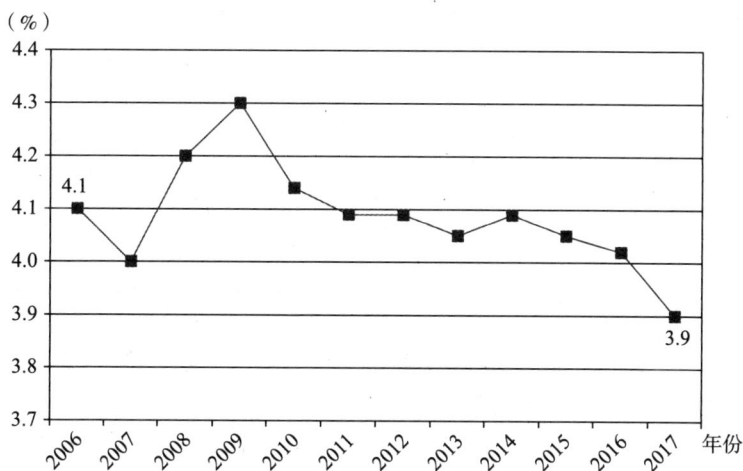

图 1 - 28　2006—2017 年中国失业率变化情况

资料来源：国家统计局，CEIC。

（5）商品服务进出口增长率

受国际金融危机影响，中国进出口增速 2009 年大幅下降，在 2010 年经历反弹后增速趋于放缓。由于全球需求复苏和"一带一路"建设稳步推进，使近年来中国进出口加速增长。2017 年，进出口增长率较前两年继续上涨，分别为 6.9% 和 9.2%（见图 1 - 29）。

（6）外商直接投资（FDI）和对外直接投资（ODI）

中国的外商直接投资总体呈现上升趋势，仅在 2008 年国际金融危机爆发后有小幅下降，随后至 2017 年延续了多年的增长趋势，达到 1363 亿美元。中国的对外直接投资在 2016 年出现了"爆发式"的增长，成为全球第二大对外直接投资大国。但是，由于随后企业海外投资政策的调控，使 2017 年中国的 ODI 也有所下降，为 1019.1 亿美元（见图 1 - 30）。

（7）汇率

2008 年至今，中国人民币兑美元汇率一直稳定在 1 美元兑 6—7 元人民币，2015—2017 年，人民币出现小幅贬值，2017 年汇率达到 1 美元兑 6.76 元人民币（见图 1 - 31）。

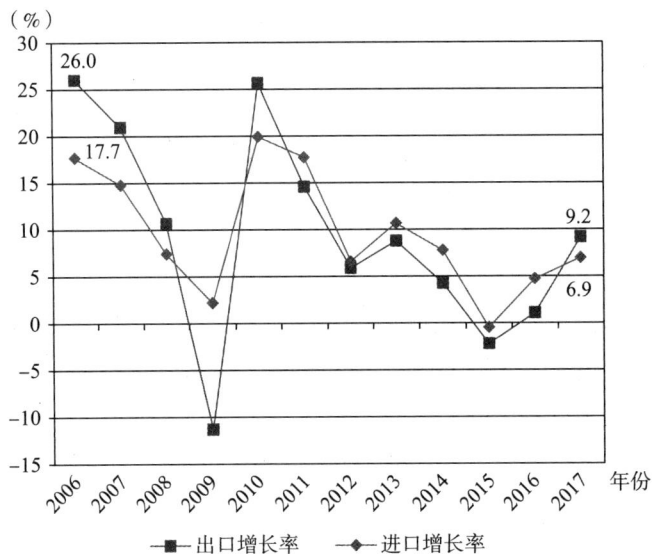

图 1–29　2006—2017 年中国商品服务进出口增长率变化情况

资料来源：国际货币基金组织。

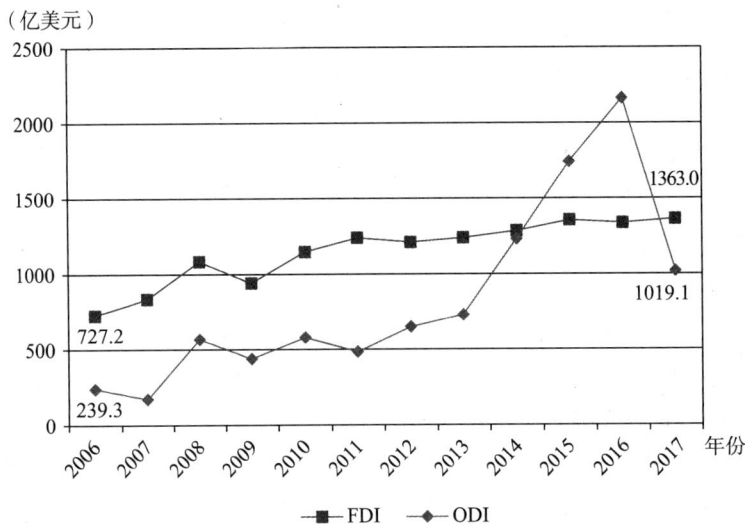

图 1–30　2006—2017 年中国 FDI 与 ODI 变化情况

资料来源：CEIC。

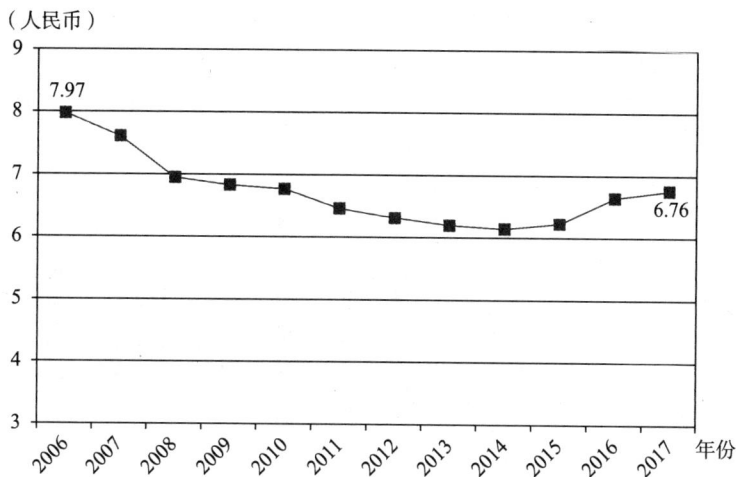

图 1 – 31 2006—2017 年中国人民币兑美元汇率变化情况
资料来源：联合国统计局。

5. 南非

南非作为非洲经济的"领头羊"，有超过 75% 的非洲大型公司驻扎于此。南非经济十分依赖于采矿业、多边的农业和金融业。由于近年来原材料价格下降和粮食歉收，以及国际需求减弱等因素的影响，南非的经济增长率逐年下降。在 2017 年全球经济向好和大宗商品价格回升的大环境下，其经济虽然有回暖的迹象，但是，总体仍处在复苏进程当中。

（1）国内生产总值（GDP）及 GDP 增长率

2008 年国际金融危机后，南非的 GDP 开始稳步增长，随后由于原材料价格下跌和国际需求不足，其增长率一直呈下滑趋势。2017 年，在农业、制造业快速增长的带动下，南非的经济增长呈现了反弹迹象，GDP 增长 1.3%，超过预期（见图 1 – 32）。

（2）人均 GDP

2017 年，南非人均 GDP 继 2011 年连续下滑多年后大幅反弹，重新回到 6000 美元以上，但较 2006 年仅上涨约 10%（见图 1 – 33）。

（3）居民消费价格指数（CPI）和生产价格指数（PPI）

从 2015 年下半年开始，南非遭遇严重干旱，粮食大幅减产致使南非由粮食出口国变成进口国，而其货币的贬值又增加了粮食等必需品的进

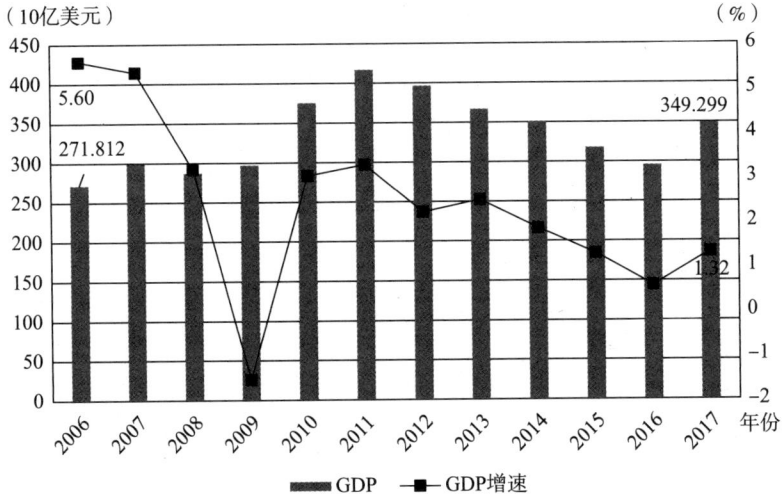

图 1 - 32 2006—2017 年南非 GDP 及 GDP 增速变化情况

资料来源：国际货币基金组织。

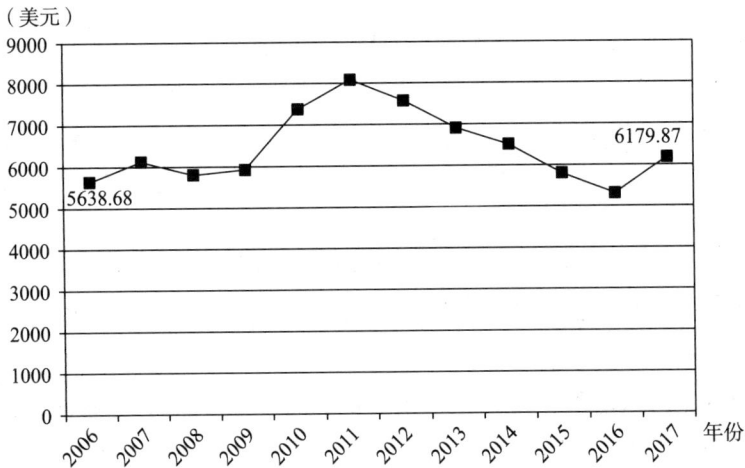

图 1 - 33 2006—2017 年南非人均 GDP 变化情况

资料来源：国际货币基金组织。

口成本，国内食品价格随之增长，加剧了通货膨胀程度。2017 年，南非摆脱了旱灾的影响，其通货膨胀率下降至 5.2%，重新回到目标通货膨胀率范围之内（3%—6%），PPI 增长率也下降至 4.9%（见图 1-34）。

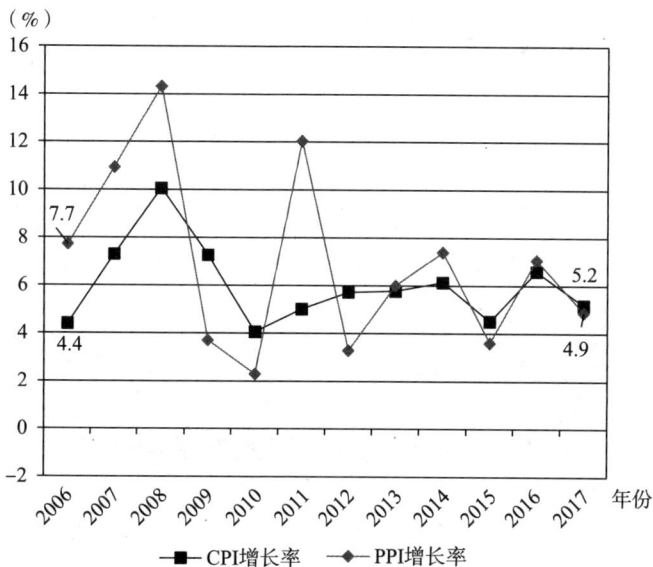

图 1-34 2006—2017 年南非通货膨胀率（CPI 增长率）及 PPI 增长率变化情况

资料来源：国际货币基金组织。

（4）失业率

受南非营商环境不佳、经济扩张低迷的影响，南非的失业率常年居高不下，虽然南非政府在 2010 年提出"新增长路线"发展战略，计划通过设立经济特区、建设基础设施项目等措施来增加就业岗位，争取在十年内把失业率降至 15%，然而，就业状况并未得到改善，失业率反而不断攀升，在 2017 年达到 27.5%（见图 1-35）。其中，青年失业问题尤为突出，15—24 岁的青年失业率接近 56%。

（5）商品服务进出口增长率

2006—2017 年，南非商品服务进出口增长变化基本一致，均在 2009 年触底反弹。2013 年以后，南非出口增长率持续下降，2017 年出现了负增长。南非进口增长率波动较大，在 2016 年负增长后，2017 年实现了 1.9% 的增长速度（见图 1-36）。

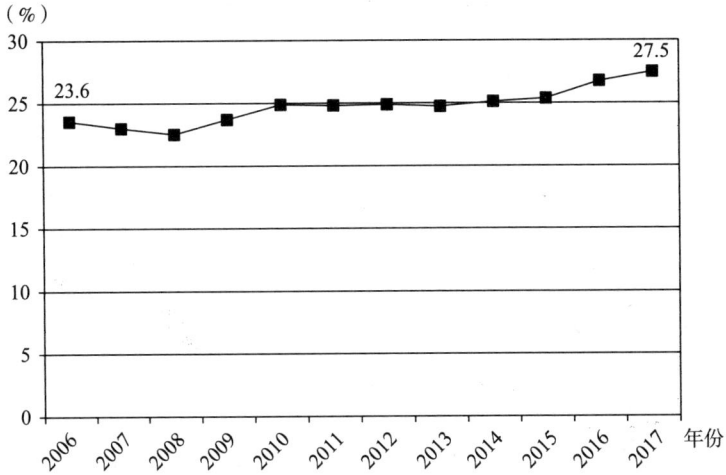

图1-35 2006—2017年南非失业率变化情况

资料来源：Statistics South Africa。

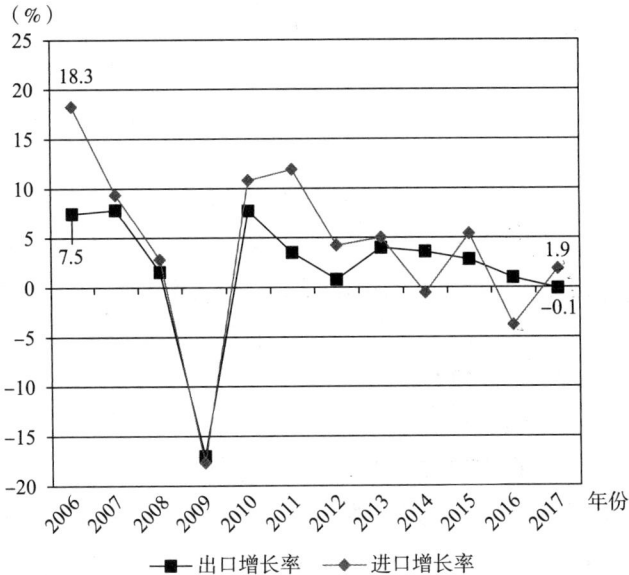

图1-36 2006—2017年南非商品服务进出口增长率变化情况

资料来源：国际货币基金组织。

（6）外商直接投资（FDI）和对外直接投资（ODI）

2008 年国际金融危机前，南非的外商直接投资上涨迅猛，但是，由于经济表现欠佳，南非的对外直接投资逐年下滑。国际金融危机后，ODI整体呈上升趋势，2017 年达 73.8 亿美元。相反，南非的 FDI 自 2013 年开始急剧下滑，南非政府于 2015 年通过《投资促进与保护法案修正案》，不允许投资者将有关投资争议提交国际仲裁解决，因此，南非 FDI 的下滑趋势一直延续到 2017 年（见图 1 -37）。

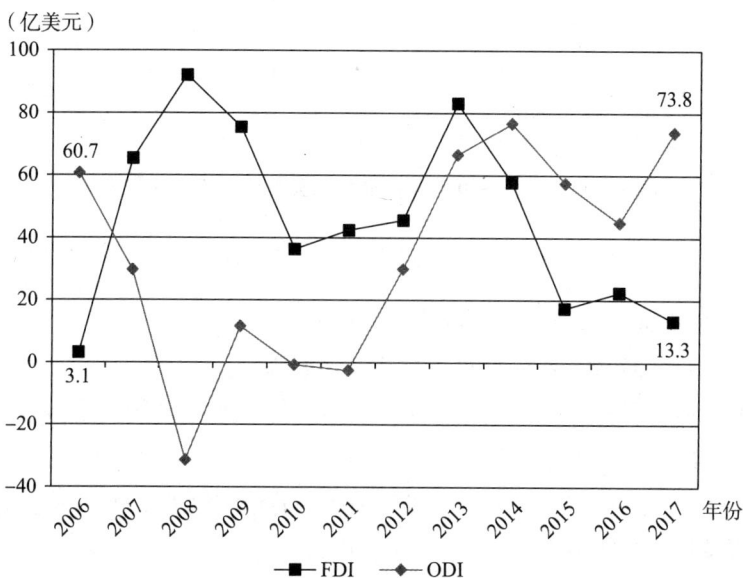

图 1 -37　2006—2017 年南非 FDI 与 ODI 变化情况

资料来源：CEIC。

（7）汇率

2006—2017 年，南非兰特兑美元汇率贬值将近 100%，其货币贬值很大原因在于经济发展长期表现疲弱，经济增速放缓，且政治不稳定。2017 年，南非的信用评级被下调后，南非兰特继续贬值。同年底，市场对新执政党非洲人国民大会主席拉马福萨的当选十分看好，加之美元的疲软，南非兰特升值较多（见图 1 -38）。

（兰特）

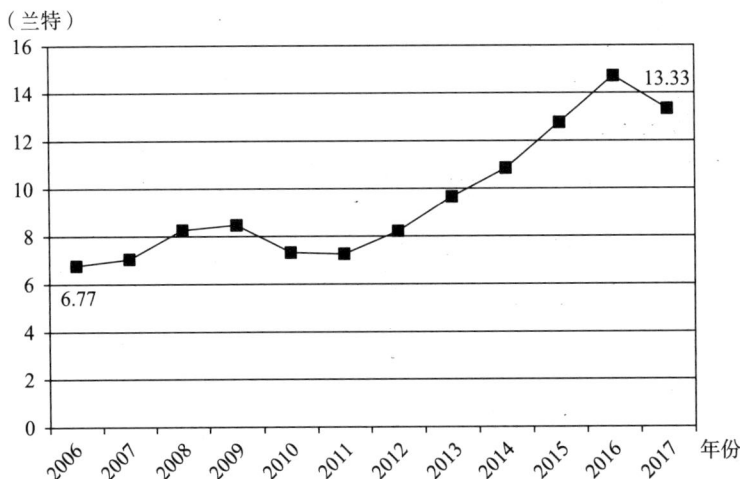

图1-38 2006—2017年南非兰特兑美元汇率变化情况

资料来源：联合国统计局。

（二）其他新兴市场国家经济发展概况

1. 新兴市场国家经济发展的地域差异较大

亚洲新兴经济体一马当先，维持较高的增长水平。2017年GDP增长率为6.5%，与2016年基本持平。菲律宾、越南等国GDP增长率超过6%，分别为6.4%和6.1%。亚洲新兴板块的稳定复苏反映了制造业活跃水平的提升，对经济增长产生可持续的拉动力。

中东、北非新兴经济体增长表现紧随其后。2017年GDP增长率为3.2%，较2016年的2.3%有显著的提升。受石油等能源类大宗商品价格回升的推动，伊拉克的实际增长率由2016年的−2.4%猛增至2017年的10.3%，科威特也由2016年的1.1%提升至2.5%。在经济制裁解禁后，伊朗石油等部门对经济增长也发挥了显著的出拉动效应，增长率由2016年的0.38%提升至2017年的4.5%。

拉美国家普遍面临政府赤字较大、通货膨胀高企、汇率波动加剧等风险。例如，阿根廷2017年一般政府赤字占GDP的7.1%，墨西哥也触及了3%的安全警戒线。阿根廷2017年的消费物价指数（CPI）同比增长25.6%，出现了严重的通货膨胀；巴西的通货膨胀率也高达9.0%。这些指标显示，拉美国家的社会脆弱性增加，政府应对或调控经济的力量有所下降。

2. 新兴市场国家整体失业率较高，青年失业问题值得警惕

2017 年，多数新兴市场国家就业人数增长放缓，甚至出现负增长，导致失业率小幅上升，各国普遍面临青年失业人数较多的严重问题。

埃及、土耳其和希腊失业率仍无转好的迹象，高达两位数，15—24 岁的青年失业问题尤为突出。土耳其整体失业率达 11%，其中，青年失业率达 20%。埃及整体失业率达 12%，主要是由于政府治理能力较弱，缺乏相应的促进就业的政策。尽管欧洲地区整体经济复苏明显，但是，希腊面临的问题仍较为严峻，2017 年失业率达 21.5%，青年失业率高达 46%。

3. 新兴市场国家物价水平总体回落，但表现不尽相同

2017 年，受食品价格回落、货币升值等影响，新兴市场国家物价水平总体回落，但是，由于国际资本流向变化、国内经济形势以及地缘政治局势等多种因素的影响，新兴市场国家各国的国内物价波动出现了分化，而且部分国家仍然面临较大的通货膨胀压力。

除金砖国家外，智利、哥伦比亚和秘鲁的通货膨胀率 2017 年下降较多，分别从 3.8% 降至 2.2%、7.5% 降至 4.3% 和 3.6% 降至 2.8%。卡塔尔的通货膨胀率最低，仅为 0.4%。印度尼西亚、韩国和波兰的通货膨胀率虽然较 2016 年有所上升，但总体上通货膨胀压力不大。墨西哥、土耳其和埃及通货膨胀率 2017 年急剧上升，其中，墨西哥、土耳其的通货膨胀率分别上升至 6.0% 和 11.1%，埃及的通货膨胀率高达 23.5%。

4. 新兴市场国家外商直接投资增长乏力且分化明显

2017 年，新兴市场国家 FDI 发展仍面临诸多挑战，增长形势远低于预期，并呈现出分化格局。

墨西哥是新兴市场国家中对外商直接投资最开放的国家之一，也是全球第十五大外商直接投资接受国。由于邻近美国，墨西哥接受外商直接投资的最主要国家为美国和西班牙，且集中在制造业和金融服务业，2017 年，墨西哥接受外商直接投资流量达到 311 亿美元。外商对印度尼西亚的投资主要集中在采矿业、公共事业、机器和电子行业，2017 年，印度尼西亚接受外商直接投资流量达到 221 亿美元。而巴基斯坦由于局势不稳定，导致投资环境不佳，其外商直接投资流量较少，仅有 27.5 亿美元。

二 新兴市场国家经济合作的
内在关联性和必要性

新兴市场国家在 20 世纪初期大多数是殖民地、半殖民地国家。资本主义制度建立以后，这些国家虽然接触到了先进的生产方式，但工业发展一直受到其宗主国的压制，只充当原料供应地和产品倾销地。虽然亚非拉地区在第二次世界大战以后基本上都独立为主权国家，但是，由于历史和其他原因，经济发展一直较为缓慢。正是因为新兴市场国家有着相似的历史阶段，其相互之间的经济合作更具有关联性和必要性。

（一）助力新兴市场国家经济发展

首先，通过经济合作增加对落后的基础设施投资支持，补齐新兴市场国家发展短板。包括金砖国家在内的新兴市场国家的经济社会发展普遍受到基础设施发展滞后的掣肘。追求快速发展但资金不足的新兴市场国家通常受到自筹资金不足的拖累，如大停电给印度造成了 6.6% 的年度产出损失。基础设施缺乏的主要原因是投资不足，仅仅靠世界银行、亚洲开发银行等少数几个国际开发性机构远远不能满足需求。金砖国家亟待通过大规模投资来改善基础设施，金砖国家新开发银行和亚洲基础设施投资银行的成立将为发展中国家基础设施投资提供重要的资金来源，也将为提高资金输出国的投资回报率提供机会。

其次，经济合作能有效地促进经贸发展。国家之间贸易和投资活动、生产、仓储、运输设备购置、出口基地以及品牌建设等多个环节和层次，需要投资、融资、保险等金融服务和支持。新兴市场国家加强经济合作，不仅可以提供更多的投融资路径和适当的经济援助，也可以加大相互之间在海外市场的拓展，如兼并收购、实现技术升级、资源能源、知识产权等项目的重点支持，促进贸易的发展。

最后，经济合作有助于促进新兴市场国家产业结构升级和经济创新发展。新兴市场国家均存在产业层次较低、结构不合理、创新发展缓慢、可持续发展挑战大等问题，要实现可持续发展，迫切需要经济支持以加大高新产业、低碳产业、绿色产业、现代制造业和先进服务业等的培育和发展。新兴市场国家通过双边和多边合作项目，推动建立支持绿色投资的可持续发展经济体系。

（二）推动新兴市场国家金融体制改革和政策创新

国际经济合作需要参与合作各方改革协调经济运行、监管制度和经济政策等。经济合作引导新兴市场国家经济体制改革与政策协调。缺乏相似或相近的体制机制与政策取向，多边经济合作将难以正常运转。以金砖国家为例，其信贷、保险政策、治理结构和机制等差异较大，金砖国家建立共同的国际性金融机构以及协调国际金融政策等，无疑会对各自的金融体制和政策的协调提出挑战，这就要求金砖国家加强管理机制和政策协调。通过在金融合作中共同改革金融管理体制和调整金融货币政策等，来优化金砖国家经济体制与管理机制。

（三）加速新兴市场国家融入全球价值链

新兴市场国家进出口对经济的带动作用明显，正在越来越深入地融入全球价值链。首先，新兴市场国家人口较多，人口结构一般都偏向年轻化，拥有庞大的国内市场和潜在市场，进口需求强劲。其次，新兴市场国家劳动力充足，在劳动密集型产品的生产上具有竞争优势。资源的丰富也使其在资源密集型产品的生产上具有竞争优势，出口增长迅猛。但是，由于新兴市场国家工业化起步较晚，具备后发优势，政府应制定相对开放的政策以获得资金和技术，实现经济的腾飞。

新兴市场国家通过加强经济合作，可以更快、更好地融入全球价值链。以中国为例，中国目前处于全球价值链的中心位置，向下进口自然资源丰富的发展中国家的生产原料，向上利用发达国家的资金和技术，凭借完善的工业体系成为制造业大国。因此，新兴市场国家应利用彼此的资金、技术和自然资源，以经济全球化为契机，加速融入全球价值链。

（四）协助新兴市场国家抵御政治经济风险

新兴市场国家一般都是出口大于进口，对外贸易在经济发展中发挥的作用较大，对经济全球化的依赖性相对较强。因此，新兴市场国家的经济合作，可以有效地提高其与发达国家谈判的能力，有利于制定更合理、完善的国际规则，抵御外来的政治风险。例如，新兴市场国家在面对不合理的经济制裁时，可以联合起来以提高共同的议价权，在谈判过程中取得有利的地位，在某个新兴市场国家遭受不公平的经济制裁时予以集体声援。同时，由于新兴市场国家一般都有庞大的国内市场，因此，在受到贸易保护主义措施制裁时，可以积极面向新兴经济体开拓市场。

同样，新兴市场国家也可以在内部寻找替代商品进口，以对贸易制裁行为进行反制。例如，2018 年 3 月，美国决定对进口钢铁和铝分别征收25% 和 10% 的关税，掀起了波及全球的贸易战。美国此次征收的对象不仅包括欧盟、加拿大等发达国家，也包括中国、俄罗斯、墨西哥等新兴市场国家。面对美国政府的不合理制裁，新兴市场国家纷纷采取反制措施，墨西哥宣布对美国钢铁、猪肉、苹果等一系列产品征收报复性关税，俄罗斯将对美国的修路机械产品征收进口关税，中国政府也宣布对原产于美国的产品加征 25% 的关税。

三 下一个金色十年金砖国家务实合作展望

金砖国家合作机制已经走过十余个年头，历经国际金融危机等重大挑战的考验，探索出了一条新兴市场国家和发展中国家团结合作、互利共赢的新路，金砖国家合作硕果累累，空间巨大。未来金砖国家合作的起点更高，正如中国国家主席习近平指出的，十年合作中培育出的金砖精神，将是金砖国家合作不竭的力量源泉。在全球发展的新形势下，金砖国家合作将与时俱进，不断创新、发展和深化。

（一）打造南南合作新平台

南南合作是发展中国家之间的重要合作机制，既是发展中国家自力更生、谋求进步的重要渠道，也是确保发展中国家有效地融入和参与世界经济的有效手段，在推动发展中国家崛起和促进世界经济强劲持久、平衡、包容增长中发挥了重要作用。金砖合作机制是南南合作的重要平台之一，通过多年的探索和实践，走出了一条新兴市场国家和发展中国家团结合作、互利共赢的新路。中国国家主席习近平在 2017 年厦门峰会上提出了"金砖＋"合作模式，旨在进一步深化"一带一路"倡议，加强与其他新兴市场国家和发展中国家的联络、互动、对话及合作，通过深化合作，更好地体现发展中国家的共同立场和集体意愿。

未来，金砖国家之间的合作要放眼更广泛的空间、更开放的模式，应将金砖国家合作放在南南合作和"一带一路"倡议框架之下，发挥辐射作用，在金砖国家实现经济持续高速增长的同时，鼓励和支持更多具有代表性和良好发展前景的新兴经济体参与到金砖国家合作机制中，建立更广泛伙伴关系，带动世界经济的平衡发展。

（二）进一步拓展金砖国家贸易合作

贸易是金砖国家合作的重要领域，当前，金砖国家已在经贸合作方面取得了显著进展。2017 年，金砖国家国际贸易总额达 3.2 万亿美元，占世界国际贸易总额的 15%，在世界贸易格局中的地位不断提升。未来随着金砖国家的经济转型，对外贸易将稳步增长。然而，当前金砖国家贸易合作主要受制于相关合作机制尚未建立或者不健全、不完善，为了解决这些深层次问题，金砖国家应通力合作，化解分歧。

首先，金砖国家应相互督促各国扩大开放程度。由于金砖国家总体投资贸易便利化水平不高，在全球普遍处于较为靠后的地位，对商品货物进口还存在较多贸易壁垒。因此，金砖国家应进一步提高对外经济开放水平，推动金融流动的便利化。

其次，应大力推动开展金砖国家自贸区谈判。自由贸易是全球经济发展的大趋势，尽管当前全球化进程遭遇逆风，但从长期来看，自由贸易仍然是世界经济发展的主流。

再次，在推动金砖国家自贸区谈判的同时，可同步开展金砖国家内部两两之间的双边自贸谈判。目前，中国已与东盟、瑞士、新加坡、巴基斯坦、澳大利亚等国家和地区开展了双边自贸区谈判，在双边自贸区建设方面经验丰富，未来可在金砖国家中发挥示范作用。

最后，应建立金砖国家大通关制度。金砖国家应以一体化通关为重点，改革海关监管体制，优化作业流程，合作建立金砖国家大通关机制。金砖国家各国海关应加强信息互换、监管互认、执法互助。金砖国家应共同探索通关监管方式创新，促进金砖国家间新经济、新贸易、新业态的发展。

（三）深化金砖国家金融合作

在全球经济发展与治理变革面临困境的背景下，金砖国家将加强内部改革转型和相互合作作为重振增长动力、转变增长模式和提高全球经济金融治理改革参与权的应对之策。其中，金融合作作为内推发展、外促合作的重要手段，近年来备受关注，而且，经过多年的艰苦努力，已经取得显著进展，并正在产生广泛而深刻的影响。但是，由于金融合作所涉及的领域宽广、复杂以及与金砖国家政治、经济、外交等政策取向的多样性及利益的敏感性，金砖国家需要秉承务实、互利的原则，寻求合作最大公约数，形成强大的利益交汇点，充分发挥各自的政治智慧，力促富有成效的合作。同时，金砖国家在深化自身金融体制和经济体制改革以适应金融合作的过程中，除了需要协同政策，还需要相互借鉴经验。金砖国家发展与合作愿景的相似，金融体制机制改革、金融政策创新的有效协调是金融管理创新能力等的共同提升，都能为金融合作的深化与成功打下了坚实基础，进而有力地推动金砖国家全面务实合作、经济转型创新与稳定持续发展。

（四）扩展民间交流与文化合作

金砖国家人文交流是金砖国家合作机制的重要组成部分，发展金砖国家人文交流合作机制是深化金砖国家伙伴关系的重要路径。目前，金砖国家人文交流合作覆盖的领域在不断扩展，其涵盖的内容也不断细化与深化。

总的来说，金砖国家人文交流合作机制的形成是一个自上而下，由宏观架构搭建到微观议题确立、讨论，再到具体活动执行和具体措施实施的过程。放眼金砖国家未来人文交流合作机制的发展，需要处理好三个层面人文交流合作机制的相互关系：一是要处理好与金砖国家成员国之间双边人文交流合作机制的相互关系；二是要处理好与金砖国家成员国之间其他多边人文交流合作机制的相互关系；三是要处理好与其他国际多边人文交流合作机制的相互关系。只有处理好这三个层面的关系，金砖国家人文交流合作机制才能得到健康有序的发展，人文交流与合作才能有的放矢，服务于金砖国家伙伴关系的巩固与深化。

四　投融资合作是深化金砖国家合作的重要基础

（一）金砖国家投融资合作发展潜力大

随着贸易合作的深入推进，投资领域的合作潜力逐步显现。2006—2017 年，金砖国家投融资合作呈现出整体上升的趋势。在此期间，2011年，FDI 流入量达到 12 年间的最高值，为 2974.4 亿美元，占世界份额的19.0%，2014 年，FDI 流入量占世界份额达到峰值，为 21.2%；2014 年，FDI 流出量及占世界份额均达到最大值，分别为 2090.1 亿美元和 15.9%。

金砖国家之间投融资合作发展迅猛，优势互补，潜力巨大。俄罗斯与印度之间主要是石油资源和农业领域的相互投资；印度与巴西之间在矿业投资领域合作势头良好，在农业、制造业领域的合作潜力较大；印度主要利用信息技术等服务业优势，对南非开展投资合作，开拓非洲市场；南非凭借其非洲中心的优势，对金砖国家其他成员国家的投资吸引力较大，其跨国公司从区域战略布局考虑，对南非的投资呈现出增长趋势。就增量而言，中国对金砖国家其他国家每年新增的直接投资总额超过 20 亿美元，相当于 2006 年之前的存量总和。

金砖国家成员间的投资额虽较小，但在持续提升。近年来，来自金砖国家的跨国公司已表现出在金砖国家内部投资的更大兴趣。越来越多的印度公司、中国的跨国企业正在或计划在其他金砖国家投资。例如，中国北京汽车国际公司在南非建造了 8.23 亿美元的组装设施，为当地和地区市场生产汽车；中国中车股份有限公司在印度投资 6300 万美元生产铁路运输设备；中国的华为公司计划在印度建厂制造智能手机。除此之外，中国的阿里巴巴、小米和滴滴出行在 2015 年和 2016 年也在印度投资。联合国贸易和发展组织发布的《世界投资报告（2017）》显示，金砖国家之间的并购活动在 2015—2016 年快速增长，从 2015 年的 30 亿美元增长到 2016 年的 220 亿美元（见图 1-39）。

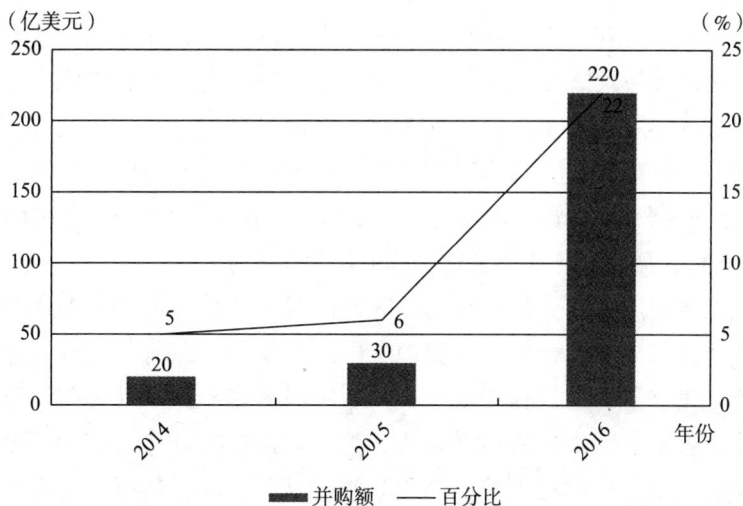

图 1-39　2014—2016 年金砖国家内部跨境并购额和占世界百分比

资料来源：联合国贸易和发展组织：《世界投资报告（2017）》，2017 年。

（二） 新开发银行和应急储备安排是投融资合作的重要平台

设立金砖国家新开发银行①和金砖国家应急储备安排②标志着金砖国家投融资合作迈上新台阶。发展中国家改善基础设施状况的需求极为迫切，据世界银行测算，发展中国家在基础设施建设上的资金缺口高达 1 万亿美元，但世界银行等传统多边开发性金融机构只能提供大约 40% 的融资。新开发银行旨在为金砖国家、其他新兴市场、发展中国家基础设施和可持续发展项目筹集资金，作为对现有多边和区域金融机构的补充。2014 年，在巴西福塔莱萨金砖国家领导人第六次会晤期间，新开发银行协议正式签署，标志着历史上首个由新兴市场国家自主建立并主导的国际多边开发银行的成立。新开发银行法定资本 1000 亿美元，初始认缴资本 500 亿美元，由创始成员国平等出资，总部设在中国上海。

与新开发银行偏向长期投资方面的资金支持不同，应急储备安排主要用于应对短期国际流动性压力，加强金融稳定，补充现有国际外汇储备安排，加强全球金融安全网。2013 年 9 月，在俄罗斯圣彼得堡举行的 G20 峰会期间，金砖国家领导人明确应急储备安排初始规模为 1000 亿美元，并确定各成员国的出资比例，即中国出资 410 亿美元，为最大股东，巴西、俄罗斯、印度分别出资 180 亿美元，南非出资 50 亿美元。2014 年，上述协议在巴西福塔莱萨金砖国家领导人第六次会晤期间顺利签署。

新开发银行和应急储备安排是一种全新的南南合作方式，不仅为发展中国家的经济发展提供了多方位保障与支持，也为发展中国家参与全球的治理提供了一种全新方式，是对现有国际金融体系的有益补充。新开发银行和应急储备安排为当今世界上国与国之间投融资合作树立了典范，为金砖国家投融资合作及南南合作的发展和深化提供了重要的平台。

（三） 投融资合作推动金砖合作的深化与发展

在经济金融全球化时代，投融资合作对经济社会的驱动作用日益显著，金砖国家投融资合作成为促进本国经济发展、参与国际经济金融合作和治理更加重要的选择。近年来，金砖国家在全面推动金砖国家合作过程中，投融资合作不断拓展深化。另外，投融资合作内容的不断丰富也为金砖国家合作奠定了共识基础和制度基础，使金砖国家合作的层次

---

① 参见本书附录"案例一：金砖国家新开发银行"。
② 参见本书附录"案例二：金砖国家应急储备安排"。

进一步提升。

第一，投融资合作深化了金砖国家合作共识。为进一步深化投融资合作，金砖国家需要凝聚合作共识，在金融发展战略、体制机制创新、国内外合作政策、推动国际新秩序构建等诸多方面，加强互信、协调与互动。

第二，投融资合作促进了金砖国家合作体制改革协调和政策互动。深化金砖国家合作应根据投融资合作的需要，共同推动合作机制改革，包括推进金融自由化、放宽利率管制、改善金融服务，如加快金砖各国的货币国际化进程，放开资本项目跨境流动限制，开放金砖国家货币银行间的市场交易，推动境内银行为境外项目提供贷款业务，以及提升相关部门与海关、工商税务等部门的密切合作。这些都为金砖国家投融资合作提供了制度上的支持与保障。

第二章 金砖国家投融资合作的目标与实践

一 完善全球金融治理体系

（一）全球金融治理体系现状

全球金融治理是指各国政府部门、国际组织与非政府组织、跨国公司以及其他市场主体，通过协调、合作、达成共识等方式，参与全球金融事务的管理，规避和预防系统性金融风险，维护经济金融稳定，以建立或维护良性的国际金融秩序的过程。一言以蔽之，全球金融治理就是在国际金融领域做到主体"协调一致、趋利避害"。

完善全球金融治理是构建人类命运共同体的实践要求，有助于建设新型国际关系，推动全球治理体系朝着更加公正合理的方向发展，其提出和实施具有必然性。

其一，进入 21 世纪后，金融市场全球化和自由化进程进一步加快，新的金融产品层出不穷，交易方式推陈出新，国际金融市场相互连接，相互依赖，跨境资产、负债及其规模越来越大，不确定因素与日俱增。在这种情况下，要全面了解、掌握跨国银行或投资公司详情，有效地进行监管，对于任何一国而言，都是力所不及的。

其二，现存的国际金融体系制度安排还存在很大的局限性，原有的以西方增长为中心的机制建构已不能满足世界经济增长中心转移的需要。比如，国际货币基金组织、世界银行等国际金融机构没有充分履行或者说不具备完全能力行使对国际金融市场应尽的协调职责等；无约束的美元本位制加上缺乏连贯性的美国宏观经济政策，极易导致国际金融危机频繁爆发，各国在外汇储备问题上受制于美国国内的货币政策，面临外汇储备随时贬值的风险。这也导致国际汇率体系存在众多不确定因素，美国可以通过发行货币将汇率的脆弱性风险转嫁给债权国，而债权国却不能以同样的方式向美国转嫁汇率风险。这无疑在国家贸易与投资方面损害了新兴市场国家尤其是金砖国家的利益。

其三，各国金融监管当局在国际金融监管方面缺乏必要的沟通和协调，不仅不同国家之间存在金融监管差异，在一国家内部也存在跨部门的监管差异。

其四，多级的国际贸易体制、区域投资合作机制以及不断涌现新的全球金融规则、协议，导致各种新情况、新问题层出不穷，客观上也需要各市场主体适时地参与全球金融治理，以减少金融外部风险，推动全球金融体系顺利、健康发展。

（二）金砖国家投融资合作有助于推动国际金融治理体系的变革

依托金砖国家新开发银行及各国的投融资实践，金砖国家已经成为推动国际金融合作机制建设和重塑国家金融秩序的新生力量。作为国际政治经济格局中重要的参与者，金砖国家通过广泛参与全球资本有效配置，优化金融监管方式和手段，逐步扩展对外投资的地域分布、资产种类、辐射影响，对世界经济企稳回升发挥着日益强大的作用。随着整体能力的增强，金砖国家在国际社会，特别是在反对贸易保护主义、维护金融安全、维护和发展开放型世界经济、平衡地区发展和多边外交等方面，开始承担越来越多的义务与责任，推动完善全球金融治理体系。

现阶段，很多专家学者对全球金融治理保持乐观态度，纷纷看好二十国集团和新兴经济体的发展，尤其是看好金砖国家投融资合作对全球金融治理发展的推进作用。金砖国家之间有诸多共同的利益，这为投融资合作奠定了坚实的基础。俄罗斯金砖国家研究国家委员会主席尼科诺夫（Nikonov）表示，金砖国家之间投融资合作有利于激发处于发展阶段的金砖国家及其他新兴经济体的经济潜力，深入推进全球金融治理。南非发展银行首席执行官德拉米尼（Dlamini）也认为，国际金融危机爆发后，现行的国际金融体系已越来越难以把握新兴市场的发展需求；而金砖国家的投融资合作，将有利于应对流动性和融资不足的挑战，可以间接地增加金砖国家在国际金融体系中的谈判筹码，更好地完善和融入全球的金融治理。

金砖国家已积极参加全球金融治理体系，并主动参与和关注诸如《巴塞尔协议Ⅲ》谈判、世界贸易组织议程对话、二十国集团峰会以及

《全面与进步跨太平洋伙伴关系协定》（Comprehensive Progressive Trans - Pacific Partnership，CPTPP）谈判、世界银行和国际货币基金组织配额与投票权改革等一系列全球活动，谋求现有的国际金融制度框架的完善。

二 助力各国实现经济结构改革

（一）金砖国家内部结构改革任务依然艰巨

巴西总统更迭和经济疲软使改革乏力。巴西政府和国会之间的紧张局势、巴西石油公司腐败案持续发酵等政治问题加剧了未来经济发展的不确定性。此外，巴西主要依托于初级产品来发展经济，国内制造业则处于停滞或萎缩状态。长期落后的基础设施建设已成为制约经济发展的"瓶颈"。为此，巴西政府除继续对进口工业品维持一定的关税之外，还在政策层面提出了一些应对措施，使初级产品出口实现增值，同时支持创新。

俄罗斯资源型经济结构亟待转型。俄罗斯对资源型经济过度依赖，国际能源价格持续下跌对其造成了巨大冲击，自由市场竞争环境短期内难以形成。俄罗斯经济对能源和原材料行业的依赖已经成为其经济发展的痼疾。这导致俄罗斯经济对于外部环境波动的敏感性较高，尤其是油价的涨跌，能够对俄罗斯经济造成直接影响。摆脱过度依赖资源和原材料的现状，积极研发高新技术、实现经济创新发展成为俄罗斯政府和专家的共识。

印度长期"二元"结构性问题根深蒂固。印度贫富差距与产业发展差距大，服务业占印度GDP的比重超过了50%，但制造业比较落后。此外，印度信息产业高速发展与落后的基础设施并存。印度主要评级和研究机构CRISIL首席经济学家达马科特·乔希表示，印度经济增长模式大约在2000年之后从以农业为主转变成主要靠服务业和消费支撑。服务业在印度经济起飞时实现了很大的发展，但制造业并没有出现大幅提振，而制造业是除农业以外劳动力最为密集的部门，印度现在需要振兴制造业，以解决严峻的就业问题。

中国供给侧结构性改革面临体制障碍。国有企业改革、财政金融、价格体制、土地制度、社会保障等关键环节和重点领域的市场化改革尚未取得实质性突破，经济发展方式转变迟滞，经济动力活力不足。此外，去产能、去库存、去杠杆等进程都发展较缓，未达到社会预期，迫切需要创新工作方式。

南非对外依赖程度过高，削弱了自主性。南非经济对大宗商品特别是矿产品的出口依赖度较高，但受成本上涨和矿井储备减少的影响，南非采矿行业开始陷入困境。南非政府开始实施新经济增长战略，以促进南非矿业、制造业、交通业、农业、旅游业、绿色产业、金融业、高新技术产业等行业全面快速发展，致力于解决高失业率和电力短缺等问题。

（二）金砖国家团结一致，维护经济全球化，促进经济结构改革

当前"逆全球化"潮流正在上升，在这种贸易保护主义抬头的情况下，金砖国家更需要团结一致，进一步推动贸易自由化，走出缓慢发展的泥潭，同舟共济，共谋发展，寻求共赢。

金砖国家经济正经历新旧动能转换，亟须通过较深层次的结构性调整，以及金砖国家投融资领域的合作，挖掘新的经济增长点，不断提高劳动生产率和潜在增长率。金砖国家应当完善合作机制，打造全球经济增长新引擎，并通过有效的沟通协调，探索金砖国家经贸合作、政策环境、金融风险等多领域、多议题的共识，在加强金砖国家内部合作基础上推动与其他国家的合作。

金砖国家已经认识并高度重视科技创新在产业发展中的作用，也都制定了各自的战略规划来促进本国技术创新和产业升级。中国发布了《国家创新驱动发展战略纲要》，全面启动实施"科技创新2030——重大项目"，实施《新一代人工智能发展规划》，"大众创业，万众创新"蓬勃开展。科技创新研究重点领域包括：航空航天和国防、饮用水、食品、生物群落和生物经济、社会科学技术、气候、数字经济和数字社会、能源、核能、卫生。

俄罗斯在2016年12月正式实施《俄罗斯联邦科学技术发展战略》，聚焦领域包括航空航天、大洋、极地开发与研究；先进的数字和智能制造技术、机器人制造系统；节能环保型经济，提高碳氢原料的开采和深加工效率；个性化医疗与精准医疗，合理利用包括抗生素在内的各类药物。

印度2013年发布了《科学技术和创新政策》，并将继续实施《印度十年创新路线图（2010—2020年）》。

南非 2016 年出台了《研究基础设施路线图》，扩大南非国家研究网络建设，建立高性能计算中心，制定天文学国家战略，大力发展以 SKA 大科学项目为重点的研究基础设施建设。重点领域包括天文、信息通信、新能源、新材料、医学等。

加强金砖国家的投融资合作，有利于促进产业向高附加值的知识型创造活动转移。资源型国家可以通过吸收外国投资来发展加工制造业，逐步提高国内增加值，从资源比较优势向规模经济跨越。劳动密集型国家在全球价值链中升级的关键在于提升产品的技术水平，提高生产率，增加值创造能力，向技术更高、更复杂的环节发展。

三 促进金砖国家基础设施建设及产业合作

（一）加速基础建设，为发展保驾护航

目前，以金砖国家为代表的新兴经济体的经济发展大多都受到基础设施老旧和不足的制约。印度一半以上的国土还未开通公路，同时铁路系统运力严重不足；俄罗斯虽在铁路和公路设施上有一定基础，但普遍设施陈旧，与实现新经济发展的需求不相匹配；南非电力设施急需更新换代，全国大部分公路路况很差；巴西的交通基础设施非常不完善。

国际货币基金组织的《世界经济展望》报告指出，许多发展中国家对于基础设施的投资量严重不足。世界银行 2016 年年初的报告也指出，新兴经济体每年可以吸收大约 2 万亿美元的基础设施投资，其中有一半目前尚未得到满足，而且这一差距将会扩大。根据预测，新兴经济体的基础设施投资需求未来十年每年都会翻番。政府预算是新兴经济体基础设施建设的最大资金来源，约占总金额的 75%。当前，无论是这些国家自身还是金融类国际组织所能提供的资金都较为有限。从国内来看，巴西、南非、印度的经常账户逆差较大，其国内储蓄不足以满足基础设施投资需求。中国和俄罗斯的经常账户虽然呈现顺差，但是，由于国内储蓄投资转换机制不健全、资本市场等长期融资欠发达、外汇储备不能直接用于国内投资等原因，中国和俄罗斯仍存在较大的融资缺口。从外部融资来看，2008—2012 年，国际复兴开发银行（IBRD）贷款和国际开发协会（IDA）对金砖国家的信贷总额为 717.2 亿美元，其中，对俄罗斯的

信贷仅为6.5亿美元。2016年，金砖国家对国际货币基金组织的信贷使用仅为419.3亿美元。其中，巴西对国际货币基金组织的信贷使用仅为38.8亿美元。多边国际开发机构数百亿美元的资金供给，相对于新兴经济体投资建设的资金需要而言，只是杯水车薪，难以满足金砖国家以万亿美元计的基础设施融资需求，从而迫切需要金砖国家创新融资渠道，以多样、灵活、广泛的投融资合作来促进发展。

大多数发展中国家正处于工业化和城镇化的高速发展阶段，对基础设施建设的需求较大，加强金砖国家的投融资合作，将会为基础设施建设提供更多的资金来源，促进市场要素的充分流动，为经济发展保驾护航。

（二）扩大产业合作，发挥优势，升级发展

在产业合作方面，金砖国家是由新兴市场大国组成的群体，有着共同的利益诉求和经济合作的基础与条件。金砖国家的崛起与合作将产生推动经济增长的大国效应。由各国国内需求构成的巨大市场潜力，将扩大经济规模，加深各国产业分工程度，促进经济快速增长。

金砖国家的资源禀赋和经济结构存在较强的互补性，形成了较好的合作基础。比如，中国和俄罗斯经常项目顺差，对外净输出资本；印度和巴西经常项目逆差，需要通过国外资本流入来弥补。同时，俄罗斯和巴西是资源能源的供应者，而中国和印度是资源能源的消费者，对进口依赖较大。在农业领域，中国和印度是世界上人口最多的国家，对农产品有巨大的需求，而俄罗斯和巴西是农产品大国，有巨大的农产品供应能力和生产潜力。在基础建设领域，中国基础设施建设能力和技术水平在全世界居于前列，可以为其他金砖国家提供工程承包、建设、运营、设备供应等方面的服务。此外，金砖国家在发展过程中也形成了自身的比较优势，产生了优势部门和产业，如印度的无线电传输和软件技术，南非的运输设备技术和矿业开采技术，巴西的农业技术、支线飞机技术，俄罗斯的军工技术以及中国的制造业、互联网技术等。在此基础上，经济和贸易结构匹配的国家之间可以互相合作，取长补短，共谋发展。同时，金砖国家合作会将产业优势进一步扩大，形成优势互补的产业体系。

除优势互补之外，金砖国家在国际前沿领域也可以通过投融资合作进行先进技术的研发工作，例如，新能源、新材料、生物医药、信息技术、智能制造等。加强能力建设，升级发展，突破金砖国家在高技术领域的发展"瓶颈"，推动国内产业结构向高端迈进。

在过去十年，金砖国家加强投融资合作，探索新的投融资合作模式和机制，改善基础设施，提高贸易及其他产业合作便利化水平。国家开发银行也参与了很多重大项目，促进了金砖国家基础设施建设。例如，以直接融资模式支持南非 Transnet 国有铁路运输公司向中国中车、中国南车、中国北车采购机车项目①，以投贷联动模式支持中国长江三峡集团收购巴西水电站项目②和以本币保函模式支持中国国家电网中标巴西美丽山输电线项目③，极大地促进了投融资模式的创新，降低了企业融资成本，在推动金砖国家基础设施建设的同时，提高了经济和社会效益。

四 深化金砖国家之间的经贸往来

（一）金砖国家各国经贸合作现状

1. 货物贸易整体呈现上升趋势

联合国贸易和发展会议数据库（UNCTADstat）数据显示，2006—2016 年，金砖国家贸易增长很快，2016 年总进口额、出口额较 2006 年分别增长了 94 个和 84 个百分点。从趋势来看，2006—2011 年金砖国家货物进出口贸易整体呈现快速上升趋势，仅在 2009 年受国际金融危机的冲击而出现大幅下降；2011—2016 年，增速有所放缓，其中，2015 年、2016 年出现较大幅度下降，这与金砖国家贸易环境及政策的变化有一定的关系（见图 2 - 1）。在整体贸易盈余方面，金砖国家货物出口总额始终大于进口总额。

2. 服务贸易整体呈现逆差状态

与货物贸易发展趋势类似，金砖国家服务贸易进出口总额在 2006—2014 年呈现出快速增长趋势，分别增长了 179 个和 103 个百分点；2015 年出现小幅下降，降幅近 5%；2016 年，服务贸易继续下降。总的来看，

---

① 参见本书附录"案例三：南非 Transnet 国有铁路运输公司与国家开发银行项目"。
② 参见本书附录"案例四：投贷联动支持中国长江三峡集团收购巴西水电站项目"。
③ 参见本书附录"案例五：本币保函创新支持中国国家电网中标巴西美丽山输电线项目"。

其服务贸易进口总额大于出口总额的趋势越来越显著，2016 年，服务贸易逆差额高达2713.1 亿美元（见图2–2）。

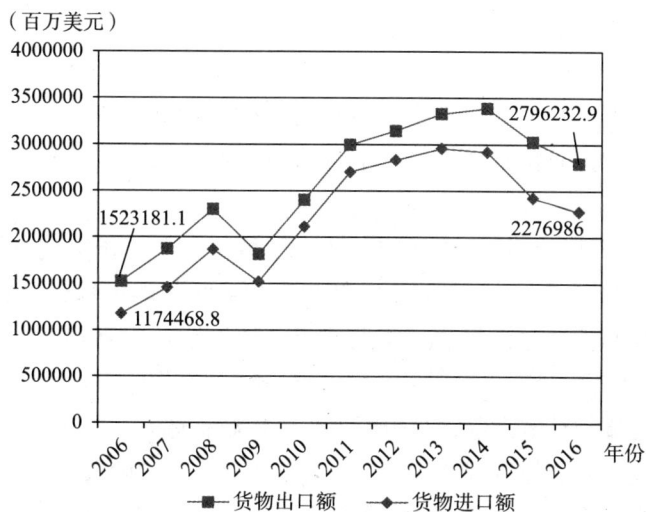

（百万美元）

1523181.1

2796232.9

1174468.8

2276986

图 2–1　2006—2016 年金砖国家货物进出口总额

资料来源：UNCTADStat。

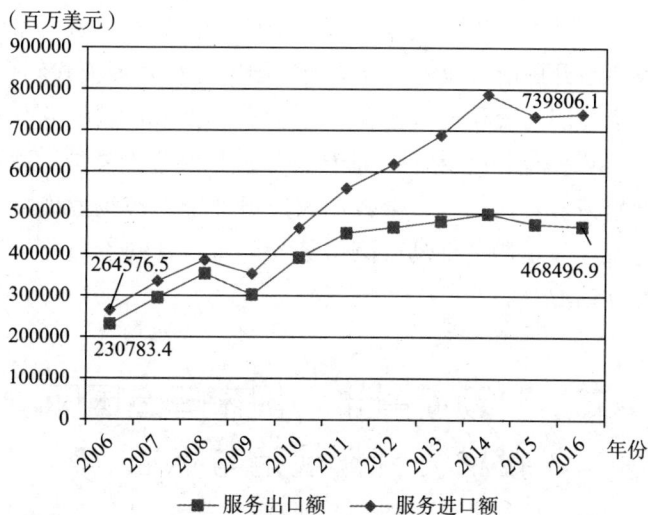

（百万美元）

264576.5

739806.1

230783.4

468496.9

图 2–2　2006—2016 年金砖国家服务进出口总额

资料来源：UNCTADStat。

（二）金砖国家投融资合作有助于降低对其他国家的依赖

2013 年 3 月颁布的《金砖国家贸易投资合作框架》提出了金砖国家内部加强合作的新原则、新概念、新模式和新机制，以及在部长级会议基础上，推动相关合作机制落地实施的安排。然而，虽然政府主导和推动的力度较大，但企业、社团等民间力量参与渠道不多，国家层面的贸易投资合作框架并没有变为实实在在的企业红利和个人利益。因此，尽管多年过去了，但相关合作机制推进依然缓慢，无法满足金砖国家经济发展的实际需要。

金砖国家已注意到这些问题并致力于解决。金砖国家建立了财长和央行行长、财政和央行行长副手、知识产权局长、能源部长、农业部长、环境部长等部长级会议机制，定期举行工商论坛等配套活动。金砖国家还成立了经贸联络组、电子商务工作组、海关工作组，以推进各层次间的协调与交流。总体来看，金砖国家合作机制整体"松而不散"，个别领域具有较完备的合作机制，适应了金砖国家合作发展阶段的需要。

2017 年 9 月 3—5 日，金砖国家领导人第九次会晤在福建厦门举行。金砖国家经贸部长会议达成了包括《金砖国家投资便利化合作纲要》在内的 8 项成果，经济技术合作首次纳入金砖国家经贸合作议程。其中，《金砖国家经济技术合作框架》指出，金砖国家将根据成员国的合作意愿和具体需求，围绕贸易投资便利化、电子商务、服务贸易、知识产权等领域，有重点地开展能力建设，分享金砖国家经济发展模式和合作理念，推动金砖国家经济发展和技术进步，共同落实好《联合国 2030 年可持续发展议程》。秉持厦门峰会精神，金砖国家应推动金融领域大联通，促进经贸的全面繁荣。具体而言，金砖国家应抓住金融市场发展机遇，不断完善现有金融合作机制，推动金融市场参与者、基础设施提供者和监管机构的良性互动。

五　引领新兴市场国家塑造国际投融资合作规范与标准

（一）现有的国际投融资规则约束较多

2008 年国际金融危机之后，为了保护和创造新的就业机会，发达国家转向了实体经济。放慢对外转移制造业的节奏，并且采取了财税等措施吸引跨国公司资金回流到国内。与此同时，经历危机的跨国公司对其全球投资也进行重组。这导致国际资本对发展中国家的投入减少，更多地在发达国家之间流动。在国际金融危机的大背景下，各国投资政策呈现"推进投资自由化"和"投资保护主义"两种倾向并行的特点，且"投资保护主义"抬头迹象明显。投资保护主义将对世界经济造成严重影响，尤其是对新兴经济体影响更大。

目前，国际投资规则还处于碎片化状态中，分散且内容不一，不仅缺乏综合性的多边制度，也缺乏一个有效运作的国际机构。金砖国家经济结构转型过程中都在一定程度上伴随着现有国际投融资合作规范的约束。

（二）金砖国家探索投融资合作新模式

金砖国家作为完善国际金融秩序的倡议者，在投融资方面加强合作，有助于积累经验，引领逐步建立和塑造国际投融资合作规范与标准。共同摸索建立符合新兴国家发展情况的国际投融资合作规范与标准，对实现投资自由化和便利化，探索投资监管方式，维护投资东道国和投资国的利益，释放金砖国家的经济活力都是十分有益的。

探索在新兴经济体之间关于保护投资者权益，解决投资的市场准入，营造良好的投资环境，平衡投资者与东道国利益方面的经验，在金砖国家合作框架下提出有特色的合作规范，将有利于促进金砖国家经济发展，提升金砖国家在未来多边国际投资规则制定的话语权，也将为其他新兴经济体提供借鉴和指引。此外，金砖国家之间已经开始构建知识分享与投融资国家合作新机制。金砖国家注重提升与国际智库合作水平，加强智库能力建设合作，加强重点问题研究，通过举办国际论坛、示范项目咨询等，深化知识和发展经验分享，有助于金砖国家之间的政策沟通及各方发展战略对接。

第三章 金砖各国投融资重点领域与产业

一 巴西

（一）发展规划

自巴西总统米歇尔·特梅尔上台执政后，设立了"投资伙伴计划"，负责执行"增长计划"以弥补劳工党推行的"经济加速增长计划"和"物流投资计划"所造成的空白，加大对巴西基础设施领域的投资，推动其薄弱环节的发展。

2016 年 9 月 13 日，政府主持召开了"投资伙伴计划"委员会第一次会议，公布了包括机场、港口、铁路、公路等多个领域在内的 34 个特许经营权项目清单，于 2017 年陆续招标。巴西政府希望通过这批项目改善经济颓势，增加就业岗位，弱化中央政府的职权，刺激私人领域参与的积极性。

巴西通信部 2016 年 5 月发布了"智慧巴西"的国家宽带发展计划，计划到 2019 年投入 18.5 亿雷亚尔（约合 5.29 亿美元），使巴西拥有光纤网络的城镇数量由 53% 提高至 70%，使宽带网络覆盖巴西 95% 的人口。

根据计划，多个大型网络基础设施建设项目将陆续开工实施，包括在亚马孙部分区域铺设网络，以及 2017 年发射一颗国防和通信地球同步卫星。巴西通信部还宣布，将建设 6 条海底光缆，连接巴西与欧洲、非洲和美国，用以提高网络数据传输能力和保障通信安全，为巴西网络连接降低 20% 的成本。此外，政府还将通过设立信用担保基金的方式帮助网络小供应商向银行融资，参与中小城市网络建设。未来，"我的生活，我的家"居民住房保障计划中新建的房屋也将建设宽带网络设施。全国约 3 万所城市和农村公立学校将开通宽带、无线网，并建立多媒体中心。

（二）重点产业

1. 农林牧业

巴西土地资源丰富，气候条件优越，全国可耕地面积达 1.53 亿公顷，占国土面积的 18%。农业在巴西经济中占据重要地位，农业产值占其国内生产总值的 21%。巴西同时还是全球农产品出口大国，农产品出口是巴西国民经济的支柱产业，农产品出口量几乎占总出口量的 50%。其中，大豆产量居全球第 1 位，出口量居全球第 2 位；玉米产量居全球第 3 位，出口量居全球第 2 位。出口量位居世界第一的产品还有蔗糖、咖啡、橙汁、烟草和酒精。

2. 石油天然气

巴西从 20 世纪 50 年代开始进行石油天然气勘探开发，目前，石油天然气行业的产值占巴西国内生产总值的 12%。就石油及能源行业发展规划来看，根据 OPEC 的研究，到 2020 年，巴西在全世界的石油储量排名，将从现在的全世界第 15 名跃升至第 8 名。根据 ANP 的数据，到 2035 年，巴西油气产量在全球的排名将会从目前的第 9 位上升至第 6 位。储量和产量的增加，将会带动巴西石油出口量的增加。

3. 汽车工业

汽车工业约占巴西工业总产值的 40%，已逐步发展成为巴西工业的重要支柱产业，对巴西经济发展发挥了重要作用。目前，世界著名汽车企业均在巴西投资设厂，其中，包括德国的戴姆勒和大众、美国的福特和通用、法国的标志和雷诺以及英国的陆虎等。

4. 纺织业

巴西是世界主要的纺织服装生产国之一，是全球第五大纺织品生产商和第四大成衣制造国。巴西有 33000 家纺织企业，年产服装 68 亿件。巴西是全球第四大纺织品出口商，其纺织品和服装公司中也有很多世界级企业。

5. 服务业

服务业对巴西经济发展举足轻重，不仅是产值最高的产业，也是创造就业机会最多的行业。主要包括不动产、租赁、旅游业、金融、保险、信息、广告、咨询和技术服务等。其中，旅游业有 80 多年的历史，游客多来自拉美、欧洲和美国。根据 2016 年全球旅游竞争指数排名，巴西在全球 136 个国家中排名第 27 位。其中，巴西在自然资源方面排在第 1 位，在文化层面排在第 8 位，但在基础设施、旅游价格等方面还需要改善。2016 年，巴西共接待外国游客 660 万人，为巴西带来旅游收入 60.24 亿美元，较 2015 年增长 6.2%。

（三）外商投资

2017 年，巴西吸引外商直接投资额为 703.3 亿美元，比 2016 年降低 10.1%。2009—2011 年，巴西外商直接投资额呈上升态势，并于 2011 年达最高值为 961.52 亿美元，然而，自 2014 年起，巴西外商直接投资逐步减少，其主要是由于通货膨胀率居高不下、关键工业领域库存高企、大宗商品疲软、失业情况恶化、政局动荡，从而引发消费衰退，企业投资信心受挫，经济发展停滞。

2017 年，巴西吸纳直接投资额前十位的国家（地区）分别为美国、荷兰、英属维尔京群岛、卢森堡、德国、法国、西班牙、智利、墨西哥、意大利，分别占巴西外商直接投资总额的 18.36%、18.05%、15.03%、7.13%、5.34%、5.25%、3.83%、2.69%、2.53%、2.52%（见表 3 - 1）。同时，2008—2017 年，巴西累计吸纳外商直接投资额前十位的国家（地区）分别为荷兰、美国、卢森堡、西班牙、日本、法国、瑞士、英国、德国、英属维尔京群岛，分别占巴西外商直接投资总额的 18.60%、15.15%、9.89%、7.55%、5.29%、5.02%、3.88%、3.29%、3.19%、3.17%。由此可见，欧美等发达国家依然是巴西外商直接投资的主要力量，其目的在于获取巴西丰富的矿产资源。

表 3 - 1　　　　　　　2017 年巴西累计外商直接投资额
前 20 位的国家（地区）　　　　　　单位：亿美元

序号	国家（地区）	投资额	序号	国家（地区）	投资额
1	美国	110.78	11	瑞士	12.88
2	荷兰	108.94	12	英国	11.71
3	英属维尔京群岛	90.69	13	中国香港	11.23
4	卢森堡	43.05	14	巴哈马群岛	11.22
5	德国	32.21	15	挪威	9.39
6	法国	31.68	16	中国	6.43
7	西班牙	23.09	17	日本	5.37
8	智利	16.20	18	开曼群岛	4.69
9	墨西哥	15.27	19	韩国	4.54
10	意大利	15.21	20	葡萄牙	3.18

资料来源：巴西中央银行。

结合巴西社会经济发展规划及巴西重点产业的优势和现状，当前，外资主要集中在电信、电力、油气、房地产、金融、医疗等领域，从资金和技术两个方面推进产业升级。2017 年，巴西吸引外商直接投资的主要领域，按照比重排名前十的行业分别是：电力和天然气、商业（除机动车外）、交通业、机动车及相关部件、石油和天然气开采、基本冶金、化学产品、食品、储存及运输和金融服务（见图 3 - 1）。

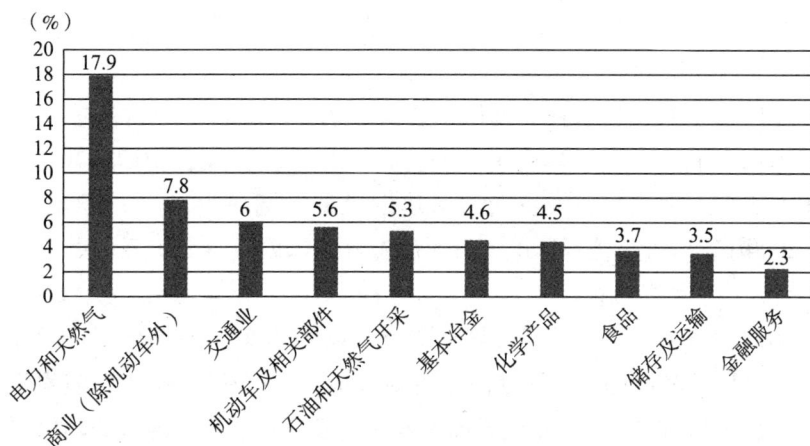

图 3 - 1　2017 年巴西吸引外商投资前十大行业

资料来源：CEIC 和巴西中央银行。

2008—2017 年，外商对巴西投资累计最多的领域是服务业，投资累计额为 2850.62 亿美元，占外商直接投资累计总额的 47.96%，同时，巴西外商直接投资累计总额前十位的产业为贸易（除车辆外），石油和天然气开采，基础冶金，财务和辅助服务，电力和天然气，金属矿物提取，化学产品，机动车、拖车、半拖车和相关部件，食品，电信，共占外商直接投资累计额的 58.74%。

综上所述，巴西应继续加强服务业的招商力度，外商投资重点产业为贸易（除车辆外），财务和辅助服务，电力和天然气，石油和天然气开采，金属矿物提取，机动车、拖车、半拖车和相关部件，化学产品等，一方面可充分利用现有的外商投资基础，另一方面可以升级巴西出口弱势产业，优化产业结构，推进经济全面发展。

二　俄罗斯

（一）发展规划

在俄罗斯总统普京再次当选后，俄罗斯将继续实施《2020 年前俄罗斯联邦社会经济长期发展构想》，重点进行产业结构调整，扩大投资，发展创新经济，加快对传统工业的升级改造，改善基础设施建设，稳步推进国有企业私有化。

2018 年 3 月，普京在年度国情咨文中表示，俄罗斯经济增速应超过世界平均水平，计划人均国内生产总值在 21 世纪 20 年代中期提升到当前的 1.5 倍。未来六年，俄罗斯公路建设投资将翻一番，达 11 万亿卢布（约 2000 亿美元），俄罗斯电力行业设施升级计划吸引 1.5 万亿卢布（约 260 亿美元）私人投资。

2018 年 5 月 7 日，普京签署总统令，规划了 2024 年前俄罗斯联邦的战略发展任务和目标。总统令内容主要包括：政府在 2024 年以前须将俄罗斯贫困人口减少 1/2，保证居民收入稳定增长，退休金的增长幅度要高于通货膨胀率。到 2024 年，要将人口平均寿命提高到 78 岁。未来六年，每年新增或改造住房需满足 500 万户家庭的需要。到 2024 年，俄罗斯要进入全球五大经济体，未来六年，每年都要保证俄罗斯 GDP 增长高于全球平均值，通货膨胀率不超过 4%。

在能源发展方面，2015 年 3 月，俄罗斯出台 2035 年前能源发展战略草案设想。到 2035 年，天然气产量将从 6400 亿立方米增加到 8050 亿—8800 亿立方米，石油年产量 5.25 亿吨，难以开采石油和大陆架石油在俄罗斯石油总产量中的比重到 2035 年将占 25%，年产量将达 1.3 亿吨。石油出口量将从 2.2 亿吨增加到 2.7 亿吨。此外，到 2035 年液化天然气产量将增长 5 倍；煤炭产量将达到 4.35 亿吨，出口量将增长 20%；电力需求将增长 15%；能源投资总额将达 2.5 万亿美元。

同时，俄罗斯政府确定了财政拨款优先发展的经济领域，包括农业（包含农业服务）、加工业（包括食品生产）、化工、机械制造（航空、船舶、汽车生产等）和住房建设。此外，优先投资项目还有运输行业，包括空运（空港、空运商业、运输基础设施），通信与电信，以及电、气、水和其他资源的生产和分配。

2016 年 2 月,俄罗斯工业贸易部制定了 2017 年度俄罗斯农业扶持发展规划,政府计划投入资金 1400 亿卢布,其中,预算补贴 1273 亿卢布。作为规划重点,将有部分资金用于贫困家庭购买俄罗斯农副产品的生活补贴。2017 年 7 月,俄罗斯联邦政府总理梅德韦杰夫签署实施《2030 年前俄联邦农业机械行业发展纲要》的命令。根据该纲要,到 2030 年,俄罗斯农机生产商在国内市场占有率将不低于 80%,出口比重不少于国内销售量的 50%。预计到 2021 年,俄罗斯国际市场总销量为 1750 亿卢布,到 2025 年将达 2020 亿卢布,到 2030 年为 2650 亿卢布。

(二) 重点产业

1. 石油天然气工业

石油天然气工业长期以来在俄罗斯经济中发挥着核心作用,乌拉尔牌石油价格是俄罗斯制定国家财政预算的重要依据。2016 年,俄罗斯石油(包括凝析油)产量为 5.5 亿吨,同比增长 2.5%;原油加工量 2.85 亿吨,同比下降 1.3%;出口石油 2.55 亿吨,同比增长 4.2%。当年俄罗斯天然气开采量为 6400 亿立方米,同比增长 0.7%;出口量为 1987 亿立方米,同比增长 7%。

2. 冶金行业

俄罗斯矿产资源丰富,铁、铝、铜、镍等金属矿产的储量和产量都居于世界前列,矿石开采和冶金行业在俄罗斯经济中发挥重要作用,冶金行业是俄罗斯重要的工业部门之一,其产值约占俄罗斯国内生产总值的 2.8%,占工业生产的 10.2%。冶金产品是俄罗斯主要出口商品之一。从出口创汇额来看,俄罗斯冶金行业占俄罗斯所有行业创汇额的 17%,仅次于燃料动力综合体,居第 2 位。

3. 国防工业

俄罗斯国防工业继承了苏联庞大国防的大部分,从设计、研发、实验到生产体系都较为完整,部门较为齐全,是世界上少有的能生产海、陆、空、天武器和装备的国家。在俄罗斯国内装备更新速度有限的情况下,俄罗斯国防工业大力发展对外合作与出口,2016 年,俄武器出口超过 150 亿美元。在俄罗斯出口武器名单中,占据首位的是军用飞机,随后依次为海军舰艇、陆军装备和防空武器。

（三）外商直接投资

2017 年，俄罗斯外商直接投资额为 278.86 亿美元，比 2016 年减少 14.3%。自 2014 年以来，由于乌克兰冲突、克里米亚收复引发的国际制裁，天然气、石油价格暴跌以及卢布贬值等因素的影响，引发了俄罗斯经济衰退，营商环境恶化，对外国资本的吸引力大幅削弱。同时，其他新兴经济体的高速发展对俄罗斯外商直接投资产生了一定的冲击，因此，俄罗斯外商直接投资波动性较大，且处于低速发展阶段。

2017 年前三季度，俄罗斯外商直接投资额前十位的国家（地区）分别是塞浦路斯、巴哈马、卢森堡、新加坡、英国、瑞士、百慕大、德国、英属维尔京群岛、爱尔兰，分别占外商直接投资总额的 25.33%、18.88%、13.66%、7.44%、6.53%、5.61%、4.76%、4.18%、3.71%、3.33%（见表3-2）。同时，2008—2017 年9 月，俄罗斯外商直接投资累计额前十位的国家（地区）分别为塞浦路斯、荷兰、英属维尔京群岛、卢森堡、爱尔兰、英国、巴哈马、百慕大、新加坡、德国，分别占俄罗斯外商直接投资累计额的 14.92%、8.30%、8.20%、8.11%、7.27%、6.52%、6.05%、4.61%、4.20%、4.20%。由此可见，西欧及"避税天堂"地区是俄罗斯外商直接投资的主要来源。

表 3-2　　　　　2017 年前三季度俄罗斯外商直接
投资前 20 位的国家（地区）　　　　单位：亿美元

序号	国家（地区）	投资额	序号	国家（地区）	投资额
1	塞浦路斯	64.17	11	中国香港	5.35
2	巴哈马	47.85	12	法国	5.24
3	卢森堡	34.60	13	泽西岛	5.20
4	新加坡	18.86	14	美国	4.36
5	英国	16.54	15	瑞典	3.12
6	瑞士	14.23	16	匈牙利	1.84
7	百慕大	12.06	17	哈萨克斯坦	1.29
8	德国	10.58	18	伯利兹	1.00
9	英属维尔京群岛	9.40	19	土耳其	1.00
10	爱尔兰	8.44	20	阿联酋	0.88

资料来源：俄罗斯联邦中央银行。

　　2017 年前三季度，外商对俄罗斯直接投资最多的行业为采矿和采石，占外商投资总额的 21.29%。俄罗斯外商直接投资前十位的行业为采矿和采石，金融和保险活动，制造业，建筑业，批发和零售贸易、修理汽车和摩托车，专业、科学和技术活动，信息和通信，电、气、蒸汽和空调供应，房地产，行政和支持性服务，共占外商直接投资的 67.30%（见表 3-3）。

表 3-3　　　　2017 年前三季度俄罗斯外商直接投资产业结构　　单位：亿美元

产业	投资额	产业	投资额
农、林、渔业	-3.63	房地产	4.94
采矿和采石	77.41	专业、科学和技术活动	17.08
制造业	32.71	行政和支持性服务	0.73
电、气、蒸汽和空调供应	10.80	公共行政和防务、强制性社会保障	0.00
供水、废水处理、废物综合管理和修复活动	-0.36	教育业	0.13
建筑业	21.16	人类健康和社会工作活动	0.60
批发和零售贸易、修理汽车和摩托车	18.30	艺术、娱乐和休闲	0.54
运输和储存	-2.91	其他服务活动	0.00
住宿和食品服务活动	0.69	雇用家庭活动、区别于商品和服务的家庭自用产品活动	0.00
信息和通信	15.19	境外组织和机构活动	0.00
金融和保险活动	56.00	未分配	4.02

　　资料来源：俄罗斯联邦中央银行。

　　2010—2017 年 9 月，俄罗斯外商直接投资累计额前十位的产业为批发和零售贸易、修理汽车和摩托车，采矿和采石，金融和保险活动，制造业，其他服务活动，建筑，房地产，电、气、蒸汽和空调供应，专业、科学和技术活动，农、林、渔业，累计达 3059.17 亿美元。

　　因此，俄罗斯应发挥其矿产优势，利用国内政策，支持其采矿业与冶金业的发展。此外，俄罗斯需大力引入外资以发展金融和保险活动，批发和零售贸易，制造业，建筑业，专业、科学和技术活动，纺织业，电力，天然气，行政和支持性服务及医药业。这样，既可优化俄罗斯产业结构，又可满足俄罗斯市场需求。

三　印度

（一）发展规划

2014—2015 财年年末，印度政府公布了 2015—2020 年新五年对外贸易政策，这是莫迪政府成立以来出台的首个五年对外贸易政策。新政策是按照莫迪总理提出的"印度制造"和"数字印度"计划而制定，旨在刺激印度制造业和服务业出口，促进就业增长。"印度制造"计划是印度政府将印度打造为制造业大国的一项重要战略举措。该战略将汽车、制药、信息技术、可再生能源、电子等 25 个行业确立为重点发展领域，通过简化审批程序，努力为国内外投资者创造良好的商业环境。在"数字印度"这一框架下，印度政府将投资 1.13 万亿卢比（约 170 亿美元）用于推进技术运用，使公民广泛参与数字和金融服务，保障公民实时享有网络和移动平台服务，全面提升公民的数字素养，创造安全可靠的网络空间，规范电子政府，推动各级政府之间电子文件流转。

与往年相比，新政策主要内容及变化包括：一是对劳动密集型和高增长潜力行业的商品和服务出口增加两项激励措施。二是未制定年度出口目标，而是制定了一个五年联合出口目标，即到 2020 年，印度商品和服务出口将达 9000 亿美元。三是政策的修订期限由原来的每年一次改为每两年半修订一次。四是特定商品的网上出口交易、来自特别经济区的出口、开拓特定欧盟市场等将获得政府相应激励。五是出口至与印度签订了自由贸易协定的国家的商品和服务享受较高幅度激励。

（二）重点行业

1. 农业

印度拥有世界 10% 的可耕地，耕地面积约 1.8 亿公顷，是世界上最大的粮食生产国之一，农牧产品丰富，牛奶、水果、茶产量位居全球第一，且印度三面环海，渔产丰富，各类水产品是政府扶持的重点出口产业之一。印度实施"农村生机国家计划"，着重提高农村发展潜力，为农村提供更多就业机会。具体措施包括：加大农业技术研发方面的投入，继续推进农地产权改革，改善物流体系和市场营销体系，为小农户提供更多的市场机会，加大对农业的金融支持力度。

2. 汽车行业

印度是世界上主要的汽车市场之一。得益于印度的物流和地理优势，全球所有的汽车巨头都在印度投资，以寻求潜在的市场机遇。印度的港口联系紧密，紧邻南亚和非洲，这种优良的地理区位有利于印度成长为区域性的制造和出口国。总体而言，由于印度政府的亲商立场，汽车生产商和供应商将长期保持对印度市场的信心并在印度持续投资。

3. 健康科学

印度生命科学行业是亚太地区规模最大且发展迅速的市场。在药物制剂和原料方面，印度是亚洲第二大市场，其有望在 2020 年前成为全球第五大市场之一。印度是全球第三大制药国，占全球药物生产的 8%。鉴于印度国内制药市场在未来的高速增长，全球最大的 20 家制药公司中有 18 家在印度设立了子公司。在生物技术方面，印度生物技术领域是亚太地区第三大市场，目前主要被国内生产者占领，就目前来看，外国公司仅占 20%。印度生物技术领域具有无限的、尚未开发的潜能，吸引了来自国内外的目光。印度政府在五年计划中通过公共资金来支援生物技术领域的发展，在下一个五年计划中斥资 37 亿美元用于该领域的建设。在医疗器械和设备方面，印度医疗器械领域排在世界前 20 名，每年人均医疗器械花费不到 3 美元，而其他新兴市场国家如中国则接近 7 美元，由此可见，印度的医疗器械市场潜力十分巨大。

4. 服务业

在服务部门，较为突出的改革是"数字印度"，政府的目的是把印度转变为一个数字化的知识经济体，并通过改善民众与政府的互动提升公民的管理水平。该计划以信息技术作为许多产业及各种消费服务交付的核心（包括在线政府服务访问，在线信息接收，以及零售、出租车、教育、金融和医疗在线服务）。该计划还可能在信息技术、电子和相关产业创造数以万计的就业岗位。"数字印度"成功地吸引了大量外国直接投资。据分析机构估计，30% 左右的外国直接投资与迅速扩张的电子商务部门有关。具体来看，印度的科技行业最近几年的投资出现了上升趋势。

（三）外商直接投资

2008—2011 年，印度受到国际金融危机的影响，外商直接投资逐年降低，而 2012—2017 年，印度外商直接投资额迅速恢复，但在 2016 年达顶峰后有所下降，2016—2017 年度①，印度外商直接投资额为 422.1 亿美元，这一方面是因为印度大力推行"印度制造"，加强招商引资力度；另一方面是由于国际大宗商品价格波动减轻了印度通货膨胀压力，激发经济增长潜力。

截至 2017 年 3 月，印度外商累计投资前十位的国家分别为毛里求斯、美国、英国、新加坡、日本、德国、荷兰、瑞士、韩国、法国，分别占外商直接投资总额的 21.77%、16.50%、14.46%、10.15%、9.31%、6.19%、5.37%、5.20%、2.01%、1.46%（见表 3-4）。

表 3-4　　　　　　　印度外商投资累计额前十位国家（地区）　　　　单位：亿美元

国家（地区）	外商投资额	国家（地区）	外商投资额
毛里求斯	779.85	德国	221.32
美国	590.37	荷兰	192.01
英国	517.45	瑞士	185.99
新加坡	363.02	韩国	71.97
日本	333.05	法国	52.28

资料来源：印度财政部。

2017 年，在印度外商直接投资的 15169 家企业中，企业数最多的领域为服务业，占企业总数的 66.68%。与此相对，印度外商直接投资市场价值最高的领域为制造业，占外商投资企业总值的 50.19%。具体从领域和产业来看，外商直接投资更青睐于计算机软件与硬件（16.1%）、电信（14.1%）和服务业（13.2%）。

按累计外资流入资金计算，服务业（包括金融、银行、保险等行业，占 17.62%）、电信业（8.51%）、电脑软硬件业（7.4%）、建筑业（6.06%）和汽车产业（5.32%）是对印度的投融资合作排名前五的重点领域。

因此，印度外商投资重点领域为制造业与服务业，而重点产业为信息和通信、金融和保险、食物产品、机械和设备、批发和零售业、汽车

---

① 印度的财务年度是指上一年度 4 月到次年 3 月，如 2008—2009 年度为 2008 年 4 月至 2009 年 3 月。

产业、电力、煤气、化学品和化工产品。印度应加速工业化、现代化发展速度，挖掘可持续发展潜力。

四　中国

（一）发展规划

根据《中华人民共和国国民经济和社会发展第十三个五年规划纲要》，中国将在 2016—2020 年维持中高速增长，经济年均增长率保持在 6.5% 以上，中国的经济总量将由 2015 年的 67.7 万亿元提高到 2020 年的 92.7 万亿元。届时，国内生产总值和人均国内生产总值将比 2010 年翻一番。

《中国制造 2025》是中国政府实施制造强国战略第一个十年的行动纲领，是中国政府立足于国际产业发展方向做出的全面提升中国制造业发展质量和水平的重大战略部署，其目标是：中国到 2025 年迈入制造强国行列，到 2035 年，制造业整体达世界制造强国阵营中等水平，到 2045 年，综合实力进入世界制造强国前列。该纲要推动实行五大工程，包括制造业创新中心建设工程、强化基础工程、智能制造工程、绿色制造工程和高端装备创新工程。

2013 年 9 月和 10 月，中国国家主席习近平分别提出建设"新丝绸之路经济带"和"21 世纪海上丝绸之路"的合作倡议（简称"一带一路"倡议），致力于建立和加强沿线各国互联互通伙伴关系，发掘区域内市场的潜力，促进投资和消费，助力交通运输、铁路建设、装备制造业、建筑业等相关产业的联动发展。

中国为"绿色发展"设定了更为严厉的约束性指标：单位国内生产总值用水量、能耗、二氧化碳排放量将分别下降 23%、15%、18%，森林覆盖率从 21.66% 升至 23.04%、空气质量优良天数比率从 76.7% 升至 80% 以上。

从 2015 年开始，中国力推供给侧结构性改革，以去产能、去库存、去杠杆、降成本、补短板为重点，加快推进科技体制改革，促进高科技含量、高附加值产业的发展，加快生态文明体制改革，为绿色低碳产业发展提供动力。

（二）重点产业

1. 自然资源

中国地质条件多样，矿产资源有 171 种，其中，钨、稀土、铝、钒和钛等探明储量居世界首位，煤、铁、铅、锌、铜、磷灰石等储量居世界前列。

2. 金融业

目前，中国已形成了银行、保险、信托、证券、租赁等功能比较齐全、分工合作、多层次的、政策性金融和商业性金融协调发展的金融机构体系。无论从宏观金融还是金融行业内部，都形成了比较优良的金融环境，促进金融行业的健康发展。自中国金融市场逐步开放以来，金融监管也逐步提升，形成良好的态势，逐步朝着健康、有序的方向发展，使大量外国资本涌入中国市场。

3. 重点领域

中国国家发展和改革委员会办公厅在《增强制造业核心竞争力三年行动计划（2018—2020 年）》中对九个重点领域关键技术产业化提出了实施方案。这九个重点领域分别是：轨道交通装备、高端船舶和海洋工程装备、智能汽车、智能机器人、现代农业机械、高端医疗器械和药品、新材料、制造业智能化和重大技术装备。

此外，《中国制造 2025》明确了十个重点发展的领域，包括新一代信息技术产业、高档数控机床和机器人、航空航天装备、海洋工程装备及高技术船舶、先进轨道交通装备、节能与新能源汽车、电力装备、农机装备、新材料、生物医药及高性能医疗器械等。

（三）外商直接投资

自经济进入新常态，中国实际利用外资保持稳步增长的趋势。2017 年达到最高值，为 1363 亿美元，但 2006—2017 年，中国实际利用外资年增长率大幅降低。一方面是由于中国经济增长对环境要求越来越高，从而对外商资本的筛选标准更为严格；另一方面新兴经济体高速发展，吸引国际资本的能力逐渐增强，从而对中国外商直接投资产生了一定的冲击。

2017 年，中国外商直接投资前十位的国家（地区）为中国香港、新加坡、中国台湾、韩国、日本、美国、荷兰、德国、英国、丹麦，分别占实际投入外资总额的 79.38%、3.88%、3.80%、2.96%、2.62%、

2.52%、1.74%、1.24%、1.20%、0.66%（见表3－5）。由此可见，中国外商直接投资结构正逐步调整，由以欧美为核心转变为以东亚发达经济体为核心，这一方面是因为地域相邻，文化相通，投资成本较低，东亚国家（地区）具有较强的投资积极性；另一方面是中国经济发展势头良好，营商环境稳定，且拥有巨大的潜在消费市场，可以对东亚各国（地区）经济可持续发展产生重要的推动作用，因而东亚各国（地区）纷纷将目光投向中国。

表3－5　　　　　　**2017年中国外商投资前十位国家（地区）**　　　单位：亿美元

国家（地区）	外商投资额	国家（地区）	外商投资额
中国香港	989.2	美国	31.3
新加坡	48.3	荷兰	21.7
中国台湾	47.3	德国	15.4
韩国	36.9	英国	15.0
日本	32.7	丹麦	8.2

资料来源：中华人民共和国商务部。

2017年，中国外商直接投资前五位的产业是制造业，信息传输、计算机服务和软件业，房地产业，租赁和商务服务业，批发和零售业，外商直接投资额均超过100亿美元，共占外商直接投资总额的73.0%（见表3－6）。2010—2017年，中国外商直接投资累计额前五位的产业为制造业、房地产业、租赁和商务服务业、金融业、批发和零售业，累计达8092.71亿美元，占外商直接投资总额的79.51%。此外，从行业分布看，金砖其他国家投资主要集中在服务业领域，占60%以上；制造业领域占30%，农业领域占10%以下。

表3－6　　　　　　**2017年中国外商直接投资产业结构**　　　单位：亿美元

产业	外商直接投资	产业	外商直接投资
农林牧渔业	10.74	房地产业	168.55
采矿业	13.01	租赁和商务服务业	167.38
制造业	335.06	科学研究、技术服务和地质勘查业	68.43

产业	外商直接投资	产业	外商直接投资
电力、燃气及水的生产和供应业	35.21	水利、环境和公共设施管理业	5.69
建筑业	26.19	居民服务和其他服务业	5.67
交通运输、仓储和邮政业	55.88	教育	0.77
信息传输、计算机服务和软件业	209.18	卫生、社会保障和社会福利业	3.05
批发和零售业	114.78	文化、体育和娱乐业	6.98
住宿和餐饮业	4.19	公共管理和社会组织	0.00
金融业	79.21	国际组织	0.00

资料来源：中华人民共和国统计局。

综上所述，中国外商直接投资的重要产业为制造业、房地产、租赁和商务服务业、批发和零售业、金融业、农林牧渔业。中国应优化出口贸易结构，加速可持续发展和产业结构调整，完善营商市场环境，改善经济发展方式。

五　南非

（一）发展规划

受国际环境和本国经济发展放缓影响，南非政府近年来收紧了外资促进保护、签证、矿产资源开发等多项政策，土地改革不确定性较大。根据南非政府2010年制定的"新增长路线"，南非积极促进基础设施建设，农业、采矿、绿色经济、制造业、旅游和服务业六大重点领域发展，2012年公布了《2030国家发展规划》，制定到2030年发展目标，并配套制定了公路、铁路、电站等大规模基础设施建设规划和旨在发展海洋经济、医疗产业发展的《帕基萨计划》。此外，南非政府还牵头规划和实施非洲国家联盟"南北交通走廊"计划，并与周边国家积极展开能源项目合作，重视对核电等可再生能源开发建设。

南非政府在能源、矿业及金属工业方面制定了相关发展规划。南非在电力建设方面投入不足，新建电源投产滞后，南非及其周边国家的电力供应不足必将带来更多的兴建项目。南非政府将在电力行业加大投入及引进资产，以促进经济发展，并且进一步明确产权制度，放宽资源产业投资限制。

（二）重点产业

1. 农业

南非农业较发达，可耕地约占土地面积的13%，但高质量土地仅占可耕地面积的22%。农业、林业和渔业就业人数约占总人口的6%，其产品出口收入占南非矿业出口收入的15%。南非农业生产受气候变化影响明显，其盛产花卉、水果和红酒等，是全球第九大羊毛生产国，各类罐头食品、烟、酒、饮料等畅销海外。南非政府发布的空间战略一体化项目，要求加强农业物流和农村基础设施建设，改善农业和农村基础设施投资，通过仓储设施、交通、农场围栏、灌溉设施、农业问题研发、农业加工设施、水产养殖和农村旅游建设支持农村发展。

2. 自然资源

南非自然资源丰富，已发现60多种矿产资源，其中，红柱石、萤石、金、铂族金属储量位居世界第一，蛭、锆、铬、锰储量位居世界第二，磷酸盐和钒储量位居世界第三，且南非政府鼓励外商开展矿产原料加工，提升国家收入和产品附加值。另外，南非平均年日照2500小时，是全球太阳能资源最丰富的国家（地区）之一。

3. 工业

总的来说，南非政府在几乎全部行业都对外开放，鼓励外国企业投资。南非《2030国家发展规划》规定，南非政府必须实现经济发展多样性，包括进一步发展如采矿业等能源密集型产业，同时有序开展技术密集型产业、商业和服务业等。为促进本国汽车行业发展，南非政府发布了《汽车投资计划》，对汽车行业的新增投资和对旧有生产性的升级改造提供优惠政策，以增加汽车生产能力、稳定就业和加强汽车产业链发展。同时，汽车制造业也享受许多优先鼓励投资政策，包括外国投资补贴、本地生产税收优惠、长期投资返还等。

4. 旅游业

南非拥有极为丰富的自然和人文旅游资源，是世界上著名的旅游度假胜地，是非洲接待国际游客最多的国家，即使在经济放缓的形势下，南非的旅游业也实现连续七年的增长。旅游业是当前南非发展最快的行业，增速在全球列第三位，产值约占GDP的8.7%，从业人员达140多万人。世界经济论坛《2017 年旅游竞争力报告》显示，南非在 136 个经济体中名列第 53 位。

（三）外商投资

2017 年，南非外商直接投资流量为 13.3 亿美元，比 2016 年下降约 9 亿美元。2008—2010 年，南非受到国际金融危机的影响，外商直接投资大幅缩减，降至 42.4 亿美元；2011—2013 年，全球经济进入复苏阶段，由于矿产资源、劳动力资源丰富，南非再度受到全球资本关注，外商直接投资进入高速增长阶段；2014—2016 年，国际大宗商品价格回落，南非营商环境恶化，外商直接投资锐减，年均减幅为 23.07%。

从资金流入国来看，截至 2016 年，63.3% 的外商直接投资来源于欧洲，英国、美国、荷兰、比利时、卢森堡、德国、瑞士和中国是南非的主要投资来源地。

从行业分布上来看，2016 年，金融服务业，制造业，采矿、采石业，运输、仓储和通信业，批发零售、餐饮业，是外商主要投资的行业，其分别占 42.1%、20.8%、20.5%、10.4%、4.5%（见图 3-2）。南非的金融体系相当发达，金融业法律法规健全，货币和金融市场成熟，为外资的注入提供了良好的平台。金融服务业是外商直接投资额中占比最大的产业。南非位居世界汽车工业大国之列，是全球汽车及零部件制造和进出口主要国家之一，几乎所有主要汽车品牌在南非都设有工厂。

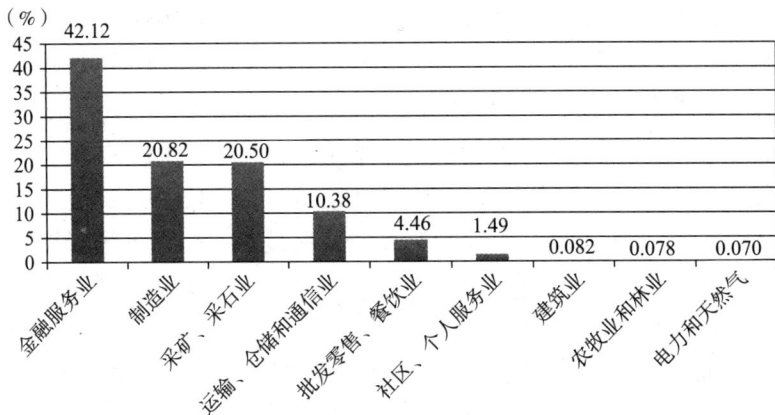

图 3-2 2016 年南非外商直接投资产业占比

资料来源：南非储蓄银行。

　　综上所述，南非外商投资重点领域为服务业和制造业，重点产业包括矿产资源加工、新能源、农产品加工、电子机械、金融业、医药品、电信、金属加工机械。南非应充分发挥自然资源丰富、市场潜力巨大的优势，推动南非经济发展从可持续发展潜力匮乏的消费型模式转变为容纳更多劳动力的生产型模式，逐步消除"二元经济"结构，促进南非经济、社会平衡发展。

第四章　金砖国家投融资合作
急需完善的几个方面

一　营商环境

金砖国家合作机制建立以来，合作基础日益夯实，领域逐渐拓展，其合作影响已超越金砖国家范畴，成为促进世界经济增长、完善全球治理、促进国际关系民主化的建设性力量。为了进一步促进金砖国家间的优势互补及深化合作，金砖国家都在积极改善本国的营商环境。然而，根据世界银行2017年营商环境指数，金砖国家的排名差距仍然较大。其中，俄罗斯排名最高，在设立企业、合同执行、电力取得、注册财产等方面均领跑其他金砖国家。南非与中国排名较为接近，分别为第74位与第78位，在取得建筑许可证、设立企业以及跨境交易方面都需要进一步提升。印度与巴西在190个国家中排名较低，究其原因，一方面国内政局的动荡增加了投资的商业风险，另一方面国内配套设施及制度的不完善也使外国投资者持谨慎观望的态度。

（一）税收体系复杂，企业赋税较重

巴西共有各种捐税58种，分为联邦税、州税和市税三级。巴西政府对税收采取分级征收和管理的办法。由于巴西税收体系高度分散化，各地执行的税率差别很大，因此，缴税需要耗费较长时间。在企业税收成本方面，巴西的企业所得税税率较高，而且企业还要缴纳其他税收及各种社会性开支，因此，税收负担十分沉重，这极大地压缩了企业的利润空间。特梅尔政府上台后，提出为企业减轻税负，但市场普遍认为，在巴西国会于2016年12月通过"未来20年财政开支上限不超过上年通货膨胀"的财税改革法案后，政府财政支出压力大增，在社会开支、外交

国防等刚性预算难以削减的情况下，无力实施大规模减税措施。根据世界银行 2017 年营商环境指数，巴西缴纳税款这一指标在 190 个经济体中排在第 181 位。

印度是一个联邦制国家，联邦政府享有税收立法权和征收权，但各邦和地方政府也有一定的课税权，地方税种名目繁多，税率各有不同。在南亚地区，印度的税收水平相对较高，税负占毛利率比重高达 60.6%，远高于南亚平均水平的 40.9%，也高于经济合作与发展组织平均水平的 40.9%。同时，印度政府在税收方面对外国投资几乎没有优惠政策；相反，外国公司所得税的税率高于印度当地企业所得税的税率。

中国涉外税制中规定外商投资企业和外国企业的所得税法定税率为 33%，同其他国家相比，这一税率水平偏高。虽然中国涉外税制对外商投资企业和外国企业所得税有一些优惠，但是，随着对涉外税制中优惠措施的调整，势必会影响这些企业的整体税收负担水平。此外，中国存在税前扣除不规范的现象，也直接影响到企业税收负担的高低。根据世界银行 2017 年营商环境指数中的纳税情况，中国在 190 个国家中排在第 131 位，同比下降 4 位。

（二）基础设施落后，亟待加强建设

巴西交通基础设施发展水平在拉美国家中位居前列，但设施老化和不足的问题比较突出。巴西的港口处于满负荷状态，机场建设落后，经常导致物流阻塞和拖延现象。巴西铁路系统同样处于不发达状态，造成大宗商品运输主要依靠公路，但是，由于路况欠佳，车速缓慢，堵车现象严重。普遍的时间延误和高昂的运输成本已经严重削弱了巴西投融资的国际竞争力。根据世界银行 2016 年公布的全球物流绩效指数，巴西的国际物流绩效指数为 3.088，排在第 55/160 位。此外，巴西电力供应结构性矛盾突出。巴西全国 70% 以上的电力供应依靠水力发电，因此，天气和季节因素对巴西发电能力的影响十分显著。自 2014 年以来，巴西东南—中西部、东北部等地区均不同程度地面临电力短缺问题。巴西不得不扩大火力发电规模，进口更多的液化天然气来满足电力需求。2015 年，由于供电紧张，巴西电力部门提高了电价。2016 年 4 月，随着水力发电量的恢复，巴西取消了电力附加费，使电价有所下降。目前，巴西政府已出台电力投资计划，准备扩大风力发电，以改变对水电过度依赖的现状。但在中短期内，电力供求矛盾仍是制约巴西经济和投资的重要障碍。

俄罗斯幅员辽阔，地理环境复杂多变，公路交通较落后，铁路和航空、水运有一定的基础，但多为在苏联时期建造，较为陈旧。目前，俄罗斯政府正大力投资改善基础设施建设，但除莫斯科、圣彼得堡等大型城市外，基础设施陈旧的现状并没有得到根本改观。根据世界银行2017年公布的全球物流绩效指数，俄罗斯的国际物流绩效指数为2.57，排在第99/160位。

印度的铁路、公路等基础设施建设滞后于其他发展中国家，并且严重阻碍了其制造业的发展。印度拥有当今世界最大的铁路网络之一，全长超过6.4万千米，但是，尚无时速超过200千米的高速铁路。交通设施的落后不利于投融资的发展。同时，印度的电力短缺问题尚未解决。印度政府虽然正积极探索新能源开发，但是，其国内长期以来电力供应不足的问题仍然十分严峻，在某种程度上也对经济发展造成了阻碍，印度应改变长期依靠煤炭发电的局面。

（三）劳动成本上升，劳动生产率低

巴西教育质量低下的问题一直没能得到有效解决。尽管巴西各级教育的普及率明显提升，但辍学率和留级率非常高。在经组织的PISA测试中，巴西学生的成绩在拉美国家中处于中等偏下水平，与经济合作与发展组织成员国的差距十分明显。因此，巴西的劳动力供给以非熟练劳动力为主，缺少具有较高知识水平和劳动技能的专业人才。此外，劳动生产率的不断下降是困扰巴西多年的问题，其根本原因在于巴西劳动力整体素质较低，缺乏合格的专业技术人才，加之企业创新能力不足，使劳动生产率难以提高。

俄罗斯存在劳动力缺口。2016年，俄罗斯就业人数为7270万，就业市场上从业人员最紧缺的是建筑业、制造业、贸易、教育和不动产等行业。俄罗斯在劳动力资源方面存在较大缺口。同时，俄罗斯已步入老龄化社会，劳动力不足使俄罗斯的长期经济发展面临一定挑战。目前，为解决这一危机，俄罗斯引入独联体地区移民，但无法完全解决老龄化给俄罗斯可持续增长带来的威胁，应对这一问题加以重视。

虽然中国劳动生产率增速较快，但劳动生产率水平仍然较低。根据中国统计局国际统计信息中心2016年发布的国际比较报告，中国的劳动生产率水平仅为世界平均水平的40%，其7318美元的单位劳动产出远低于世界平均水平的18487美元，与美国的98990美元相比差距更大。此

外，中国将逐渐步入老龄化时代，加之人工成本的持续攀升，在一定程度上影响了外商投资。

南非社会矛盾较为严重，2016 年，南非通货膨胀率达到 6.6%，失业率 26.7%，劳资矛盾激化，罢工事件频发，政府面临经济发展慢、失业率高、贫富分化、社会治安差等压力。南非工会势力大，工人维权意识强，外国投资者需要妥善处理与当地工会的关系。

（四）关税较高，相关政策并未完全实施

长期以来，印度对本土企业采取较大保护力度，进口关税保持在较高水平，包括基本关税、教育税、抵消税、反倾销税、安全税等。自国际金融危机以来，印度对中国商品采取的贸易保护主义措施已经对中国商品出口到印度造成了巨大的障碍。印度对酒精饮料、黄金珠宝、葡萄干、蔬菜征收 100% 的基本关税，水果、饮料的基本关税在 30% 左右，家用电器、服装、医药产品、化妆品等的基本关税为 25% 左右。工业品的平均关税水平在 15% 左右，手机、传真机等关税为 15%，个人电脑、鼠标、打印机等为 10%。

（五）行政机构庞大，行政效率低下

巴西拥有庞大的政府机构，但办事效率低下，腐败现象时有发生。企业经营活动经常受到手续繁杂、缺乏透明度、办理时间过长、审查过于严格等负面因素干扰。世界银行《2017 年营商环境报告》显示，巴西开办企业、获得建筑许可证和获得电力三项指标在全部 190 个经济体中分别排在第 175 位、第 172 位和第 47 位，其中前两项低于拉美地区平均水平。

印度政府行政机构复杂，办事效率低下，严重阻碍了外国资本在印度投资设厂。虽然莫迪政府提出"小政府、大治理"的措施，大刀阔斧地削减不必要的行政机构，出台相关法律，减少行政程序，但效果仍不理想。根据世界银行 2017 年营商环境指数，在印度开办企业的程序大约需要 14 个行政程序，耗费 26 天时间，获得电力许可需要 5 个行政程序，耗费 47 天时间，获得建筑许可证需要 40 个行政程序，耗费 164 天时间。

腐败和官僚主义是商业起步阶段最主要的障碍。俄罗斯发起一系列针对高级官员的反腐败活动，也强化反腐败立法。但是，反腐败行动收效甚微。以世界银行 2017 年营商环境指数中的开办企业、获得建筑许可和获得电力的情况来衡量俄罗斯的行政效率，俄罗斯三项指标的排名在

190 个国家中分别为第 26 位、第 115 位、第 30 位。同时，与区域平均水平相比，俄罗斯在办理时间和程序上高于地区平均水平，反映出俄罗斯的行政效率有待提高。

中国政府行政机构设置较为冗杂，有时会有机构、职能重叠的现象，容易导致人浮于事、效率低下。根据世界银行 2017 年营商环境指数中的开办企业、获得建筑许可和获得电力的情况来衡量中国的行政效率，中国 2017 年三项指标分别排在第 127 位、第 177 位、第 97 位。尤其在获得建筑许可方面，需要经过 22 个行政程序，耗费 244 天时间，行政效率需要进一步提高。

南非政府行政组织机构庞大，运行效率亟待提高，其较低的行政效率已经成为南非经济发展的阻碍之一。根据世界银行 2017 年营商环境指数中的开办企业、获得建筑许可和获得电力三项指标来衡量南非的行政效率，南非 2017 年三项指标分别排在第 131 位、第 99 位、第 111 位。虽高于区域平均水平，但与金砖国家相比，行政效率有待提高。

二 法律风险

金砖国家均为发展中国家，遍布四大洲，既有属于普通法系的印度和南非，也有属于大陆法系的俄罗斯和巴西，法律文化复杂多元，差异较大。与发达国家相比，金砖国家整体法治状况处于中等偏低水平，法律透明度不足，司法系统效率偏低。综观金砖国家的法律体系与司法环境，各国对外资收购土地都有着极为严格的限制或禁止。此外，巴西、南非、俄罗斯对引进劳务都持消极态度，相比于雇用外籍劳工，他们更倾向于雇用当地劳工以降低本国的失业率。腐败问题是金砖国家共同面对的难题。严重的官僚主义及腐败问题不仅增加了执法成本，也阻碍了执法能力的提升。根据最新的世界法治指数，在全部 113 个国家中，南非排在第 43 位，巴西排在第 52 位，印度排在第 66 位，中国排在第 80 位，俄罗斯排在第 92 位。

（一）法律对外资收购土地有一定的限制

巴西 1995 年颁布了第 6 号宪法修订案，取消巴西公司和外资公司之间的差别，给予所有在巴西注册的外资企业国民待遇，解除了 1971 年巴西土地法对在巴西居住、经营的外国自然人和法人购买土地的限制。但在 2008 年，巴西议会对土地法以及 1995 年第 6 号宪法修订案等条款重新进行解读。2010 年 8 月，巴西总统批准联邦咨委会对 1971 年 10 月巴西颁布的《土地法》限制外国人购买土地的解释。尽管目前巴西联邦政府有关限制外籍个人或企业购买土地的法令在巴西某些州并未完全落实，但总体而言，外资在巴西购地仍面临较大的法律风险。有巴西媒体报道，特梅尔政府正在考虑有条件放松外资购买土地限制，但遭到部门机构反对，未来是否会放开外资购地面临较大的不确定性。

印度政府统计显示，工业发展"瓶颈"的 70% 要归结于征地问题，尽管土地成本一般只占工业项目的 1%—4%，但是，征收进度缓慢和程序复杂往往将土地成本推高到工业项目成本的 20%。按照印度法律规定，政府或企业要购买土地，必须取得至少 80% 当地居民的许可。莫迪政府试图推出《全国土地获取法》，放宽对工业与基础设施置地的限制。这项法案在人民院获得通过，却没有获得联邦院的支持，暂时搁置。未来土地收购问题仍然是阻碍印度获得外国投资、促进基础设施建设的重要障碍，平衡投资者与农民的利益是印度政府需要解决的重大难题。

（二）对雇用外籍劳工限制较多

由于巴西国内一直面临就业问题，不鼓励引进劳务，因此，对于雇用外籍劳工限制较多。根据《巴西劳动法》，在巴西设立的外国子公司均可聘用外籍雇员，但巴西本国劳工在人数和工资收入上均不得低于企业全部劳工人数和工资总额的 2/3。外籍劳工必须有特殊技术专长，有高等学历者，必须有两年以上的专业工作经验；有中等学历者，必须有三年以上的专业工作经验。他们申领到第五类临时签证（或称短期工作签证）后，才可在聘用他的巴西企业工作。聘用外籍人员的手续到巴西劳工部移民局办理，需提交系列文件，且所有文件均需译成葡文，并加以公证和领事认证。这对于赴巴西工作的劳务人员是一个巨大的障碍，尤其是短期劳务人员，雇用成本十分昂贵。

俄罗斯于 2001 年 12 月颁布的《俄罗斯联邦劳动法》，对劳动关系进行梳理与提供法律保障。该法对劳动关系以及与其相关的间接关系，包括劳动的组织与管理、劳动安置、职业培训和进修、监督遵守劳动法和缴纳社会保险情况、解决劳动纠纷等进行法律调节。在外来劳务方面，俄罗斯采用配额管理方法。根据《俄罗斯联邦外国公民法律地位法》规定，在外国公民签订劳动合同，并取得俄罗斯工作许可证的情况下，可以在俄罗斯从事相关的劳动活动。但是，近年来，俄罗斯不断缩减外来劳务配额。从 2006 年起，俄罗斯政府计划每年削减 50% 的非独联体外来劳务配额，对其他地区人员赴俄劳务产生冲击。

根据南非《移民法》和《外国人管理法》，外国人只能持有南非内政部签发的"工作许可证"，并在"工作许可证"规定的单位工作才是合法的。政府对引进外国劳工严格限制，原则上说，能在当地找到合适人选的就业机会就不能提供给外国人。南非《劳工法》严格规定，雇主必须与员工签订正式雇佣合同。

（三）腐败问题严重，执法能力有待提高

巴西国内腐败问题严重。自 2016 年下半年以来，巴西总统特梅尔先后牵扯"奥德布雷西特腐败案"和"JBS 腐败案"，丑闻不断。此外，被指控腐败的远不止特梅尔一人，涉及现任和前任政府的大量高级官员。根据世界银行 2016 年公布的全球治理指数中的法治得分，巴西法治得分为 –0.19，同比减少 0.11。

在国家利益突出的领域，俄罗斯法院较少做出不利于政府的判决，特别是涉及自然资源、媒体或安全领域。另外，国际和国内仲裁执行率低。根据世界银行 2016 年公布的全球治理指数中的法治得分，俄罗斯法治得分为 –0.72，同比下降 0.01。

腐败、洗钱等成为印度经济发展中的重要顽疾，莫迪政府甚至采取废钞令这样的大胆措施来打击腐败，虽然取得了一定效果，但尚未从根本上改善印度的执法能力，彻底解决行政腐败、效率低下等问题。根据世界银行 2016 年公布的全球治理指数中的法治得分，印度法治得分为 –0.06，同比提高 0.03。此外，印度存在宪政性风险。印度政局虽然极其稳定，但印度政权的统一性和执行力却存在巨大的风险。印度统一建国成为一个单一制中央政府的国家，但并未大刀阔斧地整合中央权力。无论立法权、司法权还是行政权，中央与地方分权自治处于势均力敌的格局。由于印度存在 1000 多个地方政党、1000 多种地方语言，再加之地方封建大家族势力的盘根错节，印度中央政府的统一性和执行力明显削弱。因此，在经济层面上，表现为"全国市场的统一性不强、中央政令法规的执行力极弱"。

中国共产党第十八次全国代表大会以来，中国采取了一系列的措施

解决腐败问题，加大了对腐败的惩治力度。目前，中国腐败问题有所改善，但要根治腐败还需要时间。根据世界银行2016年公布的全球治理指数中的法治得分，中国法治得分为 -0.22，同比上升0.19。

南非腐败问题十分严峻，已经影响到执政党的地位以及投资者的信心，前总统祖马本人也多次受到腐败指控。根据世界银行2016年公布的全球治理指数中的法治得分，南非法治得分为0.0558，同比下降了0.1119。

（四）外资投入的限制或禁止事项较多

巴西不允许外国投资者在核能、医疗卫生、养老基金、海洋捕捞、邮政等领域投资。航天企业仅允许少量外资股份存在，在民航企业的股份不得超过20%。这在一定程度上限制了外资的投资领域。

在俄罗斯，外资禁止投资的行业为赌博业、人寿保险业。2008年5月，普京签署了《有关外资进入对国防和国家安全具有战略性意义行业程序》（以下简称《战略法》）的联邦法，该法第5条明确规定13大类42种经营活动被视为具有战略性意义行业，主要包括：国防军工、核原料生产、核反应堆项目的建设运营、用于武器和军事技术生产必需的特种金属和合金的研制生产销售、宇航设施和航空器研究、密码加密设备研究、天然垄断部门的固定线路电信公司、联邦级的地下资源区块开发、水下资源、覆盖俄罗斯领土一半区域的广播媒体、发行量较大的报纸和出版公司等。根据《战略法》的规定，外国国家、国际组织及其控制的组织（包括设立在俄罗斯境内的组织），不得通过交易取得战略公司的控制权或收购、占有或使用战略公司的固定生产资产。而在外资投入的限制事项方面，根据《战略法》规定，若外国国家、国际组织及其控制的组织意图经交易取得对俄罗斯国防和国土安全存在战略意义的公司，需要取得由俄罗斯总理负责的政府委员会的事先批准。这些特定行为包括：直接或间接处置战略公司法定股本中超过25%有投票权的股份的行为；直接或间接处置战略公司法定股本中超过5%有投票权股份的，且在具有联邦重要性的地区进行地质底土勘探和（或）地质勘探、采矿的行为；其他阻碍战略公司管理层决策的行为。

中国商务部发布的2017年《外商投资产业指导目录》列出了外商投资限制和禁止的负面清单。其中，限制外商投资的产业包括汽车整车、专用汽车制造，电信公司，银行，保险公司，证券公司，证券投资基金管理公司，期货公司等。此外，禁止外商投资产业包括稀有和特有的珍贵优良品种的研发、养殖、种植以及相关繁殖材料的生产（包括种植业、畜牧业、水产业的优良基因），稀土勘查、开采、选矿，邮政公司、信件的国内快递业务，人体干细胞、基因诊断与治疗技术开发和应用，互联网新闻信息服务，网络出版服务，网络视听节目服务，互联网上网服务营业场所，互联网文化经营（音乐除外），互联网公众发布信息服务等。

（五）环境立法严苛，程序复杂

巴西在环境方面的要求严格，环境许可证的审批时间长，项目可能具体涉及多级政府（联邦、州和市）审批。开展或运营一个可能对当地环境或社区居民利益造成影响的项目，如果没有达到相关的环境要求，可能会导致项目公司及其母公司的民事和行政责任，甚至刑事责任。

南非环境保护要求也较为严格。以海洋经济为例，南非海洋管理相关法律众多，凡对环境、社会、经济、文化遗址产生影响的开发、建设活动均实行严格的影响评价制度；近岸污水排放、海洋倾废、机动船舶出海实行许可证制度；渔业资源实行配额管理制度；油气开采之前须提交环境管理规划书。根据南非《全国海岸带综合管理法》规定，南非政府有权要求终止对海岸环境产生不利影响的任何计划或活动。

三 汇率风险

投融资是促进金砖国家经济发展的重要组成部分，而全球的汇率波动是影响国际投融资的重要因素。通过选择合适的币种和汇率政策，来应对包括美国货币政策的溢出效应在内的多种风险是未来金砖国家合作面临的重要问题。

（一）金砖五国货币政策和汇率制度现状

1. 巴西

（1）货币政策方面，巴西实行通货膨胀目标制。巴西国家货币委员会对未来两年的通货膨胀与容忍区间制定目标，由巴西中央银行制定货币政策来实现既定目标。中央银行货币政策委员会继而设立政策利率的目标水平，由公开市场操作部通过采取公开市场操作的手段使隔夜 SELIC 利率接近利率目标。自 2006 年至今，巴西国家货币委员会制定的通货膨胀目标和容忍区间分别为 4.5% 和 2%，实际通货膨胀水平在 2.5%—6.5%，均落在容忍区间范围内。

（2）汇率制度方面，巴西使用自由浮动的汇率制度。巴西最早实行固定汇率制度，并伴随兑美元的汇率变化而逐步贬值。为了防止本币出现剧烈贬值，巴西政府大量减少持有的外汇储备，由此造成国际收支失衡，继而带来金融危机。1999 年的大量资本外逃造成盯住汇率无法维持，巴西中央银行不得不将固定汇率制度改为浮动汇率制度。在该种制度下，汇率通过市场化机制形成，中央银行通过银行间结算市场间接干预最终汇率的形成。

2. 俄罗斯

（1）俄罗斯中央银行采用多目标制的货币政策。《俄罗斯中央银行法》要求俄罗斯银行在每年年末公布未来三年货币政策的主要目标、对国家未来经济状况的分析，以及各种情况下相对应的货币政策等。通过公布明确的中期货币政策，稳定市场对未来货币走势的预期，达到稳定汇率和抑制通货膨胀的目标。俄罗斯 2018 年的通货膨胀目标范围在 3%—4%，通常使用法定存款准备金率和再融资利率两种货币政策工具实现政策目标。

（2）俄罗斯施行有管理的浮动汇率制度。俄罗斯政府最初实行固定汇率政策。汇率不完全由市场供求决定，而是由外汇交易所与银行间外汇市场上货币的比价来规定汇率浮动区间，即"外汇走廊"。1998 年，国内的恶性通货膨胀导致货币危机，俄罗斯不得不放弃汇率的目标区间，实行有管理的浮动汇率制度。俄罗斯中央银行参照"一揽子"美元和欧元（0.9 美元、0.1 欧元）管理卢布汇率，通过银行间货币交易维持汇率在浮动区间内。

3. 印度

（1）印度实行多目标的货币政策。印度储备银行制定货币政策并负责实施，重点主要在于通货膨胀预期管理。储备银行通过间接市场化操作，调节流动性和短期利率，主要使用的政策工具有政策利率、市场稳定计划、流动性调节便利和公开市场操作等。

（2）汇率政策方面，印度实行有管理的浮动汇率制度，但不设定预定浮动区间。卢比的汇率由货币市场供求决定，汇率管理目标是：保证货币的价值反映基本面，在必要时提供外汇保持市场环境健康、抑制投机和汇率过分波动，帮助国家维持充足的外汇水平，帮助消除外汇市场上的约束，促进外汇市场健康发展。

4. 中国

（1）中国实行多目标的货币政策，并在不同的历史时期给多目标赋予不同的权重。中国货币政策目标是保持人民币币值稳定，运用的政策工具有基准利率、再贴现、存款准备金、公开市场操作、商业银行贷款等。

（2）中国目前的汇率政策是有管理的浮动汇率制。1994—2004年，中国采取的是盯住美元的汇率管理机制。随着人民币面临越来越大的升值压力，中国的外汇储备迅速增加。2005年，中国人民银行宣布实行"一揽子"的汇率决定机制，根据货币市场供求对汇率进行调节，逐步推动汇率形成机制。在此后的三年内，人民币升值累计超过26%。近年来，人民币的外汇弹性逐年增强，汇率呈现双向浮动。

5. 南非

（1）在受到了严重的汇率冲击之后，南非从2000年开始实行通货膨胀目标制的货币政策，放弃汇率而选择通货膨胀目标作为政策的名义锚。2000年2月，南非政府正式引入通货膨胀框架，设立2002年的通货膨胀目标。货币政策委员每半年会公布货币政策回顾，并公布政策声明。实行通货膨胀目标制度之后，南非中央银行在货币政策的落实方面更加迅速，货币政策与其他政策措施之间的协调更加顺畅。通货膨胀目标的设定提高了南非货币政策的透明度与中央银行的问责效率，大大提升了中央银行货币模型的预测效果。

（2）汇率制度方面，南非采用的是由市场决定的浮动汇率制度。1984年，由于南非实行种族隔离制度，国际社会对南非的制裁迫使当局采用双轨制的手段直接管理汇率。1992年大选之后，南非政局变化，对外汇市场和汇率的改革再次启动，单一汇率制度取代双重汇率制度，南非开始实行市场供求关系决定的浮动汇率制度。

（二）美国经济政策对全球的影响

作为世界上最发达的经济体，美国的经济形势和政策变化对世界其他国家的投融资有着重要且深刻的影响。美元是全球货币市场中最常见的主要货币，大部分货币的交易都是相对美元进行的。因此，美元的变动对世界其他国家汇率波动有直接影响，是国际投融资分析决策时需要考虑的重要因素。

在经济全球化进程中，美国的货币政策溢出效应日渐增强。2004—2005 年，美联储通过连续 17 次加息，将利率从 1% 调高至 5.25%，造成房地产泡沫的破灭，并进一步引发了国际金融危机。2007—2008 年，美联储为应对国际金融危机引起的严重经济衰退，连续 10 次下调利率至 0.25%，随后进入了长达 7 年的"零利率"时代。自 2015 年年底至今，美联储连续 7 次加息，将利率调升至 2%。此轮加息引发"全球联动"，对新兴市场国家造成了一定的影响。短期溢出效应推动美元汇率上升，致使全球资本流向发生改变，新兴市场货币承受巨大的压力，短期跨境资本流出。此外，美元的持续升值，导致新兴经济体债券展期成本显著上升，美元债务风险加大。最后，美联储加息提速，打压国际大宗商品价格，导致资源出口型的新兴经济体利益受损，抑制其贸易发展。

2017 年特朗普政府上台后，开启了美国 31 年以来最大规模的税收制度改革。公司所得税从 35% 下降至 20%，同时还鼓励美国的企业将海外获得的利润带回美国本土。此项政策将在全球范围内产生巨大影响，更多的资本涌入美国，减少了其他国家可能获得的外商直接投资。

（三）汇率变动对金砖国家投融资合作的影响

汇率变动一般分为两个层面。其一是汇率走势变化，即货币的升值贬值；其二是汇率波动程度的变化，即波动平稳程度的变化。

1. 汇率的走势会影响外商直接投资

东道国货币的贬值会使外商直接投资的相对成本降低，尤其是降低了劳动力成本，因此，外商直接投资的资本回报率增加，有助于促进外商直接投资的增加。反之，一国货币的升值会增加投资的相对成本，不利于吸引外商直接投资。近年来，学者发现，汇率走势对不同种类的外商直接投资影响方向不同。通过对中国外商直接投资的实证研究发现，币值上升不利于吸引贸易型外商直接投资，但有利于吸引非贸易型外商直接投资。

（1）印度

2013—2016 年，印度卢比持续贬值，外商直接投资总量呈上升趋势。2017 年，卢布小幅升值，外商直接投资总量也随之减少（见图 4 - 1）。

（2）巴西

整体来看，2013—2016 年，巴西雷亚尔较 2006—2009 年大幅贬值，而从外商直接投资总量来看，在货币贬值期间（2013—2016 年）的 FDI 明显高于货币升值期间（2006—2009 年）的 FDI（见图 4 - 2）。

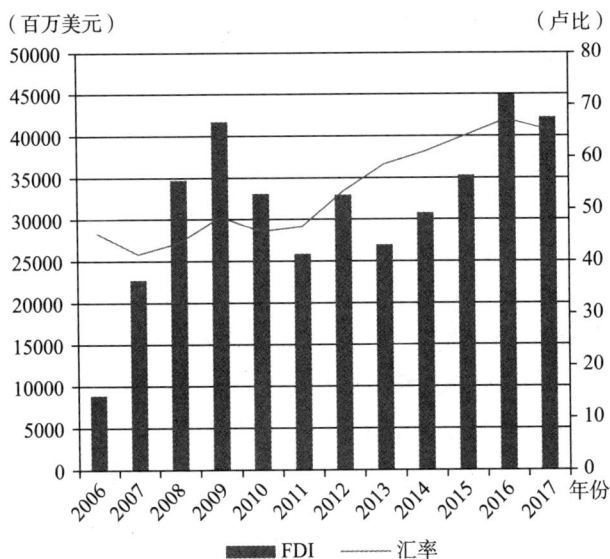

图 4 - 1　2006—2017 年印度汇率及 FDI 变化情况

资料来源：国际货币基金组织和 CEIC。

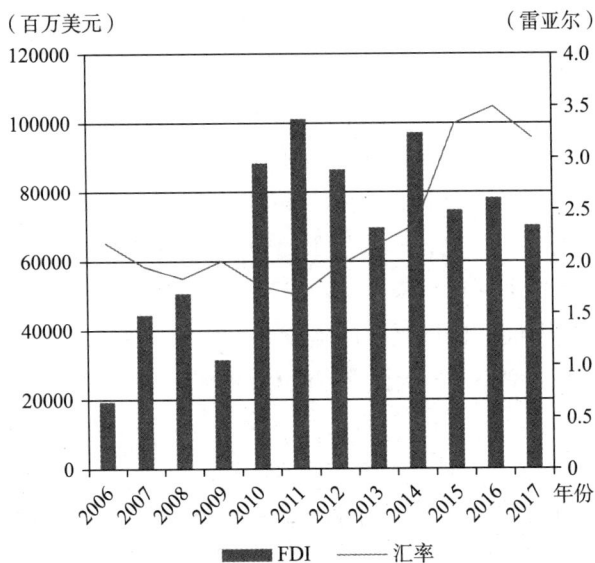

图 4 - 2　2006—2017 年巴西汇率及 FDI 变化情况

资料来源：国际货币基金组织和 CEIC。

2. 汇率波动使跨国投资面临更多的风险和不确定性

外商直接投资的收益可能由于汇率的剧烈波动而损失殆尽，甚至面临亏损的风险。不确定性增加将大大削弱对外商直接投资者的吸引力。对汇率波动的预期也不利于外商做出直接投资的决策。此外，汇率波动增加了外商直接投资的成本。即使可以使用对冲工具，也会给跨国企业带来成本的提升。因此，汇率波动的增加不利于经济体吸引投资，是国际投融资合作的不利影响因素。

（1）中国

在金砖国家中，中国汇率的波动幅度相对最小，外商直接投资总量也相对最为平稳。自 2001 年至今，人民币基本维持在 6.5% 以内的窄幅波动，仅有 2008 年和 2015 年波动稍大，在 8%—10%。正因如此，投资者对于人民币汇率波动通常保持乐观预期，从外商直接投资来看，基本保持稳步增长态势（见图 4 – 3）。

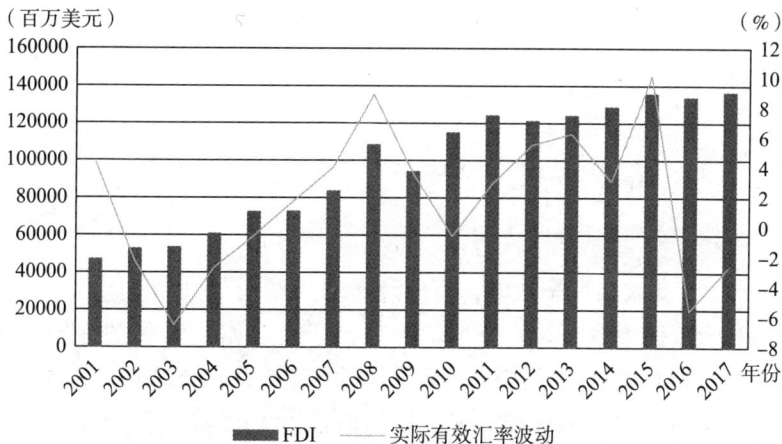

图 4 – 3　2001—2017 年中国汇率波动率及 FDI 变化情况

资料来源：世界银行和 CEIC。

（2）南非

2002—2004 年，南非兰特的汇率波动高达 30%，此时的外商直接投资总量急剧减少。2011—2016 年，汇率相对趋于平稳，外商直接投资较 2002—2004 年有明显涨幅。2017 年，汇率波动再次突破 12%，外商直接投资较 2016 年有一定程度的下降。总体来看，南非兰特汇率波动幅度较大，外商直接投资稳定性较低，说明汇率波动对外商直接投资存在较大的不利影响（见图 4-4）。

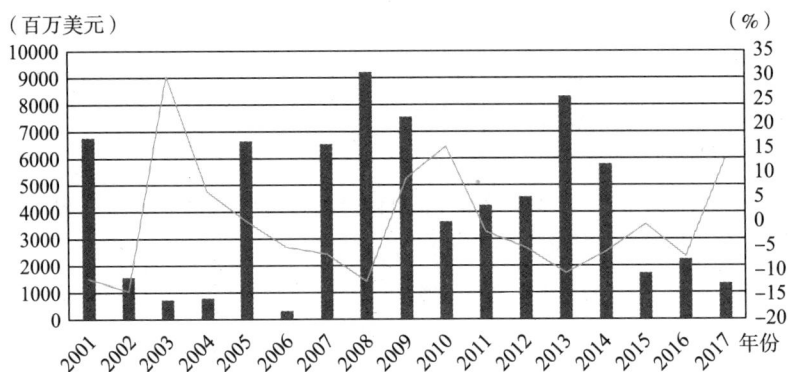

图 4-4　2001—2017 年南非汇率波动率及 FDI 变化情况

资料来源：世界银行和 CEIC。

四　经济结构转型与产业革命对接面临挑战

（一）全要素生产率疲弱，产业升级遇"瓶颈"

IMF 的数据表明，2007—2017 年，由于全要素生产率的疲弱，发达国家、新兴市场国家的经济增速年均分别下降约 5% 和 12%，其负面影响分别约占发达国家、新兴市场国家年均增长损失的 47% 和 85%。金砖国家以需求侧刺激推动的短周期复苏难以长期维系，以供给侧结构性改革来提振全要素生产率成为当务之急。

金砖国家在面临转型发展中需要解决以下重要问题：一是保持高劳动生产率产业的持续发展；二是高劳动生产率产业具有普遍前向与后向联系；三是大量吸收劳动力；四是促进整个经济的积累与创新。从就业部门分布来看，南非、印度、巴西和中国的主要就业人口均在劳动生产率低于总体水平的部门，尤其是印度，该国近 60% 的人口在农业就业。这显示出通过结构转型提升劳动生产率，进而促进经济增长的巨大潜力。

此外，金砖国家经济转型目前面临以下三个方面的问题：

其一，大部分金砖国家仍然以开采自然资源（如矿产资源）方式保持贸易和经济增长，这种发展既受一国资源禀赋以及资源产品价格的限制，其高劳动生产率也与其资本密集型行业特征息息相关，吸收的劳动力资源有限。此外，还会产生"寻租"、腐败、社会分配不公以及收入差距拉大等问题。

其二，金融、保险、房地产和商业服务业具有较高劳动生产率，但吸收的劳动力数量相对有限，对劳动力素质要求相对较高，金砖国家劳动力素质现阶段还有较大提升空间，难以超越第二产业的发展程度实现跨越式发展。

其三，金砖国家旅游业等劳动密集型服务业虽然有助于吸纳就业，但其缺陷是劳动生产率仍然处于相对较低的水平，且对经济其余部分的拉动力不足，对于经济实现可持续增长的积累与创新贡献有限，同时呈现出明显的顺经济周期现象，难以推动经济持续稳定增长。

（二）产业规划尚未对接，缺乏整体规划以促进经济结构转型

金砖国家各自都有明确的国民经济和产业发展规划，但产业发展规划对接程度有限，尚未建立一个集中化程度更高的经济发展框架。中国在 2016 年发布了《中华人民共和国国民经济和社会发展第十三个五年规划纲要》，阐明国家战略意图，明确政府工作重点，引导市场主体行为，对国家重大建设项目、生产力分布和国民经济重要比例关系等做出规划，为国民经济发展远景规定目标和方向。俄罗斯制定了《发展工业和提高工业竞争力纲要》，旨在激发工业领域发展潜能，提高工业企业在国内外市场上的竞争力，以再工业化推动经济发展。莫迪上台后，推出"印度制造"计划，力争把制造业占印度经济的比重从 18% 增加到 25%。巴西发布了"工业强国计划"。南非 2017 年 5 月发布最新"工业政策行动计划"（IPAP），寻求在不稳定的全球经济背景下，建立一个集中化程度更低、竞争力更强的经济和制造业框架。

然而，推进金砖国家共同的可持续发展议程，尚未在各国发展基础上建立综合性的发展规划或单个产业发展规划。各国的产业发展侧重点没有从互补、互联的角度实现金砖国家内部的对接，未能实现资源和优势的相互补充，也未从产业融合的角度寻求最佳的发展路径。

（三）研发投入不足，产业升级投融遇到"瓶颈"

创新和研发是产业升级的重要动力，科技创新需要源源不断的资金投入作为支持。然而，对于科技研发的投入，金砖国家还有较大的投入缺口。

目前，世界上公认的创新型国家，其研发投入占 GDP 比重一般在3%以上，如北欧一些发达国家的研发投入占 GDP 比重为 3%—3.5%，而金砖国家的研发比重均不到 3%。2016 年，印度和南非研发支出占GDP 比重相对较低，分别为 0.65% 和 0.8%，其次是俄罗斯和巴西，分别为 1.1%、1.3%，均处在较低水平。根据中国科技部统计，2017 年，中国的研发支出占 GDP 比重约为 2.15%，位于金砖五国之首（见图 4 - 5）。根据另一个测算指标，研发人员全时当量，俄罗斯为 83 万人/年，印度为 53 万人/年，中国最高，为 388 万人/年，南非仅为 4 万人/年（见图 4 - 6）。

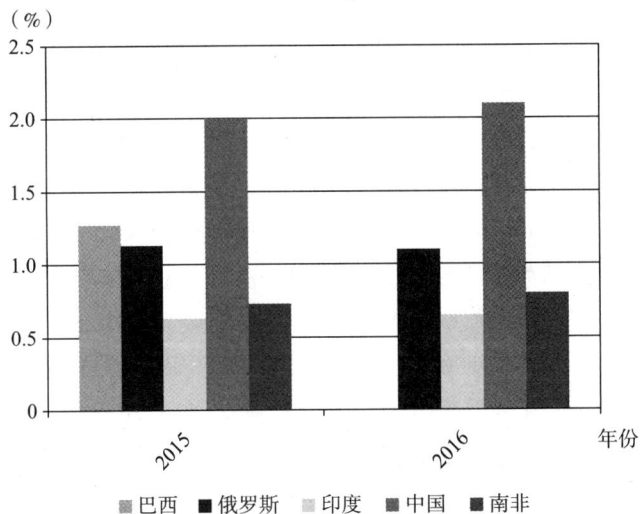

图 4 - 5 2015—2016 年金砖国家研发支出及其占 GDP 比重情况

资料来源：Human Sciences Research Council、Eurostat、MCTIC、Department of Science and Technology 和中国国家统计局。

（万人/年）

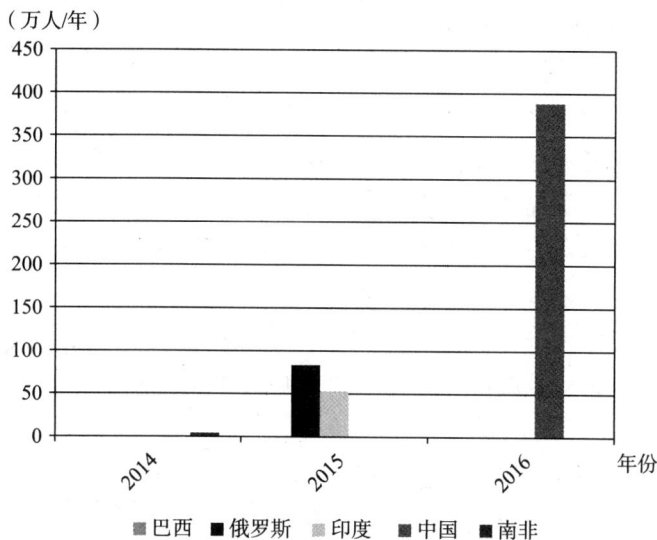

图 4−6　金砖国家研究人员全时当量

资料来源：国家统计局：《金砖国家联合统计手册（2017）》。

以中国为例，其他指标与创新型国家也有差距，产业升级和科技创新尚有较长的路要走。其一，中国的科技贡献率约为50%，而发达国家已高达70%。其二，中国的科技成果转化率不到30%，而发达国家通常达到60%—70%。其三，中国的核心技术与关键技术的对外依存度为50%—60%，而国际先进国家的技术对外依存度仅为30%。

技术的结构性改革与投融资具有高度联结性。技术的结构性改革恰似一场赛跑，研发投入增加迅速，金融供给及时有效，有利于供给侧结构性改革目标的实现。金融创新与科技革命的融合速度非常关键，直接影响需求侧与供给侧的结构平衡。此外，金融创新撬动社会资本对研发的投入，创新成果及创新者将被赋予更高的市场价格。然而，金砖国家在研发领域的投入明显不足，针对研发投入的金融资本尚有空间。

（四）产业链配合与生产标准化程度有待提高

金砖国家之间的优势产能合作是覆盖多个环节的全方位合作。优势产能是研发设计、生产制造、市场销售、服务配套等多个环节全产业链优势的综合。然而，金砖国家内部在原材料、研发设计、专业人才、制度标准等方面缺乏统一的标准，生产配套能力弱成为制约生产制造能力、产业国际竞争力的"短板"。

在产品生产过程中，生产的各个环节可以实现空间分离，布局在不同国家，实现全球化生产。就发展的角度而言，形成金砖国家之间生产合作最根本、最关键的环节是标准的统一。某一国具有独立和完备的生产制造能力，能实现国内产品生产。但要形成金砖国家之间的分工协作、生产配套、技术合力、实现规模效应，则需建立一套完备的生产标准并进行对接，将金砖国家内部生产的优势加以利用。因此，金砖国家之间的生产制造合作是以标准对接为基础、覆盖多个环节、强化生产配套能力、连接产供销、打通技术研发、产品制造和生产销售各个环节的全方位合作。

（五）产业革命的培育基础薄弱

金砖国家中，中国和印度对产业革命的培育基础较好。中国和印度分别在制造业和信息技术服务业取得较大发展，并以此确立了新兴大国的地位，但区域内的科技产业培育基础差异化程度较大，并且在产业培育基础的发展上未能达成一致。

第一，金砖国家拥有资源和人口数量优势，但想要掀起航空航天和汽车等领域的制造业革命，还需要具备引入先进技术，创造吸引外来技术的良好的营商环境。然而，金砖国家仍然维持较保守的投资政策、知识产权保护政策等，对吸引外国直接投资和知识转移未能提供最优质的环境。

第二，缺乏知识成果迅速转换的产业环境。金砖国家普遍拥有熟练的劳动力，也逐步注重教育培训，例如，印度拥有强大的高中和大学教育体系，学生被全世界的跨国公司认可。然而，金砖国家教育体制变革和知识产品的转化缺乏迅速转换的产业根基，受过高等教育的学生掌握的高科技技能难以在工作环境中运用，短期内需要金砖国家政府和私营部门设立职业技能培训中心来提升就业能力，中长期则需要靠牢固的产业发展和转型的根基，连接知识成果的迅速转换路径，以实现产业革命对金砖国家整体产业结构的升级和优化。

第三，缺乏对可再生能源等新兴资源的应用共识。相对于欧洲等发达国家，金砖国家自然矿产及能源相对丰富，较多国家还处于用资源能源换发展速度的阶段，未形成对清洁能源应用的共识。金砖国家中，仅中国计划在 2020 年后允许出售可再生能源车辆，在追求清洁环境上处于相对领先的地位，其他金砖国家尚未在可再生能源领域达成长期政策共识。

【案例：南非报业 Naspers 入股腾讯项目】

2002 年，南非报业旗下的 MIH 以拥有腾讯 46.3% 的股权，成为腾讯的第一大股东。2018 年 3 月，MIH 首次出售腾讯 2% 的股票，但仍以 31.2% 的股票份额位列腾讯第一大股东。此案例带来如下启示：

（1）思维转变引领合作创新。在纸媒数字化没能全面满足时代发展需求的情况下，南非报业开始全媒体转型之路。南非报业具备技术优势，更重要的是思维转型、组织结构转型，推动媒体与社会的融合过程。

（2）投融资加速企业转型。南非报业积极寻求海外投资机会，并通过投资人的形式将资金注入符合自身发展理念的公司，为所投企业提供现金流，并分享互联网行业爆发所产生的巨额红利。[1]

---

① 参见本书附录"案例六：南非报业 Naspers 入股腾讯项目"。

第五章　创新金砖国家投融资机制，
促进务实合作互利共赢

一　探索构建金砖国家多边评级机制

（一）当前国际信用评级机构存在的问题

信用评级机构对于融资者的信用评级直接决定了发债能否成功以及融资成本的高低。目前，金砖国家各国在基础设施建设等方面有着较大的资金需求，而获得国际信贷和投资的前提是信用评级。金砖国家一方面可以利用现有评级体系，另一方面也可以新建适用于金砖国家的信用评级体系，并在此基础上互相认可，以降低融资成本。

目前，全球提供信用评级主要有标准普尔（Standard and Poor's）、穆迪（Moody's）和惠誉（Fitch）三大机构，现阶段，国际三大评级机构存在较大的局限性。

第一，等级分析偏向稳定，相关信息处理过程缓慢，信用等级缺乏实时性。

第二，缺乏问责制度，评分等级都是基于各国机构分析员的主观观点和建议，缺乏问责机制来保证评级的真实性。

第三，标准单一，评级机构对新兴市场国家和发达国家采用同一套评级体系，缺乏一套金融指标来区分新兴经济体和发达经济体的金融发展程度。

第四，评级缺乏透明度，存在偏见。

第五，主权评级服务很难获得。

以上这些局限性在一定期限内无法改变，因此，金砖国家自身建立信用评级机构势在必行。

（二）构建新开发银行信用评级机制的必要性与可行路径

债券的风险和收益水平是影响债券发行的基本要素，因此，发展金砖国家债券增信担保机制，提高金砖国家政府和企业债券的信用等级，对于本币债券市场的发展十分重要。债券的信用等级一般由债券的发行人和担保人中较高者决定。因此，可以从以下两方面加强担保机制建设：一是由新开发银行为本币债券的发行提供担保；二是建立金砖担保基金，为本币债券的发行提供信用增级。

首先，新开发银行可以凭借自身的较高信用等级为本币债券的发行提供担保服务。欧洲投资银行（EIB）及其下属的欧洲投资基金（EIF）在此领域的经验值得借鉴。EIB 和 EIF 通过广泛的传统担保工具支持欧洲中小企业融资；同时，EIF 在新兴的资产证券化领域十分注重担保工具的创新，通过为证券化产品的发起人提供担保来帮助它们实现资金来源的多样化，通过转移信用风险的方式降低经济成本和监管成本。近年来，EIB 和EIF 已经成为欧洲中小企业信用增级的领导者，其多边开发银行的地位和3A 评级使与之合作的金融机构能够对其担保的资产采用零风险权重。

其次，可以通过建立金砖国家信用担保基金对本币债券的发行提供担保。除欧洲投资基金的经验外，日本信用保证协会为本国企业融资和债券交易提供担保便利的经验也值得借鉴。2004 年，日本宣布建立"亚洲债券保险制度"，为在东亚国家投资的日本企业发行的外国债券提供担保，帮助日本企业在投资国筹集资金，这项举措为日资企业在东亚国家通过发行债券筹集资金开辟了道路。金砖国家通过合资建立金砖国家担保基金，完全可以发挥类似日本信用保证协会的功能。该基金可以建在新开发银行旗下，这样，在运作上就可采用欧洲投资银行及欧洲投资基金的模式。

（三）构建金砖国家信用评级机构的主要目标、对象、步骤和要素

1. 构建金砖国家信用评级机构的主要目标

金砖国家信用评级机构将对新兴市场的发行者进行信用评级，让用户能在信用评估结论与发行者之间权衡评级的信用风险。金砖国家信用评级机构以及提供的信用评级服务，主要说明发行者在偿还外币债务方面的信用度；使用的评级服务既非国家体系，也非全球体系，而且所提供的信用评级将对新兴市场中众多的发行者进行信用风险评估。

2. 构建金砖国家信用评级机构的对象

构建金砖国家信用评级机构的对象有：公司部分的债务，包括银行贷款、债券、信用债券及其他资本市场工具；公共部分的债务，针对国有企业和城市地方机构；结构性金融交易和金融机构评级。金砖国家信用评级机构应当发展内部主权风险评估，这对于遍布不同国家的发行者进行外币债务评级很重要。随着金砖国家信用评级机构的建立和发展，其评级服务范畴扩展到其他国家，金砖国家信用评级机构可以拓展进行主权评级服务。

3. 金砖国家信用评级机构的步骤和要素

建立金砖国家信用评级机构，具体可分三个阶段进行。

第一阶段，金砖国家信用评级机构的评级业务应从新开发银行为金砖国家所提供的外币贷款着手。它还应着重为国际货币基金组织、世界银行和亚洲开发银行等多边机构提供的外币贷款进行信用评级，包括为在金砖国家内部银行合作机制下指定成员开发银行对所提供的贷款进行评级。在这个阶段，金砖国家信用评级机构需要获得金砖国家成员国的支持。成员国应鼓励新开发银行、亚洲基础设施投资银行及本国其他成员开发银行等多边机构在其管辖领域内为项目提供资金时使用金砖国家信用评级机构。

第二阶段，提高金砖国家信用评级机构的普及度，使基于金砖国家和新兴市场债务的银行及金融机构使用金砖国家信用评级机构的信用评级。典型用户将是金砖国家各国国内面向金砖国家或其他新兴市场外汇敞口的银行。应当利用第一阶段所获得的经验与信誉，鼓励更多的群体使用金砖国家信用评级服务。

第三阶段，信用评级机构应以壮大成员队伍为目标，向其他新兴市场国家如墨西哥、菲律宾、印度尼西亚和泰国等提供服务。一旦信用评级机构在各个新兴市场国家积累了更多的证券评级经验，它就能通过在新兴市场给国家主权信用评级实现资本化。

在建立过程中，需要有良好声望的评级机构的强力支持。金砖国家信用评级机构成为一家在新兴市场具有良好声望的评级机构，依赖于其创始成员对市场的判断。每个创始成员国需要使用本国的专业经验，并凭借对整个新兴市场中国家风险因素的深入理解，树立风险基准，这是金砖国家信用评级发展壮大的基础。因此，金砖国家信用评级机构至少在初创的几年里，有必要获得一家在新兴市场拥有丰富经验的知名信用评级机构的支持。股权均在多边机构与金砖国家成员国开发银行和金融机构之间平均分配，以确保股权结构的多元化与独立性。金砖国家信用评级机构的长远目标应当是分散自身股权，有利于其他散户和机构投资者。

4. 股权结构、持股机构和后续运营

第一，股权结构。股权分散，由成员开发银行、金融机构和知名信用评级机构共同持有。在创始阶段，股权应包括两个部分：其一，成员国开发银行、出口担保机构和各个金砖国家成员国的其他金融机构。来自这些国家的私营金融机构也可以被邀请加入股权结构，以确保股权结构多元化。其二，一家全球公认的知名信用评级机构持有一定的股份。这家评级机构可以其广受认可的信用评级经验，为金砖国家信用评级机构提供管理经验、制定评级方法的专业技术以及员工培训。

第二，确保评级独立于发放贷款的持股机构。确保作为信用评级机构股东的贷款机构（比如银行和多边机构）和信用评级机构的管理层之间保持一定距离，因为这些股东是金砖国家信用评级机构所公布评级的潜在使用者，股东和金砖国家信用评级机构管理层之间泾渭分明。

第三，摆脱政治和利益冲突等方面的影响。考虑到信用评级机构将以来自金砖国家的金融机构、成员国开发银行和多边机构的股权出资为特征，其评级可能被视为具有政治倾向，有利于一个或多个金砖国家，从而破坏了其独立性和可信度。上述信用评级机构必须具备多元化的股权结构。国家可以是间接股东，即通过一个诸如新开发银行、成员国开发银行或金融机构等类似的多边机构获得股权，但不能直接通过股权出资。随着信用评级机构的扩张，必须确保股权一直保持多元化，而且单个国家不得独自控制机构的经营。

第四，在后续运营阶段，需要引入后评价机制，确保其评级质量不断提升。金砖国家信用评级机构的新兴市场体系一旦确定，其普及可能引致来自全球知名评级机构的竞争，后者可能采纳这一体系或开发自身的新兴市场体系以迎合这一细分市场的要求。虽然这可能被视为潜在竞争和对金砖国家信用评级机构的商业活力的一个威胁，但其最终目标与金砖国家信用评级机构一样，使投资者的资金有效地流向新兴经济体的核心部门。因此，在后续阶段，如果其他评级机构选择金砖国家信用机构的评级结果作为融资依据，那将会提升金砖信用评级体系的市场认可度和接受度，使投资者有据可依，降低融资风险和提高融资安全系数。

二 推动发展金砖债券市场

债券市场是发行和买卖债券的场所，同时也是金融体系中不可或缺的一部分。尤其是对于发展中国家来说，债券市场对于改善融资结构，减少对银行的过度依赖，增强金融、经济体系的稳定性，具有至关重要的作用。

（一）推动发展金砖债券市场需具备的条件

金砖国家国内债券市场的发展已经日趋完善，由于一国的资源有限，仅靠国内融资还不足以满足资金的需求。国际债券市场能够帮助机构或企业从国外获得资金，从而大大拓宽了融资渠道。另外，由于新兴市场国家发展较快，一般来说，债券利率也高于同类型的发达国家债券利率，这也是吸引国际投资重要的因素。

根据统计，在金砖国家中，2017 年第四季度中国的未偿付国际借债水平较高，达到了 1.947 亿美元，印度和南非则相对较低，分别只有 0.419 亿美元和 0.346 亿美元（见图 5 - 1）。虽然金砖国家的外债总量总体呈上升趋势，然而，相对于同时期美国的 24.3 亿美元的国际借债总额来说，差距仍旧相当大。因此，金砖国家应当以发达国家为目标，继续推动其债券市场的发展。

1. 加大资本账户的开放程度

资本账户的开放程度直接影响到国家的对外融资，只有放开限制，更多的国外资本才能够流入债券市场，扩大金砖国家债券的规模。随着金融全球化的发展，新兴市场国家先后逐渐放松资本账户的管制。但与发达国家相比，金砖国家各国仍保留着较高程度的资本控制。目前，金砖国家，特别是印度和南非，对于资本流的控制依旧非常严格。诚然，资本账户的开放也并非一蹴而就的，过快的开放会导致资本流动的波动性增加，给金融系统稳定性带来风险，因此，这是一个循序渐进的过程。可以考虑首先在金砖国家之间相互协商，进行对等的投资开放，促进金砖国家之间的经济融资合作，扩宽各国外汇储备的使用渠道，降低对美

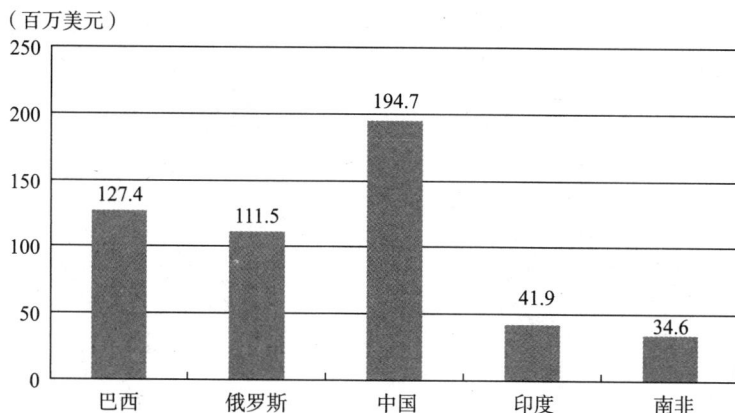

图 5 - 1　2017 年第四季度金砖国家未偿付国际借债情况

资料来源：Bank for International Settlements。

国金融市场的依赖。与此同时，完善当地的金融市场，并配合相应的监管条例措施，例如，针对短期流动的国际资本，征收额外的税收或者其他额外的限制。

2. 大力推广发展离岸金融市场和本币债券

欧洲货币市场是指在货币发行国以外进行该国货币存贷的市场，俗称"离岸金融市场"，产生于 20 世纪 60 年代，90 年代后迅速发展起来。离岸金融市场对各国有很大的吸引力，因为它是一个完全自由开放的、富有竞争力的市场。它不受任何国家的政府管制和纳税限制，存贷利差较小，资金高度灵活，手续简便，业务方式主要凭信用。发展本币债券可以减少一国的融资成本，同时也能够推进本国货币的区域化甚至国际化。另外，部分国家如中国和俄罗斯，拥有巨额的外汇储备，但主要投向发达国家市场，这样导致了对美元资产的过度依赖。促进金砖国家之间的本币债券交易，可以很好地缓解这一问题。

从 2017 年第四季度金砖国家未偿付国际债券（按发行货币分类）的统计来看（见图 5 - 2），金砖国家美元债券均占发行总量的 75%—95%，而发行的本币债券均不足总量的 15%。其中，巴西和俄罗斯只有 3% 左右。从目前的情况来看，本币债券市场相对于美元债的规模还有相当大的差距，这从一个侧面说明了它还有很大的提升空间。

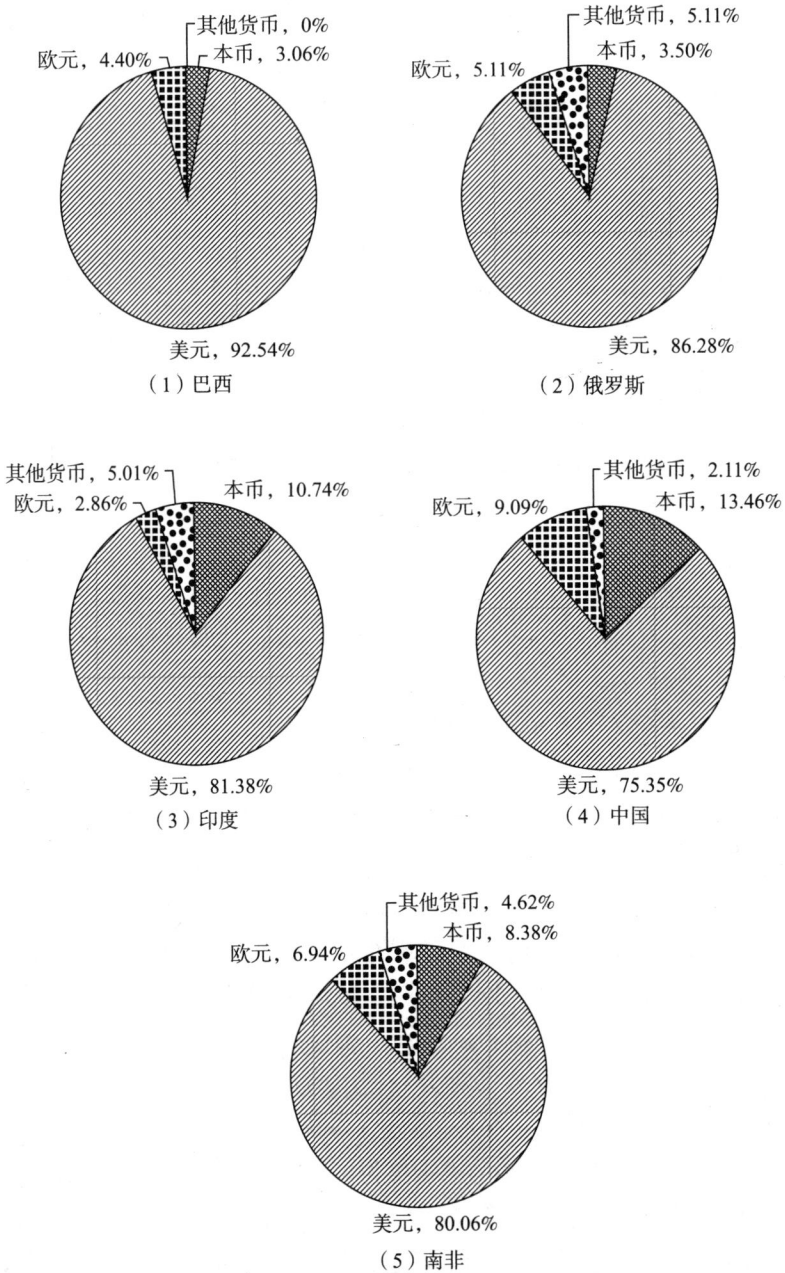

图 5－2 2017 年第四季度金砖国家未偿付国际债券情况

注：因为四舍五入；百分比之和不等于100%。

资料来源：国际清算银行。

由于新兴市场国家的金融发展还尚不完善，经济底子相对于发达国家来说较弱，投资者面临的风险也相对较高，从而会导致货币价值波动较大。因此，新兴市场国家在发行外债时，国外投资者由于担心货币贬值，而不希望购买以发展中国家本币为计算单位的债券。因此，金砖国家需要完善金融体系，建立良好的风险对冲机制。金融衍生品能够有效地对冲债券的风险，在进行债券交易的同时，通过使用远期、期权、货币互换等方式，固定好远期的汇率，这样，有助于投资者规避汇率风险；针对债券本身的违约风险，投资者还可以购买信用互换类衍生品如信用违约互换，一旦债券发生违约，互换卖方将会针对违约的部分予以补偿，从而大大降低违约的损失。

（二）推动发展金砖国家债券市场的举措

1. 加强金砖国家之间的相互合作，建立应急保险机制

金砖国家的优势在于经济发展迅速、收益率高。然而，投资者担心债券本身的违约风险，一旦出现违约风险，将传递到其他金融部门及金砖国家。因此，随着债券市场发展的逐步推进，应在金砖国家内部成立应急保险合作机制。

国际上的最后贷款人这一角色一般由 IMF 担任。然而，由于 IMF 并非一家中央银行，其所能够提供的资源是有限的。另外，IMF 等国际金融机构的话语权主要掌控在发达国家手中，一旦发生金融危机，其提供援助贷款有很强的政治性和局限性。例如，2009 年的欧债危机，为了得到 IMF 以及欧盟的援助，希腊政府必须接受苛刻的财政整顿条件，一定程度上反而恶化了当地的经济。因此，金砖国家之间可共同成立应对相应风险的基金，对于违约的债券（特别是主权债），在满足一定条件下予以流动性援助，充当一个最后贷款人的角色，有效地降低风险，增强投资者信心。

2. 加强与国际金融组织的合作，扩大融资规模

由于海外投资人对于金砖国家的发债人了解有限，一般企业直接通过发行债券的方式很难在国际上凑集到资金。当有国际金融组织作为中间人时，其发行债券的信用等级一般会较高，投资者更容易接受。各国应当加强与国际金融公司、亚洲开发银行等国际金融组织的合作，在拓展自身业务渠道的同时，为成员国债券融资提供更多路径，让更多金砖国家企业得到融资机会。

3. 增进金砖国家银行间市场合作

银行间市场的建设是一个国家债券市场发展的核心要素之一。目前，金砖国家银行间市场仍处于严重的分割状态。金砖国家银行间市场的制度法规、资信评级、会计风险审核及交易、清算结算系统等方面存在明显的差异，银行间市场的成熟度差距仍然比较大。金砖国家应加强银行间市场合作与交流，通过协商加强银行间市场的会计审核准则和相关法律法规的兼容性，放宽金砖国家之间投资者准入条件，丰富投资者结构，实现各金砖国家投资者在资金、信息、技术等方面的互补合作，同时，建立金砖国家银行间市场跨境电子交易平台，进一步减少交易成本。

4. 完善监管制度，推进信息的公开化

信息的不对称导致了投资者对金砖国家债券的担忧，逆向选择使高风险的债券更多地充斥于市场。作为市场的管理者，政府应当制定准则并督促其实施，加大企业信息的披露，完善债务合约和法律规范。从政治角度来看，本国的审计和监管可能产生欺诈行为，因此，应同时加强金砖国家之间信息监管的合作，并且设立相应的监督机制。

总之，推进债券市场的发展可以优化金砖国家的金融体系，降低和缓解金融系统风险，并使区域内资金达到有效配置。资本账户的开放，推行本币债券，建立保险机制，促进国际组织、银行间的合作以及完善市场监管将有助于加速这一进程。在推行过程中，金砖国家各国应通力合作，积极探索，推进制度创新。

三　深化本币结算、货币互换

美元、欧元、英镑和日元是国际贸易结算的主要货币，而金砖国家的货币基本属于不可自由兑换货币，贸易结算需要通过上述国际硬通货来实现，硬通货的获得和积累要受到这些国家的出口能力和净出口盈余的约束。自2008年国际金融危机以来，美元和欧元等主要货币的币值出现较大的波动，世界各国面临着汇率变化风险。随着金砖国家贸易量的逐年增长，使用美元等非本币货币导致的外汇兑换成本也日益增加。金砖国家可以推动贸易本币结算等方面的合作，使货币配置多元化，有利于国家金融体系稳定和促进贸易便利，同时也能够摆脱金砖国家对美元或其他硬通货的过度依赖。

（一）金砖国家之间本币结算存在的问题

第一，金砖国家之间对于推动本币结算和合作基础较薄弱。金砖国家的合作在一定程度上属于区域多边合作，区域金融合作程度取决于本地区经济一体化程度，金砖国家在地理区位和经济一体化方面的紧密程度还不高。

金砖国家经济发展结构差异较大，增长可持续性动力不足。另外，金砖国家之间的经济联系往往远不如各自与发达国家的经济联系紧密。例如，中国与美国、日本、欧盟和韩国的经贸往来多于中国和金砖国家经贸往来，俄罗斯与欧盟的贸易量也高于与金砖国家的贸易量，巴西与美国的经贸关系也超过了和金砖国家的关系。中国大力推行与各国国家的本币结算，但仍处于刚起步的阶段。金砖国家需要增强互信和合作意愿，深入交流和探讨，寻求官方利益契合点达成共识。

第二，现阶段金砖国家之间的贸易产品和方式较单一。例如，俄罗斯和巴西主要出口能源类产品；中国、印度贸易结构的雷同等。金砖国家成员国之间，应继续扩大相互间贸易规模，优化贸易结构，提升本国出口产品的竞争力和吸引力。中国和印度均是原材料需求大国，而俄罗斯和巴西则是原材料出口大国，这对于在金砖国家之间形成需求与供给对接、在大宗商品交易中采用金砖国家货币计价结算是十分有利的。因此，推广本币结算可从大宗商品入手，再随着贸易的扩大逐步推广。

第三，银行本币结算制度还不够完善。例如，商业银行缺乏应对本币结算风险的相关制度。由于商业银行总行没有设立专门用于规避本币结算风险的专项拨备，只能由各分支银行自行承担风险。另外，银行本币结算服务的水平还需要进一步提高，双边的货币结算方式还主要在汇款方面，信用证、托收等业务仍旧比较少。在推进国家本币结算的同时，各国也应当督促国内商业银行完善相应的业务，以应对日益增长的结算需求。

第四，金砖国家之间的资本流动限制较多。例如，俄罗斯对银行跨境调运的现钞征收高关税，大大增加了成本，并且影响到银行本币现钞的头寸平补，制约了本币结算的发展。对于这一点，各国需要加大沟通与协商，增加互信和合作意愿，并加大推动资本账户的开放。

第五，主权货币流出后需要解决回流问题。金砖国家应当积极开展资本市场合作，允许回流的本币资金在国内开设账户，进行债券、股票等投资。在本国债券市场上，引进合作的投资者，发行双边本币债券以分散风险，推动双边债券市场的发展。

（二）金砖国家之间货币互换存在的问题

相对于发达国家，新兴市场国家底子弱、金融稳定性低，为应对流动性不足的风险，金砖国家之间应当建立起一系列合作，以推动中央银行的多边货币互换。一方面，货币互换是交易双方按照事先商定的规则，互相交换不同货币、相当金额的本金及利息支付，到期后再换回本金的交易。双方的事先约定被称为货币互换协议。按照参与主体不同，货币互换可以在商业机构之间进行，也可以在中央银行之间进行。商业机构货币互换的主要目的是降低筹资成本和规避汇率风险；中央银行则是通过互换提供流动性支持，体现加强合作、共同应对危机的意愿，并以此增强市场信心，促进地区金融稳定。与 IMF 提供的流动性救援机制相比，货币互换在使用条件、可获得性和救助速度方面都有很大的优势。另一方面，多边货币互换协议的签订也有助于推动金砖国家之间的直接投资与增长。互换的货币可以直接分配给本国相关的商业银行，由银行授信给贸易企业，便于互换货币落实到贸易融资、结算和资金融通、信用证开立等具体交易活动中。

在实际操作过程中，货币互换还存在一些问题：

第一，互换仍旧以美元为基础。由于进行外汇干预的货币主要是美元，货币互换中购买和回购所使用的汇率以美元即期汇率为基础（例如，2000 年东盟 10 国和《中日韩清迈协议》达成了规模为 920 亿美元的互换协议，其中大部分为美元互换。）"去美元化"与贸易结算相辅相成，需逐步优化贸易结构，从贸易方面逐渐摆脱对美元的依赖，以加强本币作为储备货币的地位。因此，推动本币的结算也能够改善货币互换的机制。

第二，货币互换机制并不能规避系统性风险。某一金砖国家出现流动性问题，通过其他成员国的货币互换，能够起到一定的缓解作用。然而，当大多数成员国都出现了此类问题时，金砖国家的多边货币互换将遇到较大难度，并导致市场对所有新兴市场国家信心的下降，从而引发系统性风险。金砖国家依旧需要和 IMF 等国际组织合作，建立相应的机制以防范系统性风险。

第三，与 IMF 的挂钩一定程度上制约了多边货币互换机制。由于缺乏区域内独立监测机构，目前，多边货币互换机制多参考 IMF 的监测机制来防范道德风险，使其被定义为对 IMF 等国际金融援助机制的补充。与 IMF 贷款条件挂钩会受到其融资制度的制约而无法发挥应有的作用，丧失必要的灵活性和即时性。例如，在 2013 年的"双 I 危机"中，印度尼西亚的本币汇率和资本市场大幅波动，但其并未利用多边货币互换机制来缓冲；印度卢比相对美元在 3 个月里下跌了 20%，虽然曾经寻求其他新兴经济体在外汇方面协调干预，但最后却接受了日本的资助。因此，金砖国家之间需要调整并改善协议计划，适当放宽储备的使用条件，并且要建立较完善的风险评估体系判别危机性质，区分资本收支危机、经常收支危机或复合型危机，才能制定适合于该国或该区域的处理办法。

深化本币结算和货币互换仍需要多边国家的紧密合作，虽然面临重重挑战，但推动两者的发展将进一步完善金砖国家的投融资体系，有利于提高国家和区域的福祉，提升新兴市场经济体在国际经济中的地位。

【案例：货币互换基金】

为解决新兴市场国家的货币错配问题，货币互换基金（TCX）由开发性金融机构、专门小额信贷投资机构和其他捐助者于 2007 年设立，投资者包括荷兰和德国政府，以及 22 个多边与双边机构。TCX 的投资者和客户以本地货币向其借款人提供融资，同时利用货币互换和利率互换将货币风险转移至 TCX，从而免受汇率与利率波动的影响。私人部门的交易对手也通过货币与利率互换降低自身承担的风险。TCX 则通过对冲工具来对冲自身所承担的汇率与利率风险，能够持续为客户提供货币互换的金融服务。金砖国家可参考货币互换基金，在本币合作基础上建立更加广泛的货币互换机制。[①]

【案例：俄罗斯外贸银行营运资金贷款项目】

2014—2015 年，国家开发银行与俄罗斯外贸银行（The Bank for Foreign Trade）（以下简称"俄外贸银行"）沟通协商，共同开发了以支

---

① 参见本书附录"案例七：货币互换基金"。

持中俄贸易项目为融资目的的金融机构境外人民币项目，额度120亿元人民币，期限3年，截至当前已提款96亿元。该项目对国家开发银行未来与境外其他金融机构大规模开展金融机构境外人民币合作、支持"一带一路"经贸合作以及人民币国际化战略有着里程碑式的意义。

该项目对巩固中俄两国战略合作伙伴关系有重要意义。该项目为近年来我国与俄罗斯金融机构开展境外人民币合作单笔金额最大的贷款融资，也是国家开发银行践行国家"一带一路"金融合作、推动人民币国际化战略的重大举措，具有开创性的里程碑意义。该项目为未来中资银行与境外"一带一路"国家金融机构开展以贸易融资为着力点的贷款合作开创了先例和示范。该项目的实施将加快推动人民币成为国际市场交易的计价结算货币，提升人民币在国际市场中的购买力，实现人民币国际化。同时，开展境外人民币合作有助于推动我国与俄罗斯及其他地区经贸关系发展，保持对外贸易的稳定增长。①

四　建设金砖国家多边投融资模式、"智库＋金融"合作模式

（一）建立开发性与商业性金融相配合的多边合作模式

开发性金融的特点是支持符合国家发展战略的业务，更适用于中长期项目，而商业性金融是市场化的，网点多、覆盖面大，对中短期业务优势明显。开发性金融能够发挥"逆周期"的作用，而商业性金融是"顺周期"的。金砖国家开发性金融合作发展应以开发性金融为核心，逐步扩大合作范围，集合可利用的资源，使合作方式多样化。

1. 充分发挥不同类型金融机构的作用

一方面，要以开发性金融和政策性金融为杠杆，为重点项目的孵化和启动提供融资支持。对于有一定盈利能力，但投资周期较长、回报较慢的项目主要由开发性金融提供融资保障；对于需要利用资金扶植或者补贴的"走出去"行业，则由政策性金融覆盖，但应考虑财政的承受能

---

① 参见本书附录"案例八：俄罗斯外贸银行营运资金贷款项目"。

力。另一方面，对于中短期海外投资，可通过商业性金融提供市场化的融资方式，带动商业性资金和各方力量参与投资建设，形成合力，力争取得良好效果。同时，对于符合国家政策导向的重要海外投资项目，各种资金也可在项目生命周期的不同阶段进入，相互配合，提供金融支持。考虑到政策性资金成本较低且不以营利为主要目标，可在项目开发阶段或无利润时期介入，提供财政补助或贴息，同时应避免承担过多财政负担；开发性资金可以在项目的低利润期进入，一方面为项目提供较低成本的资金支持，另一方面也可将项目做大做好，分享成长红利；商业性资金可以待项目成熟、回报稳定后进入，此时项目已经运行一段时间，积累了一定资信，即使在市场上融资，成本也会更低。

2. 加大公私合营项目（PPP）在基础设施建设中的应用

充分调动社会资本和民间资本共同参与收益率较高的投资项目。对于收益比较好的项目，应由社会资本和私人资本联合参与，共同投资建设。亚洲基础设施投资银行、丝路基金、国家开发银行等金融机构参与的投资项目周期较长，有必要建立国际公私合营业务模式来分散风险，以提高融资的可持续性。金砖国家需要改善投资环境，对各利益相关方的风险进行优化，并配合相应的监管制度，选择合适的私人合作伙伴，增加成功的概率。同时，金砖国家可以和已有的开发性金融机构合作，更好地利用全球资源，并建立起信息共享机制。

（二）提升"智库＋金融"在金砖国家可持续发展中的作用

通过智库合作，既可以增信释疑，融通文化，为拓展和深化合作奠定民意基础；又可以通过宣传介绍金砖国家的合作成就，提升了影响力和吸引力。金砖国家成员国智库合作交流不断深入，对全面推进安全、经济、人文等领域合作发挥了"推动器"和"黏合剂"的作用，成为金砖国家成员国加深了解、增强互信的重要纽带，为金砖国家的发展集聚了更多资源与潜力。与此同时，金砖国家各成员国都面临发展重任，需要破解经济社会结构性难题，各国应加强智库合作，为金砖国家实现新发展提供智力支持。

金砖国家合作需要兼顾资金和知识合作，对内可以帮助金砖国家加深了解，增信释疑；对外能够增强金砖国家整体影响力，具体举措有以下两项：

1. 纵横联合多类型多机构，加强智库建设与国际智库交流合作

其一，定期开展知识分享和经验交流，发挥"智库＋金融"积极作用，如人员互访、共同举办学术活动等。在此基础上，还应进一步建立交流与合作网络，可由金砖国家具有影响力的智库牵头，使交流合作常态化、机制化，对金砖国家之间的信息交流和决策参考起到重要作用。

其二，加强金砖国家的联合研究，由金砖国家智库双方或多方共同承接研究项目，合作成果由参与方共同发布，传播金砖国家智库的声音。以多种方式加强合作课题研究，以高度的创新精神，加快推进金砖智库建设，并积极探索金砖国家智库的组织形式和管理方式。

其三，建立联合研究机构。加强金砖国家智库之间的国际交流，建立联合研究机构以加强智库国际平台建设。金砖国家智库合作应将"走出去与请进来"相结合，大力开展各种长期或短期的国际合作。联合研究机构可常设一国，也可以在金砖国家之间轮值工作，并将其打造成具有重要影响力的国际智库交流平台。

其四，增强智库全球意识。关注能源供应、环境保护、气候变化、可持续发展、贸易自由化、公共外交、全球治理等国际重大问题的研究，提高金砖国家处理国际事务的能力。拓宽聘请金砖国家专家交流和研究的渠道，更好地为金砖国家决策提供参考。培育一批有国际影响的智库人才，提高智库开放程度，提升研究人员独特的视野和研究水平。

2. 通过智库建立长期规划，推动制度建设

一是通过智库建立长期规划。建设金砖国家特色新型智库，提升智库核心竞争力，从"全能选手"的误区中走出来，明确智库定位，针对金砖国家共同的、热点的重大现实问题、长远问题、战略问题进行前瞻性研究，并系统地提出具有建设性、可操作性的政策建议。智库建设需从金砖国家整体经济和社会发展的角度入手，以建立规划并推动机制建设为目的，注重智力产品，提升研究质量，打造竞争力强、专业水平高、能拿"硬方案"的高端国际化龙头智库。

二是通过规划推动投融资项目落地。长期综合规划对于一个国家或地区实现跨越式发展来说至关重要，开发性金融机构可通过银政企合作推进市场建设、信用建设和制度建设，弥补市场空白和缺失，并以投融资服务基础设施重点项目，配套商业金融推动项目落地，最终实现国家发展目标。

【案例：金砖国家银行合作机制】

2010年4月15日，中国国家开发银行、巴西开发银行、俄罗斯开发与对外经济活动银行和印度进出口银行在巴西利亚共同签署《金砖国家银行合作机制备忘录》，标志着金砖国家银行合作机制正式成立。2011年4月13日，南非开发银行加入合作机制。自合作机制成立以来，各成员行积极开展多双边金融合作，为促进金砖国家经济发展和经贸合作发挥了重要作用，先后签署多边合作协议如《金砖国家银行合作机制银行间本币授信协议》《金砖国家银行合作机制信用评级结论共享合作备忘录》等，涉及本币授信、信用证保兑服务、可持续发展和基础设施融资等多个领域，有力地推动金砖国家金融合作和经贸投资便利化。①

五　建立金砖国家框架内
可持续投融资模式

金砖国家合作目标应瞄准共同的可持续性发展，其独特之处在于呼吁金砖国家成员国共同采取行动，致力于消除贫穷，促进经济增长，满足教育、卫生、社会保障和就业机会等社会需求，为社会综合发展奠定可持续投融资的良性循环基础。另外，投融资的具体领域需要与可持续发展结合，金砖国家的投融资领域也将集中在绿色发展、民生、教育及社会保障领域，承担发展重任，破解经济社会结构性难题。

（一）发挥开发性金融特有优势，以发展为首要任务

具体而言，以发展为首要目标，包括消除极端贫困并减少不平等现象；设立环境与社会安全保障措施，并建立信息交流、问责和补救机制；在可持续发展中展现金砖国家的领导力；创立公众咨询与讨论机制；采取真正的民主治理结构。在金砖国家合作过程中，只有通过更具有地域和发展的开发性金融合作机制的设计，才能实现金砖国家的区域经济合

---

① 参见本书附录"案例九：金砖国家银行合作机制"。

作可持续发展目标。

（二）进一步挖掘合作各方利益的汇聚点

随着二十国集团逐渐取代八国集团成为全球治理的主导力量，金砖国家应在全球治理过程中以制度建设参与者的身份，更紧密地团结在一起，通过均衡各方的经济和非经济利益，来挖掘利益汇聚点。要进一步聚焦对不完善、不合理的国际旧规制的改革，借助多边对话机制，使各方在全球经济治理问题上达成一致意见，为金砖国家乃至发展中国家在国际贸易与投资过程中谋求更加公正、公平的国际环境。在合作的过程中，关注各国经济的可持续增长，将各国的"走出去"和"引进来"结合在一起，实现在经济上的优势互补与相互促进。对竞争性产业，积极开展国际技术合作，在节能减排、技术领域等，应以项目研发为主，形成研发团队，促进各方在技术上突破。在互补性产业发展中，充分发挥各方优势，加强经贸往来，形成稳定的经济增长点，形成经贸深化与金融合作的互动。同时，进一步深化各国在政治上的互信，加强各国在文化上的交流，通过官方与民间的双轨交流，促进各国在安全、粮食、能源、气候、科技、教育等领域的合作。

（三）加快完善区域金融合作的机制建设

加快金融监管机制的建立。监管与金融业的全球化、区域化必须齐头并进。金砖国家新开发银行的成立，简化了金砖国家之间贸易与融资的程序，为金砖国家之间的投融资等金融服务提供了便利，解决了各国在基础设施建设领域的资金问题，而金融监管功能的缺失会增加区域的系统性风险。随着金砖国家新开发银行及应急储备安排的成立，建立金融监管机制迫在眉睫。在监管机制建设过程中，应以尊重各国金融主权为基本原则，以公开透明、平等互利为导向，实现金融监管的公平与效率。首先，建立资本流动监控、危机预警等机制。其次，加快信用等级评价体系建设，对全球和区域的宏观经济进行有效评估。此外，应加速出台金砖国家新开发银行和应急储备安排的各项管理制度，以提高金砖国家新开发银行的管理水平。借鉴欧洲复兴开发银行、美洲开发银行、亚洲开发银行的组织架构、决策过程、管理制度等，建立一套符合新兴市场国家的银行管理制度，形成金砖国家新开发银行的企业文化，树立良好的形象。

（四）促进产业结构优化升级，合理调整经济发展模式

满足金融合作所需，稳定金融外部环境。在产业结构优化升级过程中，兼顾发展传统的劳动密集型产业和技术资本密集型产业，提升金砖国家在全球产业分工中的核心竞争力，在全球价值链中寻求更高的位置。充分利用以新开发银行为核心的金砖国家投融资体系，加大基础设施建设，提升人力资本水平，并利用金砖国家各成员国市场技术与能源互补优势，提高自然资源利用率，形成新的开放而又充分的产业结构体系。在经济发展模式调整过程中，以稳定经济增长为目的，合理发挥比较优势，利用金砖国家广阔的市场及现有合作成果，减少因投资和基础设施建设不足、社会收入差距大、贫困和社会基础薄弱等带来的影响，调整经济结构和收入分配结构，提升国家整体实力。

（五）敦促多边发展银行和绿色气候基金等重要基金投资各国绿色增长

发挥国际金融的杠杆作用，引导资金向低碳基础设施投融资建设领域倾斜，提高增长质量，实现可持续发展。新成立的亚洲基础设施投资银行和新开发银行等可以通过投资绿色基础设施，扩大业务范围，扩展国际影响力。投资过程中，要加强对项目所在地环境的保护、与当地城镇化进程的融合及对当地就业的促进等，以气候变化和可持续的基础设施投资为依托，形成自身独特的国际影响力。此外，还应鼓励"主权财富基金"投资低碳领域。主权财富基金作为一种特殊的具有特定目标的公共投资基金，可以作为多边发展银行如亚洲基础设施投资银行等的融资来源，引导其投向低碳领域，扩展融资规模。

【案例：中国工商银行收购南非标准银行项目】

中国工商银行和南非标准银行在 2007 年 6 月达成以股权为纽带的战略合作共识，中国工商银行以约 54.6 亿美元的对价收购了南非标准银行 20% 的股权，股权交割于 2008 年 3 月完成，中国工商银行成为标准银行集团第一大股东。南非标准银行全球首家中国非洲银行业务中心于 2017 年正式成立，进一步加深中国与非洲的双边贸易合作关系。该收购成为金砖国家银行之间投融资合作的典型范例，中国工商银行与标准银行集团均加大了对非洲涉及中国企业的项目信贷投放力度，仅中国工商银行

审批的非洲贷款金额一年就高达近百亿美元，积极推动了中非经贸合作往来便利化。中国工商银行与标准银行将继续通过综合化金融服务、多元化融资渠道，为中非产业合作提供支撑，并积极响应政府间货币互换、自贸区等创新金融需求，提高金融便利性，推动中非经贸合作不断深化。①

六　探索数字经济（区块链等）在投融资领域的应用

金砖国家将会成为产业革命区域空间和经济合作的典型载体，将借助产业革命机遇，充分发挥技术外溢与干中学效应，促进金融创新与投融资发展。在数字经济领域，区块链技术助力于金砖国家实现全球价值链竞争的"弯道超车"。

（一）金砖国家探索区块链投融资应用的意义

利用区块链技术建立金砖国家跨境支付结算系统，不仅能够大幅提升金砖国家之间跨境结算的效率，还可以打破美国的金融特权，对国际货币金融体系产生根本性的影响。在当前国际货币体系下，美元是各国跨境支付和结算的主导货币，在美国控制下的环球同业银行金融电信协会（SWIFT）和纽约清算所银行同业支付系统（CHIPS）成为美元国际结算的必经通道。区块链是当前全球金融科技发展中潜在影响力最大的技术之一，有可能从根本上改变现行的国际货币金融体系。

区块链本质上是一个去中心化的巨大分布式账本数据库，具有去中心化、去中介化、加密安全性等特征，它有可能改变传统国际货币结算体系的"中心—外围"模式（以美国控制的 SWIFT 和 CHIPS 系统为中心，其余系统是外围），从而在较大程度上削弱美国的金融特权。金砖国家内部可积极推动基于区块链技术的合作，尝试建立基于该技术的跨境支付结算体系，并以此为契机在国际货币金融体系改革当中占据有利地位。

---

① 参见本书附录"案例十：中国工商银行收购南非标准银行项目"。

首先，金砖国家货币当局和金融机构应通过合作，共同建立行业标准，引导区块链国际监管新规则。目前，全球银行业区块链应用还处在发展的初级阶段，面临一系列技术与模式选择，存在监管合规以及应用领域等多种不同的可能性。包括区块链金融科技公司、大型银行以及监管机构在内的三股力量，未来将会极大地影响区块链的应用方向及标准，其中监管将成为区块链技术应用的主导力量。

其次，在金砖国家内部实施区块链合作后，未来金砖国家在参与国际规则谈判过程中可以发挥更大的影响力。金砖国家之间可以通过监管机构协商，建立行业监管及相应的技术标准，制定游戏规则，从而把握市场先机。

最后，建立金砖国家区块链合作平台，鼓励金融机构、金融科技公司与政府合作，争取尽早建立基于区块链技术的金砖国家跨境支付系统，从技术上将彻底打破美国在国际货币支付领域的垄断，这对于保障金砖国家的金融安全，具有重大价值。

（二）区块链自身的特征及在金砖国家投融资领域切入点

基于区块链本身的去中心化、去信任化、可追溯等特征，区块链技术能实现点对点的价值转移，通过资产数字化和重构金融基础设施架构，可达成大幅度提升金融资产交易后清算、结算流程效率，降低成本的目标，可解决金砖国家之间支付所面临的现存问题。

1. 去中心化

在中心化的结构体系中，系统由中心节点控制和进行决策，在去中心化的结构中，每个节点都是平等的，不拥有整个系统的控制权，系统决策由所有参与节点在共识机制作用下共同决定。市场经济是典型的去中心化系统，每个经济主体都在"看不见的手"引导下决定生产和消费而不受外界干预，本质上是双方交易去中心化。在金砖国家区域内，可以通过此手段绕过美国的货币支付系统，在各成员国中形成平等的支付体系。

2. 去信任化

去信任化并非不可信或不需要信用，而是指用技术规则加持信用，通过算法实现自我约束，任何恶意欺骗系统的行为都会遭到其他节点排斥，因此，不依赖中央权威机构的信用背书，可以在一定程度和一定范围内取代传统信用建立方式，完成点对点之间信任关系的建立。在区块链技术构建的信用系统中，参与者不需要依赖任何人提供信用背书，随着参与者的增加，破坏系统的难度加大，系统安全性也将上升。现阶段金砖国家尚未建立统一的信用体系，而通过区块链的应用则可以完成不可撤销的信用保障，可以通过区块链技术的应用促进信用体系的建设。

3. 可追溯性

区块链技术具有数据不可篡改和可追溯特性，可以用来构建监管部门所需要的、包含众多手段的监管工具箱，以利于实施精准、及时和更多维度的监管。在区块链中，任一区块都记录着上一个区块全部信息，任何一笔交易都可追溯，任何节点上都保留着完整的区块链。在金砖国家区域内，每一笔交易都可以通过区块链保存详细的交易信息，以利于在区域内逐步建立完整的信息集合体系。

区块链技术能使数据在交易各方之间公开透明，从而在整个供应链条上形成一个完整且流畅的信息流，这可以确保参与各方及时发现供应链系统运行过程中存在的问题，并有针对性地找到解决问题的方法，进而提升供应链管理的整体效率。区块链所具有的数据不可篡改和时间戳的存在性证明的特质能很好地运用于解决供应链体系内各参与主体之间的纠纷，实现轻松举证与追责。最后，数据不可篡改与交易可追溯性两大特性相结合，可以根除供应链内产品流转过程中的假冒伪劣问题。

现阶段，在金砖国家之间最可行的应用为区块链信用证及代开信用证。目前，信用证开立后大多以纸质形式传递，安全性低、校准难，银行间信用证开立目前没有电子化渠道，多为信开，在发生信用证修改、到单、通知等情况，目前没有直接信息交互通道；以中国为例，信用证目前多使用 Swift MT999、MT999 或二代支付的报文不能使用中文，报文较短不能满足用户需求。

以中国建设银行通过润和软件公司的应用为例，他们的合作实现了信用证的简单应用：信用证申请人通过填写在线电子申请书（在区块链上进行）给开证行 A，开证行 A 将信息放在信用证电子信息上并传递给通知行 B（该信息不可修改、不可抵赖），通知行 B 在将信用证电子通知书传递给信用证受益人。

（三）金砖国家探索区块链可能的应用场景

1. 金砖国家在支付、结算、供应链领域的痛点

在支付领域，金砖国家跨境金融机构间的对账、清算、结算的成本较高，也涉及了很多的手工流程，这不仅导致了用户端和金融机构中后台业务端等产生的支付业务费用高昂，也使小额支付业务难以开展。在资产管理领域，股权、债券、票据、收益凭证、仓单等资产由不同的中介机构托管，提高了资产交易成本，也容易带来凭证被伪造等问题。

在清算和结算领域，不同金融机构间的基础设施架构、业务流程各不相同，同时涉及很多人工处理的环节，极大地增加了业务成本，也容易出现差错。在用户身份识别领域，不同金融机构间的用户数据难以实现高效的交互，使重复认证成本较高，间接地带来了用户身份被某些中介机构泄露的风险。

在供应链领域，供应链是一个由物流、信息流、资金流共同组成的，并将行业内的供应商、制造商、分销商、零售商、用户串联在一起的复杂结构。区块链技术作为一种大规模的协作工具，天然地适合运用于供应链管理。供应链由众多参与主体构成，不同的主体之间必然存在大量的交互和协作，而整个供应链运行过程中产生的各类信息被离散地保存在各个环节各自的系统内，信息流缺乏透明度。这会带来两类严重的问题：一是因为信息不透明、不流畅导致链条上的各参与主体难以准确了解相关事项的状况及存在的问题，从而影响供应链的效率；二是当供应链各主体间出现纠纷时，举证和追责均耗时费力，甚至在有些情况下变得不可行。

2. 区块链技术在金砖国家之间的具体应用方式与场景

区块链技术可从信用体系建设、流程简化、提高交易安全性等方面对支付体系加以优化。具体应用方式如下：

第一，区块链技术开源且透明，所有区块上交易记录、资产都能以分布式的数据系统形式体现，可便于验证交易内容的真实性和完整性，提高了系统可追责性，而区块链与大数据等信息技术综合使用将有效分析财务记录、购买习惯和工作表现，并对一切影响信用的因素进行评分，有助于建立双边信任或多边互信，解决金融活动中的信任问题，降低系统的信任成本。

第二，通过程序设计，区块链技术可实现自动化，程序对区块链上

数据的自动处理简化了结算操作环节，操作环节减少也降低了风险发生的概率，对提升风险控制水平和提高金融机构竞争力具有重要作用，同时，节省的部分人力、物力可进入生产性领域，创造实际经济价值。

第三，传统清结算系统为中心结构，中心出现故障问题或被攻击能致使整个网络瘫痪，区块链技术使每个节点都保存一份数据副本，能够有效地化解系统故障，抵御外部恶意攻击，任一部分出现问题都不会影响整体运行。

（1）支付领域的应用。在支付领域，区块链技术的应用有助于降低金融机构间的对账成本及争议解决成本，从而显著提高支付业务的处理速度及效率，这一点在跨境支付领域的作用尤其明显。另外，区块链技术为支付领域所带来的成本和效率优势，使金融机构能够更好地处理以往因成本因素而被视为不现实的小额跨境支付，有助于普惠金融的实现。

（2）资产数字化的应用。各类资产，如股权、债券、票据、收益凭证、仓单等均可被整合进区块链中，成为链上数字资产，使资产所有者无须通过各种中介机构就能直接发起交易。上述功能可以借助行业基础设施类机构实现，让其扮演托管者的角色，确保资产的真实性与合规性，并在托管库和分布式账本之间搭建一座桥梁，让分布式账本平台能够安全地访问托管库中的可信任资产。此外，资产发行以可根据需要灵活采用保密或公开的方式进行。

具体业务应用包括资产证券化（ABS）领域应用，一是缩短发行周期，提高效率。联合多方参与者建立多中心管理平台，提高业务操作效率。二是信息共享，交叉验证。部分信息共享，增强信息透明度，实现多个参与方之间信息交叉验证、信用相互背书。三是提高产品流动性，降低融资成本。为参与者提供全流程管理功能，形成多方参与的正向证券化生态圈。

信用证领域应用。一是贸易企业、开证行、通知行、物流企业、税务部门或企业组成联盟链。二是跨机构信息通过区块链的共识机制和分布式账本保持同步，降低通信协作成本，实现行业互惠。三是贸易信息、信用证信息、物流信息、电子发票登记在区块链上不可篡改，有助于提升交易、信用证可信性，降低造假风险。四是区块链完整地记录了信用证流程，历史记录都可以追踪和查询，增强了业务信息透明度，用户可以及时了解到业务进展。

福费廷领域应用。基于链上的贸易业务和单据真实可信，拓展福费廷业务，降低风险，帮助出口商以更低成本融资，改善其财务情况。

投标保函领域应用。一是跨系统业务协作。连接行外申请系统与行内审批系统，实现传统业务线上高效协作处理。二是电子化存证。将电子签约合同的 Hash 值（文件指纹）存入区块链，方便随时查询校验，对接公证处，快速出具司法鉴定报告和公证书，强化司法效力。三是全流程监控。监管机构通过部署节点，可以实现对投标保函业务的全流程监管。

（3）智能证券的应用。金融资产的交易是相关各方之间基于一定的规则达成的合约，区块链能用代码充分地表达这些业务逻辑，如固定收益证券、回购协议、各种掉期交易以及银团贷款等，进而实现合约的自动执行，并且保证相关合约只在交易对手之间可见，而对无关第三方保密。基于区块链的智能证券能通过相应机制确保其运行符合特定的法律和监管框架。

（4）供应链金融的应用。应收账款融资领域应用。业务流程：核心企业确认应付账款，签发白条；一级供应商进行签收；一级供应商根据自身情况选择转让、融资或持有到期；供应商可随时在线发起白条面额以内的融资申请；融资申请实时到账。业务优势：实现基于核心企业信用的应收账款凭证（白条）在供应链上的多级流转；支持拆分、转让和融资，有效惠及除一级供应商外的多级供应商，实现了核心企业信用的多级传导；通过引入外部金融机构，为应收账款提供低成本融资利率。

货押融资领域应用。业务流程：货物入库，仓单出具，物权转让给做市商；做市商向客户支付白条；客户根据自身情况选择转让、融资或持有到期；供应商可随时在线发起白条面额以内的融资申请；融资申请实时到账。业务优势：流通方式改变，仓单—票据（白条），票据的付款独立于基础合同，流通性更好；白条可拆分转让，改善融资能力；白条上加上核心企业的承付使票据的流通性更好；通过保理商或银行，对接ABS、再保理，资产的标准化程度更高。

（5）清算和结算的应用。区块链技术的核心特质是能以准实时的方式，在无须可信的第三方参与的情况下实现价值转移。金融资产的交易涉及支付和证券两个重要方面。通过基于区块链技术的法定数字货币或者是某种"结算工具"的创设，与前文所述的链上数字资产对接，即可完成点对点的实时清算与结算，从而显著降低价值转移的成本，缩短清算、结算时间。在此过程中，交易各方均可获得良好的隐私保护。

（6）客户识别的应用。全世界的金融机构都是受到严格监管的，其中很重要的一条，就是金融机构在向客户提供服务时必须履行客户识别（KYC）责任。在传统方式下，KYC是非常耗时的流程，缺少自动验证消费者身份的技术，因此，无法高效地开展工作。在传统金融体系中，不同机构间的用户身份信息和交易记录无法实现一致、高效的跟踪，使监管机构的工作难以落到实处。区块链技术可实现数字化身份信息的安全、可靠管理，在保证客户隐私的前提下提升客户识别的效率并降低成本。

（7）物流交易的应用。在物流过程中，利用数字签名和公私钥加解密机制，可以充分保证信息安全以及寄、收件人的隐私。例如，快递交接需要双方私钥签名，每个快递员或快递点都有自己的私钥，是否签收或交付只需要查一下区块链即可。最终用户没有收到快递就不会有签收记录，快递员无法伪造签名，因此，可杜绝快递员通过伪造签名来逃避考核的行为，减少用户投诉，防止货物的冒领误领。而真正的收件人并不需要在快递单上直观展示实名制信息，由于安全隐私有保障，所以，更多的人愿意接受实名制，从而促进国家物流实名制的落实。

附录 金砖国家投融资合作案例与启示

案例一：金砖国家新开发银行

一 基本情况

金砖国家新开发银行（New Development Bank，以下简称"新开发银行"）原名金砖开发银行，于 2014 年 7 月 15 日在巴西福塔莱萨由金砖国家领导人签署协议并宣告成立。新开发银行是金砖国家合作成立的多边开发银行，旨在"为金砖国家和其他新兴市场经济体中国家的基础设施建设、可持续发展项目筹措资金"。新开发银行初始认缴资本 500 亿美元，金砖国家五国各出资 100 亿美元，法定资本为 1 亿美元；新开发银行总部设在上海，并在南非设立非洲区域中心。根据新开发银行的协议，银行"将通过贷款、担保、参股和其他金融工具来支持公共或私人项目"。此外，新开发银行还应与国际组织和其他金融机构合作，为世界银行支持的项目提供技术援助。新开发银行首任行长、理事会主席和董事会主席分别来自印度、俄罗斯和巴西。

二 机遇与挑战

新开发银行作为发展中国家主导的世界性开发性金融机构，是南南合作的重要成果。它根植于新的世界经济格局，力图改善现有全球治理体系无法解决的新兴经济体发展问题。作为新兴市场国家的开发银行，新开发银行自成立初期就面临若干的机遇与挑战。

一是合作基础不够牢固。金砖国家目前还是一个较为松散的合作框架，各成员国在国际贸易等问题上仍然存在一定冲突，合作的基础不够牢固，在深化合作的道路上还将面临诸多困难。因此，在未来的发展过程中各国需要充分沟通利益诉求，求同存异，尽量避免并及时解决冲突与分歧。中国在和金砖国家的合作过程中，也要平衡好大国战略和细节方面的让步妥协，推动新开发银行的稳步运行与发展。

二是平权决策模式可能带来效率损失。《福塔莱萨宣言》中的金砖国家新开发银行法定资本1亿美元，初始认缴资本500亿美元，由创始成员国平等出资意味着新开发银行在制度上没有哪个成员国是绝对意义上的主导决策者。这种平权决策模式的优势是充分尊重各成员意愿，劣势是在决策时可能部分损失效率，尤其是当各成员国之间存在利益冲突的时候。因此，在实行平权决策时，也应充分考虑效率问题，明确治理架构，优化决策机制，保证"发展"的根本政策出发点得到落实。

三　意义与影响

第一，建立服务金砖国家发展的开发银行，为"南南合作"提供合作典范。自2009年以来，金融体系的不平等一直是金砖国家的重要关切，如何实行切实的改革措施应对复杂多变的国际环境也多次在金砖国家领导人峰会中提起。新开发银行由金砖国家五国分摊认缴资本，民主地选举任命银行理事会、董事会和其他高层管理者，是南南合作的重要机会和窗口。新开发银行使金砖国家由原来的资金、技术接受者一定程度上转变为资源的提供者。角色的转变使各国能够以平等协商、互利共赢的原则为金砖国家提供开发性金融服务，以主动的姿态参与开发性金融事务的决策和执行当中，平等地获得基础设施开发和可持续发展的机会及资源。

第二，提升新兴经济体在国际事务中的影响力和话语权。2008年的国际金融危机暴露了全球金融体系的系统性风险，新兴经济体面临着前所未有的挑战。但是，以美国为首的发达国家牢牢地把握着金融体系的顶层设计和标准执行，阻挠新兴经济体在国际货币基金组织、世界银行等金融组织中地位和话语权的提升。在此之下推行的任何改革都建立在不损害发达国家既得利益的前提下，对新兴经济体的高速发展与赶超实质上起到了阻碍作用。新开发银行是金砖国家多年协商谈判的结果，期望在实质上打破发达国家在国际事务中的垄断话语权，是后国际金融危机时代新兴经济体实施战略合作，参与游戏规则制定的重要尝试。

第三，深化金砖国家之间的多边合作，改善全球经济金融格局。新开发银行正面临着发展的重要机遇，而金砖国家在此期间的经济形势决定了创始成员国对新开发银行的资源贡献与支持力度。在当前复杂的经

济形势下，将应急储备安排协议与新开发银行进行互补，共同发力，是
推进金砖国家框架内合作的有效途径。新开发银行主要提供经济平稳运
行时期的基础设施开发贷款，而应急储备安排协议则在经济环境恶化的
时候缓解成员国短期流动性压力。两者的结合是深化金砖国家银行间合
作机制的重要抓手，并将深刻改变全球金融格局。

案例二：金砖国家应急储备安排

一　产生背景

金砖国家的外汇风险暴露程度和当前全球金融体系能够提供的风险
防控水平的不匹配促成了应急储备安排的产生。金砖国家拥有大量外汇
储备，但是，在当前国际资本高度流动的背景下，很多成员国的外汇储
备规模不足以应对资本流动带来的潜在风险，即存在发生金融危机的可
能性。双边层面，金砖国家之间没有建立有效的防火墙，如学习西方国
家相互签署双边信贷互惠协定，也没有和美联储建立双边的货币保障协
议，一旦发生大规模资本流动以及汇率波动，可能很难从美国和其他发
达国家获得及时援助。此外，国际货币基金组织（IMF）作为金砖国家成
员的重要外部依赖，其提供的预防性工具和流动性额度等风险防控的金
融资源很难满足金砖国家的发展需求。在此情况下，金砖国家建立自己
的风险防范机制就极具重要性与紧迫性。

二　成立过程

在2012年6月的二十国集团峰会上，金砖国家领导人首次提出探索
设立应急储备安排（Contingent Reserve Arrangement，CRA）的构想。在
2013年3月27日第五次金砖国家峰会上，金砖国家正式确定出资1000
亿美元设立金砖国家应急储备安排。在2013年9月5日的G20峰会上，
金砖国家领导人在非正式会晤期间，深入讨论并在应急安排的储备规模、
运作机制、各国参与比例等关键议题和细节等方面取得了重要共识。
2014年7月15日，时任中国人民银行行长周小川代表中国政府与其他金
砖国家代表在巴西签署了《关于建立金砖国家应急储备安排的条约》，各
方同意设立自我管理的金融储备安排来应对短期国际收支压力，通过相
互提供金融支持进一步加强成员国的金融稳定。至此，应急储备安排初

步形成。

三 机制内容

应急储备安排的首要目标是通过流动性工具和预防性工具提供支持框架，本质上是货币互换协议。各成员国做出在危机情况下出资帮助的承诺，在非危机情况下无须实际出资。一旦危机发生，需要帮助的国家可以按照约定的汇率使用本国货币购买应急储备安排的可用额度，在约定期末根据约定赎回本币。金砖国家通过签订中央银行间协议，指引和规定使用流动性与预防性金融工具所必要的操作程序。

金砖应急储备安排的初始规模为1000亿美元，各成员国出资承诺分别为：中国410亿美元，俄罗斯、巴西和印度各180亿美元，南非50亿美元。各国以最大借款额为限获得可用资金额度，中国的借款倍数为1，南非倍数为2，其他三个国家的倍数均为1。

为了保障出资方资金安全，金砖应急储备安排参考《清迈倡议》多边化的要求，大部分出资仍与国际货币基金组织贷款相挂钩。各方还约定了批准互换申请与展期的具体条件（如保障债权地位等），要求信息及时报送，不发生拖欠。各方约定了应急储备安排履行时的各项义务、法律合规要求和资金支付保证等细节，制定了详细的惩罚与化解措施，应对可能发生的违约。

四 意义与启示

应急储备安排是金砖国家金融合作的重要成果，对未来金砖体制内的投融资务实合作具有深刻的战略意义。

第一，提前预防危机发生。应急储备安排的作用不仅在于危机之后的相互支持，还能够在危机发生之前起到提振市场信心的作用，提前预防危机发生。通过货币互换承诺，应急储备安排可以在危机发生之后提供正面的市场预期，降低未来不确定性，稳定市场情绪，降低外部冲击对成员国的影响，从而降低危机发生的可能性和强度。

第二，推动金砖国家经济一体化进程，促进南南合作和全球治理改革。虽然《德班宣言》没有提及增进经济一体化的目标，但实质上应急储备安排和新开发银行在推动金砖国家务实合作、促进经济一体化方面起着重要作用。改革旧机制很难依靠既得利益者推进，作为国际货币基金组织和世界银行等发达国家主导的国际金融组织的竞争机制，应急储备安排和新开发银行通过推动原有国际金融组织进行自我改革，助力全球治理改革。

第三，维护金砖国家和全球经济的稳定。在经济全球化的大环境下，世界经济的相互联系日益紧密。金砖国家虽然在地理区域上有一定距离，但是，存在日益密切的经济金融往来和相似的发展水平，这使一旦某个国家发生金融危机，危机将在金砖体制内进行传导。应急储备安排作为金砖体制内的金融"防火墙"，提升了金砖体制内的稳定性，进而促进了全球经济的稳定，为金砖国家发展提供良好的外部环境。

案例三：南非 Transnet 国有铁路运输公司与国家开发银行项目

南非 Transnet 国有铁路运输公司（以下简称"Transnet"）是国家开发银行（以下简称"开发银行"）在南非重要的合作伙伴，自 2013 年开展合作以来，双方联系密切。2013 年 3 月，开发银行与 Transnet 签署了50 亿美元金融合作协议；2015 年，开发银行与 Transnet 继续签署了一份300 亿兰特的贷款协议，用于老旧机车升级计划。

目前，开发银行与 Transnet 的合作主要以直接融资模式为主，本案例以中国中车—南非 Transnet 国有铁路运输公司机车采购项目来介绍双方合作情况。

一　借款人简介

Transnet 成立于 1990 年，是南非垄断型大型国有企业，其前身是成立于 1980 年的南非运输服务局。1990 年，南非政府对南非交通运输服务系统进一步改制，按照企业化管理，并更名为 Transnet 国营有限公司（Transnet SOC Ltd.）。

Transnet 作为南非乃至非洲最大的铁路货物运输和物流公司，下设铁路货运部、铁路工程部、港务局、港口码头部和管道部 5 个经营部门。负责南非铁路、港口等基础设施的建设、管理和货物运输服务，2017 年 3 月末，铁路营运里程 3.04 万千米，在役机车 1064 辆，运输管道 3800 千米。

2010 年，南非政府出台了《全国运输总体规划（2005—2050 年）》。在规划期内，南非将通过大规模改造，提升现有铁路网络运行效率，大力发展铁路，逐步降低公路承担客货运输的压力，实现陆上大宗货物运输由公路向铁路的战略转移。规划期内，南非政府将斥巨资对现有货运体系进行升级改造，具体执行主体为 Transnet。

2012 年 2 月 9 日，南非总统祖马宣布 Transnet 市场需求计划（Market Demand Strategy，MDS），意在通过 Transnet 基础设施建设，促进经济增长，增加就业。通过 MDS，Transnet 将在 7 年间投资 3000 亿兰特（约合253.43 亿美元），扩大现有铁路、港口、管道等基础设施，使南非成为撒哈拉以南非洲的转运枢纽，加强南非作为进入非洲大陆的大门的地位。截至 2017 年 3 月末，实际累计投资 1450 亿兰特（约合 122.49 亿美元）。

二 中国中车—南非 Transnet 国有铁路运输公司机车采购项目

2013 年 3 月，在习近平主席、祖马总统的见证下，开发银行郑之杰行长与 Transnet 签订了 50 亿美元金融合作协议。

2014 年 3 月 17 日，Transnet 公布机车采购招标结果，宣布中国南车集团公司（以下简称"中国南车"）中标 359 台电力机车、中国北方机车车辆工业集团公司（以下简称"中国北车"）中标 232 台内燃机车，中方中标份额超过 50%，合同总价款为 324.69 亿兰特，根据当时美元兑兰特汇率（1∶10.71）折算，约合 30.32 亿美元，是我国有史以来最大铁路机车车辆出口海外订单。

2014 年 9 月，国家开发银行对 Transnet 公司承诺贷款 25 亿美元，用于支付中国中车与 Transnet 采购合同，项目资本金为 5.32 亿美元，2015年 6 月 4 日，世界经济论坛非洲峰会在南非开普敦召开期间，在时任南非公共企业部部长和中国驻南非大使见证下，开发银行与 Transnet 签署了总金额 25 亿美元先期部分，贷款合同金额 15 亿美元，期限 15 年，建设期4.5 年。截至 2018 年 4 月末，累计发放 9.33 亿美元，贷款余额 9.33 亿美元，中国铁路装备企业累计向 Transnet 交付 260 台铁路机车，目前合同执行正常。

三 主要贷款条件

（一）贷款金额

该项目贷款金额为 25 亿美元。

（二）贷款用途

用于支付其向中国南车集团公司、中国北方机车车辆工业集团公司采购机车项目商务合同价款，Transnet 分别购买中国南车 359 台电力机车和中国北车232台内燃机车，合同总金额324.69亿兰特，约合30.32亿美元。

（三）期限

贷款期限为15年，建设期4.5年，以项目现金流还款。

四 项目成效及意义

第一，该项目服务于我国历史上最大的铁路机车海外订单，是开发银行发挥开发性金融优势、实践国家"走出去"战略的标志性成果，对推动国家开发银行对非业务突破具有积极意义；也是2013年3月在习近平主席、祖马总统的见证下，国家开发银行由郑之杰行长与Transnet签订的50亿美元金融合作协议的主要组成部分。

第二，国家开发银行开展对非国际合作业务以来，受制于非洲国家财政实力弱、市场投资环境差、法律法规机制不健全等因素，对非业务一直未能取得重大突破。项目所在国南非是非洲最发达的国家与最具有影响力的国家，在非洲具有绝对的"领头羊"地位，也是我国对非"一点、一线、一大片"外交战略中重要的"一点"，本项目的实施将成为开发银行与非洲基础设施国有企业合作的典范，对于打开整个非洲市场将起到重要的推动和积极示范作用。

第三，南非作为外向型、资源型经济国家，铁路是南非经济振兴计划的关键环节，本项目实施后，将降低南非物资运输成本，增强出口竞争力，将打通Vele、Makhado等新建矿山/矿井项目的运输通道，还将为南非电力公司电煤运输"公路转铁路"计划提供必要通道，对南非经济复苏有重要意义。中国和南非双方国有企业之间的此项合作，为南非方面年运力从现在的2.1亿吨增长至3.5亿吨奠定了基础，使南部非洲铁路基础设施取得巨大飞跃。同时，项目也带动了中国机车装备等优势产品出口，为南非本地直接和间接地创造了约8000个工作岗位，有力地提升了南非机车生产技术和工业化水平。

五 经验总结和借鉴意义

（1）以高访为契机，支持中资企业"走出去"。在中非关系持续发展的情况下，中国对南非投资也在不断增加，越来越多的中国企业在走向国际，同时，国家开发银行也在严格落实高访项目，助力中国企业在国际化道路上稳健前行。

（2）抓大放小，角力群雄。按照南非惯例，国家开发银行提供美元贷款，应由国家开发银行操作客户资金交易，并赚取一定的利润。为实现双方战略合作，国家开发银行给予客户充分的选择权，允许客户自由选择银行操作资金交易。

（3）巧妙地设计信用结构，严控信贷风险。以机车抵押方式担保17.75亿美元，免担保授信7.25亿美元。

中国和南非两国这种"重要国有企业 + 国家开发银行"的重大基础设施合作模式，可以在金砖国家之间复制，用于支持金砖国家在核电、铁路、公路、港口等基础设施方面的合作。

案例四：投贷联动支持中国长江三峡集团收购巴西水电站项目

为推动中资企业拓展巴西市场，国家开发银行会同中拉产能投资基金（以下简称"中拉产能"），大力支持三峡集团成功竞标巴西朱比亚、伊利亚水电站30年特许经营权，助力三峡巴西公司成为巴西第二大私营发电企业，第六大发电企业。项目的成功运作成为国家开发银行支持中资企业巴西基础设施特许经营权投资的成功案例。

一 借款人简介

中国长江三峡集团巴西有限公司（简称"三峡巴西"）成立于2013年，为三峡集团全资子公司，主营业务为巴西水电、风电项目的投资、开发、运营。截至2016年年底，三峡巴西已控股和参股17个水电站及11个风电场，是巴西第二大私营发电企业、第六大发电企业。

二 项目背景和基本情况

为增加财政收入，巴西政府于2015年11月对29个特许经营期满约600万千瓦的运营水电项目进行新一轮30年特许经营权竞标。巴西是全球第二大水电市场，电力市场机制成熟，未来发展潜力较大。此次竞标为外国投资者投资巴西电力市场提供了战略机遇。

巴西朱比亚、伊利亚水电站装机容量共499.5万千瓦，合计占总竞标装机容量的80%以上，30年特许经营权期费用共计138.04亿雷亚尔（按2015年11月美元兑雷亚尔汇率，约折合36.8亿美元），每年70%的发电量有固定电费收入（约23.81亿雷亚尔/年），剩余30%的发电量需在自由市场解决。

2015 年 12 月，国家开发银行发放全额贷款，最终促成三峡集团在 2016 年 1 月 5 日成功实现巴西朱比亚、伊利亚水电站特许经营权的交割。

三　意义与启示

（1）投贷联动，支持中国能源企业"走出去"。本项目中，国家开发银行通过银行与基金投贷结合的模式，为三峡集团收购巴西特许经营权项目提供有力的融资支持，通过引入中拉产能投资基金，降低企业当期资本金出资压力，服务三峡集团"走出去"的战略目标。

（2）发挥综合金融服务优势，为客户量身定制融资方案。考虑三峡集团信用能力和未来海外发债需求，国家开发银行为客户量身打造了"一揽子"综合金融服务方案，既满足客户融资和未来发债需求，又帮助客户对冲美元加息风险，降低客户财务成本。

（3）经济与社会效益并重，打造巴西能源基础设施合作典范。本次融资模式的创新，不仅助力客户实现业务战略，促进海外业务稳步增长，又稳固和锁定双方战略合作关系，而且可为其他中资企业在巴基础设施特许经营权项目的融资提供重要参考。此外，从社会效益考虑，在巴西政府的困难时期参与特许经营招投标，为政府补充了及时有效的资金来源，一定程度上缓解了区域电力供应和工人就业等问题。

案例五：本币保函创新支持中国国家电网中标巴西美丽山输电线项目

一　借款人简介

国家电网巴西控股公司（以下简称"国网巴西公司"）成立于 2010 年 7 月，主要从事电力传输系统的规划、建设和运营，是巴西第三大输电公司，连续三年荣获"巴西电力行业最佳公司"，在当地电力市场具备较强的综合竞争实力。

国网巴西公司于 2010 年通过并购西班牙公司所有的巴西 7 家输电特许权公司进入巴西输电市场，并于 2011 年、2012 年与巴西企业合作，以联营体形式中标 3 个输变电绿地项目，资产规模迅速上升至巴西同业前列。2014 年 2 月，国网巴西公司与巴西电力公司以 51%：49% 的股比组成的联营体，成功中标巴西美丽山水电站一期输电项目。2015 年 7 月，国网巴西公司独立中标巴西美丽山水电站二期输电项目。目前，国网巴西公司已成为在巴西成长最快、发展最好的中资企业之一。

二 项目背景和基本情况

美丽山一期特高压直流输变电项目是世界第四大水电站——美丽山水电站的送出工程，是美洲第一个 ±800KV 的千伏输电线路及两端换流站。

2014 年 2 月，国网巴西公司（股份占 51%）与巴西电力公司旗下巴西福纳斯电力公司（Furnas，股份占 24.5%）、北方电力公司（Eletronorte，股份占 24.5%）组成联营体，成功中标该项目。该项目特许经营权期限为 30 年，建设期从 2014 年 6 月至 2018 年 2 月。

2014 年 7 月，在习近平主席和巴西罗塞夫总统的见证下，国网公司董事长刘振亚与巴西国家电力公司总裁科斯塔在巴西总统府签署了《巴西美丽山特高压输电项目合作协议》。2015 年 5 月，李克强总理和罗塞夫总统出席项目奠基仪式。

该项目总投资超过 50 亿雷亚尔，除股东注资和发债外，巴西开发银行提供一定数量的雷亚尔贷款。国网巴西公司作为项目股东之一，按股份申请巴西开发银行雷亚尔贷款，国家开发银行为该部分融资提供融资性保函。2017 年 4 月，巴西开发银行为项目发放了首笔贷款。

三 意义与启示

（1）服务巴西实体经济，实现中巴合作共赢。国网巴西公司通过对美丽山输电线项目的支持，有效地推动了巴西输变电领域国家标准的提升，为巴西经济社会发展提供了稳健支持。此外，国网巴西公司长期投资和本土化运营战略，为当地社会和社区带来实实在在的利益。里约市议会向国网巴西公司总裁颁发最高等级的勋章并授予其荣誉市民的称号，充分彰显巴西当地社会对中国投融资的认可。

（2）助力中国企业投资巴西，为后续合作奠定基础。美丽山一期项目对于企业开拓拉美市场具有战略意义，有助于加强国家开发银行与国网巴西公司的战略合作关系，为后续在巴西及南美区域的合作奠定良好基础。

（3）推进融资模式创新，降低企业在巴西融资成本。国家开发银行为国网巴西公司申请巴西开发银行中长期巴西本币贷款出具保函，有效地降低企业在巴西的中长期融资成本，提高了国网巴西公司与当地银行的议价能力。

案例六：南非报业 Naspers 入股腾讯项目

一　案例背景

1995—2001 年，资本炒作和风险投资的广泛使用使欧美和亚洲的多个股票市场出现严重的互联网经济泡沫。以技术股为主的纳斯达克综合指数在 2000 年 3 月 10 日攀升到最高点 5048 点后暴跌，仅仅 5 天后就下降到了 4580 点。截至 2001 年，泡沫全速消退，大量公司把风投资金消耗殆尽，由于高额的负债不得不变卖资产甚至清盘。在这种宏观环境下，国际风险投资者对互联网行业的投资愈加谨慎。

与此同时，中国互联网行业正在发生剧烈变化。整体网络基础环境有了较大改善，个人和企业上网门槛降低，对网络服务的需求变得更加具体与务实。庞大的潜在用户数量和用户需求使互联网在中国的发展具有十分广阔的前景。

二　收购双方简介

（一）腾讯

腾讯控股有限公司（以下简称"腾讯"）成立于 1998 年，是中国目前最大的互联网综合服务提供商之一，提供互联网增值服务、电子商务和网络广告服务。腾讯以"一站式"在线生活服务为目标，通过即时通信工具 QQ、移动社交和通信服务微信等，满足用户在沟通、娱乐和资讯等方面的需求。腾讯是目前拥有专利数量最多的中国互联网企业之一，专利覆盖存储技术、分布式网络、无线技术等六个方面。2017 年，腾讯在网络游戏、数字内容、广告和云服务等多个核心业务方面均实现了稳健增长，致力于将人工智能技术应用于已有的产品和服务。作为中国互联网企业的领军者之一，腾讯深刻地改变了中国数以亿计网民的生活方式和沟通方式。

（二）南非报业

南非报业 Naspers 是 1915 年成立的南非传媒公司，曾经只拥有报纸这一单一业务。1985 年，南非报业创办了 M—NET 公司开展电子视频娱乐领域业务，使其业务范围由传统的纸媒拓展到了广播和影视行业。1997 年，库斯·贝克出任南非报业 CEO，开启了南非报业在互联网领域的发展。从业务规模和发展前景来看，广播影视类资产的前景都远远好于传统报业，因此，南非报业从未囿于纸媒的传统业务，坚定地在互联网领域寻找未来发展方向。早在1997年，南非报业CEO库斯·贝克就已经进军中国的互联网投资，但是，投资项目都宣告失败。失败的经验教训使南非报业改变了全球投资策略，决定投资于优秀的本地企业而非亲自设立运营企业。以下是南非报业的主要投资项目（见图1）：

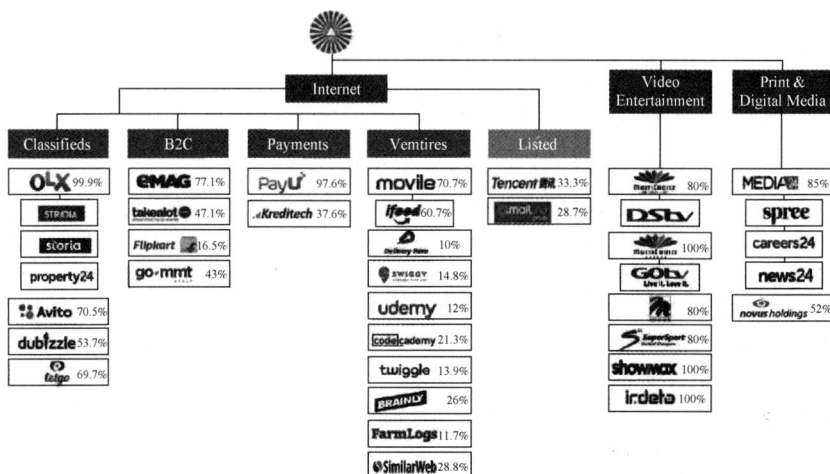

图1　南非报业主要投资项目

资料来源：公开资料。

三　收购实施过程

2001年，腾讯旗下只有单一的即时通信产品QQ（前身为OICQ）。用户数量不断增长使公司对技术和服务器的要求不断提高。一方面腾讯的资金不断消耗，另一方面缺乏成熟的盈利模式补充资金。腾讯最初融得的220万美元即将耗尽，急需二次融资。

就在此时，纳斯达克市场的崩盘导致资金供给端收紧。最开始投资腾讯的两家投资机构IDG和香港盈科都打算退出对腾讯的投资。他们认为，腾讯的商业模式不受主流市场的青睐，企业将所融资金的绝大部分投入到增添服务器当中，不可能实现短期盈利。腾讯方面多次与IDG和盈科磋商希望追加投资，但同时坚持保证腾讯创业团队的控制权。最终两家机构为腾讯提供200万美元的贷款，按照可转债方式执行，但不会继续追加投资。此时，正值南非报业关闭了三年前在中国设立的互联网服务公司，同时正积极寻找在中国的互联网投资机会。出于对互联网行业的投资需求，对即时通信工具的深刻理解，以及对腾讯未来在中国业务发展的看好，负责南非报业在中国互联网行业战略布局及合并收购的MIH（MIH Holdings Limited，米拉德国际控股集团；母公司为 Naspers）找到腾讯，希望成为腾讯第一大股东。MIH 对腾讯估价为 6000 万美元，这是当时市面上腾讯能够得到的几乎最高估值。最终盈科以 1260 万美元的价格出售腾讯全部 20% 股份，随后 IDG 资本出让 12.8% 的股份。南非报业旗下的 MIH 以 32.8% 的股份成为腾讯第二大股东。2002 年，MIH 又从其他创始人手中收购了腾讯 13.5% 的股权，成为腾讯的第一大股东。自此之后的十七年，南非报业只拿分红，没有抛售过腾讯一张股票。2018 年 3 月，MIH 首次出售腾讯 2% 的股票，但仍以 31.2% 的股票份额位列腾讯第一大股东（见图 2）。

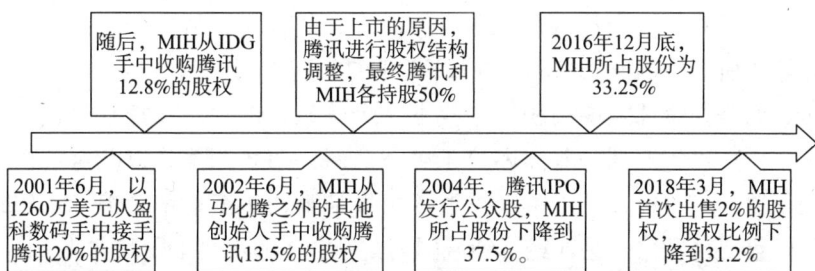

图 2　股权收购过程

资料来源：公开资料整理。

四　意义与启示

南非报业早期在企业经营方面的失败使其改变策略，不再亲自经营互联网公司，而是在全球范围内寻找优秀的企业和企业家进行投资。坚持看好中国互联网发展的投资人，南非报业发现了腾讯这家用户数量增速迅猛的公司，由此催生出两家世界级互联网巨头和总收益率 5000 多倍的股权投资界"神话"。

（一）思维转变引领合作创新

南非报业收购腾讯的案例阐释了思维转变对合作创新的重要性。作为传统的纸媒，南非报业面临着网络媒体对传统报业的巨大冲击。南非报业对此反应迅速，积极推动纸媒信息的数字化，寻求在互联网领域的业务拓展与投资机会。互联网带来的冲击反而成为它们的机遇，达到了熊彼特所言的"创造性破坏"。在纸媒数字化没能全面满足时代发展需求的情况下，南非报业进一步开始全媒体转型之路。在金砖国家的投融资合作实践中，也应该改变思维方式，以开放的心态创造性地建设合作模式与合作架构，以适应当前金砖国家在经济金融等方面遇到的挑战，从而达到"双赢"和"多赢"的结果。

（二）投融资加速企业转型

南非报业入股腾讯体现了投融资在推动组织转型中的重要作用。在国内的收费电视等业务发展前景已经较为明朗的情况下，南非报业的目光没有局限于南非本土，而是积极寻求海外投资机会，最终把目光锁定在消费者基数庞大、互联网产业方兴未艾的新兴市场——中国。经历了最初设立企业的失败，南非报业不再选择扮演业务的执行者，而是通过投资人的形式将资金注入符合自身发展理念的公司，从而分享到互联网行业爆发所产生的巨额红利。在2001年的收购之后，南非报业没有停止脚步，而是在全球范围内积极寻找下一个腾讯，进一步深挖互联网领域投资，重点投入亚洲、非洲和拉丁美洲的新兴市场国家，以及金砖国家成员俄罗斯。可以预见，未来投融资仍将是第四次工业革命浪潮下组织转型的重要推动力，是新经济领域国际金融合作的重要手段和方式。

（三）坚持正确战略方向

南非报业的早期互联网投资当中，失败案例多于成功案例，但在新兴市场投资互联网产业的逻辑和行动从未动摇过。入股腾讯之后，南非报业也曾多次经历了股价的疯狂上涨和急速下跌，但即使腾讯团队的创始人多次减持股票，南非报业截至2017年也没有减持过腾讯股票。在对未来市场前景和自身发展战略清晰明确的前提下，不因短期的市场波动和非理性行为放弃既定的投资方向，是南非报业能够超前于市场做好投资布局，并在市场爆发之后获得丰厚投资红利的重要原因。金砖国家合作的过程也面临着诸多不确定性。各国利益诉求点的不同，合作中一定会遇到各方面的困难和挑战。无论怎样，金砖国家合作是需要始终坚持的战略方向。合则两利，分则两伤。在遭遇到国际政治、金融市场等方面的不利影响时，坚持解决问题的思路与合作的态度，而不是频繁地改弦易辙，才可能获得更加丰厚的投融资合作成果。

案例七：货币互换基金

一　案例背景

新兴市场的大多数国家都不同程度地存在货币错配问题，而且发展中国家货币的汇率波动较大。货币错配指的是一个权益实体（主权国家、银行、非金融企业或家庭等）由于收支活动使用不同货币计量而导致净收入对汇率的变化非常敏感（Goldstein and Turner，2004）。此外，自1971 年布雷顿森林体系解体以来，几乎所有发展中国家的货币都经历了至少超过 20% 的贬值。开发性金融的资金主要以美元提供，以美元结算。在实际操作中，金融机构通常将货币错配的风险转嫁给最终借款方，由此导致汇率波动后，企业信用违约率上升。对于外币贷款占比较大的金融机构，货币引发的信贷风险随后会蔓延至金融系统其他机构，甚至导致其所在国家出现金融危机。

为了解决以上问题，货币互换基金（The Currency Exchange Fund，TCX）应运而生。货币互换基金为相关方（投资者、金融机构和借款人）防范风险，由此在整个金融链中起着至关重要的风险缓解功能。对于借款者来说，货币错配不再出现，借款终端违约率的降低。对小额信贷机构来说，货币互换基金提供了匹配资金的工具。借款者和小额信贷机构承担的风险降低，从而有效地解决了开发性金融机构和小额信贷投资机构股东的信用问题。

二　基金概况

货币互换基金由开发性金融机构（Development Finance Institutions，DFI）、专门小额信贷投资机构（Microfinance Investment Vehicles，MIV）和其他捐助者于 2007 年设立，旨在为货币风险问题提供解决方案。目前，货币互换基金的投资者包括荷兰政府和德国政府，以及 22 个多边与双边开发性金融机构和小额信贷投资机构。通过对冲货币风险，货币互换基金有助于新兴市场和前沿市场的可持续发展，目标是发展本地资本市场，保护货币互换基金的客户和股东。

（一）运营模式

货币互换基金专注于解决发展中国家借款客户本币融资困难的问题。货币互换基金的投资者和客户以本地货币向其借款人提供融资，同时利用货币互换和利率互换将货币风险转移至货币互换基金，从而免受汇率与利率波动的影响。一些私人部门的交易对手方也通过货币与利率互换来降低自身承担的风险。货币互换基金则通过对冲工具对冲自身所承担的汇率与利率风险，从而能够持续为客户提供货币互换的金融服务（见图3）。

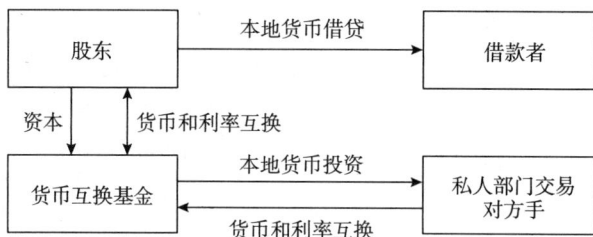

图3 货币互换基金运营模式示意

（二）对冲方式

货币互换基金按现行市场汇率定价，仅对实体经济的实际潜在风险进行套期保值。对于那些没有被商业银行或者其他货币供应商覆盖，特别是不存在离岸对冲市场、长期套期保值工具，甚至根本没有对冲市场的货币，货币互换基金在其中扮演着做市商的角色。这意味着货币互换基金自身不能对冲它所承担的货币风险，并且必须承担和管理它所需的敞口头寸。

货币互换基金通过多元化分散投资于全球多种货币的投资组合管理风险。由于汇集了市场中众多活跃货币的交易，它可以达到其他金融机构无法企及的多元化水平。这种多样化模式由投资者的强大资本提供基础支持。货币互换基金的业务活动在十年的运营中逐渐增加，目前覆盖撒哈拉以南的非洲、东欧和中亚、中东和北非、亚洲和拉丁美洲的70多种货币，提供长达30年的对冲期限定价。其机构的独特性在于货币对冲工具的运用：交易双方签订未来特定时间交换两种货币的协议，通过衍生工具，提前锁定汇率和利率。货币互换基金主要使用远期和掉期两种

金融工具:

(1) 远期合约。签订未来约定时间以指定价格购买或出售一定数量外币的协议。通常情况下,客户通过货币互换基金出售固定金额的单一本地货币,并在未来的确定日期从货币互换基金获得固定金额的美元。

(2) 货币掉期。掉期可以被描述为捆绑在一起的一系列远期。双方同意交换以两种不同货币计价的多个固定金额(通常为贷款本金和利息金额)。客户向货币互换基金出售当地货币,货币互换基金支付美元用于交换。货币互换的利息可以是固定的或围绕基准利率浮动。

(三) 客户与投资者概况

货币互换基金的股东和交易对手是开发性金融机构和私人管理的小额信贷投资机构。其中,荷兰政府和德国政府以次级可转换债及一笔首次亏损贷款的形式为货币互换基金提供了资金支持。货币互换基金的机构投资者如图4所示。

图4　当前机构投资者

目前,货币互换基金的交易对手主要是货币互换基金的投资者,投资者的客户以及其他客户(商业银行、基金、公司)。其对冲能力优先分配给其投资者和其客户。通过将本币风险转移到集中管理和多元化中心化资金池，货币互换基金使其投资者更加专注于为客户提供长期本币贷款业务。

三 意义与启示

（一）为新兴市场提供货币对冲工具

截至 2018 年，货币互换基金已经走过了 11 个年头。货币互换基金于 2017 年发布的十年影响力评估报告，对货币互换基金成立十年来对当地货币发展性影响进行了分析。结果显示，在银行客户受贬值影响、美元借款客户大量拖欠贷款的情况下，作为货币互换基金客户的小额信贷机构没有信贷违约增加。因为货币互换基金以当地货币向其客户出借国际借款，从而使当地货币的大幅贬值被货币互换基金吸收，不影响最终借款人。货币互换基金为投资者和私人机构提供了货币对冲工具，大大降低了发展中国家借款人和借款机构承担的金融风险，极大地促进了金融体系稳定和开发性金融业务的顺利开展。

（二）为金融机构提供风险管理模式的启发

货币互换基金的风险敞口主要来自市场风险，在十年的发展当中积累了大量的风险管理经验。职能方面，它在执行和非执行职能之间实现分离；组织架构方面，风险管理委员会直接汇报给管理层而非监事会，并在监事会级别上设立风险监督委员会。此外，它还引入专业机构，提供风险管理服务，协助货币互换基金应对全球市场风险。在金砖国家的投融资合作过程中，也需要积极面对汇率、利率等市场风险。因此，可以有选择地借鉴货币互换基金的职能分离设置，从合作机制和组织架构上体现对风险管理的重视；还可以考虑引入第三方专业风险管理机构、专业人才，丰富风险管理经验和知识，为金砖国家合作与开发性金融业务提供更加专业化的服务。

（三）提供多边金融合作的创新模式

货币互换基金的股东涵盖了欧洲、非洲和亚洲的众多国家，这使货币互换基金一旦受到较为剧烈的外部冲击，能够获得来自多方的金融援助。因此，货币互换基金成立之后，获得了标准普尔公司等国际评级机构的看好和支持。作为一个独立的金融实体，货币互换基金有助于为公司股东和政府提供重要的公共政策授权，通过股东力量支持官方的开发性援助，通过建立特殊目的金融实体，管理开发性金融实践中的多种风险。在未来金砖国家的多边金融合作中，可以借鉴其经验，基于共同关切建立合作关系，引进更多资本实力雄厚的金融机构提供资金支持，为金砖国家金融合作提供更强有力的风险管理能力和更加稳固的金融保障。

案例八：俄罗斯外贸银行营运资金贷款项目

2014—2015 年，国家开发银行与俄罗斯外贸银行（The Bank for Foreign Trade）（以下简称"俄外贸银行"）沟通协商，共同开发了以支持中俄贸易项目融资为目的的金融机构境外人民币项目，额度为 120 亿元人民币，期限 3 年，截至当前已提款 96 亿元。该项目对国家开发银行未来与境外其他金融机构大规模开展金融机构境外人民币合作、支持"一带一路"经贸合作以及人民币国际化战略有着里程碑式的意义。

一　项目背景和基本情况

2014 年 10 月，中国人民银行与俄罗斯联邦中央银行签署了规模为 1500 亿元人民币/8150 亿卢布的《中国人民银行和俄罗斯联邦中央银行人民币/卢布双边本币互换协议》。在此背景下，为了有效地发挥人民币在国际市场的作用和价值，更好地促进两国睦邻友好关系的发展，国家开发银行赴俄罗斯与多家俄罗斯金融机构进行会谈，最终确定与俄罗斯外贸银行利用中国跨境人民币贷款共同支持中俄进出口贸易。国家开发银行向俄外贸银行提供不超过 120 亿元人民币的授信，用于支持具有"中资因素"的中俄企业贸易融资，期限为 3 年。

二　借款人/实际控制方简介

借款人俄外贸银行成立于 1990 年 10 月，是俄罗斯第二大商业银行，其在市场地位、资产与资金总量、金融业绩与基础设施规模方面仅次于俄罗斯第一大商业银行俄罗斯联邦储蓄银行。机构遍布俄罗斯，其在独联体国家、欧洲、亚洲和非洲等地区设有 23 个分行或办事处，全球共计拥有 10 万名员工。截至 2017 年 6 月 30 日，俄罗斯外贸银行 92.2% 的股份由俄罗斯联邦政府持有，其中包括：联邦国有资产管理署（Federal Agency for State Property Management）持普通股 12.1%，国有存款保险互助会（State Cooperation Deposit Insurance Agency）持 A 型优先股 32.9%、B 型优先股 47.2%；自由流通的普通股 7.8%。

截至 2017 年 6 月末，该行总资产约合 2125.61 亿美元，总负债约合 1884.15 亿美元，所有者权益约合 241.46 亿美元，净利润约合 9.76 亿美元，资本充足率为 14.60%，不良贷款率为 6.30%，ROA 为 0.46%，ROE 为 8.20%。

截至 2017 年 6 月末，俄罗斯外贸银行占据俄国内 15.6% 的企业信贷市场、20.3% 的企业存款市场、14.5% 的零售贷款市场以及 9.7% 的零售存款业务，其中，俄罗斯外贸银行零售类贷款较 2013 年增加了 21%。当前，俄罗斯外贸银行（包括 VTB、其零售银行 VTB24 以及其收购的莫斯科银行和 ELTO 银行）机构遍布俄罗斯全国 72 个地区、341 座城市，拥有 1610 个分支机构。其中，VTB24 是俄罗斯第二大零售银行，拥有超过 12000 台自动柜员机。其国际银行业务遍布俄罗斯及其他 22 个国家，具有较强的市场地位。

三　项目执行情况

截至当前，国家开发银行累计发放的 85 亿元贷款资金主要用于中俄两国企业在冶金矿业、交通、油气、零售、木材纸浆以及食品领域的贸易合作项目中，涉及 7 个俄罗斯融资企业和 31 个中方贸易企业，其中涉及俄罗斯进口中方出口的贸易项目 18 个，涉及俄罗斯出口中方进口的贸易项目 13 个。中方向俄方出口的贸易项目融资 68 亿元人民币，占总资金使用额的 80%；中方向俄方进口的贸易项目融资 17 亿元人民币，占总资金使用额的 20%。

四　意义与启示

近年来，俄罗斯外贸银行一直致力于支持中俄贸易往来，拥有广泛的客户群。通过与俄罗斯外贸银行的合作，支持大量中俄贸易项目的开展，对推进中俄经贸关系发展、拓展中俄贸易多元化、巩固两国战略合作伙伴关系都有着十分重要的意义。

该项目为近年来我国与俄罗斯金融机构开展境外人民币合作单笔金额最大的贷款融资，也是国家开发银行践行"一带一路"金融合作、推动人民币国际化战略的重大举措。该项目为未来中资银行与境外"一带一路"国家金融机构开展以贸易融资为着力点的贷款合作开创了先例和示范。

该项目的实施将加快推动人民币成为国际市场交易的计价结算货币，提升人民币在国际市场上的购买力，推动人民币国际化进程。同时，开展境外人民币合作有助于推动我国与俄罗斯及其他地区经贸关系发展，保持对外贸易的稳定增长。

案例九：金砖国家银行合作机制

一　基本情况

为进一步丰富金砖国家经济合作的内涵，拓展务实合作领域，在金砖国家领导人会晤的框架下，2010 年 4 月 15 日，在时任国家主席胡锦涛、巴西总统卢拉、俄罗斯总统梅德韦杰夫和印度总理辛格的共同见证下，国家开发银行与巴西开发银行、俄罗斯开发与对外经济活动银行和印度进出口银行在巴西利亚共同签署《金砖国家银行合作机制备忘录》，旨在为金砖国家经济技术合作和贸易发展提供多样化的金融服务，这标志着金砖国家银行合作机制正式成立。2011 年 4 月 13 日，国家开发银行在三亚主办了第一届金砖国家银行合作机制年会暨金融论坛。成员行在银行合作机制年会上签署了《关于南非南部非洲开发银行加入合作机制的议定书》，南部非洲开发银行正式成为金砖国家银行合作机制的成员行之一。

金砖国家银行合作机制每年在金砖国家领导人会晤期间举办金砖国家银行合作机制年会暨金砖国家金融论坛活动，并签署金融论坛成果文件。自成立以来，金砖国家银行合作机制先后在五国领导人共同见证下签署多边合作协议 7 份，涉及本币授信、信用证保兑服务、可持续发展、基础设施建设和绿色融资等多个领域，有力地推动了金砖国家金融合作和经贸投资便利化。为筹备年会和金融论坛成果，金砖国家银行合作机制各成员行每年固定召开技术小组会议（局级）和工作组会议（专家）。

二　合作情况

自 2010 年金砖国家银行合作机制成立以来，国家开发银行作为成员行之一，高度重视参与银行合作机制建设，并在机制框架内加强与各成员行的合作。

一是加强与各成员行协作，共同推动多项多边合作成果。自 2011 年在中国三亚召开金砖国家银行合作机制第一届年会和金融论坛以来，各成员行在金砖国家领导人见证下共签署多边合作协议 7 份，涉及本币合作、信用证保兑、支持可持续发展和创新合作等多个领域。这些合作成果分别被纳入《三亚宣言》《德里宣言》《德班宣言》《福塔莱萨宣言》《乌法宣言》和《果阿宣言》等金砖国家领导人会晤成果文件，为服务金砖国家经贸投资便利化，深化金融合作发挥了积极作用。

二是深化双边项目合作，促进金砖国家可持续发展。从双边项目合作来看，金砖国家是国家开发银行开展国际合作的重点区域之一。六年来，国家开发银行以金砖国家银行合作机制为依托，坚持互利共赢原则，积极与成员行和当地企业开展项目合作。截至 2017 年年末，国家开发银行在金砖国家累计承诺贷款 1346 亿美元，发放贷款 869 亿美元，贷款余额 580 亿美元，项目涵盖能源、矿产、农业、电力、基础设施、加工制造、中小企业和金融等多个领域，为服务金砖国家经济可持续发展和社会包容性发展做出了贡献。从双边银行间合作来看，主要包括以下四个方面：

（1）国家开发银行与新开发银行签署双边合作备忘录，约定将在项目联合融资、资金业务、研究合作、知识共享和人员及信息交流等领域开展全方位合作。

（2）国家开发银行与巴西开发银行签署《深化全面战略合作谅解备忘录》，双方将开展包括交通、电力、市政、通信、科技、研发中心、工业园区、农业，以及环保、旅游、物流业等领域的项目合作。

（3）国家开发银行与巴西石油公司签署《全面战略合作协议》，双方将进一步开拓在融资、油气领域合作，以实现全面战略合作。

（4）2010 年 12 月，国家开发银行与印度进出口银行签署双边《战略合作备忘录》，开启国家开发银行与印度进出口银行的业务对接合作。

三是加强人员培训，促进金砖国家人文交流。国家开发银行共培训金砖国家政府部门、金融机构、合作单位的负责人、业务骨干和专家 500 人次。国家开发银行还设立奖学金，资助 13 名金砖国家优秀青年来华深造。2017 年 6 月 29—30 日，在北京举办了首届金砖国家金融创新与共同发展交流培训，与会机构不仅增进了感情，加深了解，也进一步加深了对中国经济发展模式和开发性金融理念的认识和理解。

四是持续推进机制建设。2017 年 6 月，在北京主办金砖国家本币授信、创新和高科技业务、信用评级、新兴市场经济框架研究及人员培训与经验交流五个专项工作组研讨会。与会专家围绕新兴市场国家支持创新和高科技业务可操作模式、成员行开展本币授信合作路径与模式、新兴市场国家评级机构发展路径、构建新兴市场经济金融动态研究长效合作机制和创新经验交流合作思路等议题进行交流研讨，并就进一步深化合作达成共识。

承办金砖国家智库学术分论坛和主办金砖国家银行高管与企业对话会，分享开发性金融理念、成功经验和案例，推动金砖国家"软实力"交流合作。

参加金砖国家治国理政研讨会，获得良好效果和积极反响。

主办2017年金砖国家银行合作机制年会暨第七届金砖国家金融论坛，与巴西开发银行、印度进出口银行、南部非洲开发银行、南非电力公司举行了多场双边会见。与巴西政府联合举办"巴西商业与投资机遇研讨会"，签署了多份多边合作成果文件和双边合作成果文件。在多边合作框架下，金砖国家银行合作机制5个成员行共同签署《金砖国家银行合作机制银行间本币授信协议》和《金砖国家银行合作机制信用评级结论共享合作备忘录》两个多边协议，作为年会和金融论坛成果文件，并列入《金砖国家领导人厦门宣言》。

三　意义与启示

（一）银行间合作机制使投资和国际贸易合作更加便利

金砖国家银行间合作机制的建立推动了国际贸易中的本币授信、本币结算，扩大了国际贷款规模，有效地避免了经贸投资中的外汇风险，使金砖国家之间的国际贸易和外商直接投资更加便捷，为未来金砖国家进一步深化投资和经贸领域合作奠定了良好的基础。

（二）银行间合作机制的建立有助于金砖国家及时沟通全球金融市场信息，促进金砖国家内部在金融领域的对话

智库分论坛和高管对话会有助于各成员国加强在国际经贸金融领域的对话，对于各方协调、协商并克服国际金融合作中面临的种种问题起到了积极的推动作用，最终有助于建立更加平等和高效的银行间合作体系。

（三）银行间合作机制有助于金砖国家加强在高新技术、资源、环保等领域加强投融资合作

银行间合作机制的建立为重点产业领域的项目合作搭建了桥梁。更加顺畅的投融资条件极大地便利了金砖国家在环境保护、高新技术产业

等领域开展项目合作，使金融合作助力金砖成员在实体经济的合作中实现互利共赢。

案例十：中国工商银行收购南非标准银行项目

一 案例简介

全球资本运作是当今全球化的重要特征。为了保持自身竞争力，利用规模效应增强自身盈利能力，商业银行通过海外并购，将业务触角延伸到世界上其他国家。在中国深化金融市场改革的环境下，海外并购已经成为中国商业银行实施国际化战略的重要方式。其中，中国工商银行很早就确立了国际化战略，逐步用并购等方式扩大海外机构规模。

中国在南非有巨大的投资和发展前景。非洲是中国的第三大贸易伙伴，有着丰富的自然资源，如石油、天然气等，而南非是中国对非洲国家投资中的重点，占据重要的市场地位。南非是金砖国家的重要成员，也是重要新兴经济体。2007 年，中国对南非的投资额达到 45441 万美元，2008 年更是达到了 480786 万美元。在"壮大亚洲、巩固欧洲、突破美洲"的基础上，中国工商银行把国际化的步伐迈向了非洲。

南非是世界上重要的矿产资源国，矿产种类和储量均居世界前列。南非的经济体制和非洲其他国家相比较为开放，投资环境良好，是很多中国企业对外投资的目的地。截至 2008 年，已经有超过 2000 家中国企业在南非设立生产营业机构。中国与非洲的双边贸易和对外投资增加了对中资商业银行提供的金融服务的需求。中国工商银行并购南非标准银行之前，只有中国银行和中国建设银行在非洲设有分支机构，中资银行在非洲的服务范围十分有限。为了借助南非标准银行参与非洲市场业务，通过战略投资提升股东价值，中国工商银行和南非标准银行签订了《战略合作协议》，收购南非标准银行 20% 的股份，实现了对南非标准银行的战略持股。

二 案例背景

中国自 2001 年加入世界贸易组织以来，贸易开放程度日渐提高，与各国的金融合作水平逐步深化。中国金融机构纷纷在建立境外分支机构，寻求在海外的发展。和当地银行相比，中资银行很难通过设立分支机构的方式有效地获得海外市场份额，因此，许多银行选择通过收购本土银行获得进入海外市场的机会。2008 年国际金融危机之后，不少本土银行出现了运营困难的现象，中资银行纷纷抓住机会进行海外并购。然而，由于经验的缺乏，成功的海外收购案例并不多。中国工商银行收购南非标准银行是其中较为经典的成功案例，为未来银行间的金融合作提供了经验和启示。

（一）中国工商银行

中国工商银行于 1984 年正式成立，此前主要接收中国人民银行剥离的工商业信贷业务。在经过了 20 多年的发展之后，中国工商银行于 2005 年进行股份制改革，由财政部和中央汇金公司共同成立了中国工商银行股份有限公司。2006 年，中国工商银行在上海和香港同时上市，汇金投资公司、财政部和香港中央结算代理人有限公司为三大控股股东，分别持有 37%、36% 和 25% 的流通股。

中国工商银行自 2006 年上市以来，净利润一直保持较高速度的增长，资本实力不断增强。在以一级核心资本为评价标准的银行排名中，中国工商银行在近年均排名世界前列。中国工商银行的国际化进程从 1992 年在新加坡设立第一家代表处开始，秉承"壮大亚洲，巩固欧洲、突破美洲"的原则，不断布局海外机构，逐步建立覆盖全球重要国际金融中心和贸易区域的国际化经营网络。

在成立的 30 多年中，中国工商银行把握住了两次金融危机的机会，迅速布局建设了境外经营机构。2000 年之后，尤其是 2007 年美国次贷危机后，部分国家银行业准入门槛降低，中国工商银行把握机遇多次展开海外并购，并在重点目标市场取得了瞩目的成效。

截至 2017 年年底，中国工商银行已经在全球 45 个国家和地区设立了 419 家机构，其中，通过参股南非标准银行间接地覆盖撒哈拉以南的 20 个非洲国家，与 143 个国家和地区的 1545 家境外机构建立了代理行关系，经营范围覆盖六大洲以及全球重要金融中心。目前，中国工商银行在"ONE ICBC"的整体框架下，通过统一战略、统一制度、统一文化、统筹全行的理念，向"一点接入、全集团响应、全球化服务"的目标靠近。

（二）南非标准银行

南非标准银行于 1862 年在英国注册成立，直至 1987 年渣打银行退出，南非标准银行才在真正意义上成为一家南非银行。经过 100 多年的发展壮大，南非标准银行成为非洲最大的银行，在非洲 18 个国家设立了分支机构。此外，在土耳其、阿根廷、英国和中国香港也设有分支机构。凭借着强大的分销渠道，综合多元的业务，南非标准银行成为非洲银行业中的翘楚。

南非标准银行的经营状况比较稳健，各项财务指标增速稳定，发展潜力巨大。截至 2017 年年底，南非标准银行的整体收益达到 26270 百万兰特，增幅为 14%；每股资产净值（NAV）为 9830 分，增幅为 4%；ROE 从 15.3% 增加到 17.1%。

三 案例实施过程

（一）收购准备

从 2005 年起，中国工商银行和南非标准银行的高层管理者开始逐步深入探讨了业务合作和股权合作等事宜。由于两家银行在战略布局、管理风格和市场地位等方面具有高度的相似性，双方在 2007 年 6 月的国际货币会议上就战略合作达成共识，以股权为纽带的战略合作构想初步形成。

（二）收购过程

2007 年 10 月 24 日，中国工商银行对南非标准银行的股权收购方案获得了南非储备银行的批准。10 月 25 日，中国工商银行与南非标准银行共同宣布，双方已对股权交易与战略合作事项达成协议。此次交易额约为 55 亿美元，具体的股权交易方式为：（1）中国工商银行收购的股权当中有 50% 由原有股东出售，中国工商银行收购价为 136 南非兰特/股；（2）南非标准银行按照 104.58 南非兰特/股向中国工商银行定向增发约扩充股本后 10% 的新股，作为中国工商银行收购股权中其余的 50%。两种股权交易方式互为前提。收购老股和定向增发的综合溢价约为 15%。

股权交割于 2008 年 3 月完成，中国工商银行成为南非标准银行第一大股东，向南非标准银行派出 2 名董事会成员，并建立战略合作委员会。交易过程的具体时间表如下表所示。

中国工商银行收购南非标准银行时间

时间	进程
2007 年 10 月 24 日	收购方案获得南非储备银行批准

续表

时间	进程
2007 年 10 月 25 日	中国工商银行宣布以 55 亿美元收购南非标准银行 20% 的股权
2007 年 12 月 3 日	南非标准银行股东大会通过收购议案
2007 年 12 月 13 日	中国工商银行股东大会通过收购议案
2007 年 12 月 18 日	法庭审批通过收购案合同
2008 年 1 月 23 日	中国银监会完成审查程序，批准收购案
2008 年 3 月 3 日	双方完成股权交割手续

资料来源：交易双方公告。

收购完成之后，中国工商银行和南非标银行根据《业务合作协议》，确立了在公司银行、资源银行、全球资源基金、投资银行、非洲与国际业务和全球市场业务 6 个领域展开战略合作，并根据 6 个合作领域组建合作团队，覆盖投融资业务、直接投资、托管、结算与现金管理等多个业务领域。中国工商银行和南非标银行还在股权合作的基础上，约定未来在双方中只有一方已设立营业机构的情况下，未设立机构的银行优先选择已设机构行开展业务合作。此外，中国工商银行和南非标银行合作团队还相互推荐大型集团等重点客户，为其提供更加全面的服务。

（三）收购后业务合作

收购完成之后，中国工商银行和南非标准银行在业务合作落实方面的进展十分迅速。收购完成后短短的一年中，两行已经完成共同合作的 65 个项目中的 9 个，例如，中海油服收购挪威 Awilco Offshore ASA 公司股权的融资、承贷 Premium 集团，以及联合国际出口商品融资项目。博茨瓦纳政府还选择两家银行作为银团贷款的牵头，共同为 Morupule B 燃煤电站项目提供 8.25 亿美元出口买方信贷以及 1.4 亿美元搭桥贷款服务。

在成为南非标准银行的大股东之后，中国工商银行还在 2011 年 8 月收购了南非标准银行旗下的阿根廷标准银行。中国工商银行在成为第一家收购非洲金融机构的中资银行之后，继而成为第一家进驻拉美市场的中国商业银行。2014 年 1 月，中国工商银行又宣布收购南非标准银行公众有限公司 60% 的股权。这次收购旨在通过南非标准银行伦敦子公司参与全球金融业务。此次收购后，中国工商银行对南非标准银行的持股比例达到 20.1%。

四 案例意义

(一) 成为银行间投融资合作的典型范例

收购南非标准银行是中国工商银行最大的海外投资，也是当时国内商业银行交易金额最多的海外并购。作为中国首例商业银行对非洲金融机构的并购案，这一案例是中资银行国际化进程中的重要里程碑。两家银行基于股权纽带开展战略合作，还通过人员互派等形式加深相互了解和合作程度，开创了中非金融合作先河，实现优势互补和资源共享，搭建了中非合作的金融桥梁，为未来银行间合作提供了范本。

(二) 增强业务实力，实现优势互补

通过收购，中国工商银行积极学习和借鉴南非标准银行的经验与技术，对自身产品与服务进行大力度创新，并拓展了境外业务资源。收购之前，中国工商银行的业务主要分布在公司银行和个人银行，而南非标准银行在个人与商业银行、公司与投资银行和财富管理三个领域的业务线和中国工商银行恰好可以优势互补。以收购的方式，中国工商银行吸收了南非标准银行在商业银行、投资银行和财富管理等业务上的经验，并在国内和国际业务中推行实践，提升了自身的业务能力。

(三) 提升国际竞争力，促进国际化发展

中国工商银行之所以选择南非标准银行进行合作，不仅由于其非洲最大商业银行的地位，更是由于两行具备广阔的战略合作前景。通过收购南非标准银行，中国工商银行拓展了在非洲的客户渠道，得以进入非洲市场多个新兴业务，迈出了国际化战略重要的一步。在入股南非标准银行的十年中，中国工商银行和南非标准银行在贸易融资、项目融资、资金结算、股权并购和信息科技等方面均取得了不菲的成就。创新金融服务模式方面，两行推出包括中非现金管理、跨境直联汇款等多种产品，为中资企业进入非洲投资提供资金管理、信贷融资、投资银行等多方位金融服务。

五 案例启示

(一) 收购对象和入场时机的选择是银行间投融资合作的关键

根据市场势力理论，收购可以使收购方迅速进入一个全新的市场。南非标准银行是非洲最大的银行。在收购案之前，中国工商银行在欧洲和美洲都已经设立了自己的分支机构，而非洲地区的业务仍然为空白。通过收购一家银行，中国工商银行打开了在非洲18个国家的金融业务，

获得了在非洲丰厚的客户和业务资源，以及当地金融服务的一手经验。由于选择了合适的入场时机，中国工商银行从收购中获得了丰厚的投资收益，有力地支持了中国工商银行的总体业绩。

（二）战略互补与善意收购是增强银行间投融资合作的有效途径

海外收购成功的关键因素在于对目标的选择与收购后的整合。由于中国工商银行和南非标准银行具有很强的战略互补性和合作意向，双方在收购后的整合方面较为顺利地实现了推进。经过十年的发展，双方已经取得了丰硕成果，在公司银行、投资银行、全球市场和基金等方面展开了全面的业务合作。由于中资银行在海外收购的过程中容易被"中国威胁论"的声音所影响，双方良好的合作氛围有利于中外积极推动务实合作，为中资银行树立良好形象，为未来金融机构的海外合作奠定了良好的基础。

（三）新兴市场投资是银行间投融资合作的重要方向

新兴市场的投资门槛没有发达地区高，发展中国家较高的经济增速也带来了更多的投资机会。中资银行海外合作的事实表明，我国银行在进入发达国家市场之后，即使付出很高的成本，也往往缺少话语权与决策权，因此合作效果并不尽如人意；而中国与众多发展中国家都建立了良好的经贸往来合作关系，在新兴市场拓展业务的成功率更高。在本案例中，收购完成的当年中国工商银行就收到了南非标准银行约12.13亿兰特的现金分红和5.89亿兰特的股票分红，投资收益率约为7.7%，远高于投资于国外债券的收益率。从中国工商银行境外机构指标看，在海外机构中，非洲地区对中国工商银行税前利润贡献率最大，相对投入资产最少；对比传统发达地区，投入高而效益却不够理想。因此，在未来我国金融机构的对外合作中，应更多关注新兴市场。

参考文献

［1］梅冠群：《金砖国家合作机制研究》，《中国集体经济》2017 年第
　　34 期。

［2］田丰：《金砖国家经济增长、结构转型与产能合作》，《拉丁美洲研
　　究》2017 年第 8 期。

［3］何枭吟：《第四次工业革命视域下全球价值链的发展趋势及对策》，
　　《公共管理》2017 年第 6 期。

［4］耿楠：《"工业 4.0"时代全球价值链如何变革》，《世界知识》2015
　　年第 20 期。

［5］钟源：《大数据：第四次工业革命的战略资源》，《经济参考报》
　　2016 年 6 月 21 日。

［6］陈奉先：《金砖国家应急外汇储备安排：成本收益、治理缺陷与中国
　　选择》，《南方金融》2014 年第 2 期。

［7］陈建宇：《金砖国家开发银行成立的背景与影响》，《青海金融》
　　2014 年第 11 期。

［8］代明、陈景信、姜寒：《后工业经济时代二元权益函数的实证及其例
　　证》，《科技管理研究》2016 年第 1 期。

［9］林松添、李贺：《把金砖打造成南南合作新平台》，《中国投资》
　　2017 年第 18 期。

［10］程炼：《金砖国家新开发银行："南—南"合作共赢新模式》，《紫
　　光阁》2014 年第 9 期。

［11］李永刚：《金砖国家金融合作机制研究》，《暨南学报》（哲学社会
　　科学版）2015 年第 6 期。

［12］潘庆中、李稻葵、冯明：《"新开发银行"新在何处——金砖国家
　　开发银行成立的背景、意义与挑战》，《国际经济评论》2015 年第
　　2 期。

［13］张海冰:《新开发银行的发展创新》,《国际展望》2015 年第 5 期。

［14］林跃勤:《金砖国家本币结算研究》,《学海》2012 年第 4 期。

［15］刘东民、肖立晟、陆婷:《金砖国家金融合作路径》,《中国金融》2017 年第 15 期。

［16］吕栋、汪昊旻:《双边本币结算模式与发展》,《中国金融》2012 年第 4 期。

［17］吕越:《互联网金融新模式与中小企业融资关系研究》,《现代信息经济》2016 年第 2 期。

［18］孙丹:《"去美元化"与多边货币互换——基于金砖国家应急储备安排的视角》,《国际金融》2014 年第 9 期。

［19］田慧芳:《金砖国家可持续发展合作的优先领域与政策选择》,《国际经济合作》2017 年第 8 期。

［20］王丹、鲁凤玲:《人民银行货币互换实践》,《中国金融》2012 年第 4 期。

［21］徐德顺:《拓展金砖五国信用合作新思路》,《理论导报》2017 年第 9 期。

［22］张明:《全球货币互换:现状、功能及国际货币体系改革的潜在方向》,《国际经济评论》2012 年第 6 期。

［23］张晓玫、梁洪、蒋昊然:《区块链金融模式与小微企业信贷配给》,《上海金融》2016 年第 7 期。

［24］赵忠秀、胡旭东:《新全球化中的开发性金融:金砖国家的视角》,《国际贸易》2017 年第 12 期。

［25］Preety Bhogal:《重新审视现有信用评级机构对金砖国家的意义》,节选自《印度智库观察家研究基金会报告》,2017 年。

［26］李巍:《金砖机制与国际金融治理改革》,《国际观察》2013 年第 1 期。

［27］王厚双、关昊、黄金宇:《金砖国家合作机制对全球经济治理体系与机制创新的影响》,《亚太经济》2015 年第 3 期。

［28］王信:《金砖四国国际金融实力提升对国际金融及其治理的影响》,《国际经济评论》2011 年第 1 期。

［29］汤凌霄、欧阳峣、黄泽先:《国际金融合作视野中的金砖国家开发银行》,《大国经济研究》2014 年第 9 期。

［30］桑百川、刘洋、郑伟：《金砖国家金融合作：现状、问题及前景展望》，《国际贸易》2012 年第 12 期。

［31］韩一元：《金砖国家合作发展历程与展望》，《国际研究参考》2016 年第 11 期。

［32］蔡春林、刘美香：《"金砖国家"贸易投资合作现状和机制创新方向》，《亚太经济》2017 年第 3 期。

［33］《金砖机制发展战略年度报告》（2016）2016 年。

［34］陈德铭等：《经济危机与规则重构》，商务印书馆 2014 年版。

［35］欧阳峣、张亚斌、易先忠：《中国与金砖国家外贸的"共享式"增长》，《中国社会科学》2012 年第 10 期。

［36］朱杰进：《金砖银行、竞争性多边主义与全球经济治理改革》，《国际关系研究》2016 年第 5 期。

［37］李稻葵、徐翔：《全球治理视野的金砖国家合作机制》，《改革》2015 年第 10 期。

［38］郑伟：《拓展金砖国家经贸合作的理论基础与路径选择》，博士学位论文，对外经济贸易大学，2015 年。

［39］张海冰：《世界经济格局调整中的金砖国家合作》，《国际展望》2014 年第 5—6 期。

［40］张长龙：《发展中国家争取国际经济金融新秩序的困境与出路——以金砖国家合作机制的形成为背景》，《贵州社会科学》2011 年第 7 期。

［41］林跃勤：《金融合作深化与新兴国家共同发展——基于金砖国家的一个视角》，《河海大学学报》（哲学社会科学版）2016 年第 2 期。

［42］蔡春林、刘美香：《金砖国家贸易投资合作现状和机制创新方向》，《亚太经济》2017 年第 3 期。

［43］蒲公英：《金砖国家人文交流合作机制分析》，《俄罗斯东欧中亚研究》2017 年第 4 期。

［44］UNCTAD, *World Investment Report* 2017：*Investment and The Digital Economy*, United Nations Publication, 2017.

［45］World Bank, *Global Economic Prospects*：*Broad – Based Upturn, but for How Long?*, World Bank Group, 2018.

［46］ World Bank, *Russia Monthly Economic Developments*, 2018.

［47］ IMF, *World Economic Outlook*：*Seeking Sustainable Growth—Short - Term Recovery*, Long - Term Challenges, 2017.

后　记

2017 年 9 月，金砖国家领导人第九次会晤在中国厦门成功举行。会议期间，国家开发银行研究院与金砖国家智库合作中方理事会合作发布了《金砖国家可持续发展报告（2017）》（以下简称《报告2017》），系统地分析了金砖国家经济发展状况及面临的主要挑战，提出了经济金融合作等方面的建议。

2018 年 3 月，国家开发银行作为国家高端智库培育单位，联合对外经济贸易大学启动了《金砖国家可持续发展报告（2018）》（以下简称《报告2018》）编写工作。《报告2018》是《报告2017》的延续与发展、聚焦与深入。3 月底，国家开发银行研究院组织召开了联合编写组第一次讨论会，经过对研究提纲和内容的讨论，确定《报告2018》以"创新金砖国家投融资机制，促进务实合作互利共赢"为切入点，通过全面梳理金砖国家经济发展和投融资总体情况，阐述深化投融资合作的意义和目标，分析金砖国家投融资重点领域与产业、阻碍与问题，并提出前瞻性的政策建议。

4 月，按照讨论会编写安排，国家开发银行研究院和对外经济贸易大学开始了紧张的研究和写作。在国家开发银行研究院的组织下，国家开发银行研究院、规划局、法律事务局、资金局、风险管理局、国际金融局、国际合作业务局、信息科技局、河南省分行、四川省分行、里约热内卢代表处、莫斯科代表处、印度工作组、南非工作组的业务专家参与了资料收集、整理、案例以及相关章节的编写工作。对外经济贸易大学"一带一路"PPP 发展研究中心、金融学院、区域国别研究院、世界贸易组织研究院等教授和专家参与了报告相关章节的编写工作。

在案例选择方面，我们以绿色、可持续、影响深远为基本原则，精挑细选了 10 个金砖国家典型投融资案例和合作机制，通过机构访谈和调研，获取一手信息和资料，总结案例成功经验，为今后金砖国家开展投融资务实合作走深走实提供指导借鉴。

5 月初,《报告 2018》初稿完成。国家开发银行研究院召开会议,对初稿进行讨论,对报告结构和内容提出了修改意见,并对报告进行提炼,形成了《报告 2018》中文摘要版。

5 月末,对外经济贸易大学的李小萌、李晨乐、王淳、宿玉荣、李琳、李啸初将中文摘要版翻译为英文版,约 16000 字。在金砖国家智库合作中方理事会的帮助协调下,时任对外经济贸易大学副校长的赵忠秀老师亲自背了几十本英文报告到南非,在约翰内斯堡举行的金砖国家智库会议上向参会专家介绍,供专家参阅。

6—7 月,在充分征求相关专家、里约热内卢代表处、莫斯科代表处、印度工作组、南非工作组意见的基础上,我们对报告进行了大篇幅的改写和重构,完成《报告 2018》第二稿,并翻译了英文完整版和俄语、葡萄牙语的摘要版。7 月 25 日,国家开发银行董事长在南非开普敦举行的金砖国家合作机制年会和金融论坛上正式发布《报告 2018》。《报告 2018》聚焦金砖国家投融资与此次银行合作机制年会焦点高度契合,其中,产业革命对接问题、探索数字经济(如区块链)在投融资领域的应用等与 2018 年金砖国家领导人峰会主题相呼应,为金砖国家经济及投融资可持续发展贡献“中国智慧”。

本书得到国家开发银行和对外经济贸易大学领导的高度重视。国家开发银行首席经济学家、研究院刘勇院长亲自主持并指导研究。国家开发银行研究院朱文彬副院长具体指导,全程参与,同编写团队反复讨论,修改定稿;对外经济贸易大学吴卫星教授对本书给予了鼎力支持,积极组织专家并参与写作。国家开发银行研究院李一君、龙岩统筹协调,负责主题设计,提纲起草,案例甄选,撰写和修改,统稿、校对和出版等。两个机构的大量专家参与了报告的编写,尤其是很多来自国家开发银行一线业务部门的同事将他们实际工作经验融入了报告内容。此外,来自研究院的实习生慕雅琦、吴昊翔、张馨蕊、蔡耀、周佳兮也深度参与了本书的写作、校对出版。主要负责初稿编写和第二稿编写的作者包括:第一章和第二章:龙岩、慕雅琦、吴昊翔、周念利等;第三章:慕雅琦、龙岩、吴昊翔、蓝庆新等;第四章:慕雅琦、尹燕飞、张馨蕊、龙岩、李一君;第五章:尹燕飞、宋琛、韩国新、胡勇、石文娟、李一君等;附录十个案例分别由张馨蕊、龙岩、孙湧海、周震恒、赵红涛、苏战平、杨古新、赵浩、李圣哲编写；李一君、温灏、龙岩、夏冠中、尹燕飞、慕雅琦、吴昊翔、蔡燿、周佳分参与了报告的中文、英文和俄语版本的统稿、校对和出版工作。除此之外，感谢国家开发银行办公厅、政策研究室、国际金融局、财会局等对于本书翻译、印刷、出版等的大力支持，感谢国家开发银行国际金融局努力协调本报告在金砖国家金融论坛发布，也感谢对外经贸大学国际处李小萌老师和"一带一路"PPP中心韦小泉老师的组织协调！

当今世界，经济与社会发展日新月异，本书出版之际，金砖国家发生了很多变化，我们将会持续跟踪和更新。在此欢迎读者提出宝贵建议。

国家开发银行研究院
2018 年 12 月

English Report

Chapter I Opening a Golden Decade for BRICS Cooperation and Deepening BRICS Investment and Financing Cooperation

1.1 Economic Development of Emerging Market Countries in 2017

1.1.1 BRICS Leading Emerging Market Countries' Growth

In the 21st century, the rise of emerging market economies has become an irreversible trend[1]. Emerging market countries generally have well-developed institutions of the market economy, a good speed of growth, and strong market potential. In recent years, as the world economy improves and global trade and investment revives, these countries are contributing more to world economic growth. IMF statistics show their combined GDP in 2017 to be USD 27.17 trillion, accounting for 34% of the global GDP of USD 79.28 billion, up from 22% in 2006, making them the true engine of world economic growth (Fig. 1.1).

BRICS caught more attention among the emerging market countries. An IMF report concludes that, in the past decade, BRICS countries contributed over 50% of world economic growth. In 2017, BRICS continued to show a good momentum of growth. Their combined GDP was USD 18.5574 trillion, making up 68% of that of emerging market countries (Fig. 1.1); their international

---

[1] According such authoritative organizations and agencies as the IMF, MSCI, Dow Jones, 'emerging market countries' in this report include Brazil, Chile, China, Columbia, the Czech Republic, Egypt, Greece, Hungary, India, Indonesia, Malaysia, Mexico, Pakistan, Peru, the Philippines, Russia, South Africa, Thailand, Turkey, the UAE, the DPRK, Poland, and Qatar.

trade volume was USD 3. 239 trillion, increasing its share in total international trade from 11% in 2006 to 15% in 2017 (Fig. 1. 2); they received USD 278. 1 billion of FDI, up from the USD 138. 9 billion in 2006; their ODI increased from USD 102. 8 billion in 2006 to USD 165. 4 billion in 2017 (Fig. 1. 3).

(in billion USD)

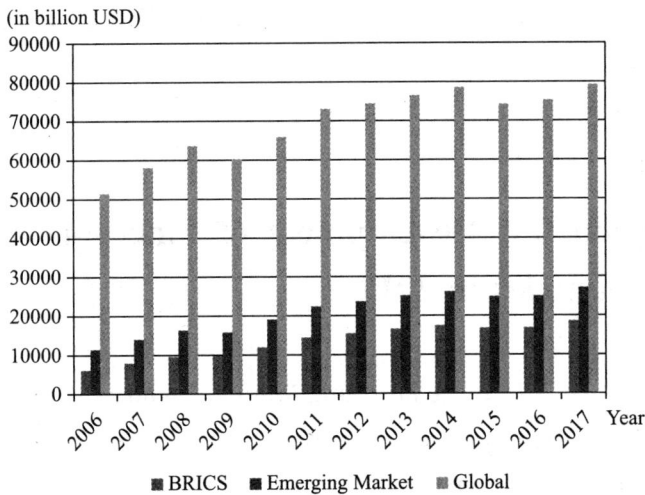

■ BRICS   ■ Emerging Market   ■ Global

Figure 1. 1   2006 – 2017 BRICS, Emerging Markets and Global GDPs
(in billion USD)

Source: International Monetary Fund

Inside the BRICS, China and India led the GDP growth in 2017, growing by over 6% ; Brazil, Russia, and South Africa were growing at 1%. GDP Per capita figures put Brazil, China, Russia, and South Africa in the ranks of medium-to-high income countries; India remained among medium-to-low income countries despite a significant increase of its per capita GDP in 2016[1]. The Chinese RMB and Indian Rupee fluctuated within a small margin of ±2% of their parities against the US Dollar, the Brazilian Real and Russian Ruble ±4% , and the South African Rand maximizes at 6% fluctuation.

---

① According to the World Bank, the per capita GDP thresholds used to categorize countries in 2017 are as follows: USD 12235 for high-income countries, USD 3956 – 12235 for medium-to-high income countries, USD 1006 – 3955 for medium-to-low income countries, and 1550 for low-income countries.

(in billion USD)

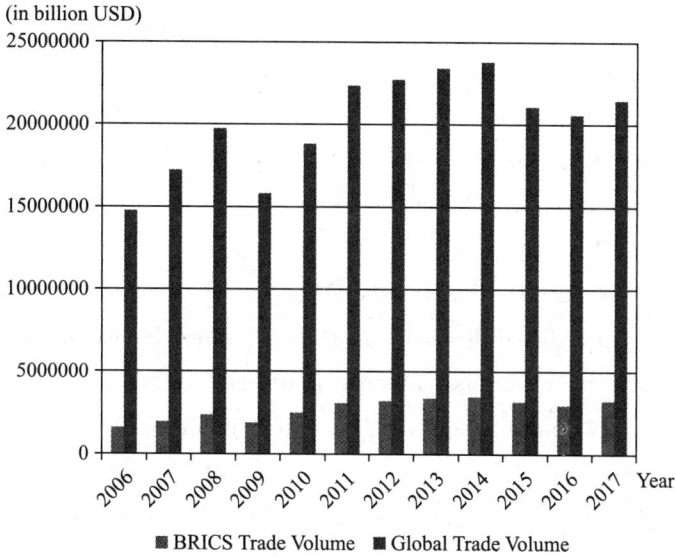

■ BRICS Trade Volume   ■ Global Trade Volume

Figure 1. 2   2006 – 2017 BRICS and Global Total International Trade Volume (in billion USD)

Source: UNCTAD, International Monetary Fund

(in billion USD)

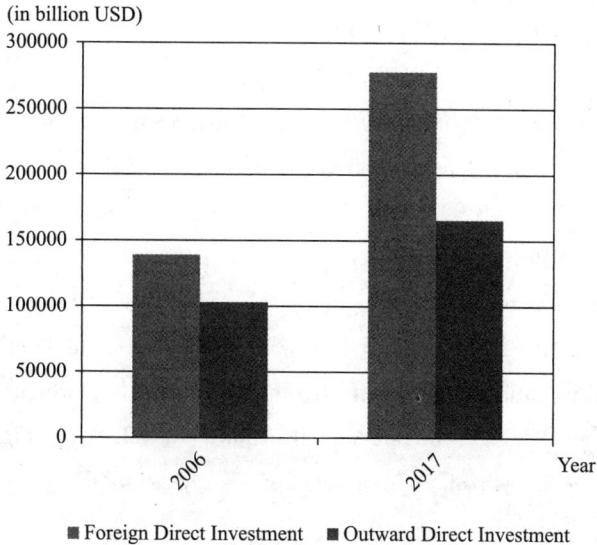

■ Foreign Direct Investment   ■ Outward Direct Investment

Figure 1. 3   2006 – 2017 BRICS FDI and ODI in 2006 and 2017 (in billion USD)

Source: CEIC

BRICS countries are committed to a balanced and inclusive economic partnership. In the early days of the group, members fought side by side with each other against the shocks of the global financial crisis. As the world economy steadily improved in 2017, BRICS countries reinforced and deepened their practical cooperation and achieved domestic economic recovery and growth.

(1) Brazil

Starting from 2011, due to labor shortage, low industrial productivity, and subdued international demand slowed down, Brazil's overall growth tends to slow down and even reverse. To steer away from recession and stimulate the economy, the government stepped up structural reform in 2017 and witnessed good results. The real economy grew, consumer confidence was stable, and the labor market improved gradually. Brazil remains an emerging market country with a strong development potential.

i. GDP and GDP Growth Rate

Thanks to a better world economy and the reform program of the government, the Brazilian economy showed a clear sign of recovery, growing for the first time since 2014. In 2017, its GDP climbed back to USD 2 trillion and its GDP grew by 1% (Fig. 1.4).

ii. GDP Per Capita

Brazil's per capita GDP grew by a small margin in 2017 to approach USD 10000, increasing by 70% from 2006 and falling by 25% from a high point in 2011 (Fig. 1.5).

iii. CPI and PPI

The year 2006 marked the beginning of a slow rise of inflation in Brazil, reaching 9% at its highest, and PPI was fluctuating significantly. In 2017, Brazil brought its inflation under effective control to 3.4%, which is the lowest in 19 years, and PPI growth rate was also down to −2.5% (Fig. 1.6). This was because the growth of grain production that year subdued the increase of food prices.

iv. Unemployment Rate

Brazil's job market continued to deteriorate in 2017, with a big increase of the number of unemployed people and unemployment rate surging to 12.8%.

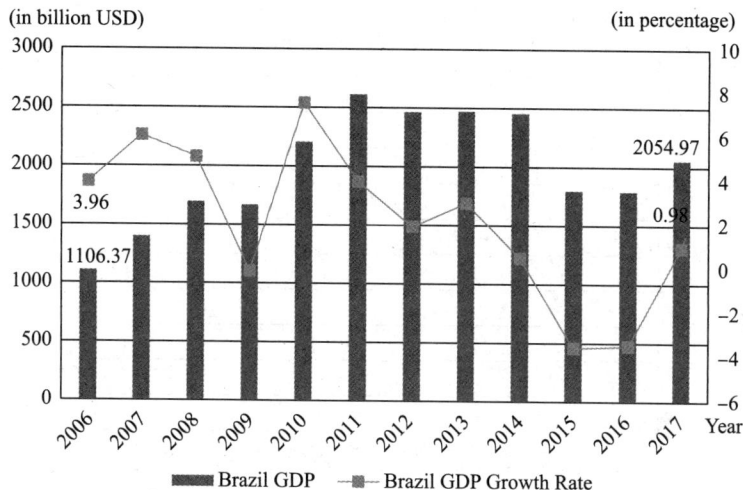

Figure 1. 4   2006 – 2017 Brazil's GDP and GDP Growth Rate

(in billion USD, percentage)

Source: International Monetary Fund

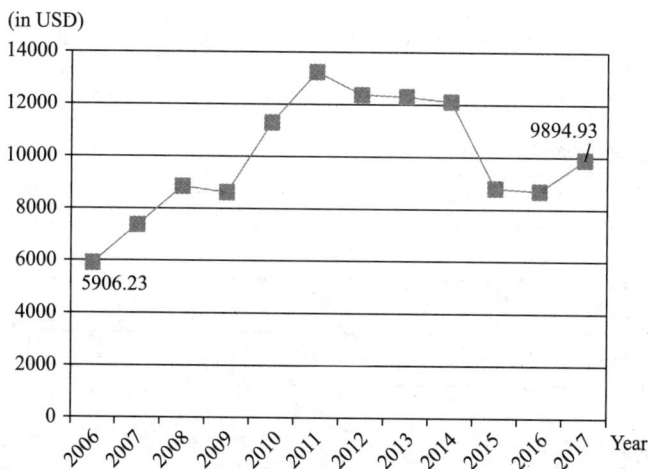

Figure 1. 5   2006 – 2017 Brazil's GDP Per Capita (in USD)

Source: International Monetary Fund

Though there was a good economic momentum, unemployment rate has been on a continuous rise since 2014. Employment challenges remain serious (Fig. 1. 7).

(in percentage)

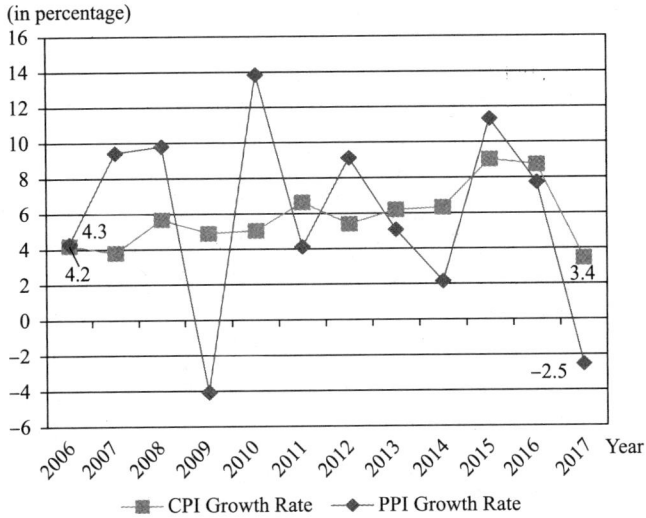

Figure 1. 6   2016 – 2017 Brazil's Inflation (CPI Growth Rate) and
PPI Growth Rate (in percentage)

Source: International Monetary Fund

As the government increases investment in infrastructure, the job market may improve.

(in percentage)

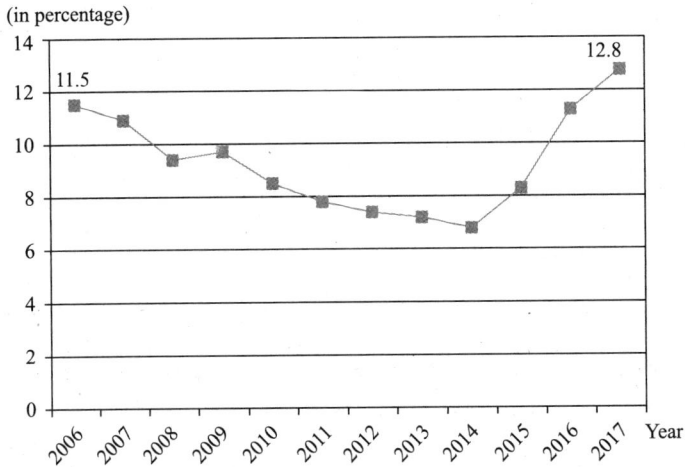

Figure 1. 7   2006 – 2017 Brazil's Unemployment Rate (in percentage)

Source: National Statistics Office

v. Growth Rates of Goods and Services Imports and Exports

With the world economy continuing to recover and commodity prices rising, Brazil's foreign trade grew much faster, becoming the main driver of economic growth. In 2017, Brazil's export and import increased by 10.9% and 3.8% respectively and the foreign trade surplus was USD 67 billion, reached the highest in 29 years (Fig. 1.8).

(in percentage)

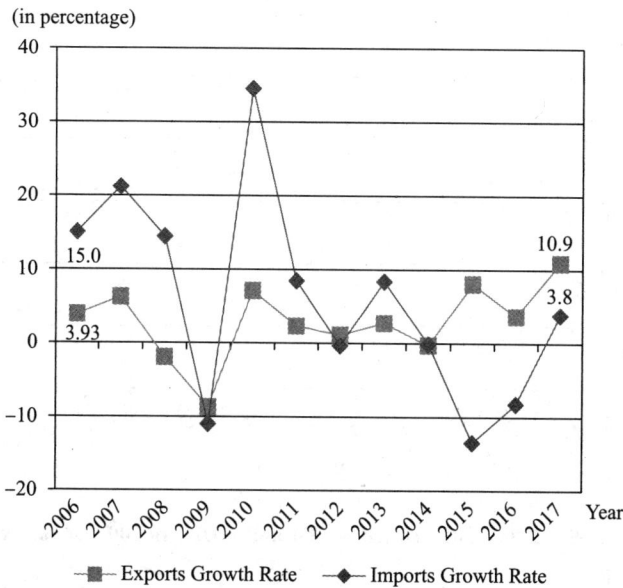

──■── Exports Growth Rate   ──◆── Imports Growth Rate

Figure 1.8   2006 – 2017 Growth Rates of Brazil's Goods and

Services Imports and Exports (in percentage)

Source: International Monetary Fund

vi. FDI and ODI

Brazil's FDI and ODI dropped slightly in 2017 to USD 70.33 billion and USD 6.27 billion. In the wake of the 2008 financial crisis, Brazil's FDI grew substantially for two years in a row before a gradual decrease in the following years. The increase in 2014 failed to alter the downward trend resulting from domestic economic and political crisis. However, Brazil remains an attractive destination for foreign investment among emerging market countries.

The 2008 financial crisis affected Brazil's foreign investment policy considerably, bringing its direct investment to below zero in 2009. The year 2017 continued the downward trend since 2014 and decreased by about 50% from that of 2016 (Fig. 1. 9).

(in 100 million USD)

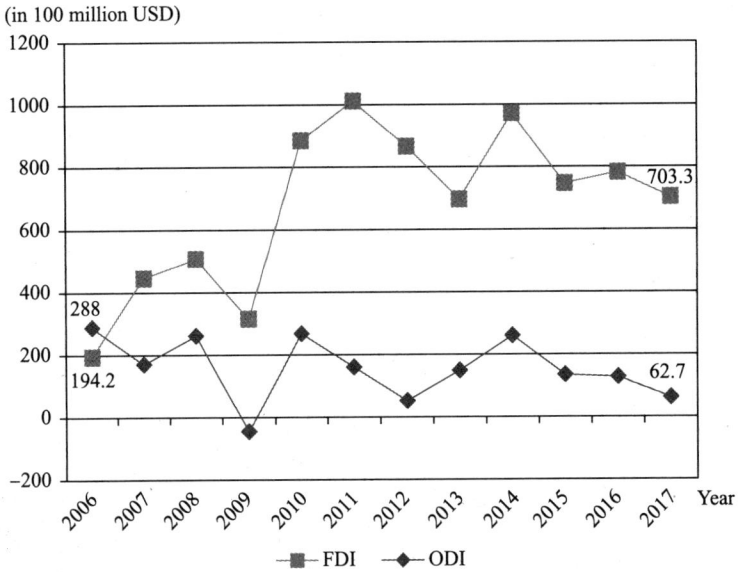

Figure 1. 9   2006 – 2017 Brazil's FDI and ODI (in 100 million USD)

Source: CEIC

vii. Exchange Rate

Between 2006 and 2011, the Real to Dollar exchange rate was at a low level and rising slowly. Starting from 2012, the Real began to depreciate and reached the lowest point in 2016, as a result of a sluggish economy, rate rise by the US Federal Reserve, and the reductions in commodity prices. Improvements in the economy in 2017 led to a slight rise of the Real against the Dollar (Fig. 1. 10).

(2) Russia

Against the backdrop of western sanctions and oil prices slide, the various policies of the Russian government to reform industrial structure and stimulate

(USD/BRL)

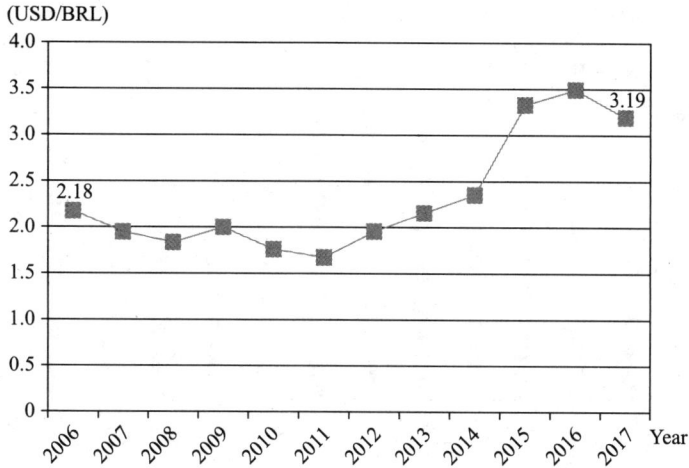

Figure 1. 10   2006 – 2017 Exchange Rate of Real Against the Dollar （USD/BRL）

Source: International Financial Statistics

the economy began to take effect. In 2017, the Russian economy slowly recovered from the downturn and showed signs of improving. Main sources of GDP growth included the mining industry, oil prices, and individual consumption, while construction and the service industry experienced a significant slide. It is forecast that the Russian economy will continue its modest recovery, and increasing risk resilience remains the guiding thought behind economic policies.

i. GDP and GDP Growth Rate

The Russian economy grew faster than expected in 2017, with its GDP growth rate increasing to 1. 55% from – 2. 5% in 2015, and total GDP growing slightly from the level in 2016 to USD 1. 528 trillion, although still lower than the 2013 peak （Fig. 1. 11）. The 2008 financial crisis had a significant impact on the Russian economy. Though the economy recovered soon, growth slowed down mainly because of western sanctions and the sharp fall in global crude oil rates.

ii. GDP Per Capita

In 2017, Russia's GDP per capita grew for the first time since 2013 to USD 10608, the highest among BRICS countries. （Fig. 1. 12） (in billion USD)   (in percentage)

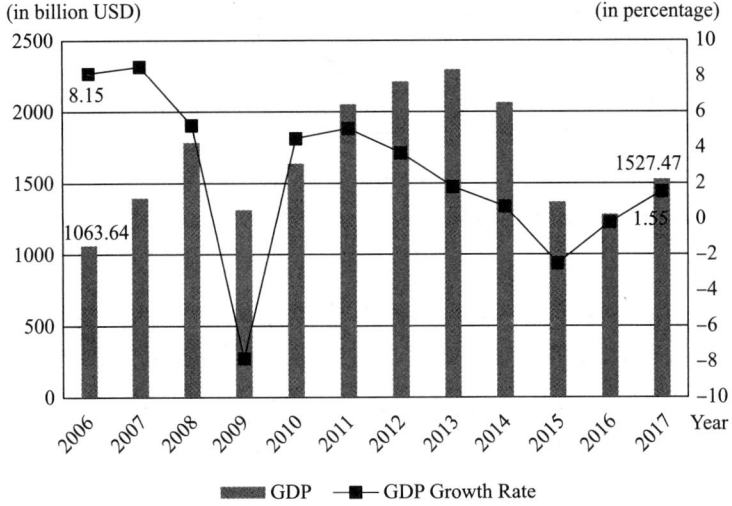

Figure 1. 11   2006 – 2017 Russia's GDP and its Growth Rate

(in billion USD, percentage)

Source: International Monetary Fund

(in USD)

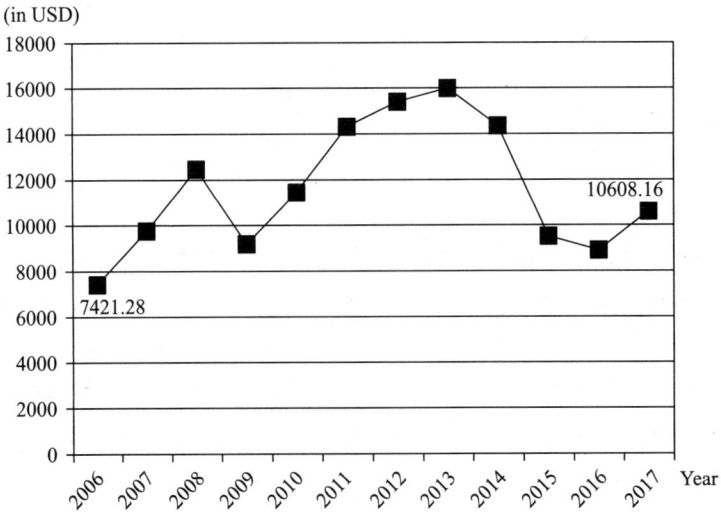

Figure 1. 12   2006 – 2017 Russia's GDP Per Capita (in USD)

Source: International Monetary Fund

iii. CPI and PPI

High inflation has been a perennial problem in Russia, with the inflation rate up to 16% in 2015. The government took it very seriously and, helped by a continuous appreciation of the Ruble, inflation kept slowing down in 2017 as in 2016 and reached a historic low of 3. 7% , lower than the 4% target rate of the central bank. PPI growth rate stabilized at 8. 4% , damping future growth uncertainties (Fig. 1. 13).

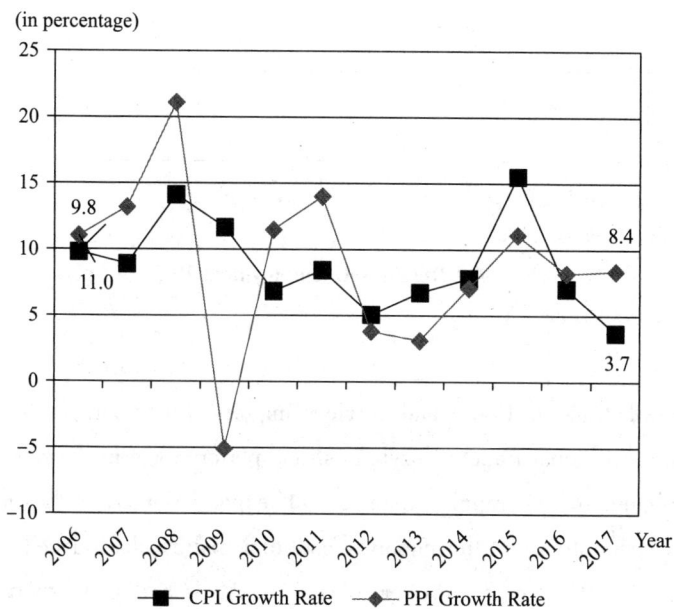

Figure 1. 13   2006 – 2017 Russia's Inflation Rate (CPI Growth Rate) and PPI Growth Rate (in percentage)

Source: Federal Reserve Bank of St. Louis

iv. Unemployment Rate

Russia's unemployment rate has been low in recent years. In 2017, it was 5. 2% , dropping from the 2016 level by 0. 3% . Unemployment rate has kept falling since the high point in 2009 (Fig. 1. 14). Some analysis concludes this fall did not happen simply because of increasing job opportunities, but was, to a significant extent, due to a reduction in the working-age population and restrictions on foreign labor.

(in percentage)

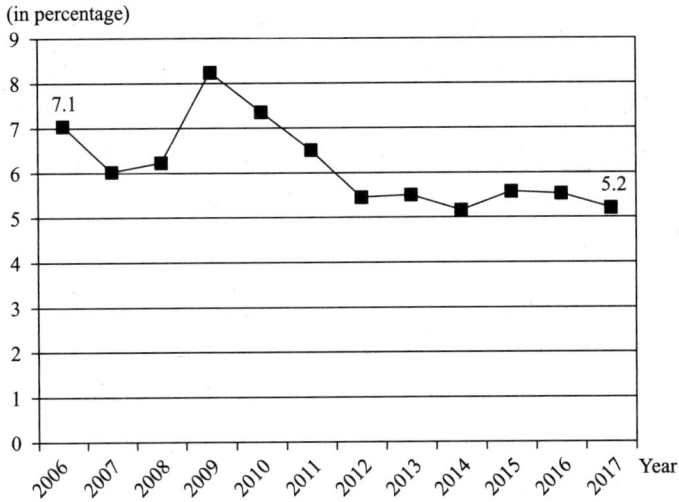

Figure 1. 14   2006 – 2017 Russia's Unemployment Rate (in percentage)

Source: Haver Analytic

v. Growth Rates of Goods and Services Imports and Exports

In terms of global trade, Russia's strong performance in the raw materials markets prompted the rapid expansion of export-oriented industries. Better customer consumption and the import substitution policy also pushed up import trade. The year 2017 saw a considerable rise in the import and export of goods and services by Russia, with an exports growth rate of 9.1% and an imports growth rate of 20.3% (Fig. 1. 15).

vi. FDI and ODI

Russia's FDI and ODI are closely correlated on the whole and tend to move in the same direction. Following a low in 2015, its FDI and ODI increased to USD 27. 89 billion and USD 38. 63 billion respectively (Fig. 1. 16). However, FDI only accounts for 2% of its GDP.

(in percentage)

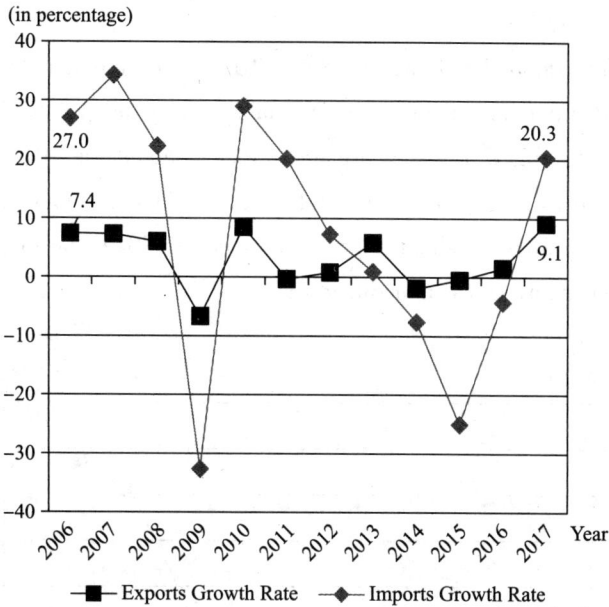

—■— Exports Growth Rate   —♦— Imports Growth Rate

Figure 1. 15   2006 – 2017 Growth Rates of Russia's Goods and Services Exports and Imports (in percentage)

Source: International Monetary Fund

(in 100 million USD)

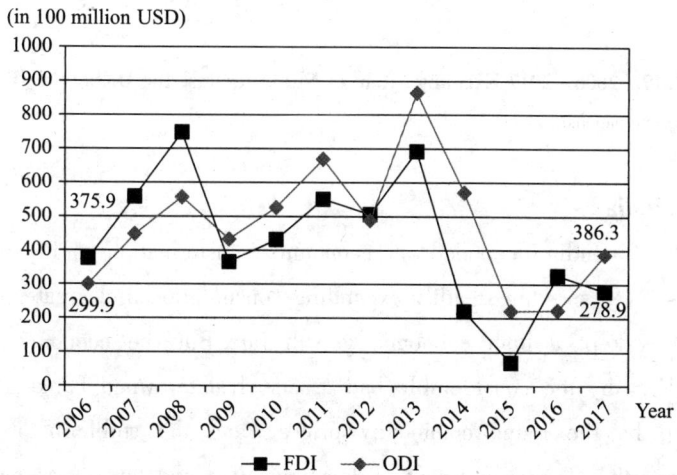

—■—FDI   —♦—ODI

Figure 1. 16   2006 – 2017 Russia's FDI and ODI (in 100 million USD)

Source: CEIC

vii. Exchange Rate

The Ruble depreciated rapidly since 2013 under the double pressure of European and American sanctions and the fall in crude oil prices. Coupled with the effect of Russia's floating exchange rate adopted in 2014 to rein in inflation, an exchange rate crisis broke out in 2016, reducing the 2014 exchange rate by 50%. A slight appreciation came in 2017 due to recoveries in the Russian economy and commodities (Fig. 1. 17).

(USD/RUB)

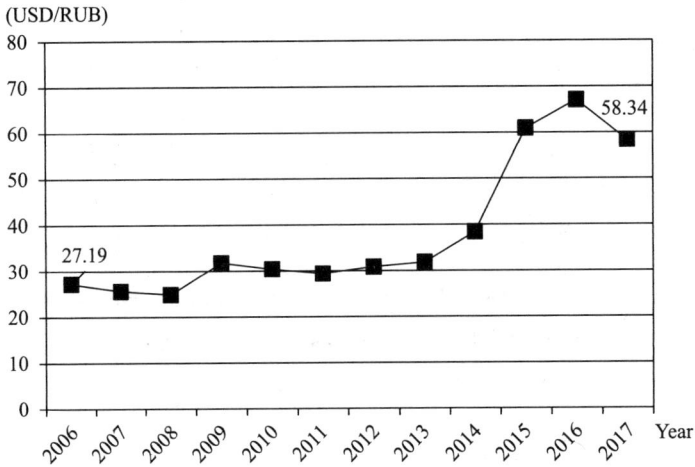

Figure 1. 17 2006 – 2017 Exchange Rate of Ruble Against the Dollar (USD/RUB)

Source: International Financial Statistics

(3) India

In 2017, India deepened its economic transformation and experienced challenges. Even so, the steadily expanding consumption and greater openness in industries kept a high economic growth rate. But the economy was still weighed down by the considerable bad assets of state-owned banks, inflation pushed up by the rising commodity prices, and the stubborn problem of 'jobless growth'. The government's demonetization and tax reform also had a negative impact on the economy.

i. GDP and GDP Growth Rate

India's GDP has been on a steady rise since 2006, reaching USD 2. 611

trillion in 2017, almost three times that of 2006. Although Indian President Narendra Modi took strong measures in structural reform to promote growth, India's GDP growth slowed down in 2017 to only 6.74%, dropping lower than China's GDP for the first time in three years (Fig. 1. 18).

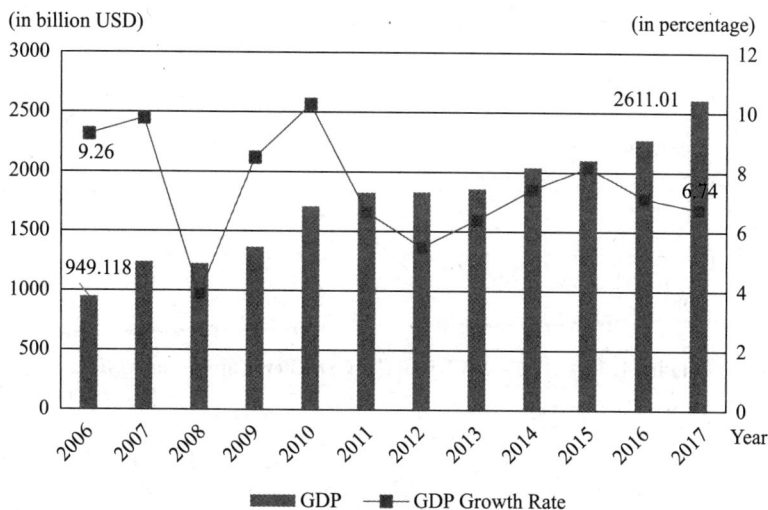

Figure 1. 18   2006 – 2017 India's GDP and Growth Rate
(in billion USD, percentage)

Source: International Monetary Fund

ii. GDP Per Capita

India's GDP per capita has been growing steadily at a modest rate since 2006, reaching USD 1982.7, the lowest among BRICS countries (Fig. 1. 19).

iii. CPI and PPI

From 2006 to 2014, India's inflation stayed above 6%. The government's demonetization policy rolled out at the end of 2016 brought inflation under effective control. The rapid fall in food prices in 2017 also eased some inflationary pressure. In 2017, India's inflation rate was down to 3. 3%, and PPI growth rate 3. 6% (Fig. 1. 20). It is projected that inflation will likely stay stable in the near future, but rising energy prices will be the main source of pressure.

(in USD)

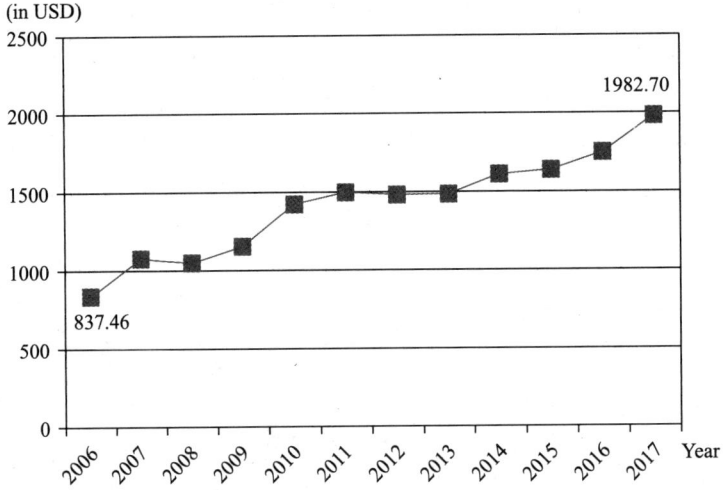

Figure 1. 19   2006 – 2017 India's GDP Per Capita（in USD）

Source：International Monetary Fund

(in percentage)

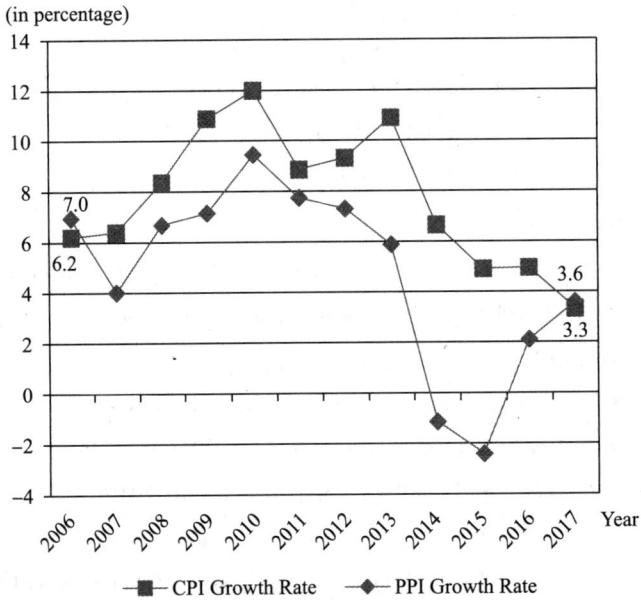

■ CPI Growth Rate   ◆ PPI Growth Rate

Figure 1. 20   2006 – 2017 India's Inflation Rate（CPI Growth Rate）

and PPI Growth Rate（in Percentage）

Source：International Monetary Fund

iv. Unemployment Rate

India's unemployment has been quite steady at a low level. In 2017, it was 3. 5% , slightly higher than that of 2016 (Fig. 1. 21). Before he took office, President Modi pledged to create 10 million jobs every year, but only 230000 were created over the past three years. His Make in India program did not bring sufficient financing support for the real economy and had a limited impact on job creation. All of this added to the uncertainties in India's job market.

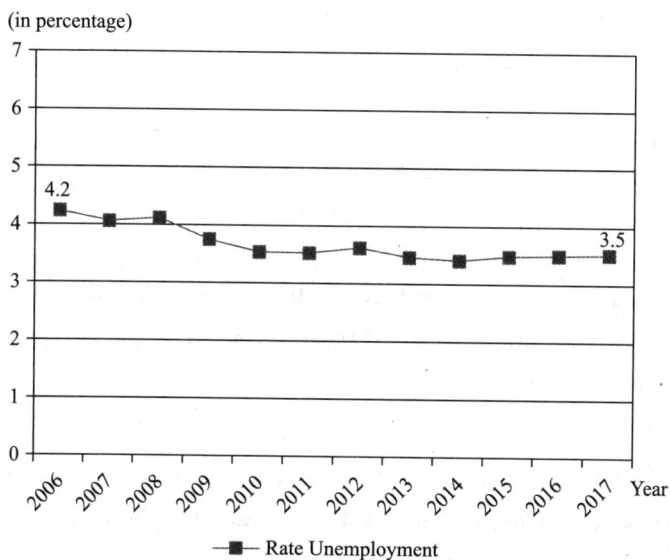

(in percentage)

—■— Rate Unemployment

Figure 1. 21   2006 – 2017 India's Unemployment Rate (in Percentage)

Source: Modeled ILO Estimate

v. Growth Rates of Goods and Services Imports and Exports

In 2017, increasing minerals trade pushed up the growth of India's goods and services import and export to 10. 6% and 7. 2% respectively. China-India bilateral trade hit a record high of USD 84. 4 billion. On the whole, the growth rates of India's import and export have been fluctuating considerably and were deeply affected by the 2008 financial crisis. Its import and export are also closely correlated, both showing signs of improvement two years after a 2015 low (Fig. 1. 22) .

(in percentage)

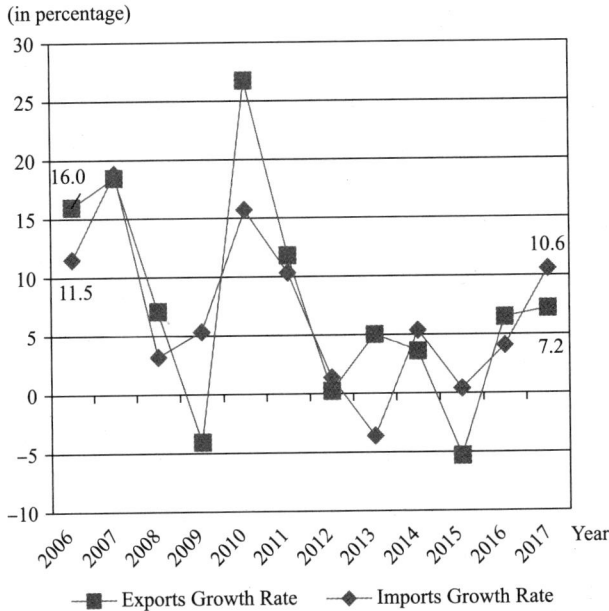

Figure 1.22 2006 – 2017 Growth Rates of India's Goods and

Services Exports and Imports (in percentage)

Source: International Monetary Fund

vi. FDI and ODI

India's FDI was growing tremendously from 2006 to 2009, with a growth rate 4.7 times that of 2006, but was then followed by a moderation. The Make in India program introduced in 2014 greatly liberated foreign investment, pushing the FDI to a peak in 2016. In 2017, its FDI was USD 42.21 billion, slightly below that of 2016. Its ODI has been falling every year since 2008 until it bottomed out in 2013. In 2017, it experienced a significant increase to reach USD 11.26 billion (Fig. 1.23).

vii. Exchange Rate

India's Rupee was depreciating against the Dollar from 2006 to 2016 under the pressure of an economic slowdown, shrinking international demand due to the financial crisis, and the rate hikes of the US Federal Reserve. The introduction of the goods and services tax strengthened foreign investors' confidence, leading to a small appreciation of the currency in 2017 from the 2016 level, signaling better performance in the future (Fig. 1.24).

(in 100 million USD)

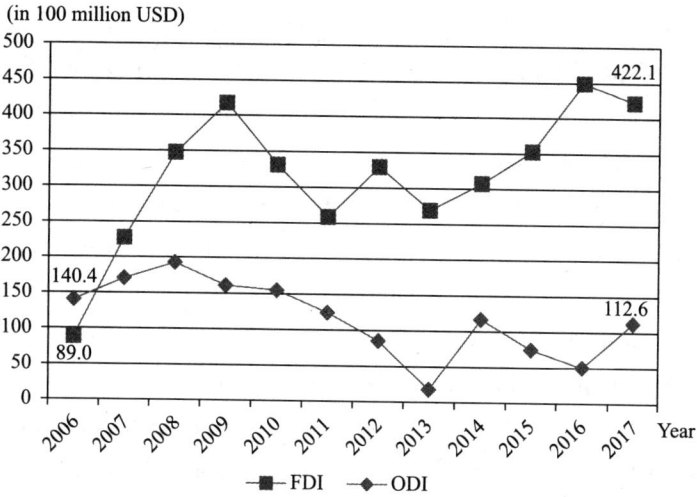

Figure 1. 23   2006 – 2017 India's FDI and ODI (in 100 million USD)

Source: CEIC

(USD/INR)

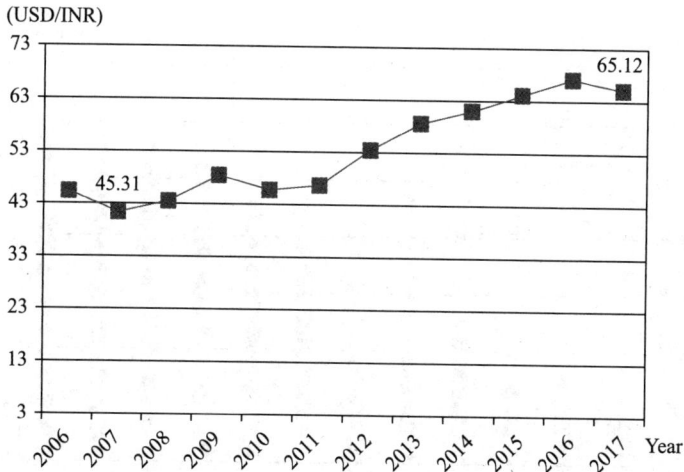

Figure 1. 24   2006 – 2017 Exchange Rate of India's Rupee Against the

Dollar (USD/INR)

Source: International Financial Statistics

(4) China

In 2017, China performed stronger than expected. After a period of post crisis adjustment, the Chinese economy entered what Chinese President Xi Jinping called in 2014 a 'new normal', characterized by a transition of the growth rate from a high level to a medium-to-high level. In 2016 and 2017, China's growth rate was steady and rising modestly, pointing to the solid fundamentals and resilience of the macro-economy. Positive factors included continuous supply-side structural reform, good performance in industrial production, improving economic structure, and faster growth in consumption than in investment.

i. GDP and GDP Growth Rate

China's GDP has been growing at a fast pace each year since 2006, topping USD 12 trillion in 2017 and 4.3 times that of 2006. Its growth in 2017 was faster than expected, albeit not as fast as 10 years ago. In 2017, it reached 6.9%, a little faster than 2016 and accelerating for the first time since 2011, leading the growth of BRICS countries (Fig. 1.25).

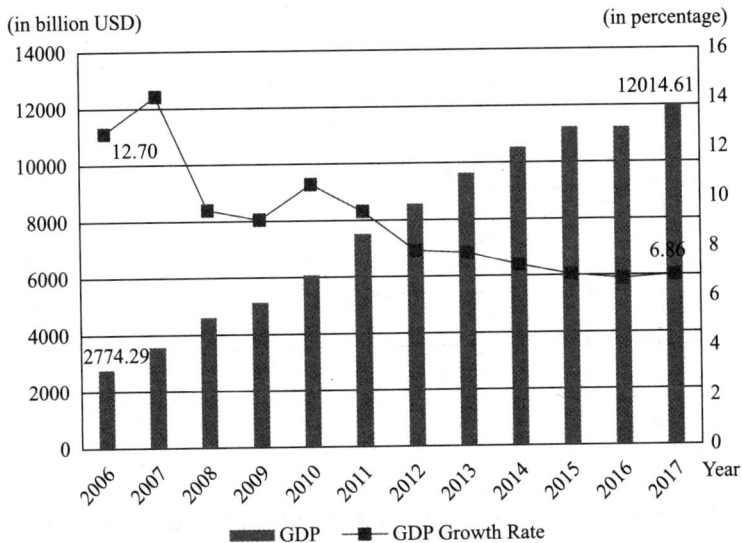

Figure 1.25   2006 – 2017 China's GDP and Growth Rate

(in Billion USD, percentage)

Source: International Monetary Fund

ii. GDP Per Capita

In 2017, China's GDP per capita continued its growth to USD 8643, four times higher than that of 2006 (Fig. 1. 26).

(in USD)

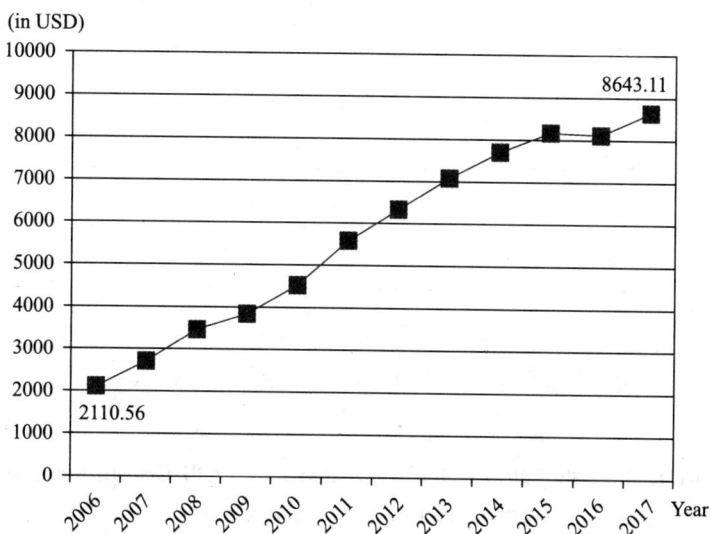

Figure 1. 26   2006 – 2017 China's GDP Per Capita (in USD)

Source: International Monetary Fund

iii. CPI and PPI

Starting from 2012, China has been keeping its inflation rate under good control at around 2% and lower than the target rate even though the economy has been growing at a faster pace. In 2017, the CPI growth rate decreased slightly to 1. 6%, and the PPI growth rate was also down by a small margin to 4. 9% (Fig. 1. 27). Falling food prices is the main reason behind the moderation in CPI.

iv. Unemployment Rate

China's unemployment rate fell below 4% in 2017, the first time since 2006. This was due to China's economic recovery, improving business performance, and the growing added value of various industries (Fig. 1. 28).

(in percentage)

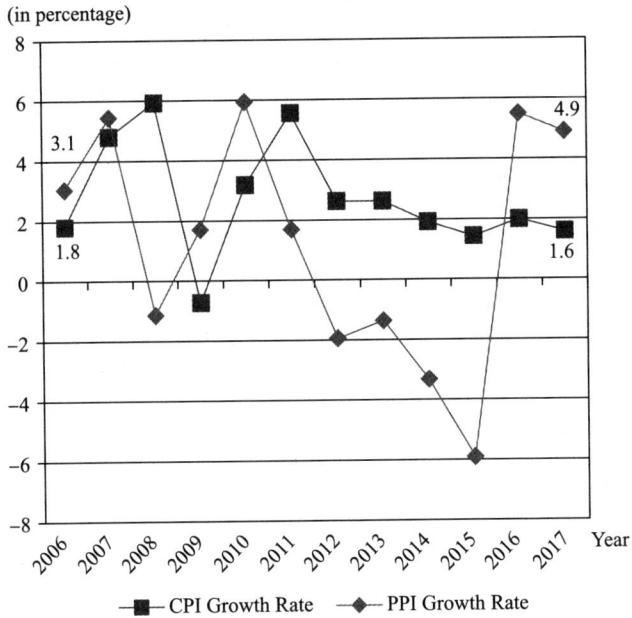

Figure 1. 27 2006 – 2017 China's Inflation Rate (CPI Growth Rate) and PPI Growth Rate (in percentage)

Source: International Monetary Fund

(in percentage)

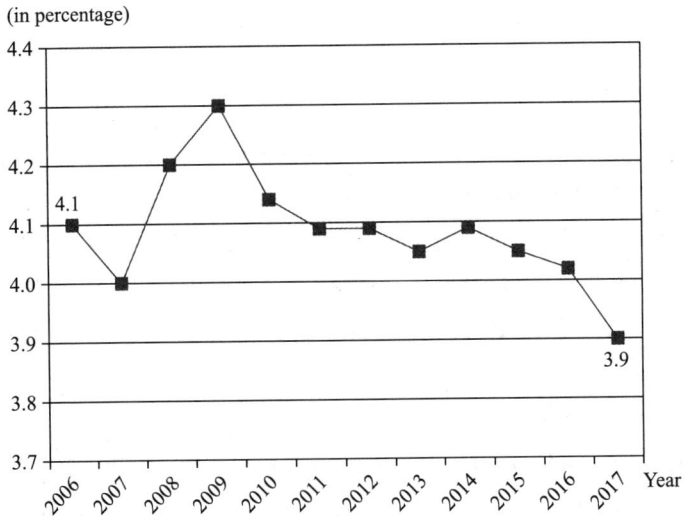

Figure 1. 28 2006 – 2017 China's Unemployment Rate (in percentage)

Source: National Bureau of Statistics, CEIC.

v. Growth Rates of Goods and Services Imports and Exports

China's import and export growth in 2009 was seriously dented by the international financial crisis and slowed down after a recovery in 2010. With the global demand recovery and progress under the 'Belt and Road' Initiative, import and export growth has been accelerating in recent years. In 2017, the growth rates continued to rise on the back of the gains of the past two years, reaching 6.9% and 9.2% respectively (Fig. 1.29).

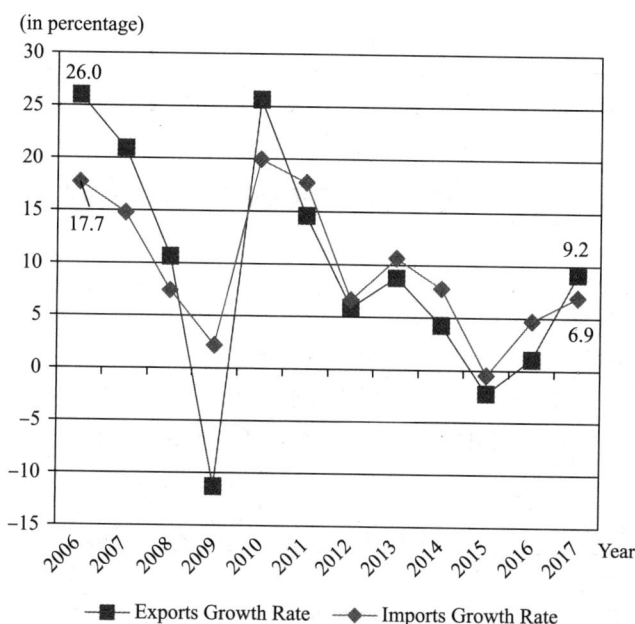

Figure 1. 29   2006 – 2017 Growth Rates of China's Goods and
Services Imports and Exports (in percentage)

Source: International Monetary Fund

vi. FDI and ODI

China's FDI was on a continuous rise overall, it only decreased followed by the financial crisis in 2009, in 2017, the upward trend continued, reached USD 136.3 billion. China's ODI experienced explosive growth in 2016, making the country the world's second largest investor. But with the adjustment of overseas business investment policy, China's ODI in 2017 moderated and stood at USD 101.91 billion (Fig. 1.30).

(in 100 million USD)

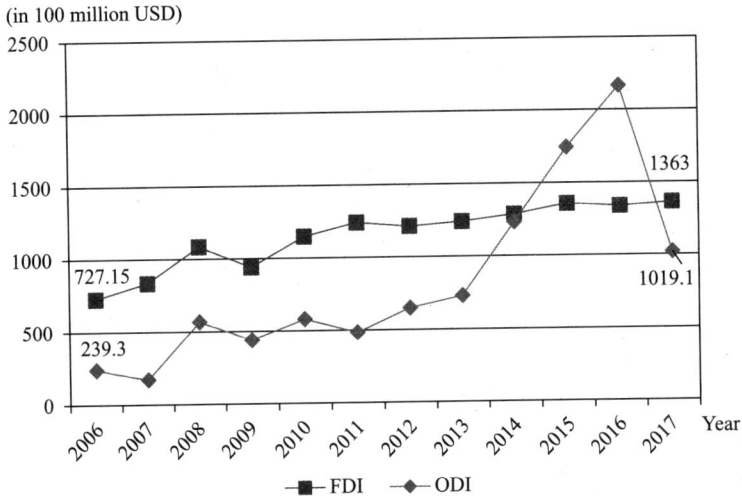

Figure 1. 30   2006 – 2017 China's FDI and ODI（in 100 million USD）

Source： CEIC

vii. Exchange Rate

The exchange rate of the RMB against the dollars has been steady at between six and seven since 2008. Between 2015 and 2017, the RMB depreciated slightly. In 2017, it was 6. 76. （Fig. 1. 31）.

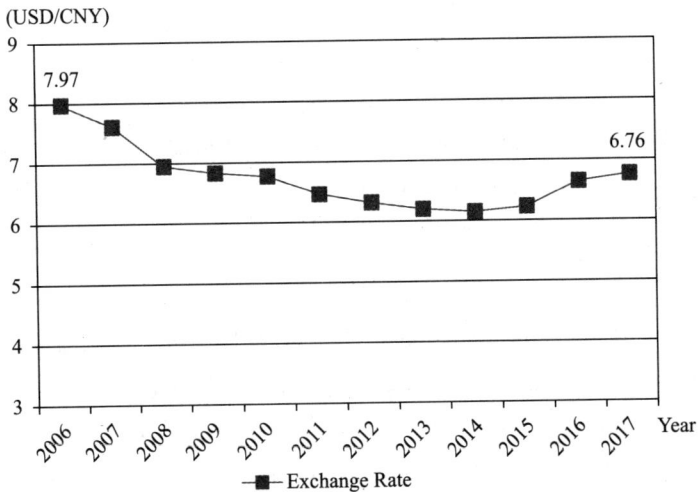

Figure 1. 31   2006 – 2017 Exchange Rate of RMB Against the Dollar（USD/CNY）

Source： International Financial Statistics

(5) South Africa

South Africa is a main engine of the African economy, hosting over 75% of large African companies. Its economy relies heavily on the mining industry, agriculture, and the finance industry. Economic growth in South Africa slowed down in recent years due to falling raw materials prices, poor harvest, and subdued international demand. With the world economy turning for the better and commodity prices rising, the economy showed signs of improving and continued its recovery.

i. GDP and GDP Growth Rate

After the 2008 financial crisis, South Africa's GDP began to grow steadily and then slid as a result of falling raw material prices and lackluster demand. In 2017, driven by the fast growth of agriculture and manufacturing, South Africa's economy bounced back and grew by 1.3%, exceeding expectation (Fig. 1.32).

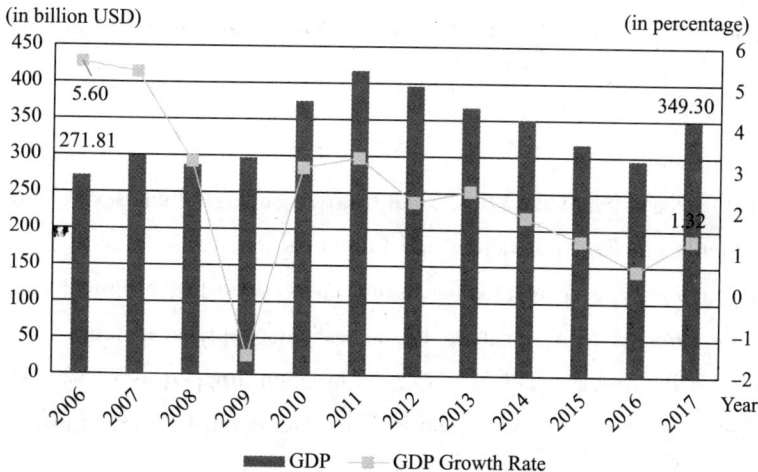

Figure 1.32   2006 – 2017 South Africa's GDP and Its Growth Rate
(in billion USD, percentage)

Source: International Monetary Fund

ii. GDP Per Capita

In 2017, South Africa's GDP per capita grew substantially after years of falling that started in 2011 and climbed back to over USD 6000, but only 10% higher than that 2016 (Fig. 1. 33).

(in USD)

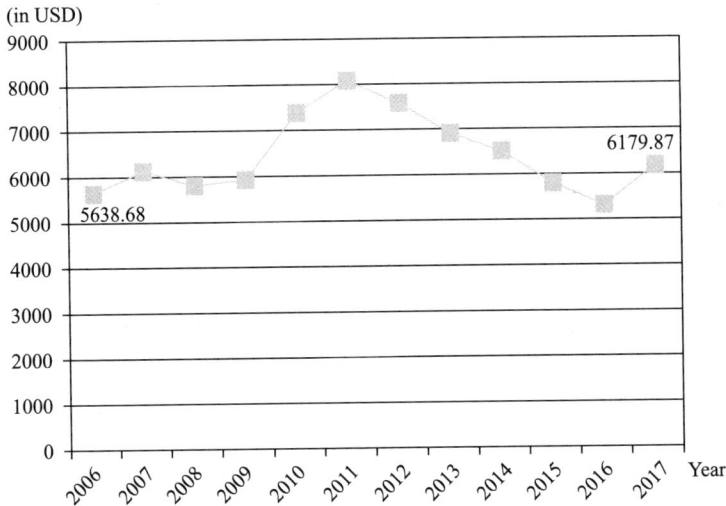

Figure 1. 33   2006-2017South Africa's Per Capita GDP 2006-2017 (in USD)

Source: International Monetary Fund

iii. CPI and PPI

In the second half of 2015, South Africa suffered from severe drought, which greatly cut food production and turned the country from a food exporter into an importer. The devaluation of its currency added to the cost of importing such necessities as food, pushing up domestic food prices and inflation. With the effect of the drought over in 2017, its inflation dropped to 5. 2%, back to the target range (3% to 6%), and PPI growth rate fell to 4. 9% (Fig. 1. 34).

iv. Unemployment Rate

South Africa's unemployment rate has been hovering at a high level due to a poor business environment and anemic economic growth. The *New Growth Path* strategy released by the government in 2010 aims to bring down unemployment rate to 15% within 10 years through the means of setting up special economic zones and infrastructure development. However, employment situation did not

(in percentage)

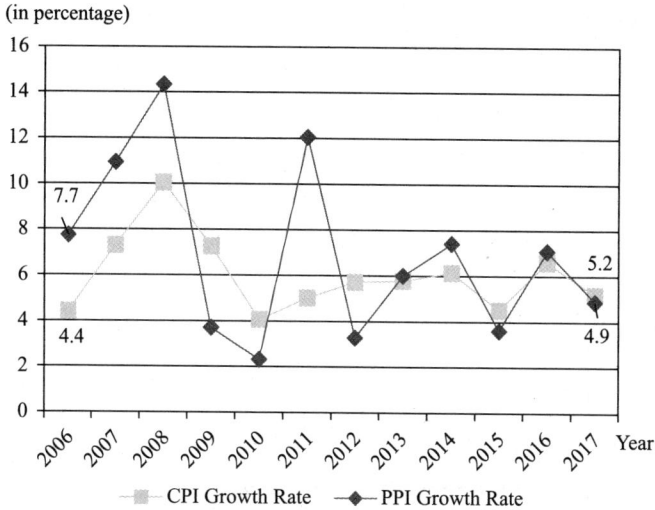

Figure 1. 34   2006 – 2017 South Africa's Inflation Rate (CPI Growth Rate) and PPI Growth Rate (in percentage)

Source: International Monetary Fund

improve and the unemployment rate inched even higher to 27. 5% in 2017 (Fig. 1. 35). Youth unemployment is a most acute problem, with an unemployment rate of those between 15 and 24 years old close to 56%.

(in Percentage)

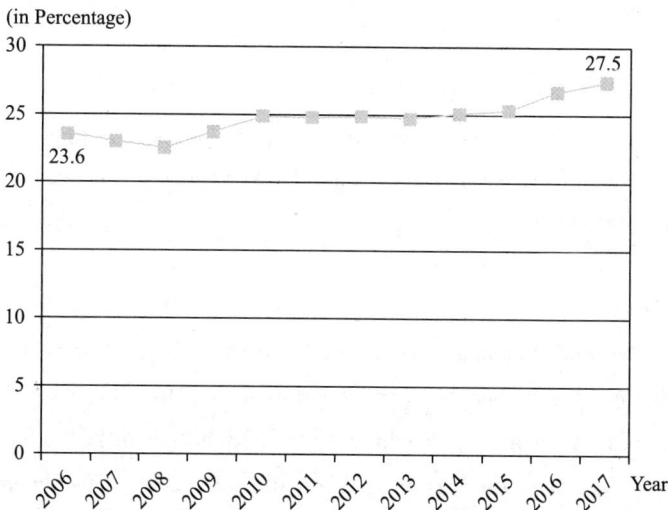

Figure 1. 35   2006 – 2017 South Africa's Unemployment Rate (in percentage)

Source: Statistics South Africa

v. Growth Rates of Goods and Services Imports and Exports

Between 2006 and 2010, South Africa's import and export were on the
same falling trend and experienced a recovery after bottoming out in 2009. After
2013, export growth rate began to fall and was in the negative territory in 2017.
Import growth rate has been fluctuating significantly. After a negative growth in
2016, import increased by 1.9% in 2017 (Fig. 1.36).

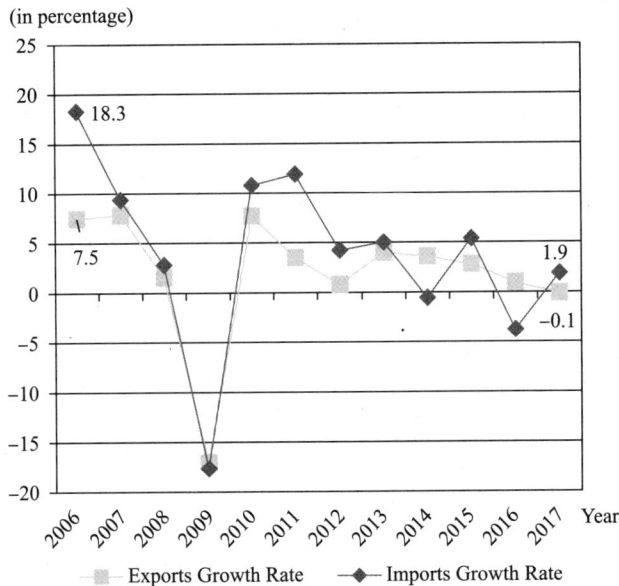

Figure 1. 36   2006 – 2017 South Africa's Goods and Services Imports and
Exports Growth Rates (in percentage)

Source: International Monetary Fund

vi. FDI and ODI

Before the 2008 financial crisis, South Africa's FDI was growing fast, but
ODI was falling due to poor economic performance. After the crisis, ODI has
been on a rising momentum, reaching USD 7.38 billion in 2017. Its FDI, on
the contrary, has been decreasing dramatically since 2013. The amendment to
the *Promotion and Protection of Investment Bill* released in 2015 prohibited
investors from referring investment-related disputes to international arbitration,
extending the FDI's downturn into 2017 (Fig. 1.37).

(in 100 million USD)

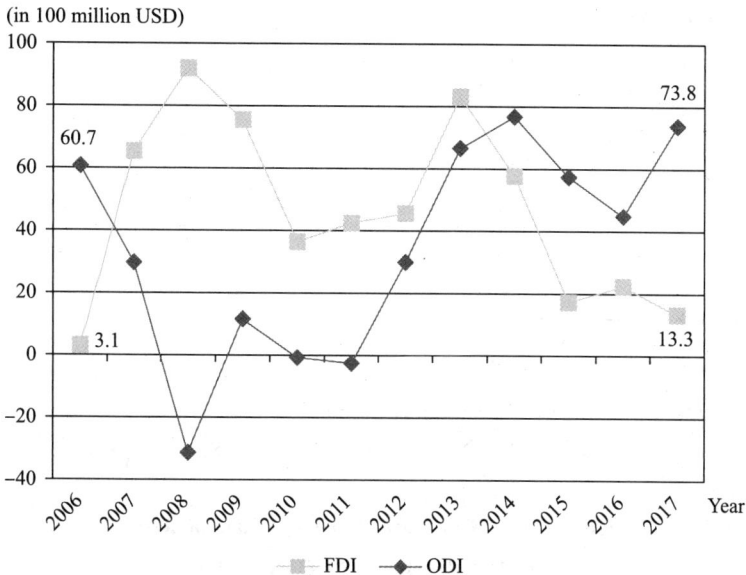

Figure 1. 37   2006-2017 South Africa's FDI and ODI（in 100 million USD）

Source：CEIC

vii. Exchange Rate

From 2006 to 2017, South Africa's Rand depreciated by almost 100% against the Dollar, mainly due to an extended period of a lackluster economy, slowdown of growth, and political instability. The downgrading of the country's credit rating in mid-2017 carried forward the depreciation. This trend was reversed by a weak Dollar and the election of Cyril Ramphosa, President of the African National Congress, as the country's president, which gave market much confidence (Fig. 1. 38).

1. 1. 2   Economic Development of Other Emerging Market Economies

1. 1. 2. 1   Marked Geographic Disparity in the Economic Performance of Emerging Market Countries

Emerging market countries in Asia have been playing a leading role in the group, growing at a fast speed. In 2017, their average GDP growth rate was 6. 5%, almost the same as 2016. The Philippines and Vietnam grew by over 6. 4% an 6. 1% respectively. Their stable recovery reflects a more active

(USD/ZAR)

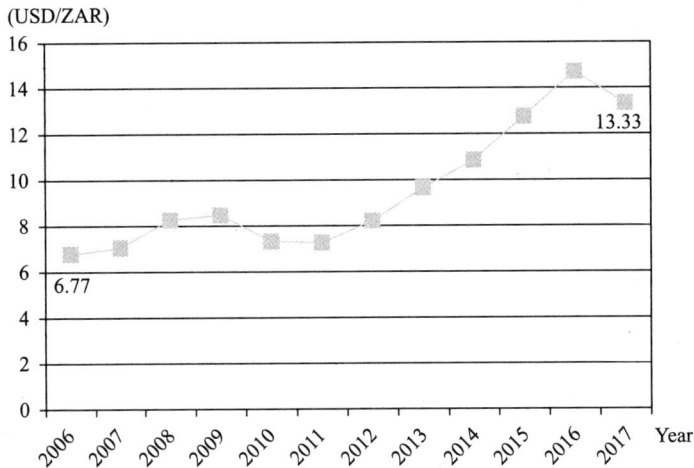

Figure 1. 38   2006 – 2017 Exchange Rate of Rand
against the Dollar（USD/ZAR）

Source：International Financial Statistics

manufacturing industry, which produces a lasting driving force on growth.

The emerging economies in the Middle East and North Africa also performed well, with a growth rate of 3. 2% in 2017, a marked improvement from 2. 3% in the previous year. On the back of rising energy commodity prices, such as oil, Iraq's real growth rate surged from -2. 4% in the previous year to 10. 3% in 2017, and that of Kuwait from 1. 1% to 2. 5%. With the easing of sanctions and the driving force of the oil industry, Iran's economic growth rate rose from 0. 38% in the previous year to 4. 5% in 2017.

Latin American countries are generally faced with such risks as a large government deficit, high inflation, and increasing fluctuations of the exchange rate. For instance, Argentina's general government deficit in 2017 amounted to 7. 1% of GDP, and that of Mexico reached the 3% threshold. Argentina's CPI in 2017 increased by 25. 6% year on year, bringing about a serious inflation. Brazil also had an inflation rate of 9. 0% . These indicators show that Latin American countries are seeing greater social vulnerability and the governments are constrained in tackling or managing the challenges.

1. 1. 2. 2 Unemployment Rate Generally High among Emerging Market Economies and Youth Unemployment Alarming

In 2017, employment growth in most emerging market countries slowed down or even entered into negative territory, leading to a small increase of unemployment rates. In addition, high youth unemployment remains a serious issue for these countries.

Egypt, Turkey, and Greece showed no signs of improvement in their double-digit unemployment rates, and unemployment among the 15 to 24 years old was particularly acute. The overall employment rate was 11% in Turkey and youth unemployment rate 20%. In Egypt, the overall unemployment rate stayed at 12% for a lack of employment promotion policies due to the weak governing capabilities of the government. Although in Europe, the economy experienced a notable recovery, Greece was still facing challenges, with the 2017 unemployment rate at 21. 5% and youth unemployment rate as high as 46%.

1. 1. 2. 3 Emerging Market Countries on the Whole Witnessing a Lower Price Level, but with Individual Differences

In 2017, sliding food prices and currency appreciation generally brought down the price levels in emerging market countries. But due to changes in the international capital flow, differences in the domestic economy, and geopolitical factors, there were also differences in the price level changes of individual countries, and inflation remained a big pressure.

Besides BRICS countries, Chile, Columbia, and Peru saw a big drop in their inflation rates in 2017 from 3. 8% to 2. 2%, 7. 5% to 4. 3%, and 3. 6% to 2. 8% respectively. Qatar's was the lowest at 0. 4%. In Indonesia, the ROK, and Poland, inflation rates rose from the 2016 levels, but not a big source of pressure. Mexico, Turkey and Egypt experienced dramatic increases in 2017, with their inflation rates surging to 6. 0%, 11. 1%, and 23. 5% respectively.

1. 1. 2. 4 Sluggish Growth of FDI in Emerging Market Countries and Significant Differences between These Countries

In 2017, emerging market countries still face challenges in attracting FDI, with the growth of the investment far below expectations. In addition, different countries faced different situations.

Mexico is one of the most open countries to foreign investment among emerging market countries, and the world's 15th recipient of foreign investment. For its geographical proximity with the US, its sources of foreign investment are mainly the US and Spain, focusing on manufacturing and financial services. In 2017, Mexico received USD 31.1 billion of FDI. Foreign investment in Indonesia mainly flowed into the mining industry, welfare programs, machinery, and the electronic industry. In 2017, Indonesia received USD 22.1 billion of FDI. Pakistan received only USD 2.75 billion of FDI because of instabilities in the country that hurt the investment environment.

1.2   Correlation and Necessity of Economic Cooperation between Emerging Market Economies

Emerging market countries were exposed to advanced means of production after the capitalist system was established. However, as colonies and semi-colonies in the early 20th century, their industrial development was crippled by their suzerain states and they only served as origins of raw materials and destinations of the dumping of goods. The many countries in Asia, Africa, and Latin America that gained independence after the two world wars have seen slow economic development due to historical and other factors. The similar historical experience makes it natural and necessary for emerging market countries to engage in economic cooperation with each other.

1.2.1   Promoting Emerging Market Countries' Development

First, it is important to carry out economic cooperation to increase funding for infrastructure development, strengthening the weak link of emerging market countries in pursuing development. This is because infrastructure is a common challenge for emerging market countries, including BRICS countries, in developing the economy and society. Eyeing for rapid development but constrained by a lack of financial resources, these countries have seen serious consequences. For example, massive power shortages in India reduce India's annual output by 6. 6% . This is mainly because of under investment. It is far from enough for only a few international development institutions, such as the World Bank and the Asian Development Bank, to meet the demand. BRICS countries are in urgent need of large-scale investment to improve infrastructure. The newly established BRICS New Development Bank (NDB) and the Asian Infrastructure Investment Bank (AIIB) will become important sources of funding for infrastructure investment in developing countries and offer more chances for funding providers to increase returns on investment.

Second, economic cooperation can facilitate trade and commerce. Commercial activities between countries, including trade and investment, production, stocking, purchase of transport equipment, developing export bases, and brand building all require financial services and support, such as investment, financing, and insurance. Economic cooperation between emerging market countries not only provides more channels for investment, financing, and economic assistance, but also supports their expansion in overseas markets, such as mergers and acquisitions, technology upgrading, and carrying out programs in energy, resources and intellectual property, thereby facilitating trade.

Third, economic cooperation will help emerging market countries to upgrade industrial structure and realize innovative development. Emerging market countries generally stand on the lower end of industrial chains; their industrial structure is not well-developed, innovation lagging behind, and sustainable development faced with serious challenges. To realize sustainable development, economic support is urgently needed to cultivate and develop high and new tech industry, low-carbon industry, green industry, modern manufacturing, and advanced services. Emerging market countries can carry out bilateral and multilateral programs to establish a sustainable development system conducive to green investment.

1. 2. 2   Supporting Financial System Reform and Policy Innovation in Emerging Market Countries

International economic cooperation requires its participants to coordinate economic policies and monitoring mechanisms. By taking part in economic cooperation, emerging market countries will be encouraged to reform their economic system and coordinate their policies. Multilateral economic cooperation will be difficult if there are no similar systems, mechanisms, and policies surrounding the economy. Take the BRICS countries for example. Their credit and insurance policies and governance structure and mechanisms are very much different from one another. The international financial institutions jointly established by the five countries and the need to coordinate their international financial policies will undoubtedly pose challenges for their capacity to coordinate their financial systems and policies. This will push them to strengthen the coordination of the management systems and policies. Financial cooperation will enable the reform of the financial management system and adjustment of financial and monetary policies, thereby improving the economic system and management mechanism in BRICS countries.

1.2.3 Accelerating the Integration of Emerging Market Countries into the Global Value Chain

Import and export have a substantial role in driving the economic growth of emerging market countries, as they are increasingly integrated into the global value chain. On the one hand, these countries, mostly populous with a young population, enjoy a huge and promising domestic market that has a strong demand for import; and on the other hand, with a sufficient labor supply and rich natural resources, they are competitive in producing labor-intensive and resource-intensive products, the export of which have been growing fast. As later comers in industrialization, they also have the particular strength to formulate open policies to access funding and technology to spur economic growth.

Emerging market countries can integrate into the global value chain faster and better by strengthening economic cooperation. For example, China, now at the center of the global value chain, imports production materials from developing countries down the value chain that are rich in natural resources, and draws on the funding and technology of developed countries up the chain to grow into a strong manufacturing country with a well-developed industrial system. Therefore, emerging market countries are well-advised to draw on funding, technology, and natural resources of each other, and take economic globalization as an opportunity to accelerate their integration into the global value chain.

1. 2. 4   Helping Emerging Market Economies against Political and Economic Risks

Emerging market countries generally export more than they import and foreign trade plays a big role in the overall economy; therefore, they rely much on economic globalization. Economic cooperation between themselves can effectively increase their capacity to negotiate with developed countries, make international rules more reasonable, and fend off external political risks. For instance, when faced with unjustified economic sanctions, emerging market countries can join forces to enhance their bargaining power, gain a favorable position in negotiation, and voice support for any emerging market country that is unfairly targeted. In addition, when trade protectionist measures hit, emerging market countries can rely on the enormous domestic markets of their counterparts. They can also look within the group for alternate products to replace import and fight back against trade sanctions. In March 2018, the US decided to levy 25% and 10% tariffs on steel and aluminum import, triggering a trade war that have implications for the whole world. The US tariffs target not only developed partners like the EU and Canada, but also emerging market countries, such as China, Russia, and Mexico. To counter these sanctions, emerging market countries took similar steps. Mexico enacted retaliatory tariffs on US steel, pork, and apples; Russia imposed tariffs on US equipment for road construction; and China declared 25% tariffs on products of US origin.

1. 3   Looking into BRICS Practical Cooperation in the Next Golden Decade

It has been a little over a decade since the inception of BRICS. Over the period, BRICS withstood the test of the international financial crisis and blazed a new trial for emerging market countries and developing countries to work together for win-win results. BRICS cooperation has been fruitful and demonstrated great potential for an even better future. President Xi Jinping noted the BRICS spirit enriched over the 10 years of cooperation would become an inexhaustible source of strength driving BRICS cooperation. In the context of global development, BRICS cooperation will stay abreast of the times and keep innovating, moving further and deeper.

1.3.1 Creating a New Platform for South-South Cooperation

South-South cooperation is an important channel for developing countries to cooperate with one another and pursue progress through their own efforts. It is also an effective means for them to get involved and integrated into the world economy, playing an important role in the emergence of developing countries and the robust, sustained, balanced, and inclusive growth of the world economy. BRICS cooperation is one of the important platforms of South-South cooperation. After years of exploration and practice, it has blazed a new trial for emerging market countries and developing countries to work with one another for win-win results. At the 2017 BRICS Summit in Xiamen, Chinese President Xi Jinping proposed the 'BRICS +' approach to deepen cooperation under the Belt and Road Initiative, and increase the contact, interactions, dialogue and cooperation between BRICS and other emerging market countries and developing countries, so as to better uphold the common position and collective will of the developing world.

Going forward, BRICS cooperation will have a broader view and more open model. BRICS cooperation should be allowed to play its role within the frameworks of South-South cooperation and the Belt and Road Initiative. In addition to their own fast growth, BRICS countries need to encourage and support more emerging market countries that are representative of the group and enjoy a bright prospect to get involved in BRICS cooperation. A more extensive partnership like this will promote the balanced growth of the world economy.

1.3.2 Further Expand BRICS Trade Cooperation

Trade is an important area of BRICS cooperation. BRICS countries have made remarkable progress in this area. In 2017, international trade between

BRICS countries reached USD 3. 2 trillion, accounting for 15% of global trade and making the group an increasingly important player in trade. With the continued transformation of BRICS economies, their foreign trade will continue to rise steadily. At present, trade within the BRICS group is mainly held back by a lack of well-developed institutions. This deep-rooted challenge should be tackled by the collective efforts of BRICS countries.

First, BRICS countries need to stay committed to openness. Currently, BRICS countries lag behind the world average in terms of their trade and investment facilitation and still suffer from many trade barriers that threaten goods and services import. They need to further open up their economies, and facilitate the flow of financial resources. Second, BRICS countries must engage in FTA negotiations. Free trade is the dominating trend in the global economy and, despite the current headwind, will remain the trend in world economic development. In addition, BRICS countries should be encouraged to carry out bilateral FTA negotiations. China has gained rich experience in building bilateral FTAs through its negotiations with ASEAN, Switzerland, Singapore, Pakistan, and Australia. This wealth of experience can be used to produce a demonstration effect for BRICS cooperation. And third, BRICS countries need to promote greater ease in customs clearance. In order to do this, they should reform the customs control system, streamline procedures, and work together to harmonize their customs clearance methods. The customs authorities in these countries need to cooperate in information exchange, mutual recognition of controls, and law enforcement assistance. They should also innovate customs control methods to support the development of new forms of economy and trade within the group.

1. 3. 3   Deepen BRICS Financial Cooperation

With challenges looming over world economic development and the reform of the global economic governance, BRICS countries will intensify their internal reforms and cooperation to produce impetus for growth, transform the growth model, and increase their participation in the reform of the global economic and financial governance. Financial cooperation, as a crucial means for promoting domestic development and foreign cooperation, has been drawing close attention in recent years. Hard efforts have already paid off in this field, producing an extensive and profound impact. However, financial cooperation covers broad areas and can be very complicated. It is also influenced by the different political, economic, and diplomatic policies of BRICS countries and the sensitivities of different interests. BRICS countries need to be clear-headed and find out the common denominator in such cooperation to maximize the convergence of interests. They would also need to show political wisdom to promote effective cooperation. To deepen the reform of their own financial and economic systems to adapt to the needs of financial cooperation, they need to both coordinate policies and learn from each other's experience. With a similar vision for development and cooperation, reform of the financial system, innovation of the financial policy, and stronger capabilities in financial management innovation, BRICS countries have a strong foundation for deepening financial cooperation and thereby support their practical cooperation, economic transformation and sustained development.

1. 3. 4 Expanding People-to-People and Cultural Cooperation

People-to-people exchange and cultural cooperation is an important part of BRICS cooperation and a crucial pathway for deepening the BRICS partnership. This area has kept expanding in breadth and depth.

Following a top-down approach, programs in this area are identified after a macro framework is put in place and subjects are determined. Three pairs of relationships are particularly important in promoting this field of work. First, the relationship between the various bilateral cultural programs within the BRICS group; second, the relationship between the other multilateral cultural programs within the BRICS group; and third, the relationship between the BRICS group and other multilateral cultural programs. Good relations in these three aspects will facilitate the healthy development and good results of BRICS cultural cooperation and help consolidate and deepen BRICS partnership.

1.4　Investment and Financing Cooperation Is an Important Foundation of Deepening BRICS Cooperation

1.4.1　Strong Potential in BRICS Investment and Financing Cooperation

With the deepening of trade cooperation, the potential for investment cooperation is revealing itself. Between 2006 and 2017, BRICS investment and financing cooperation has been on a growing trend. In 2011, the inflow of FDI reached a 12-year high of USD 297.44 billion, taking up 19% of the world economy. In 2014, it was a record high of 21.2% of the world's total, and the FDI outflow was USD 209.01 billion or 15.9% of the world's total, both figures record highs.

Drawing on the complementarity of their strengths, BRICS countries have seen their Investment and financing cooperation growing fast and demonstrating great potential. Between Russia and India, the two-way investment mainly focuses on oil resources and agriculture; between India and Brazil, there is a good momentum in the mining industry and enormous potential in agriculture and manufacturing; India is engaged in investment cooperation with South Africa and exploring the African market, tapping on its strength in information technologies and the service industry; and South Africa, a center on the African continent, is proving an attractive destination for BRICS investment and for multinational corporations that are trying to gain from the country's strategic position in the region. China's direct investment to other BRICS countries each year increases by over USD 2 billion, equaling the total stock of such investment before 2006.

Mutual investment between BRICS countries may not be a tremendous figure now, but it is growing steadily. In recent years, multinational companies of the five countries are more likely to invest within the group. An increasing number of Indian and Chinese companies are investing or planning to invest in other BRICS countries. For example, China's BAIC Group invested in an assembly plant worth USD 823 million in South Africa, producing vehicles for the country and the regional market. China's CRRC invested USD 63 million in India to produce railway transport equipment; China's Huawei is planning to establish a smart phone factory in India. Other Chinese companies like Alibaba, Xiaomi, and DiDi also invested in India in 2015 and 2016. According to World Investment Report 2017, the mergers and acquisitions within BRICS surged from USD 3 billion in 2015 to USD 22 billion in 2016 (Fig. 1. 39).

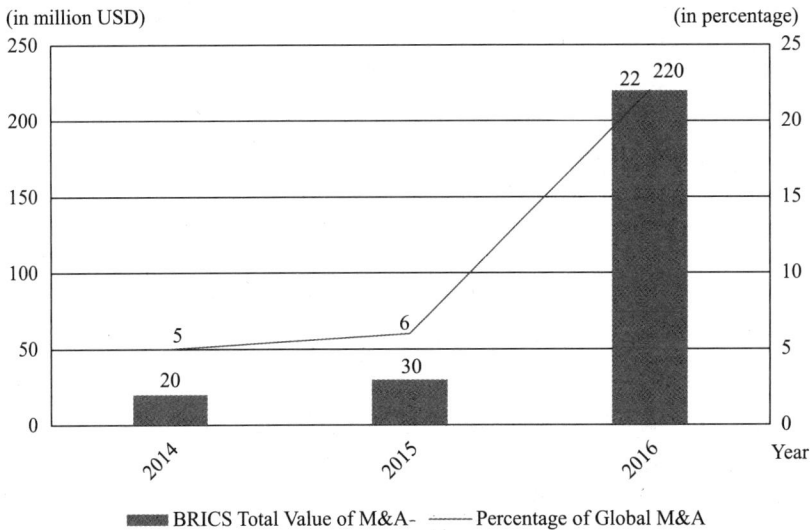

BRICS Total Value of M&A- ------ Percentage of Global M&A

Figure 1. 39 2014 – 2016 Cross-border M&A Within BRICS Countries and Its Share in the World's Total (in million USD, percentage)

Source: World Investment Report 2017

1. 4. 2 New Development Bank and Contingent Reserve Arrangement: a Crucial Platform for Investment and Financing Cooperation

The BRICS New Development Bank[1] and Contingent Reserve Arrangement[2] marks a new stage in BRICS investment and financing cooperation. Developing

---

① See details in Appendix: *Case 1: New Development Bank.*
② See details in Appendix: *Case 2: The BRICS Contingent Reserve Arrangement.*

countries have an urgent need to improve infrastructure. The World Bank put the gap in infrastructure financing in the developing world at USD one trillion, but only 40% can be covered by conventional multilateral development institutions like the World Bank. As a complement to the existing multinational and regional financial institutions, the new development bank aims to provide funding for infrastructure and sustainable development programs in BRICS countries, other emerging markets, and developing countries. In 2014, during the sixth BRICS Summit in Fortaleza, the agreement on the NDB was signed, marking the birth of the first ever international multinational development bank initiated and led by emerging market countries. Its legal capital is USD 100 billion, with an initial subscribed capital of USD 50 billion equally shared among founding members. The headquarters are in Shanghai.

While the NDB focuses on long-term investment, the CRA is created mainly for handling international short-term liquidity pressure, enhancing financial stability, complementing the current international foreign exchange reserve arrangements, and consolidating the global financial safety net. At the G20 Summit in St. Petersburg in September 2013, BRICS leaders agreed on an initial size of USD 100 billion for the arrangement and the funding proportions of the member states, with China being the largest contributor of USD 41 billion, Brazil, Russia, and India each contributing USD 18 billion, and South Africa USD 5 billion. The agreement was later signed during the sixth BRICS Summit in Fortaleza.

The NDB and the CRA is a completely new model of South-South cooperation. It provides all-round support for economic development in developing countries, offers a new way for developing countries to participate in global governance, and well complements the existing international financial system. They set up a good example for investment and financing cooperation between countries and constitute an important platform for growing and deepening BRICS investment and financing cooperation and South-South cooperation.

1.4.3 Investment and Financing Cooperation Deepening and Growing BRICS Cooperation

In the age of economic and financial globalization, investment and financing cooperation plays an increasingly important role in driving socioeconomic development. BRICS countries are also turning to this cooperation to promote domestic economic development and participate in international economic and financial cooperation and governance. Their cooperation in this area is expanding and deepening with the progress of the overall BRICS cooperation. It also elevates BRICS cooperation to a new level by building consensus and institutional foundation for BRICS cooperation.

First, investment and financing cooperation deepens consensus. In order to deepen the cooperation, BRICS countries have been building consensus and trust and increasing coordination and interactions in their financial development strategies, institutional innovations, policies for domestic and foreign cooperation, and the efforts to facilitate the development of a new international order, etc..

Second, it supports BRICS' coordination of institutional reform and policy interactions. To deepen BRICS cooperation, collective efforts should be made in institutional reforms in light of the needs of financial and investment cooperation. Such reforms include financial liberalization, flexibility in exchange rate management, improving financial services, speeding up the internationalization of BRICS currencies, lifting restrictions on the cross-border flow under the capital account, opening up the interbank trading of BRICS currencies, encouraging banks to provide loans of overseas program, and increasing the cooperation between the customs and taxation authorities and other government agencies. All of this serves as institutional guarantee for investment and financing cooperation within BRICS.

Chapter II   Goals and Practices of Investment and Financing Cooperation among BRICS Countries

2. 1   Improve Global Financial Governance

2. 1. 1   Overview of Global Financial Governance

Global financial governance is the process where market players such as the governments, international organizations, non-governmental organizations, and multinational companies, by means of coordination, collaboration and reach a consensus, participate in the management of global finance matters, prevent and mitigate systemic financial risks, safeguard economic and financial stability, and establish or maintain sound international financial orders. In a word, global financial governance sets to achieve 'concerted coordination for profits and against loss' in the global financial arena.

It is required by a community of shared future for mankind to enhance the global financial governance, which facilitates formation of new international relations, and a global governance system that is fair and reasonable. It is necessary that we promote and implement global financial governance. First, in the 21st century, the financial markets have been increasingly globalized and liberalized, as evidenced by new financial products, innovative trading methods, interconnected financial markets with enhanced inter-reliance, and greater cross-border assets and liabilities, hence the increasing uncertainties. Given this, it is beyond the capacity of a single state to have comprehensive knowledge or controls over the international banks or investment companies for proper regulation. Second, the existing financial system has substantial limitations as the system has been constructed around the Western-led economic growth and no longer meets the needs of a world with shifted economic growth centers. For example, the IMF, World Bank, and other international financial organizations do not, or do not have the fully capacity to, properly coordinate among the financial markets. The dollar standard system that is free from any restrictions, and inconsistent US macro-economic policies are prone to trigger frequent global financial crisis. Subject to the implications of US domestic monetary policies on foreign exchange reserve, countries are exposed to risks of foreign exchange reserve depreciation at all times. This has led to uncertainties within the international exchange rate system that allows the US to transfer risks of vulnerable exchange rates through currency issuance onto the creditors, but the creditors cannot do the same to the US. Without any doubt, it jeopardizes the interests of emerging countries, the BRICS nations in particular, through trade and investments. Third, the global regulators do not conduct necessary communications and coordination on financial regulation. A lack of such communications and coordination is seen among the national regulators, and even among the sectors within a single nation's regulatory system. And fourth, a multi-layered international trade system, regional investment cooperation mechanisms, and emerging financial rules and protocols have resulted in new issues and problems. It is necessary that all market players be properly engaged in global financial governance, in order to reduce external risks to the markets and to realize sound development of global financial systems.

2.1.2 Investment and Financing Cooperation among BRICS Helps Enhance Reform on Global Financial Governance

With the support of the New Development Bank and the investment and financing experiences of varied nations, the BRICS has been a new driving force in establishing financial cooperation mechanism and reshaping national financial orders. As important players in the international economic and political establishments, the BRICS is widely involved in effective allocation of global assets and optimization of financial regulatory approaches, and gradually expanding outbound investments in terms of geographies, asset types, and influences. The BRICS makes important contributions to the world economic recovery. Thanks to their elevated overall competency, the BRICS is committed to more obligations and responsibilities for improving global financial governance system, especially on countering trade protectionism, safeguarding financial security, maintaining and developing open economies, and balancing regional development and multilateral diplomacy.

Currently, many experts are optimistic about the global financial governance, with good prospects on the future of G20 and emerging economies, in particular the role that BRICS is playing in promoting the development of global financial governance through investment and financing cooperation. Shared interests among the BRICS lays solid foundation to the future of investment and financing cooperation. Vyacheslav Nikonov, head of the board of the National Committee for BRICS Studies, said that investment and financing cooperation helps stimulate economic potentials in the developing BRICS nations and other emerging economies, and enhances global financial governance. Patrick Khulekani Dlamini, CEO of Development Bank of South Africa, also believed that after the outbreak of the global financial crisis, the existing global financial system has failed to meet the development needs of the emerging markets, while investment and financing cooperation among the BRICS nations will help to address the challenges of insufficient liquidity, investment and financing, and indirectly, increase the bargaining power of the BRICS in international financial system talks, and encourage better global financial governance to the exiting one.

The BRICS are actively contributing to a global governance system through involvement in the Basel III talks, WTO agenda, G20 Summit, and Comprehensive Progressive Trans-Pacific Partnership (CPTPP) talks, World Bank and IMF quota and voting right reform, among other efforts, for enhancements to the existing global financial regulatory system.

2.2　Drive the Economic Restructuring Reform

2.2.1　BRICS Facing Arduous Tasks on Internal Restructuring

The political turmoil over the presidency and economic stagnation in Brazil has impeded the national economic reform. The future of the Brazilian economy is masked with uncertainties brought by political issues such as tension between the Brazilian parliament and congress, and continued cases on corruptions of oil companies. Additionally, the Brazilian economy is highly reliant on primary products, since the domestic manufacturing industry is stagnating or shrinking. The outdated infrastructure, for a long term, has been an impediment that holds the economy at bay. The Brazilian government, in order to address these issues, will maintain the tariffs on imported industrial products, and have activated some countering measures in the policies to create value added on the primary products export and to sponsor innovation.

The Russian resource-oriented economy should be further restructured. With over-reliance on the resources, the Russian economy has been hit with the continuous declining of energy prices worldwide, making it difficult to form free markets in a short term in Russia. The reliance on energy and crude material industries has been a malady lingering on the Russian economy. It is highly sensitive to the fluctuations of the external influences, especially the ups and downs of oil prices, which have direct impacts on the economy. It is a consensus of the Russian government and the academics that Russia should break away from the current status that it heavily relies on resources and crude materials, but devote itself to research and development of high techs, and realize innovation-driven growth of the economy.

India has a deeply-rooted dual structure problem. There have been drastic gaps between the rich and the poor as well as the persistent industrial disparities, where services industries generate over 50% of its GDP, and the manufacturing industries are much outdated. Besides, the disparities are also indicated by fast development of the Information Technology industry and the backward infrastructure. D. K. Joshi, Chief Economist of India's main rating and research institute, CRISIL, commented that the Indian economy has been mainly fueled by the services industry and consumptions from a previously agricultural economy since 2000. The services industries realized substantial growth during the economic take-off, but the manufacturing industries did not enjoy such significant improvements. As manufacturing is the most labor-intensive sector only after agriculture, India needs to revitalize the manufacturing industry to address severe unemployment issue.

In the case of China, it is facing difficulties with the supply-side structural reforms. Market-oriented reforms, in a number of key areas such as state-owned enterprise, fiscal finance, pricing mechanism, land ownership, and social security, have not made breakthroughs. The transformation on the means of economic development is delaying and the economic engine is short of vitality. In addition, the process on de-capacity, de-stocking, and de-leveraging, is relatively slower than expected. The need for innovative approaches is vital.

South Africa also has high external reliance which undermines its independence. The African economy is highly reliant on bulk commodities, minerals in particular, while its mining industry has been trapped by increasing costs and consumption of mining resource reserves. The South African government has implemented a new economic growth strategy focusing on comprehensive accelerating growth of mining, manufacturing, transportation, agriculture, tourism, green industries, financial services, and high-tech industries, and addressing the high unemployment rate as well as power shortage.

2.2.2　Concerted Efforts of BRICS to Safeguard Economic Globalization and Promote Economic Restructuring

As the world is seeing a growing trend of 'anti-globalization' and the trade protectionism is gaining ground, the BRICS needs to join hands in our efforts to safeguard free trade, and to drag the economies out of sag for shared growth and win-win outcomes.

The BRICS economies are transiting to an emerging growth mode, which should be supported by substantive economic restructuring, discovery of new growth points, higher productivity and potential growth rates as well as launch cooperation on investment and financing among the BRICS nations. The BRICS should formulate a sound cooperation mechanism, find a new engine to drive the global economic growth, seek consensus on trades, policies, and financial risks through effective communications, and further launch cooperation with the non-BRICS nations on the basis of established cooperation projects within BRICS.

The BRICS nations have fully recognized the role of technological innovation in driving the industry development, with strategic plans aiming to promote technological innovation and industrial upgrading. China has launched the *Outline of the National Strategy of Innovation-Driven Development*, activated the implementation of *Technological Innovation* 2030: *Key Projects*, and implemented the *New Generation Artificial Intelligence Development Plan* to support blooming entrepreneurship domestically. The key areas of technological innovation cover aerospace and defense, drinking water, food, biological communities and biological economy, social science and technology, climate, digital economy and society, energy, nuclear energy, and health. Russia has been implementing its *Development Strategy on Science and Technology* since December 2016 with focus on aeronautics and astronautics, oceans and poles, digital and smart manufacturing, robot manufacturing, energy-saving and environment-friendly economy with higher exploitation and deep-processing efficiency of hydrocarbon resources, tailored and precise health care that use anti-biotics and other drugs properly. India has publicized the *Science, Technology and Innovation Policy* 2013, and has rolled out the *Roadmap for Innovation 2010 – 2020*. South Africa also has launched the *Research Infrastructure Plan* in 2016, which outlines the nation's devotion to enhancing internet capacity building, establishing high-performance computing centers, formulating national strategy on astronomy, and developing key research infrastructures featuring big-scale scientific projects such as the SKA. The key areas covered in the planning include astronomy, information communications, new energy, new materials, and medical sciences.

The investment and financing projects among the BRICS nations help with the industrial transfer towards knowledge-based innovation activities with high value-added. The resource-based nations will develop domestic manufacturing capacities with the help of foreign investment, improve the domestic value-added, and transform to scaled economies from competitive edges in resources. The labor-intensive nations also benefit from the cooperation by improving the technical edges in the products, enhancing productivity and value-added capacity, thereby moving up the value chain with higher technical requirements.

2.3   Promote Infrastructure and Industrial Cooperation among the BRICS

2.3.1   Expedite Infrastructure Projects to Better Support Growth

At present, the emerging economies development which represented by the BRICS countries are constrained by the aging and inadequate infrastructure. More than half of India has no roads, and the rail system is severely underpowered. Although Russia has some basic railway and road facilities, its general facilities are old and do not match the needs of the new economy. Electric power facilities in South Africa are in urgent need of upgrading, and most of the country's roads are in poor condition. Brazil's transport infrastructure is also inadequate.

The IMF's World Economic Outlook report indicates that many developing countries are seriously underinvested in infrastructure. In early 2016, a report from Word Bank also points out that the emerging economy can absorb about USD 200 million infrastructures investment annually, half of which has not been met, and this gap will be enlarged further. According to the prediction, demand of infrastructure investment in emerging economies will double every year over the next decade. Government budgets are the biggest source of funding for infrastructure in emerging economies, which almost account for 75% of total investment.

At present, neither these countries nor international financial organizations can provide adequate funds. Domestically, Brazil, South Africa and India have large current account deficits, and their domestic savings are insufficient to meet the needs of infrastructure investment. Since the domestic saving-investment transformation mechanism is inadequate, capital marketing and other long-term financing are less developed, foreign exchange reserves cannot be directly used in domestic investment etc., China and Russia still exist large financing gap although the current account of China and Russia present surplus status. From the external financing perspective: the total amount of the credit and loan from the International Bank for Reconstruction and Development (IBRD) and the International Development Association (IDA) to the BRICS reached USD 71.72 billion from 2008 to 2012, of which only USD 650 million to Russia's credit. In 2016, the BRICS used only USD 41.93 billion in IMF credit. Brazil's use of IMF credit is only USD 3.88 billion. Multilateral international development institutions supply tens of billions of dollars, however, it is still a small amount of money and cannot meet the needs of emerging economies investment and the BRICS trillion-dollar infrastructure. Thus, the innovative financing channels need BRICS to explore, and BRICS needs to promote development via diverse, flexible and extensive investment and financing cooperation.

Most developing countries are in the stage of fast industrialization and urbanization, which have a high demand on infrastructure building. The tighter cooperation among BRICS can provide more funding for infrastructure building, also facilitate all market factors to join the market, which can further stimulate the economic development.

2.3.2 Expand Industrial Cooperation to Capitalize on the Advantages for Upgraded Growth

In terms of industrial cooperation, the BRICS, a group of major emerging economies, which share common interests and basis and conditions for economic cooperation. The rise and synergy of BRICS nations will generate the 'Power State Effects' to stimulate economic growth. The substantive potential in markets driven by domestic demands will be utilized for greater scale of economy, further segmented industrial divisions, and faster economic growth.

The BRICS nations have remarkable resources advantages and complementary economic structures, which constitute good basis for cooperation. For example, China and Russia often have current account surpluses, meaning net capital outflows, while India and Russia often have current account deficits, meaning needs for foreign capital inflows. In the meantime, Russia and Brazil are energy resource suppliers, and China and India are energy users heavily reliant on import. In the agriculture sector, China and India are world's most populous countries with huge demands for agricultural products, while Russia and Brazil are two main agricultural producers that have great supply capacity and potential productivity in the agricultural sector. In the infrastructure sector, China tops the world in infrastructure building and technology. It is able to provide the other BRICS nations with services in engineering contracting, construction, operation and equipment supply. In addition, the BRICS has developed their own comparative edges in advantageous sectors and industries, such as India's radio transmission and software development, South Africa's delivery equipment and mining technologies, Brazil's agriculture and regional airliner, Russia's military technology, and China's manufacturing and Internet technologies. On this basis, the BRICS nations are highly complementary in terms of economic and trade structures which should be utilized for shared growth. At the same time, the cooperation will further enhance the industrial edges for formation of complementary industrial systems.

In addition to complementary cooperation, the BRICS can also be engaged in the research and development of high techs with the help of investment and financing projects in the international front fields, such as renewable energy, new material, biological medicine, information technology, and smart manufacturing. Through these efforts, the BRICS sets to enhance the capacities, achieves upgraded growth, then breaks the confinement of development bottleneck in high tech areas, and drive high-end restructuring of domestic industries.

In the past decade, the BRICS has expanded cooperation in investment and financing, explored new cooperation model and mechanisms, improved infrastructures, and made efforts to facilitate trades and other industrial cooperation. China Development Bank has been involved in key projects to support infrastructure building in BRICS through direct funding for South Africa's state-owned railway company Transnet to purchase trains from

CRRC, CNR, and CSR①, through joint investment and financing on China Three Gorges' purchase of Brazilian hydro-power projects②, and through issuing local currency letter of guarantee on China State Grid's bidding on Belo Monte power transmission project in Brazil③. These projects have successfully promoted innovation on investment and financing models, which reduced financing costs for the companies, and created social economic benefits while speeded up the infrastructure building in the BRICS nations.

2.4 Deepen Trade among the BRICS

2.4.1 Trade Overview

a. Trade in Goods on an Upward Trend

According to the UNCTADstat, trade among the BRICS nations has been on a fast trajectory for the period between 2006 and 2016. The total imports and exports of 2016 increased by 94 and 84 percentage points over those of 2006. Overall, the goods trade was on overall rapid growing rate for the period from 2006 to 2011, which then slumped due to the global financial crisis in 2009. During the period from 2011 to 2016, the trade growth slowed down, with drastic declines in 2015 and 2016 caused by policy and trade environment changes (Fig. 2.1). In terms of overall trade balance, all the BRICS nations have trade surplus where exports exceed imports.

b. Deficits of Trade in Services

Trade in services share similar trends with trade in goods where significant growth was witnessed during 2006 to 2014 at rates of 179 and 103 percentage points each. In 2015, there was a moderate decline at 5%. And the decline

---

① See details in Appendix: *Case 3: South Africa's Transnet SOC Ltd and China Development Bank's Joint Project.*

② See details in Appendix: *Case 4: Support China Three Gorges Corporation's Acquisition of Brazilian Hydropower Station Project with Investmint and Loans.*

③ See details in Appendix: *Case 5: Innovative Local Currency Letter of Guarantee Supports State Grid's successful Bidding for the Belo Monfe Hydropower UHV Transmission Project in Brazil.*

(in million USD)

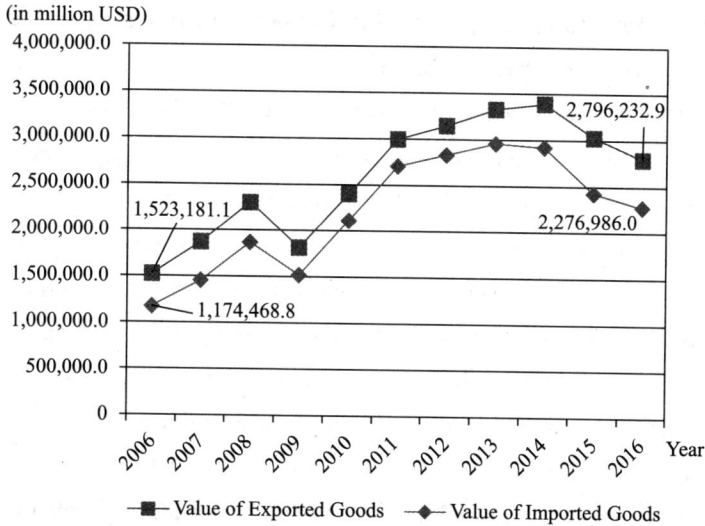

Figure 2.1   Trade in Goods in BRICS Countries (2006 – 2016) (in million USD)

Source: UNCTADstat

continued in 2016. Overall, trade in services is increasingly leaning toward higher imports than exports. In 2016, the trade deficit was as high as USD 271. 31 billion (Fig. 2. 2).

(in million USD)

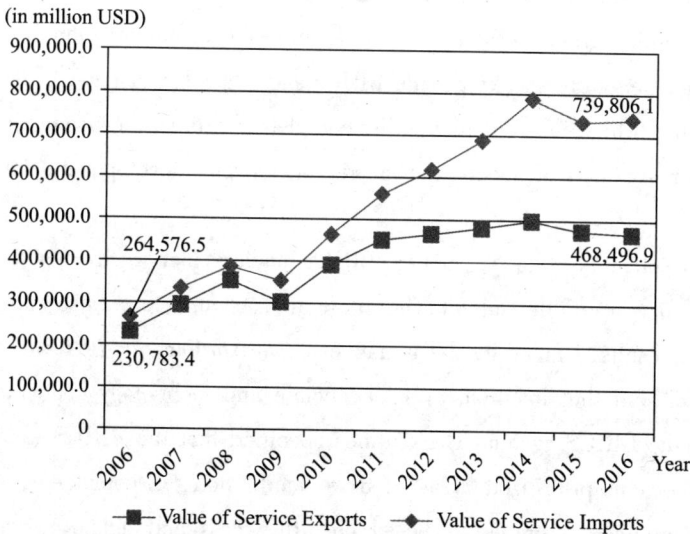

Figure 2.2   Trade in Services in BRICS Nations (2006 – 2016) (in Million USD)

Source: UNCTADstat

2.4.2 Investment and Financing Cooperation Helps Reduce Reliance on Non – BRICS Nations

The BRICS Trade and Investment Cooperation Framework, which was issued in March 2013, proposed new principle, concepts, models and mechanisms for enhancing BRICS cooperation. Based on the ministerial meetings, it sets to implement the BRICS cooperation. However, though with strong guidance and promotion from the governments, the corporate and communities are not much involved. The trade investment cooperation framework on the national level failed to benefit the companies and individuals. As a result, for so many years after, the cooperation mechanism has been on a slow progress that cannot meet the actual economic demands for the BRICS.

The BRICS nations are well aware of these issues and are devoted to finding proper solutions. Ministerial meeting mechanism, including for finance ministers and central bank governors, deputies for finance ministers and central bank governors, heads of intellectual property office, ministers of energy, ministers of agriculture and ministers of environment, has been established. Regular business forums and other supportive events are held. The BRICS has set up trade and investment liaison working group, E-commerce working group, and customs working group to facilitate coordination and communications throughout the system. Generally speaking, the BRICS has placed a dispersed cooperation mechanism, which is supplemented by complete coordination systems in certain specific areas, and it meets the needs of current development among the BRICS.

On September 3 to 5, 2017, BRICS leaders met in Xiamen of Fujian Province for the ninth summit. The trade and commerce ministerial meeting reached 8 results, including the issuance of *The Outlines for BRICS Investment Facilitation*. For the first time ever, economic and technology cooperation was listed on the BRICS agenda. The outlines specified that the BRICS would build on capacities in prioritized areas of trade facilitation, E-commerce, trade in service, intellectual property, based on willingness and actual needs of the member states, shared the economic development modes and cooperation concepts among the BRICS, which promoted economic development and technological advances, and collectively executed the UN 2030 Agenda for Sustainable Development.

In line with the spirit of the Xiamen Summit, the BRICS should advocate interconnected financial services for better development of trades and businesses. To be specific, the BRICS should capitalize on the opportunities in financial markets, improve and utilize the exiting financial collaboration mechanism continuously, and advocate good interactions among the market players, infrastructure suppliers, and regulators.

2.5   Facilitate the Emerging Economies towards Standardized Investment and Financing Activities

2.5.1   Restrictions on the Existing International Investment and Financing Rules

After the 2008 international financial crisis, the developed nations have turned to the real economy for maintaining and creating jobs. Their industrial transfer has slowed down, coupled with back-flow of funding of multi-national companies. At the same time, the companies that had survived the financial crisis had restructured. As a result, the investments, instead of being made on developing countries, are increasingly flowing among the developed nations. Against the backdrop of international financial crisis, the investment policies among nations have demonstrated two popular tendencies, which towards both 'free investment' and 'investment protectionism' in parallel, with trade protectionism gaining more ground. Investment protectionism will severely disrupt the world economies, especially the emerging economies.

As of now, the global investment rules are still 'fragmented', which are dispersed and inconsistent. There is not yet a comprehensive multi-lateral mechanism, or an efficient international organization. To some extent, all BRICS nations are subject to the restrictions of global investment and financing cooperation rules in their efforts for economic upgrade.

2.5.2 Explore New Models on Investment and Financing Cooperation

As advocates for better international financial orders, the BRICS should enhance cooperation in the sectors of investment and financing to accumulate experiences, and take the leading role in establishing standards for global investment and financing cooperation. The standardization that suits emerging economies will contribute to free investment, investment facilitation, exploration of investment regulation, safeguarding the interests of investors and hosts, and unleashing economic vitality of the BRICS.

It will also benefit the emerging economies by sorting out the approach to protect investors' interest and rights, resolve market entry issue, create investor-friendly environment, balance interests between the host and investor, as well as propose cooperation rules within the BRICS cooperation framework. These will help the BRICS develop their economies, gain a bigger say in the formulation of future global multi-lateral investment rules, and provide guidance and references for other emerging economies. Additionally, the BRICS has started to work on knowledge sharing and formation of new mechanisms on national investment and financing cooperation. The BRICS attaches great importance to enhancing cooperation with global think tanks, expanding their own think-tank capacities, focusing on prioritized research tasks, hosting international forums, and providing demonstrative project consultancy for the purpose of sharing knowledge and best practices that will facilitate policy communications and joint efforts on strategy execution among varied parties.

Chapter III   Key Areas and Industries of Investment and Financing Cooperation among BRICS

3.1   Brazil

3.1.1   Development Plan

Under the administration of Michel Temer, Brazil has launched the *Investment Partnership Program* to implement the 'Advance Plan' of Brazil, which sets to fill in the gap from the PAC program and Logistics Investment Program implemented by the Workers' Party, in an effort to increase investment on the Brazilian infrastructure and to drive the growth in weaker areas.

On September 13, 2016, the Brazilian government hosted the first committee meeting under the 'Investment Partnership Program'. The meeting announced a list of 34 franchise projects on airport, port, railway, and highway, which were open for bidding in 2017. Through offering these opportunities, the Brazilian government aims to drag the economy out of the sag, increase jobs, decentralize the authority of the central governments, and provide incentives for the private sector's involvement.

The Brazilian Agency of Telecommunications, in May of 2016, announced the 'Smart Brazil' National Broadband Plan which targets investment of 1.85 billion Real (equivalent to about USD 529 million). The program will increase the access to fiber optic network by cities and townships from 53% to 70%, and reach 95% of the Brazilian population with broadband networks.

According to the plan, multiple large-scale network infrastructure projects have been initiated, including network building in the Amazon area, and launching of a defense and communications geostationary satellite in 2017. The Agency of Telecommunications also announced the projects on laying 6 submarine optical fiber cables to connect Brazil with Europe, Africa and America for better data transaction capacity and communication security, as well as reduction of internet access costs by 20%. The government is also committed to helping small suppliers accessing the credit loans from banks through credit guarantee funds for their participation in network projects in medium and small cities. In the future, houses constructed under the resident housing program 'My House My Life' will have access to broadband networks. Over 30000 public schools in urban and rural areas all across Brazil will be equipped with broadband access, wireless access, and the multi-media centers.

3.1.2 Key Industries

a. Agriculture, Forestry and Husbandry

Brazil enjoys rich land resources, prime climate conditions, and arable area of 153 million hectares, which covers 18% of the national land area. Agriculture is an important sector in the Brazilian economy, with an output equivalent to 21% of the GDP. Brazil is also a major exporter of agricultural products, accounting for almost 50% of the total export. It is a pillar industry of Brazil of the national economy. Brazil is the world's largest producer and the second largest exporter of soy beans. It is also the largest producer and second largest exporter of corn. By amount of export, Brazil tops the world on cane sugar, coffee, orange juice, tobacco, and alcohol.

b. Oil and Gas

Brazil has been engaged in the exploration and production of oil and gas since the 1950s. The oil and gas industries generate 12% of the GDP. As far as the planning for oil and energy industries are concerned, according to OPEC's research, by 2020, Brazil's oil reserve will rank the 8th world-wide from the current ranking of the 15th. According to ANP, by 2035, Brazil's oil and gas production will rank the 6th from the current ranking of the 9th. The increased reserves will further drive up Brazil's oil export.

c. Automobile

The automobile industry creates about 40% of the gross industrial output value, and has grown to be a pillar industry of Brazil, which is playing an important role in fueling economic growth in Brazil. Now, all major automobile brands have set up facilities in Brazil, including Daimler (German), Volkswagen (German), Ford (US), GM (US), Peugeot (French), Renault (French) and Land Rover (U. K.).

d. Textile

Brazil is an important manufacturer of textile and garments, as the world's fifth largest textile producer and fourth largest garment maker. Over 33, 000 textile companies in Brazil make over 6. 8 billion pieces of clothing annually. As the fourth largest textile exporter in the world, Brazil is home to many world-class textile and clothing companies.

e. Services

The service industry carries a big weight in Brazil. It has the highest output among all industries in Brazil, and offers the most jobs. The service industry covers real estate, leasing, tourism, financial services, insurance, information, advertising, consultancy, and technology services. Brazil attracts a great number of tourists from Latin America, Europe and America with a tourism industry dated back to over 80 years ago. According to the Travel & Tourism Competitiveness Index 2016, Brazil ranks the 27th among 136 nations globally. It leads the world on natural resources, and ranks the 8th on culture. But in terms of infrastructure and tourism pricing, there is room for improvement. In 2016, Brazil received over 6. 6 million foreign visitors, which generated income of USD 6. 024 billion for the nation, up by 6. 2% over 2015.

3.1.3   Foreign Investment

In 2017, Brazil attracted foreign direct investment (FDI) of USD 70. 3 billion, 10. 1% lower than 2016. During 2009 – 2011, Brazil' FDI continued to increase and peaked at USD 96. 152 billion in 2011. However, since 2014, FDI in Brazil has trended downwards due to weakened consumer confidence, rattled investor confidence and stagnated economy led by persisting high inflation, high stocking in key industrial sectors, weak bulk commodity prices, deteriorating unemployment, and political turmoil.

In 2017, the top 10 countries (regions) as sources of direct investment in Brazil were the U. S. , the Netherlands, the British Virgin Islands (BVI), Luxemburg, Germany, France, Spain, Chile, Mexico, and Italy, each contributing 18. 36%, 18. 05%, 15. 03%, 7. 13%, 5. 34%, 5. 25%, 3. 83%, 2. 69%, 2. 53%, and 2. 52% of the total direct investment in Brazil (Table 3. 1). In the meantime, for the period of 2008 to 2017, the top 10 countries (regions) as sources of investment on an accumulative basis were the Netherlands, the U. S. , Luxemburg, Spain, Japan, France, Switzerland, the U. K. , Germany, and the BVI, each with contribution at 18. 60%, 15. 15%, 9. 89%, 7. 55%, 5. 29%, 5. 02%, 3. 88%, 3. 29%, 3. 19% and 3. 17% of the total investment. The developed nations constitute the main source of foreign investment in Brazil, mainly targeting rich mining resources in the nation.

Table 3. 1   Top 20 Countries/Regions as Source of Accumulative Direct Investment in 2017

No.	Country/Region	Value of Investment (USD 100 million)	No.	Country/Region	Value of Investment (USD 100 million)
1	The U. S.	110. 78	11	Switzerland	12. 88
2	The Netherlands	108. 94	12	The U. K.	11. 71
3	The BVI	90. 69	13	Hong Kong	11. 23
4	Luxemburg	43. 05	14	Bahamas	11. 22
5	Germany	32. 21	15	Norway	9. 39
6	France	31. 68	16	China	6. 43
7	Spain	23. 09	17	Japan	5. 37
8	Chile	16. 20	18	Cayman Islands	4. 69
9	Mexico	15. 27	19	South Korea	4. 54
10	Italy	15. 21	20	Portugal	3. 18

Source: Central Bank of Brazil

Combine with Brazil economic and social development plan as well as its industrial structure, the FDI mainly focus on telecom, electricity, gas, real estate, finance, health care and so on, which facilitate the industrial upgrade from financing and technology. In 2017, the rank of 10 most popular sectors for FDI is electricity, natural gas, commerce, transportation, motor vehicles and relevant unit, petrol and natural gas exploitation, metallurgy, chemical industry, food and finance industry (Fig. 3. 1).

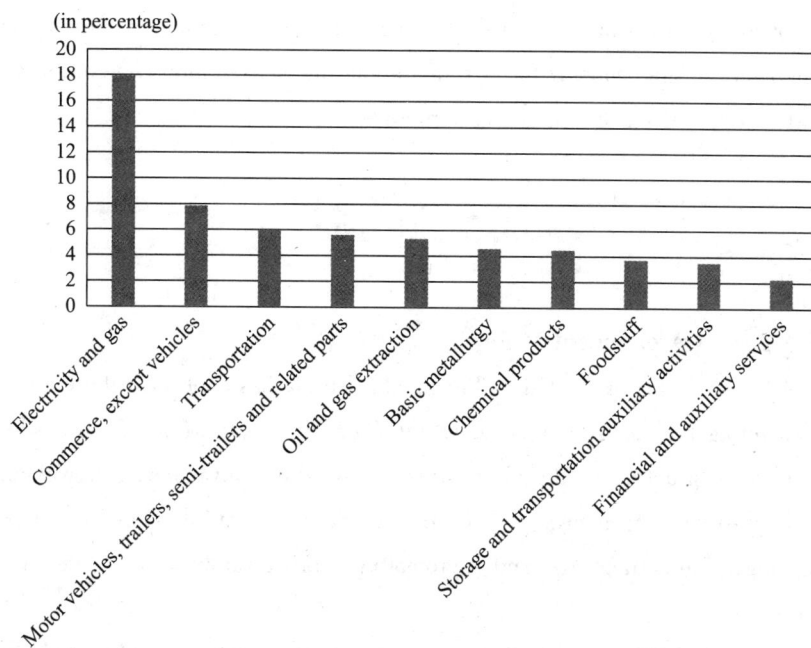

Figure 3. 1   Top 10 Industries for Foreign Investment in Brazil 2017 (in percentage)

Source: CEIC, Central Bank of Brazil

From 2008 to 2017, the top industries with the highest accumulative foreign investment is service industry, amount of USD 285. 06 billion, and account for 47. 96% of the accumulative FDI. In the meanwhile, the top 10 sectors attractive to foreign investors are, in order of proportions, electricity and natural gas, business (excluding automobiles), transportation, motor vehicles and related components, oil and gas mining, basic metallurgy, chemical product, food, storage and delivery, and financial services, accounted for 58. 74% of the total FDI.

Given the above, Brazil should further work to attract investments on the service sector with priorities placed on industries including trade (excluding automobiles), finance and auxiliary services, electricity and natural gas, oil and gas mining, metal mineral extraction, motor vehicle, trailer, semi-trailer and related component, chemical product, machinery and equipment, garment, and accessories. On one hand, Brazil can fully utilize the existing basis of foreign investments, on the other hand, it can promote comprehensive development of the economy through upgrading the weaker industries in terms of export and optimizing the industrial structure.

3. 2   Russia

3. 2. 1   Development Plan

After Putin was reelected as President, Russia has continued the efforts in implementing the *Long-term Development Plan for Russia Until 2020*, which prioritizes restructuring the industries, expanding investment, developing innovation-driven economy, expediting upgrading of traditional industries, improving infrastructure, and promoting privatization of state-owned enterprises.

In March 2018, President Putin, in his state of union address, said that the Russian economy will develop at a rate exceeding the world's average, and achieve an output per capita 1. 5 times of the current level by the medium term of the 2020s. In the next 6 years, the highway construction costs in Russia will increase by one-fold to RUR 11 trillion (equivalent to USD 200 billion), and an electricity industry upgrading program targets to pool RUR 1. 5 trillion (equivalent to USD 26 billion) from the private sector.

On May 7 of 2018, President Putin signed an Executive Order on National Goals and Strategic Objectives of the Russian Federation through to 2024, which specifies the goals by 2024 including cutting poverty in half; ensuring sustainable growth of real wages; ensuring the growth of pensions above inflation level; increasing life expectancy to 78 years; improving housing conditions for at least 5 million households annually; taking Russia into the top five largest economies; ensuring economic growth rates exceeding international rates, and maintaining macroeconomic stability, including inflation under 4 percent.

In terms of energy development, Russia issued the *Energy Strategy Plan Until 2035* in March 2015, which sets that by 2035, Russia will increase natural gas production from 805 billion to 880 billion cubic meters from current's 640 billion cubic meters, achieve annual oil production at 525 million tons, among which the oil production from the hard exploitation and continental shelf at 25% of the total oil production, with annual production at 130 million tons. Oil export will increase to 270 million tons from 220 million tons. In addition, the *Energy Strategy Plan until 2035* predicts growth of liquefied natural gas production by 5 times, coal production up to 435 million tons, growth of coal export by 20%, and growth of power needs by 15%, and total energy investment at USD 2.5 trillion.

The Russian government also decided to prioritize the allocations of fiscal funding in sectors including agriculture (including agricultural services), processing (including food processing), chemical, engineering, machinery manufacturing (aviation, ship, and automobiles), and housing construction. In addition, the priority investment projects also include the transportation industry, including air transportation (airport, air commerce, transport infrastructure), communications and telecommunications and the production and distribution of electricity, gas, water and other resources.

In February 2016, the Ministry of Industry and Trade issued the Agriculture Support Plan 2017. The plan sets to allocate funding of 140 billion RUR, among which 127.3 billion RUR is budget subsidies. As prioritized under the planning, some funds will be used to subsidize the poor families on buying Russia-made agricultural and sideline products. In July 2017, Russian Prime Minister Dmitry Medvedev signed the order on the *Strategy for the Development of Agricultural Machinery in Russia For the Period Until 2030*. According to the strategy, Russia targets to bring the indicator of the number of modern Russian agricultural machinery and equipment to at least 80% by 2030, at the same time, it is planned to increase the volume of supplies of modern Russian agricultural machinery abroad to 50% of domestic consumption. It is also estimated that the overall international sales will reach RUR 175 billion by 2021, 202 billion RUR by 2025, and 265 billion RUR by 2030.

3.2.2 Key Industries

a. Oil and Natural Gas

Oil and natural gas industry, for a long time, has played a central role in the Russian economy. The price of Urals oil is a key indicator of the national budget making. In 2016, Russia produced 550 million tons of oil (including condensate), up by 2.5% year-on-year. The crude oil processed was 285 billion tons, 1.3% lower year-on-year. The oil export was 255 million tons, up by 4.2% year-on-year. The natural gas output was 640 billion cubic meters, up by 0.7% year-on-year, while the gas export was at 198.7 billion cubic meters, up by 7% year-on-year.

b. Metallurgical Industry

Russia is abundant in mineral resources with world-leading reserves and production capacities of iron, aluminum, copper, and nickel. The mining and metallurgical industry is critical to the Russian economy. The metallurgical industry is a pillar industry, with an output that covers 2.8% of the GDP, and 10.2% of the industrial production. The metallurgical products are key export in Russia. From the earns of foreign exchange through export, the metallurgical industry generates 17% of the foreign exchanges, only next to fuels and energy complex.

c. National Defense

The defense industry in Russia builds on the legacies of the enormous defense system of the Soviet Union. Enjoying a complete system of design, research, development, experiment, and production, Russia is one of the few nations in world that has capacities for making maritime, land, air, and space arms and facilities. Given that the domestic needs for upgrading and refreshing the arms is limited, the defense industry in Russia has been seeking external cooperation, with an arms export over USD 15 billion in 2016. Military aircraft tops the list of arms exports, followed by naval vessels, army equipment and air defense weapons.

3.2.3 Foreign Investment

In 2017, foreign direct investment in Russia was USD 27.89 billion, which is down by 14.30% over 2016. Since 2014, the international sanctions on Russia for the conflicts in Ukraine and its overtake of the Crimea region, the plummeting prices of natural gas and oil, and depreciation of RUR etc., have caused an economic recession in Russia. The business environment is severely deteriorated, which is much less-appealing to the foreign capital. Also, the fast-growing emerging economies have impacted the FDI in Russia. So, the FDI in Russia has remained volatile at low growth rates.

For the first three quarters of 2017, the top 10 nations/regions as source of FDI are Cyprus, Bahamas, Luxemburg, Singapore, Britain, Switzerland, Bermuda, Germany, the BVI, and Ireland, which accounts for 25.33%, 18.88%, 13.66%, 7.44%, 6.53%, 5.61%, 4.76%, 4.18%, 3.71%, and 3.33% of the total FDI (Table 3.2). Also, during 2008 to September of 2017, in relation to FDI on an accumulative basis, the top 10 nations/regions are Cyprus, the Netherlands, the BVI, Luxemburg, Ireland, the U.K., Bahamas, Bermuda, Singapore, and Germany, which accounts for 14.92%, 8.30%, 8.20%, 8.11%, 7.27%, 6.52%, 6.05%, 4.61%, 4.20%, and 4.20% of the accumulative FDI. From these, the Western Europe and the tax heavens are main sources of foreign investment in Russia.

Table 3.2 Top 20 Countries/Regions as Source of FDI in Russia for First Three Quarters of 2017

No.	Country/Region	Value of Investment (USD 100 million)	No.	Country/Region	Value of Investment (USD 100 million)
1	Cyprus	64.17	11	Hong Kong, China	5.35
2	Bahamas	47.85	12	France	5.24
3	Luxemburg	34.60	13	Jersey	5.20
4	Singapore	18.86	14	The U.S.	4.36
5	The U.K.	16.54	15	Sweden	3.12

continued Table

No.	Country/Region	Value of Investment (USD 100 million)	No.	Country/Region	Value of Investment (USD 100 million)
6	Switzerland	14. 23	16	Hungary	1. 84
7	Bermuda	12. 06	17	Kazakhstan	1. 29
8	Germany	10. 58	18	Belize	1. 00
9	The BVI	9. 40	19	Turkey	1. 00
10	Ireland	8. 44	20	The United Arab Emirates	0. 88

Source: Central Bank of the Russian Federation

For the first three quarters of 2017, mining and quarrying attracted the most FDI in Russia, accounting for 21. 19% of the total foreign investment. The top 10 industries appealing to FDI, collectively accounting for 67. 30% of the total foreign investment, are mining and quarrying, financial services and insurance, manufacturing, construction, wholesale and retail trade, repair of automobiles and motorcycles, professional services, scientific and technical activities, information and communications, electricity, gas, steam and air conditioning supply, real estate, administrative and supportive services (Table 3. 3).

Table 3. 3   Industrial Distribution of Foreign Investment in Russia for First Three Quarters of 2017

Industry	Value of Investment (USD 100 million)	Industry	Value of Investment (USD 100 million)
Agriculture, forestry, and fishing	– 3. 63	Real estate	4. 94
Mining and quarrying	77. 41	Professional services, scientific and technical activities	17. 08
Manufacturing	32. 71	Administrative and supportive services	0. 73

continued Table

Industry	Value of Investment (USD 100 million)	Industry	Value of Investment (USD 100 million)
Electricity, gas, steam and air conditioning supply	10. 80	Public administration and defense and compulsory social security	0. 00
Water supply, waste water treatment, waste comprehensive management and rehabilitation activities	- 0. 36	Education	0. 13
Construction	21. 16	Health care and social work	0. 60
Wholesale and retail trade, repair of automobiles and motorcycles	18. 30	Art, entertainment, and leisure	0. 54
Transport and storage	- 2. 91	Other services	0. 00
Accommodation and food service	0. 69	Household employment, household self-use product and activities other than commodities or services	0. 00
Information and communications	15. 19	Overseas organization and institutional activities	0. 00
Financial services and insurance	56. 00	Unassigned	4. 02

Source: Central Bank of the Russian Federation

For the period from 2010 to September of 2017, the top 10 industries with the highest accumulative foreign investment are wholesale and retail trade, repair of automobiles and motorcycles, mining and quarrying, financial services and insurance, manufacturing, other services, construction, real estate, electricity, gas, steam and air conditioning supply, professional services, scientific and technical activities, and agriculture, forestry, and fishing. They accumulatively attracted FDI of USD 305. 917 billion.

In conclusion, Russia should make full play of its resources and formulate domestic policies to support development of the mining and metallurgical industry. In addition, Russia should work to enhance foreign investments on industries including financial services and insurance, wholesale and retail trade, construction, professional services, scientific and technical activities, textile, electricity, gas, administrative and supportive services and pharmaceutical industry. These efforts will improve the Russian industrial structure, and serve the needs of the Russian market.

3.3　India

3.3.1　Development Plan

By the end of the fiscal year 2014-2015, the Indian government issued the new five-year trade policy for 2015 to 2020, which is the fifth in its kind issued by the Modi administration. The new policy is in line with Modi government's 'Made in India Campaign' and 'Digital India Program', which are aiming at stimulating the manufacturing and service export and enhancing employment rate. The 'Made in India Campaign' is a strategic effort implemented by the Indian government for making India a manufacturing power, which targets 25 industries as priority areas including automobiles, pharmaceuticals, information technology, renewable energy, and electronics, and sets to provide business-friendly environment for domestic and foreign investors through streamlined approval process. Under the framework of 'Digital India Program', the Indian government aims to invest 1.13 trillion Indian Rupee (equivalent to USD 17 billion) on technological application to provide universally accessible digital and financial services, available services in real-time from online & mobile platforms, universal digital literacy, safe and secure cyber-space, electronic access to government services, and e-Governance & e-Services across the governments at various levels.

Compared to the previous policies, the new one has some key changes which includes, first, provision of two incentives on product and service export on labor-intensive industries and industries with high growth potential; second, stipulation of a five-year collective export goal, instead of annual export goals, which means that by 2020, India's export of product and service will reach USD 900 billion; third, the extension of policy review period has changed from annual to every 2.5 years; fourth, provision of governmental incentives for on-line trade, export from special economic zones, and penetrating specific EU markets; and fifth, higher incentives for export to countries/regions that have free trade agreement relationship with India.

3.3.2   Key Industries

a. Agriculture

India owns one tenth of the world's arable land, with agricultural acreage at 180 million hectares. It is one of the biggest food producers globally known for diversified agricultural and husbandry products. Among which, India tops the world in milk, fruits and tea production. As surrounded by sea on three sides, India is also resourceful in fishing, with the fishing products as one of the prioritized areas of government funding. India implements a 'rural vitality national program' that improves the potential in rural development and creates more jobs for the rural area. The detailed measures under the program include: increasing investment on rural technology research and development, enhancing rural land property ownership reform, improving logistics system and marketing, creating market opportunities for small famers, and providing financial supports on agriculture.

b. Automobile

India is one of the biggest automobile market in the world. Thanks to the edges in logistics and geography, all the main automobile produces have made investments in India in hope for potential market opportunities. India ports are closely connected and neighbor South Asia nations and Africa. The geographic advantages contribute to India's status as a regional manufacturer and exporter. Overall, automobile manufacturers and suppliers, over a long term, will remain confidence in India as a promising market due to the business-friendly approach by the Indian government.

c. Health Sciences

The health sciences industry in India is one of the largest and fastest developing markets in the Asia-Pacific region. Indian, as the second largest markets in Asia on pharmaceutical preparations and raw materials, is expected to be the fifth largest market globally by 2020. India is the world's third largest pharmaceutical producer that produces 8% of the global pharmaceutical products. Considering the potential high growth of the pharmaceutical industry in India, 18 of the top 20 pharmaceutical companies have set up their subsidiaries in India. In terms of bio-technology, India is the third largest market in the Asia-Pacific region. Dominated by domestic companies, this market only has 20% share by the foreign companies. India's bio-technical market has high potential to be developed, which attracts the attention domestically and globally. The Indian government, in its five-year plan, devotes public funding to support the growth of bio-technologies. In the next five-year plan, a total of USD 3. 7 billion will be used on this area. The health care industry in India, in terms of medical equipment and facilities, ranks among the top 20 worldwide. The per capital cost on medical equipment and facilities is under 3 dollars in India, while it is as high as 7 dollars in other emerging nations such as China. The medical equipment industry thus enjoys a great prospect.

d. Service Industry

In the service industry, a significant reform on 'Digital India' has been implemented. Through this flagship program, the Indian government sets to turn India into a digitally empowered society and knowledge economy, as well as improve the civil management via better interactions between the government and people. This program targets to digitalize the key delivery of a variety of industries and consumption services (including e-Governance, online information, retail, taxi, education, financial services and online medical services). It will also create tens of thousands of jobs in IT, electronics, and relevant industries. 'Digital India' has successfully attracted a large amount of foreign direct investment. According to a research firm, around 30% FDI is relevant to the fast-expanding e-commerce sector in India. Overall, the tech sector in India has seen an upward trend in investments.

3.3.3 Foreign Investment

From 2008 to 2011, under the implications of the international financial crisis, India's FDI has decreased over these years. However, the FDI has soon recovered and gained stable momentum for growth from 2012 to 2017 and decreased after reached the peak in 2016. In the fiscal year 2016-2017[①], India witnessed FDI at USD 42. 21 billion. It is partially attributed to the 'Made in India Campaign' that has a goal of attracting FDI, and it has also been driven by decreasing inflation thanks to the fluctuations of bulk commodity prices.

As of March of 2017, the top ten countries/regions as source of FDI in India are Mauritius, the U. S. , the U. K. , Singapore, Japan, Germany, the Netherlands, Switzerland, South Korea, and France, each accounts for 21. 77% , 16. 50% , 14. 46% , 10. 15% , 9. 31% , 6. 19% , 5. 37% , 5. 20% , 2. 01% , and 1. 46% of the total FDI (Table 3. 4).

Table 3. 4   Top 10 Nations/Regions as Source of Accumulative Foreign Investment in India

Nation/Region	Value of Investment (100 million USD)	Nation/Region	Value of Investment (100 million USD)
Mauritius	779. 85	Germany	221. 32
The U. S.	590. 37	The Netherlands	192. 01
The U. K.	517. 45	Switzerland	185. 99
Singapore	363. 02	South Korea	71. 97
Japan	333. 05	France	52. 28

Source: Ministry of Finance of India

In 2017, among the 15, 169 companies in India with FDI, the service industry tops the list, where 66. 68% of companies in this industry are directly invested by foreign investors. At the same time, manufacturing has attracted the highest FDI by value, which is 50. 19% of the total value of foreign invested companies. From the industrial point of view, foreign investors are in preference

---

① The Indian fiscal year is from April to the end of next March, e. g. fiscal year 2008 – 09 means from April of 2018 to March of 2009.

of computer hardware/software (16. 1%) , telecommunication (14. 1%) , and services (13. 2%) .

By industry and sectors, in terms of accumulative inflow of foreign investment, the top 5 for investment and financial cooperation are the service industry (including financial services, banking, and insurance) (17. 62%) , telecommunications (8. 51%) , computer hardware and software (7. 4%) , construction (6. 06%) , and automobile (5. 32%) .

Foreign investment in India concentrates on the manufacturing and service industries, while the key areas include information and communications, financial services and insurance, food products, machinery and equipment, wholesale and retail, automobile industry, electricity, gas, chemicals and chemical products. India should further accelerate industrialization and modernization for realizing the potentials for sustainable development.

3. 4   China

3. 4. 1   Development Plan

According to the 13*th Five-year Plan for Economic and Social Development of the People' s Republic of China* (2016-2020) , China aims to maintain medium to high growth rates for this period at an average annual growth rate of above 6. 5% , achieving an economic aggregate of 92. 7 trillion Yuan in 2020 from 67. 7 trillion Yuan of 2015. By 2020, the GDP and per capita income in China will double those of 2010.

The *Made in China 2025* program is the action plan for the first ten years under the manufacturing power strategy, and a strategic imitative to comprehensively upgrade the quality and strength in China' s manufacturing. It is the goal of the program that China will be a manufacturing power by 2025, and as a second step Chinese manufacturing will reach an intermediate level among world manufacturing powers by 2035, and by 2045, China will become the leader among the world' s manufacturing powers. Five main projects have been planned under the program, including innovation center projects, enhanced infrastructure projects, smart manufacturing projects, green manufacturing projects, and high-end equipment innovative projects.

In September and October of 2013, Chinese President Xi Jinping announced the initiatives on 'New Silk Economy Development Zone' and '21st Century Maritime Silk Road' (the 'Belt and Road' Initiative) that are devoted to establishing and enhancing inter-connected partnerships among the countries in these regions, realizing the potentials in regional markets, promoting investment and consumption, and facilitating coordinated growth of the transport, railway projects, manufacturing, construction industries.

China has also set stricter restriction indicators on 'Green Development', by lowering the thresholds on the unit-GDP water consumption, energy consumption and carbon dioxide emission by 23%, 15% and 18%, raising the forestation rate to 23.04% from 21.66%, and rate of days of good air quality to above 80% from 76.7%.

Since 2015, China has been a strong advocate of the supply-side structural reform, featured by de-capacity, de-stocking, cost lowering and weak link strengthening. China sets to speed up the technological system reform, promote development of high-tech and high value-added industries, expedite the reform of bio-civilization, and fuel the growth of green industries.

3.4.2   Key Industries

a. Natural Resources

China, rich in geological conditions, has 171 types of mineral reserves, with the world's largest known reserves in tungsten, rare earth, aluminum, vanadium and titanium, and leading reserves in coal, iron, lead, zinc, copper, and apatite.

b. Financial Services

Now China has set up a financial system that has complete functions of banking, insurance, trusts, securities trading, and leasing, has divided roles and responsibilities on multiple layers, and has coordination between the government-led financing and commercial financing. A sound financial services landscape has been formulated both from a macroeconomic view and an internal view of the industry. It will further facilitate the growth of the industry. Since

China decided to liberalize the financial markets, it is also enhancing the financial regulations. Good momentum has been built that guarantees orderly development of the industry and has enhanced inflow of foreign capital.

c. Key Areas

The *Three-year Action Plan on Enhancing Core Competency of Manufacturing* (2018-2020) issued by the National Development and Reform Commission, provided the implementation plan on 9 key technological sectors, which are rail transportation equipment, high-end ship and marine engineering equipment, smart car, intelligent robot, modern agricultural machinery, high-end medical instrument and pharmaceuticals, new materials, smart manufacturing, and major technical equipment.

In addition, the *Made in China 2025* program identified 10 key areas, including new generation information technology industry, high-end CNC machine tool and robot, aeronautic and astronautic equipment, marine engineering equipment and high-tech ship, advanced rail transportation equipment, energy saving and new energy car, electricity equipment, agricultural machinery equipment, new materials, biomedicine, and high performance medical equipment.

3.4.3 Foreign Investment

As the Chinese economy is in 'the New Normal', China has maintained steadily growth in actually utilized foreign capital, which peaked in 2017 at USD 136.3 billion. During 2006 – 2017, annual growth rate of actually utilized foreign capital in China has slowed down significantly. On one hand, China has higher environmental requirements and screening standards on foreign-funded projects and foreign investors thanks to its economic growth, and on the other hand, the fast-growing emerging economics have been increasingly appealing to the foreign investors, and that has impacted the foreign investments in China.

In 2017, the top ten countries/regions as source of foreign investments are Hong Kony, China, Singapore, Taiwan, China, South Korea, Japan, the U.S., the Netherlands, Germany, the U.K., and Denmark, each accounting for 79.38%, 3.88%, 3.80%, 2.96%, 2.62%, 2.52%, 1.74%, 1.24%, 1.20%, and 0.66% of the total foreign investments

(Table 3. 5). It is clear that China's foreign investment structure is upgrading from a great focus on the Europe and the U. S. to developed economies in Eastern Asia. For one thing, this shift has been driven by the adjacent geographies, connected cultures, and lower investment costs, which resulted in strong investment enthusiasm in Eastern Asian countries (regions). For another, the Eastern Asian nations/regions have incentives to invest in China for China's good growth momentum, stable markets, and huge potential in consumption markets. The Eastern Asian partners have shifted their attentionto China, through making investments, to fuel the sustainable development in the region.

Table 3. 5   Top Ten Nations/Regions as Source of Foreign Investment in China of 2017

Nation/Region	Value of Investment (USD 100 million)	Nation/Region	Value of Investment (USD 100 million)
Hong Kong, China	989. 2	The U. S.	31. 3
Singapore	48. 3	The Netherlands	21. 7
Taiwan, China	47. 3	Germany	15. 4
South Korea	36. 9	The U. K.	15. 0
Japan	32. 7	Denmark	8. 2

Source: Ministry of Commerce of the People's Republic of China

China's FDI in 2017 has been led by five areas, including manufacturing, information transfer, computer service and software, real estate, leasing and commercial service, and wholesale and retail, each exceeding investment of USD 10 billion, and collectively for 73. 0% of the total FDI (Table 3. 6). During 2010 – 2017, the top 5 industries for attracting accumulative FDI were manufacturing, real estate, leasing and commercial service, financial services and wholesale and retail, with an accumulative investment at USD 809. 27 billion, which was 79. 51% of the total accumulative investment. From the industrial distribution, the investments from the BRICS nations have concentrated on the service industry at above 60%. The manufacturing industry has had less than 30% of BRICS investment while the agriculture sectors less than 10%.

Table 3. 6   **China's FDI Industrial Structure in 2017**

Industry	Value of Investment (USD 100 million)	Industry	Value of Investment (USD 100 million)
Agriculture, forestry, husbandry, and fishing	10. 74	Real estate	168. 55
Mining	13. 01	Leasing and commercial service	167. 38
Manufacturing	335. 06	Scientific research, technical service and geological survey	68. 43
Electricity, gas, and water production and supply	35. 21	Water, environmental and public facilities management	5. 69
Construction	26. 19	Resident service and other services	5. 67
Transport, storage and mailing	55. 88	Education	0. 77
Information transfer, computer service and software	209. 18	Health, social security and social welfare	3. 05
Wholesale and retail	114. 78	Culture, sports and entertainment	6. 98
Accommodation and catering	4. 19	Public administration and social organizations	0. 00
Financial services	79. 21	International organizations	0. 00

Source: National Bureau of Statistics

Overall, the FDI in China is mostly made on the manufacturing, real estate, leasing and commercial services, wholesale and retail, financial services, and agriculture, forestry, husbandry, and fishing. Improve the export trade structure will help expedite sustainable growth and industrial restructuring for a better market and commercial environment, and also improve growth modes in China.

3.5   South Africa

3.5.1   Development Plan

Subject to the implications of international environment and economic slow-down domestically, the South African government has tightened a number of policies on foreign investment protection, visa, and mineral resource development. The land reform in Africa also faces uncertainty. According to the 'New Growth Path' (NGP) issued in 2010 by the South African government, it targets 6 areas for prioritized development, including infrastructure, agriculture, mining, green economy, manufacturing, tourism, and service industry. In 2012, the government issued the *National Development Planning* 2030 that have set targets for the period until 2030. And to supplement the planning, the government has launched large-scale infrastructure projects on highway, railway, and power station, and issued the *Operation Phakisa* on maritime economy and medical care. Besides, the South African government has led the planning and implementation of the 'North-South Corridor' among the African Union members, and has worked with the neighbors on energy projects, such as development of nuclear power and other renewable energy projects.

The South African government has also formulated planning on energy, mining and metal industries. Due to under-investment on electricity and delayed production of new power stations, the under-powered South Africa and its neighbors have markets for new power projects. The government needs to enhance investment and bring in assets for the electricity industry to promote economic growth, further clarify the property ownership rules, and extend the limits on resource industry investment.

3.5.2   Key Industries

a. Agriculture

South Africa has an advanced agricultural sector. The arable lands take up 13% of the total land, but only 22% of the arable land are high quality lands for plantation. Around 6% of the population work in agriculture, forestry and fishing, which outputs 15% of export revenue from the non-mining sectors. Though vulnerable to climate changes, South African is the world's ninth largest producer of wool, and a big producer of flowers, fruits, and wines, with export of canned food, cigarettes, and wines to all over the world. The spatial strategic integration program issued by the South African government sets to enhance the agricultural logistics and infrastructures in rural areas, improve investments on agriculture and rural infrastructure, and support rural developments through storage facilities, transportation, farm fencing, irritation, rural issues research, agricultural processing, aquaculture, and rural tourism.

b. Natural Resources

Endowed with natural resources, South Africa has over 60 kinds of mineral resources, with the world's highest reserves in andalusite, fluorite, gold, and platinum group metal, the second highest reserves in vermiculite, zirconium, chromium, manganese, and the third highest reserves in phosphate and vanadium. It is encouraged by the South African government to engage foreign investors in mining and processing in order to generate national income and value-added of products. South Africa, with an average annual insulation of 2500 hours, has the top solar resources globally.

c. Industries

Overall, the South African government has opened almost all industries to foreign investors. The *National Development Strategy* 2030 requires that the government must realize diversified economic growth, including developing energy-intensive industries such as mining, and also launching technology-intensive industries, commerce and service industries domestically. To promote the development of domestic automobile industry, the government has issued the *Automotive Investment Scheme* that provides incentives for creating new investments and upgrading outdated capacities, in order to stabilize employment and enhance development of industrial chain. In the meanwhile, automobile manufacturing plays a key role and is prioritized for preferential policies as well, including foreign investment subsidies, local production taxation incentives, and long-term return of investment.

d. Tourism

South Africa is gifted with natural and cultural resources for tourism. It is home to the world's most famous tourist attractions, which receives the most foreign visitors among the African nations. Even in the economic slowdown, the tourism industry in South Africa still realized growth for 7 years in a row. Tourism is the fastest growing industry in South Africa, at the world's third highest growth rate. It outputs value equivalent to 8.7% of GDP and employs over 1.4 million people. According to the *Travel & Tourism Competitiveness Report 2017* by the World Economic Forum, South Africa ranks the 53rd among 136 economies worldwide.

3.5.3   Foreign Investment

In 2017, South Africa had a flow of FDI at USD 1.33 billion, which is USD 0.9 billion lower than in 2016. During 2008 – 2010, the South African economy was hit by the global financial crisis and saw substantial decrease of FDI to USD 4.24 billion. During 2011 – 2013, the global economy has been on a recovery trajectory. Thanks to the abundant mining and human resources, South Africa has been back on the radar of global investors, with high growth of FDI. For the period 2014 – 2016, as the global bulk commodity prices fell, the foreign investment has dropped along with deteriorating business environment, at an average annual decreasing rate of 23.07%.

In terms of capital inflow, as of 2016, 63.30% FDI was from Europe, and the main contributors were the U.K., the U.S., the Netherlands, Belgium, Luxembourg, Germany, Switzerland and China. From the distribution of industries, in 2016, the financial services, manufacturing, mining, transport, storage and communications, as well as wholesale and retail have attracted the most FDI in South Africa, each at 42.1%, 20.8%, 20.5%, 10.4%, and 4.5% (Fig. 3.2). South Africa has an advanced financial system with laws and regulations and mature monetary and financial markets, providing a solid platform for injection of foreign capital. The financial services industry is the top industry for attracting foreign investment by value. South Africa is also a power in automobile manufacturing as a main producer, importer and exporter of cars and components. Almost all brands have facilities set up in South Africa.

(in percentage)

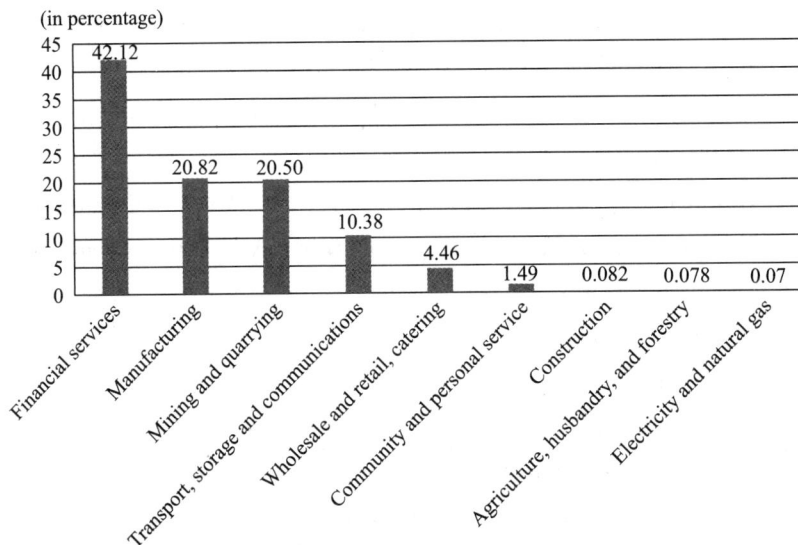

Figure 3. 2   The Proportion of Foreign Direct Investment Industry in South Africa in 2016 (in percentage)

Source: South African Reserve Bank

Given the above, the key sectors of foreign investment in South Africa are the service industry and manufacturing industry. The key areas include mineral resources processing, new energy, agricultural products processing, electronic machinery, financial services, pharmaceuticals, telecommunications, and metal processing machinery. South Africa should further capitalize on its advantages in natural resources and market potential to transform itself towards a labor-intensive production model from a consumption-driven model that is defective in sustainability, solve the issue on 'dual economy', and seek balanced development of the economy and society.

Chapter IV   Investment and Financing Cooperation among BRICS Countries: What Are the Aspects Needed to Be Improved Urgently?

4.1   Business Environment

Since the founding of the BRICS Cooperation Mechanism, the foundation for cooperation has been increasingly solidified and we gradually expand our cooperation to new fields. The cooperation has exceeded the geographic scope of the five countries and has become a constructive force for promoting world economic growth, improving global governance, and promoting the democratization of international relations. In order to further promote the complementary advantages and deepen the cooperation among BRICS countries, we are actively improving our business environment. However, according to the World Bank's Business Environment Index in its *Doing Business 2017 Report*, the rankings of BRICS countries still have large gaps with each other. Among them, Russia has the highest ranking, leading other BRICS countries in businesses setting-up, contract implementation, acquisition of power, and property registration. South Africa and China are close, ranking the 74th and the 78th respectively, and need further improvement in construction permits, businesses setting-up and cross-border transactions. India and Brazil rank relatively low in the total 190 countries. The root cause is that the domestic political turmoil has increased the commercial risks of investment. In addition, the imperfections of domestic supporting infrastructures and mechanisms have also made foreign investors to be cautious and hold a wait-and-see attitude. .

4.1.1 Complex Taxation System and Heavy Corporate Tax

Brazil has a total of 58 kinds of taxation, being divided into three levels: federal tax, state tax and city tax. The Brazilian government adopts a system of multi-level tax collection and management. Due to such a highly decentralized taxation system, tax rates vary widely across different regions and the taxation process takes quite a long time. In terms of corporate taxation costs, Brazil's corporate income tax rate is high, and companies also have to pay other taxes and various social expenses. As a result, the tax burden they bear is extremely heavy, which greatly reduces the company's profitability. After the Temer Administration came to power, the government proposed to reduce the tax burden for enterprises. However, the market generally believes that after the Brazilian parliament passed the fiscal reform bill, which stipulates that the fiscal budget limit for the next 20 years shall not exceed the inflation of the previous year. In December 2016, the government's pressure of fiscal expenditure has increased greatly, and it is unable to implement large-scale tax cuts since it is difficult to reduce rigid budgets such as social, diplomatic and defense spending. According to the World Bank's Business Environment Index 2017, Brazil's tax payment index ranks only the 181st out of the 190 economies in total.

India is a federal state. The federal government retains the right of legislation and taxation. However, states and local governments also have some taxation power. Local taxes are numerous and their tax rates vary. In the south part of India, tax levels are relatively high, with a percentage as high as 60.6% of the gross profit on average, much higher than that of the South Asian average of 40.9%, and also higher than the OECD average of 40.9%. At the same time, the Indian government has almost no preferential policies for foreign investment regarding taxation. On the contrary, the tax rate of foreign corporate income tax is higher than that of their local counterparts in India.

In China's foreign-related tax system, the statutory tax rate for foreign-invested enterprises and foreign-funded enterprises is 33%, which is higher than other countries. Although China's foreign-related tax system does offer some preferential policies for foreign-invested enterprises and foreign corporate income tax, with the adjustment of preferential measures in the foreign-related tax system, the overall tax burden of these enterprises will be inevitably affected. In addition, China's pre-tax deduction is not well-regulated, which also directly affects the taxation burden for the corporations. According to taxation-related statistics in the World Bank's 2017 Doing Business Index, China ranks the 131st out of the 190 countries in total, down by 4 places in a year-on-year manner.

4.1.2   Backward Infrastructures in Urgent Need of Improvement

The development of Brazilian transport infrastructure ranks the first among Latin American countries, but the facilities are inadequate and being worn-out. Brazil's ports are at full capacity and the construction of the airport is backward, which often leads to logistical obstruction and delays. The Brazilian railway system is also underdeveloped, causing bulk commodities to rely mainly on highways. However, due to poor road conditions, the speed is slow and traffic jams are serious. The frequent delays and high transportation costs have severely weakened Brazil's international competitiveness in investment and financing. According to the World Bank's global Logistics Performance Index announced in 2016, Brazil's international Logistics Performance Index is 3.088, ranking 55/160. In addition, the structural contradictions in Brazil's power supply are outstanding. More than 70% of Brazil's electricity supply depends on hydroelectricity, so weather and seasonal factors have a significant impact on its power generation. Since 2014, the southeastern, mid-west, and northeastern regions of Brazil have been faced with power shortages in varying degrees. Brazil had to expand the scale of thermal power generation and import more liquefied natural gas (LNG) to meet its electricity demand. In 2015, the Brazilian electricity sector increased the electricity prices due to power shortages. In April 2016, with the restoration of hydroelectric power, Brazil canceled the electricity surcharge, resulting in a drop-in electricity price. At present, the Brazilian government has issued an investment plan in the energy industry to prepare for the expansion of wind power, so as to change the over-reliance on hydropower. However, in the short to medium term, the contradiction between supply and demand of electricity is still a major obstacle to the Brazilian economy and investment.

Russia has a vast territory featuring complex geographical environment of all kinds. Russia's road traffic is relatively backward while the country has a certain foundation for railways, aviation, and water transportation. However, these are mostly constructed during the Soviet period and, relatively, outdated. At present, the Russian government is investing heavily in improving the construction of infrastructures. However, apart from large cities such as Moscow and St. Petersburg, the status quo of outdated infrastructure has not been fundamentally changed. According to the Global Logistics Performance Index released by the World Bank in 2017, Russia's international Logistics Performance Index is 2.57, ranking 99/160.

India's infrastructure such as railways and highways lags behind other developing countries and seriously hinders the development of its manufacturing industry. India has one of the largest railway networks in the world today, with a total length of more than 64000 kilometers. But there is no high-speed railway that exceeds 200 kilometers per hour. The backwardness of transportation facilities is not conducive to India's development of investment and financing. At the same time, the power shortage in India has not yet been resolved. Although the Indian government is actively exploring the development of new energy sources, its long-standing problem of insufficient power supply is still very serious, which hinders economic development to a certain extent. India should change its long-term dependence on coal-based power generation.

4.1.3 Increasing Labor Costs and Low Labor Productivity

The poor quality of education in Brazil has not been effectively solved. Although the education at all levels in Brazil has been promoted significantly, the drop-out rate and repetition rate are very high. In the OECD PISA test, Brazilian students scored at a lower level in Latin American countries, and the gap with other OECD member countries was quite significant. Therefore, Brazil's labor supply is dominated by unskilled laborers and lacks professionals with higher knowledge levels and labor skills. In addition, the constant decline in labor productivity is a problem that has plagued Brazil for many years. The basic reason is that the overall quality of the Brazilian workforce is low, and there is a shortage of qualified professionals and technical personnel. In addition, the lack of innovative capability of Brazilian enterprises has made it even more difficult to increase labor productivity.

Russia has a labor shortage too. In 2016, the number of employees in Russia was 72.7 million, and the most significant shortage of employees in the job market is in construction, manufacturing, trade, education and real estate, forging a huge deficiency in labor resources. At the same time, Russia has entered an aging society, and the lack of labor force has brought certain challenges to Russia's long-term economic development. At present, in order to resolve this crisis, Russia has introduced immigration from the CIS region, but it has not been able to completely address the threat to Russia's sustainable growth posed by aging. This issue should be seriously taken care of.

Although labor productivity in China is growing faster, labor productivity levels are still low. According to the International Comparison Report released by the China Statistics Bureau's International Statistical Information Center in 2016, China's labor productivity level is only 40% of the world average, and its average unit labor output of USD 7318 is far lower than the world's average of USD 18487 with a huge gap of 98990 in between. In addition, China will gradually enter the era of aging. With the continuous rise in labor costs, these factors are, to a certain extent, affecting the foreign investment.

South Africa's social conflicts are more serious. In 2016, South Africa's inflation rate was 6.6%, the unemployment rate was 26.7%, the contradiction between labor and capital was intensified, and there were frequent strikes. The government faces pressures such as slow economic development, high unemployment, polarization between rich and poor, and poor public order. The South African trade unions are powerful and workers have a strong sense of rights protection. Foreign investors need to properly handle the relationship with local trade unions.

4.1.4   Higher Tariffs and Incompletely-implemented Policies

For a long time, local companies in India have enjoyed great protection while India's import tariffs have remained at relatively high levels, including basic tariffs, education taxes, offset taxes, anti-dumping taxes, and safety taxes. Since the financial crisis, the protectionist measures taken by India against Chinese goods have created huge obstacles to the export of Chinese goods to India. India imposes a basic tariff of 100% on alcoholics, gold/jewelry, raisins and vegetables. The basic tariff on fruits and beverages is about 30%, and the basic tariff on household appliances, clothing, pharmaceutical products, and cosmetics is about 25%. The average tariff for industrial products is around 15%. The tariffs for mobile phones and fax machines are 15%, and for personal computers, PC mice, and printers are 10%.

4.1.5 Complex Government Institutions and Low Administrative Efficiency

The Brazilian government has a huge amount of agencies, but it is inefficient and corruption happens from time to time. Business is often interfered by negative factors such as complicated procedures, lack of transparency, long processing time, and excessively strict review. According to the World Bank's *Doing Business 2017 Report*, Brazil's business starting-up, acquisition of construction permits, and access to electricity index ranked the 175th, the 172nd, and the 47th in all 190 economies. The first two are even lower than the Latin American average.

The Indian government's administrative structure is complex and its efficiency is low, which seriously hampers the investment of foreign capital in India. Although the Modi government proposed 'small government, big governance' measures, drastic cut in unnecessary administrative institutions, and introduced relevant laws to reduce administrative procedures, the outcome is still not satisfactory. According to the World Bank's 2017 Doing Business Index, the process of starting a business in India involves 14 steps and it takes 26 days on average. It takes 5 steps and 47 days to get a power license. For obtaining a construction permit, it takes 40 steps throughout the procedure and 164 days in total.

Corruption and bureaucracy are the main obstacles in the beginning period of doing business. Russia has launched a series of anti-corruption campaigns against senior officials and also strengthened its anti-corruption legislation.

However, anti-corruption actions have had little success. The administrative efficiency of Russia can be measured by statistics from the World Bank's Doing Business Index 2017 regarding the prerequisites for starting a business, obtaining construction permits and accessibility to electricity: the 26th, 115th and the 30th for ranking among the 190 economies in total. Regionally, at the same time, Russia has longer processing time and more complex procedures than the regional average, reflecting that Russia's administrative efficiency needs to be improved.

The Chinese government's administrative institutions are more complex and sometimes have institutions with overlapping functions, which can easily lead to overstaffing and inefficiency. According to the World Bank's 2017 Doing Business Index, which measures the administrative efficiency of China in terms of starting a business, obtaining a construction permit, and obtaining electricity, China's three indicators in 2017 ranked the 127th, the 177th, and the 97th respectively. In particular, in terms of obtaining construction permits, 22 administrative procedures are required which could take as long as 244 days, indicating that the administrative efficiency needs to be further improved.

South Africa's government administrative organization is large and its operational efficiency needs to be improved. Its lower administrative efficiency has become one of the obstacles to South Africa's economic development. To measure the administrative efficiency of South Africa, according to the World Bank's 2017 Doing Business Index, rankings of the three indicators regarding the establishment of new enterprises, the acquisition of construction permits and access to electricity South Africa were the 131st, the 99th, and the 111st respectively. Although they are higher than the regional average levels, the administrative efficiency still needs to be improved compared with other BRICS countries.

4. 2   Risks in Legal Affairs

The BRICS countries are all developing countries spreading over four continents. India and South Africa are both in the common law system while Russia and Brazil belong to the civil law system. The legal cultures are complex and diverse. Compared with developed countries, the overall rule of law of BRICS countries is at a lower level, with less legal transparency and lower efficiency of the judicial system. In terms of the legal system and judicial environment of the BRICS countries, all countries have extremely strict restrictions or prohibitions on the acquisition of land by foreign investors. In addition, Brazil, South Africa and Russia hold a negative attitude toward the inflow of foreign labor services. Instead of employing foreign workers, they are more inclined to hire local workers to reduce their unemployment rate. Corruption is a common problem facing the BRICS countries. Serious bureaucracy and corruption issues not only increase the cost of law enforcement, but also hinder the improvement of law enforcement capabilities. According to the latest World Rule of Law Index, South Africa ranks the 43rd out of 113 countries, Brazil ranks the 52nd, India ranks the 66th, China ranks the 80th and Russia ranks the 92nd.

4.2.1 Legal Restrictions on the Foreign Acquisition of Land

Brazil enacted the *Constitutional Amendment No. 6* in 1995, canceling the differences between Brazilian companies and foreign companies, granting national treatment to all foreign-invested companies registered in Brazil, and dissolving the restrictions on the purchasing of land by foreign natural or legal persons living and operating in Brazil which is stipulated by the 1971 *Land Law*. However, in 2008, the Brazilian Parliament reinterpreted the provisions of the *Land Law* and the *1995 Constitutional Amendment*. In August 2010, the Brazilian President approved the Federal Advisory Committee's interpretation of the *Land Law* enacted by Brazil in October 1971 restricting foreigners from purchasing land in Brazil. Although the Brazilian federal government's decree on restricting the purchase of land by foreign individuals or businesses has not been fully implemented in some Brazilian states, foreign investment in Brazil still faces significant legal risks in general. According to the Brazilian media, the Temer Government is considering relaxing the prerequisites for foreign investment in land, but that has been opposed by many departmental agencies.

Whether it will open up foreign investment in the future still faces great uncertainty.

According to statistics from the Indian government, 70% of bottlenecks in industrial development are due to land acquisition problems. Although land costs generally account for only 1-4% of industrial projects, the slow progress of land acquisition and complicated procedures often push up the actual cost of land to about 20% of the total cost. According to the Indian law, either the government or a business must obtain permission from at least 80% of the local residents before they can purchase a piece of land. The Modi government has attempted to introduce the *National Land Acquisition Act* to ease the restrictions on industrial and infrastructure land use. The bill was passed at the People's Court, but it has not been supported by the Federal Institute and has thus been shelved. The issue of land acquisition in the future is still an important obstacle to India's access to foreign investment and infrastructure construction. Balancing the interests of investors and farmers is an important problem that the Indian government needs to solve.

4. 2. 2   Restrictions on the Employment of Foreign Workers

Since Brazil has always faced employment problems and does not encourage the introduction of foreign labor services, it has many restrictions on the employment of foreign workers. According to the Brazilian Labor Law, foreign affiliates established in Brazil can employ foreign employees, but the number of Brazilian workers must not be less than 2/3 of the total number and their wages being at least 2/3 of the total salary too. Foreign workers must have special technical expertise. Persons with advanced education must have more than two years of professional working experience while those with a secondary education must have more than three years of professional working experience. They must apply for the fifth type of temporary visa (or short-term work visa) before they can work for a Brazilian employer. The procedure for hiring foreigners through the Immigration Bureau of the Brazilian Ministry of Labor requires the submission of a series of documents which must be translated into Portuguese and certified by the notary and consulate. This is a huge obstacle for laborers working in Brazil, especially for short-term laborers, and the cost of employment is very expensive.

Russia promulgated the *Russian Federation Labor Law* in December 2001 to sort out and provide legal protection for labor relations. The law regulates labor relations and its indirect relationships including the organization and management of labor, labor placement, vocational training and advanced studies, supervision of compliance with labor laws, payment of social insurance, and settlement of labor disputes. In terms of foreign labor services, Russia adopted quota management methods. According to the *Legal Status of Foreign Citizens of the Russian Federation*, foreign citizens can engage in relevant labor activities in Russia when they obtain a Russian working permit based on a labor contract. However, in recent years, Russia has continuously reduced foreign labor quotas. From 2006 onwards, the Russian government plans to cut 50% of the non-CIS quotas for labor services each year, which will have an impact on personnel from other regions to Russia.

According to South Africa's *Immigration Law* and *Foreigner Management Law*, foreigners can only hold a 'working permit' issued by the Ministry of the Interior of South Africa, and work for the employers specified on the work permit. The government imposes strict restrictions on the introduction of foreign workers. In principle, employment opportunities that can already find suitable candidates at home will not be provided to foreigners. The South African *Law on Labor* strictly stipulates that employers must sign formal employment contracts with their employees.

4.2.3 Serious Corruption Problem and Imperfect Law Enforcement

Corruption in Brazil is serious. Since the second half of 2016, Brazilian President Temer has been involved in the 'Odbrecht corruption case' and 'JBS corruption case' with scandals continuing to emerge. In addition, the corruption alleged not only involves Temer himself but a large number of senior officials in the current and former governments. According to the rule of law marking in the Global Governance Index published by the World Bank in 2016, Brazil's rule of law score was −0.19, down 0.11 year-on-year.

In areas where national interests are prominent, Russian courts are less likely to make judgments against the government, especially in the areas of natural resources, media or security. In addition, the implementation efficiency of international and domestic arbitration is low. According to the rule of law score in the Global Governance Index published by the World Bank in 2016, the Russian rule of law score was −0.72, down by 0.01 year-on-year.

Corruption and money laundering have become major problems in India's economic development. The Modi government has even adopted such bold measures like cash ban to combat corruption. Although it has achieved certain results, this has not fundamentally improved India's law enforcement capabilities and completely solved corruption, administrative inefficiency and other issues. According to the rule of law score in the Global Governance Index published by the World Bank in 2016, India's rule of law score was −0.06 points, a year-on-year increase of 0.03 points.

In addition, there is a constitutional risk in India. Although the political situation in India is extremely stable, there is a huge risk in the unity and implementation *capacity* of the Indian government. India won its independence and became a unitary system with a central government, but it did not integrate the central power in a profound way. In terms of legislative power, judicial power, or administrative power, the battle between the central and local governments is in a balance-of-power situation. Since there are more than 1,000 local political parties and more than 1000 local languages in India combined with the fact that local feudal and large family forces are intertwined, the unity and implementation of the Indian central government have been significantly weakened. As a result, on the economic level, the unity of the national market is not strong, and the implementation capacity of central government regulations is extremely weak.

Since the 18th National Congress of the Communist Party of China, China has taken a series of measures to solve corruption and has stepped up its efforts to punish corruption. At present, corruption in China has been mitigated, but it takes time to eradicate it. According to the rule of law score in the Global Governance Index released by the World Bank in 2016, China's rule of law scored −0.22, which was a year-on-year increase of 0.19.

Corruption in South Africa is very serious and has affected the status of the ruling party and the confidence of investors. Former President Zuma himself has also been accused of corruption on many occasions. According to the rule of law score in the World Bank's 2016 Global Governance Index, the South African rule of law score was 0.0558, down 0.1119 year-on-year.

4.2.4 Restrictions or Prohibitions on Foreign Investment

Brazil does not allow foreign investors to invest in nuclear energy, health care, pension funds, marine fishing, postal services, etc. Aerospace companies only allow a small number of foreign shares to exist, and the shares in civil aviation enterprises must not exceed 20%. This has limited the investment fields of foreign capital to a certain extent.

In Russia, the industries that foreign investment is prohibited are gambling and life insurance. In May 2008, Putin signed the federal law *Industrial Procedures Related to the Entry of Foreign Capital for Strategic Defense of National Defense and National Security*. Section 5 of the Act clearly stipulates that the 13 categories of 42 kinds of business activities are considered to be of strategic significance. It mainly includes: defense and military industry, production of nuclear materials, construction and operation of nuclear reactor projects, development and production of special metals and alloys necessary for production of weapons and military technology, research on aerospace facilities and aircraft, research on password encryption equipment, and natural monopoly departments as well as fixed-line telecommunication companies, development of federal-level underground resource blocks, underwater resources, broadcasting media covering half of Russian territory, newspapers with large circulation, and publishing companies. According to the provisions of the *Strategy Law*, foreign countries, international organizations, and the organizations they control (including those established in Russia) must not obtain control of a strategic company or acquire, occupy, or use a company's fixed production assets through transactions.

Regarding the restrictions on foreign investment, according to the *Strategic Law*, if foreign countries, international organizations, and the organizations controlled by them intend to obtain a company with strategic significance for Russian national defense and homeland security through trade, they need to obtain a prior approval by the governmental committee led by the Russian Prime Minister. These specific actions include: the direct or indirect disposal of more than 25% of the voting shares in the authorized capital of the strategic company (alone); the direct or indirect disposal of more than 5% of the voting shares in the authorized capital of the strategic company (plus) geological exploration and/or geological prospecting and mining activities in the area considered of federal importance; as well as other actions that impede the decision-making of strategic company management.

The Catalogue of Foreign Investment Industry Guidance 2017 issued by the Ministry of Commerce of China lists the restrictions and prohibitions in the form of a negative list for foreign investment. Industries that restrict foreign investment include automobile vehicles, special automobile manufacturing, telecommunications companies, banks, insurance companies, securities companies, securities investment fund management companies, and futures companies. In addition, the foreign investment is prohibited from research and development, breeding, planting, and production of related reproductive materials (including crops, animal husbandry, and aquaculture's excellent genes) of rare and unique precious varieties, rare earth exploration, mining, ore dressing, postal companies, domestic express delivery services, human stem cells, development and applications of the gene diagnosis technology, online news information services, network publishing services, network audiovisual program services, online access service business sites, online cultural management (except music), online public Information services, etc.

4. 2. 5   Strict Environmental Legislation and Complicated Procedures

Brazil has strict environmental requirements and the approval of environmental permits takes a long time. According to the specific circumstances of the project, multiple levels of government (federal, state and municipal) may be involved in the process of starting a business. If the relevant environmental requirements are not satisfied, the development or operation of a project that may affect the interests of the local environment or the residents of the community may result in civil and administrative liability and even criminal liability of the project company and its parent company.

South Africa's environmental protection requirements are also stringent. Take the ocean economy as an example. South Africa has many laws related to maritime management. All development and construction activities that affect environmental, social, economic, and cultural heritage sites are subject to a strict impact assessment system; near-shore sewage discharge, marine dumping, and motorized ships going to sea are subject to a licensing system; fishery resources are subject to a quota management system; environmental management plans must be submitted before oil and gas exploration starts. Under the *South African National Integrated Coastal Management Act*, the South African government has the right to request termination of any plans or activities that adversely affect the coastal environment.

4. 3　Risks Regarding Exchange Rates

Investment and financing is an important part of promoting the economic development of BRICS countries, and the global exchange rate fluctuations are important factors affecting international investment and financing. Choosing the right currency and exchange rate policy to deal with various risks, including the spillover effect of the U. S. monetary policy, are an important issue for the future cooperation of BRICS countries.

4. 3. 1　Current Status of the Currency Policy and Exchange Rate System of BRICS Countries

(1)　Brazil

In monetary policy, Brazil implements the inflation-targeting policy. The Brazilian National Monetary Committee sets targets for the inflation and tolerance zones for the next two years, and the Central Bank of Brazil develops monetary policy to achieve the stated goals. The Central Bank's Monetary Policy Committee subsequently sets a target level for policy interest rates, and the Open Market Operations Department adopted an open market operation to bring the overnight SELIC interest rate close to the interest rate target. Since 2006, the inflation target and tolerance range set by the Brazilian National Monetary

Committee are 4. 5% and 2% respectively, and the actual inflation level is between 2. 5% and 6. 5%, both falling within the tolerance range.

In terms of the exchange rate system, Brazil uses a free-floating exchange rate system. Brazil first implemented a fixed exchange rate system with a gradual depreciation against the dollar. In order to prevent the devaluation of the local currency, the Brazilian government has greatly reduced its foreign exchange reserves, which has caused an imbalance in the international balance of payments. That in turn has brought about a financial crisis. The massive capital outflow in 1999 caused the pegged exchange rate to be unsustainable, and the Brazilian central bank had to change the fixed exchange rate system to the floating exchange rate system. Under this system, the exchange rate is formed through a market-based mechanism, and the central bank indirectly intervenes in the formation of the final exchange rate through the inter-bank settlement market.

(2) Russia

The Central Bank of Russia adopts a multi-objective monetary policy. The *Russian Central Bank Law* requires Russian banks to announce at the end of each year the main objectives of the next three years of monetary policy, an analysis of the country's future economic conditions, and the corresponding monetary policies in various circumstances. By publishing a clear medium-term monetary policy, Russia can stabilize the market's expectations for future currency movements, and achieve the goal of stabilizing the exchange rate and restraining inflation. Russia's inflation target ranged from 3% to 4% in 2018. It usually uses the statutory deposit reserve ratio and refinancing interest rate as two monetary policy tools to achieve the policy goal.

Russia implements a managed floating exchange rate system. The Russian government initially implemented a fixed exchange rate policy. The exchange rate is not entirely determined by the market supply and demand, but is by the prescribed currency exchange rate floating range on currency parity between the foreign exchange and the inter-bank foreign exchange market, i. e. the 'Forex Corridor'. In 1998, the country's hyperinflation caused a currency crisis and Russia had to abandon the target range of exchange rates and implement a managed floating exchange rate system. The Russian central bank manages the ruble exchange rate with reference to a basket of USD and the euro (USD 0. 9, 0. 1 euros), and maintains the exchange rate in a floating range through inter-bank currency transactions.

(3) India

India implements a multi-objective monetary policy. The Reserve Bank of India establishes the monetary policy and is responsible for the implementation. The focus is mainly on inflation expectations management. The Reserve Bank regulates liquidity and short-term interest rates through indirect market operations. The main policy tools used are policy rates, market stability plans, liquidity adjustment facilities, and open market operations.

For exchange rate policy, India implements a managed floating exchange rate system, but does not set a predetermined floating range. The exchange rate of the Rupee is determined by the supply and demand of the money market. The goal of exchange rate management is to ensure that the money responds to the fundamentals of its value and, if necessary, provides foreign exchange to maintain a healthy market environment, curb speculation and excessive exchange rate fluctuations, help the country maintain adequate foreign exchange levels, and help eliminate market constraints so as to promote healthy development of the foreign exchange market.

(4) China

China implements a multi-objective monetary policy and assigns different weights to multiple objectives in different historical periods. The goal of China's monetary policy is to maintain the stability of the value of the RMB. The policy tools used are benchmark interest rates, rediscounting, deposit reserve, open market operations, and commercial bank loans, etc.

China's current exchange rate policy is a managed floating exchange rate system. From 1994 to 2004, China adopted an exchange rate management mechanism that was pegged to the USD. As the RMB faces increasing pressure for appreciation, China's foreign exchange reserves have rapidly increased. In 2005, the Central Bank announced the implementation of a basket of exchange rate determination mechanisms to regulate exchange rates based on supply and demand in the money market, and gradually promote exchange rate formation mechanisms.

Over the next three years, the appreciation of the RMB has exceeded 26%. In recent years, the RMB's foreign exchange flexibility has been increasing year by year, and the exchange rate has been floating in both two directions.

(5) South Africa

After suffering a severe exchange rate shock, South Africa began to adopt an inflation-targeted monetary policy from 2000, abandoned the exchange rate and choosing the inflation target as the nominal anchor of the policy. In February 2000, the South African government formally introduced the inflation framework and established the 2002 inflation target. The Monetary Policy Committee will publish a review of its monetary policy every six months and publish a policy statement. After the implementation of the inflation target system, the Central Bank of South Africa has made more rapid progress in the implementation of its monetary policy, and the coordination between monetary policy and other policy measures has been smoother too. The setting of the inflation target has increased the transparency of South Africa's monetary policy and the effectiveness of the central bank's accountability, greatly improving the forecast effect of the central bank's currency model.

For the exchange rate system, South Africa uses a floating exchange rate system determined by the market. In 1984, as a result of South Africa's apartheid, the international community's sanctions against South Africa forced the authorities to adopt a dual-track approach to the direct management of exchange rates. After the general election in 1992, South Africa's political situation changed, the reform of the foreign exchange market and exchange rate started again, the single exchange rate system replaced the double exchange rate system, and South Africa began to implement a floating exchange rate system determined by supply-and-demand relationship of the market.

4.3.2   The Global Impact of U. S. Economic Policy

The U. S. being the most developed economy in the world, the changes in the economic situation and policies of the United States have had an important and profound impact on the investment and financing of other countries in the world. The USD is the most commonly used major currency in the global currency market. Most currencies are traded in relative to the USD. Therefore, changes of the USD dollar influence the exchange rate fluctuations directly in other countries in the world, and is also an important factor to consider when conducting international investment and financing decision.

In the process of economic globalization, the United States' monetary policy spillover effect is increasing day by day. From 2004 to 2005, the Fed raised interest rates 17 times from 1% to 5.25%, causing the real estate bubble to burst and further triggering the global financial crisis. From 2007 to 2008, in response to the severe economic recession caused by the financial crisis, the Fed cut interest rates to 0.25% for 10 consecutive times, and then entered a seven-year zero-interest rate era. Since the end of 2015, the Fed raised interest rates seven times in a row and raised interest rates to 2%. This round of rate hike has triggered a *global linkage* and has had a certain impact on the emerging market countries. Short-term spillovers have pushed the dollar's exchange rate up, causing changes in global capital flows, and emerging market currencies are under tremendous pressure and short-term cross-border capital outflows are huge. In addition, the continued appreciation of the USD has led to a significant increase in the cost of bond swaps in emerging economies and an increasing risk of USD debt. Finally, the Fed's rate hikes have accelerated the suppression of international commodity prices, which has led to the loss of the interests of resource-exporting emerging economies and further the development of their trade in general.

After the Trump administration came to power in 2017, U.S. opened the largest tax reform in 31 years. Corporate income tax fell from 35% to 20% while U.S. companies were encouraged to bring overseas profits back to the U.S.. This policy will have a huge impact on a global scale, attracting more capital back into the United States for investment and reducing foreign direct investment that other countries may receive.

4.3.3 Impact of Exchange Rate Changes on the Cooperation of Investment and Financing among BRICS Countries

The changes in exchange rates is generally divided into two parts. One is the exchange rate fluctuation itself, that is, the appreciation/depreciation of the currency. The second is the degree of exchange rate fluctuations, that is, how dramatic the fluctuation goes.

Firstly, the trends of exchange rates will affect foreign direct investment (FDI). The depreciation of the host country's currency will reduce the relative costs of foreign direct investment, especially the labor costs. Therefore, the return on capital of foreign direct investment will increase, which will help increase the foreign direct investment. On the contrary, the appreciation of a country's currency will increase the relative cost of investment, which is not conducive to attracting foreign direct investment. In recent years, scholars have found that exchange rate trends have different kinds of influence on different types of foreign direct investment. Through empirical research on foreign direct investment in China, it has been found that the rising currency value is not conducive to attracting tradable foreign direct investment, but conducive to attracting non-tradable foreign direct investment.

(1) India

Between 2013 and 2016, the Indian Rupee continued to depreciate, and the total foreign direct investment volume showed an upward trend. In 2017, the Rupee appreciated slightly and the total foreign direct investment also decreased accordingly (Fig. 4. 1).

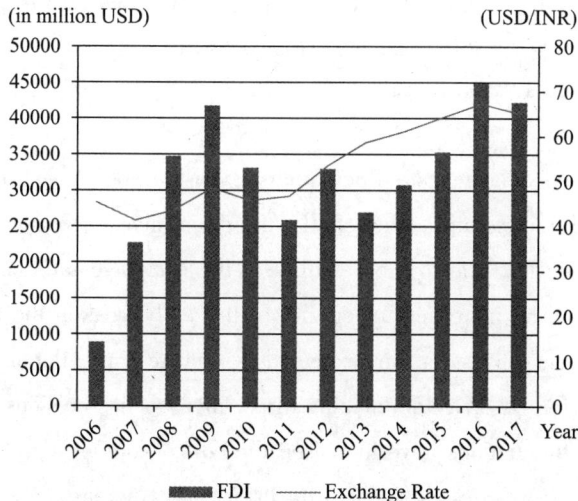

Figure 4. 1   India exchange rate and FDI 2006 – 2017（in million USD, USD/INR）
Source: International Monetary Fund, CEIC

(2) Brazil

Overall, the Brazilian Real in 2013-2016 depreciated significantly from 2006-2009, and from the total foreign direct investment, the FDI during the currency depreciation period (2013-2016) was significantly higher than that of the currency appreciation period (2006-2009) (Fig. 4. 2).

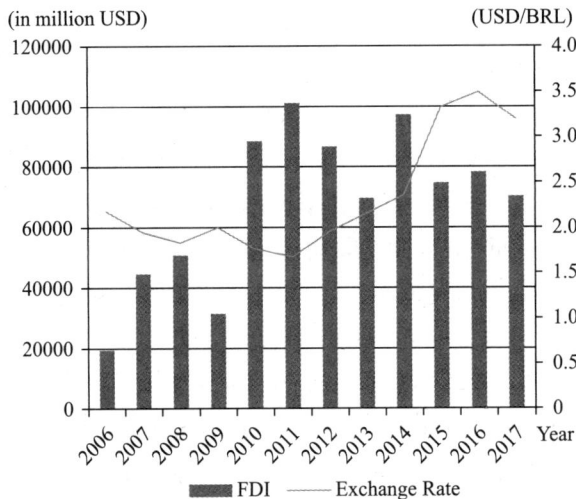

Figure 4. 2　Brazilian Exchange Rate and FDI from 2006 to 2017

(in million USD, USD/BRL)

Source: International Monetary Fund, CEIC

Secondly, exchange rate fluctuations expose transnational investment to more risks and uncertainties. First of all, the direct investment income of foreign investors may be lost due to the volatility of the exchange rate, and even face the risk of loss. The increased uncertainty will greatly weaken the attractiveness of foreign direct investors. An expected exchange rate fluctuation is also detrimental to foreign investors making direct investment decisions. In addition, exchange rate fluctuations have increased the cost of foreign direct investment. Even hedging tools are used, it will bring cost increases to multinational companies. Therefore, the increase in exchange rate fluctuations is not conducive to the economy to attract investment, which is an adverse factor affecting international cooperation of investment and financing

(3) China

In the BRICS countries, China's exchange rate fluctuations are relatively small, and foreign direct investment quotas are also the most stable. Since 2001, the RMB exchange rate fluctuated less which remained within 6.5%, while from 2008 to 2015, the fluctuation became larger, ranged from 8% to 10%. Thanks to the relative stable exchange rate of RMB, investors are optimistic about the fluctuation. For the FDI of China, it maintains a steady growth momentum (Fig. 4.3).

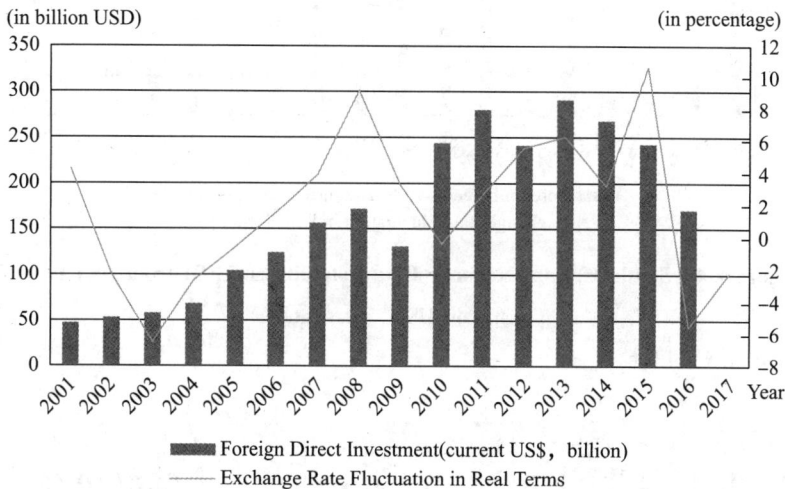

Figure 4.3   China's Exchange Rate Volatility and FDI from 2001 to 2017

(in billion USD, percentage)

Source: World Bank.

(4) South Africa

In 2002-2004, the fluctuation of the exchange rate of the South Africa Rand was as high as 30%, and the total foreign direct investment at that time was drastically reduced. From 2011 to 2016, the exchange rate has stabilized and foreign direct investment has gradually increased compared to the period of 2002-2004. In 2017, the fluctuation exceeded 12% again, it thus showed a decreased of FDI compared to 2016. In general, the fluctuation of the South African Rand exchange rate is relatively dramatic while the stability of foreign direct investment is relatively low, indicating that the exchange rate fluctuations have a large adverse effect on foreign direct investment (Fig. 4. 4).

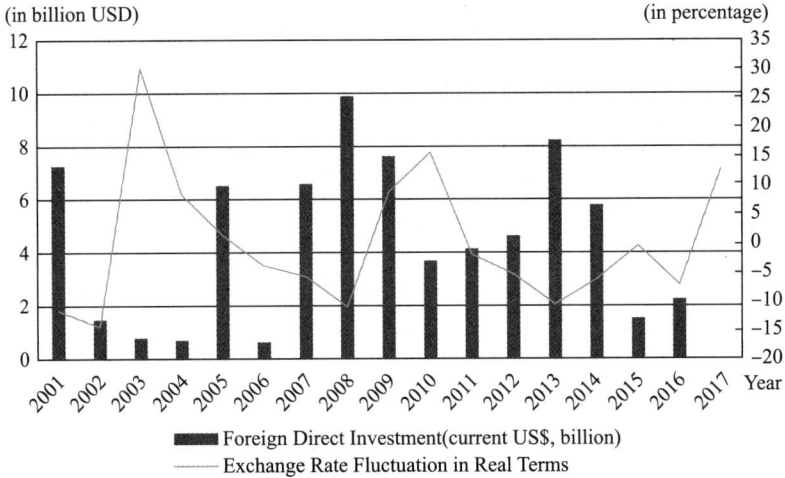

Figure 4. 4 South African Exchange Rate Volatility and FDI from 2001 to 2017

(in billion USD, percentage)

Source: World Bank

4. 4 Challenges in Connecting Economic Structural Transformation with Industrial Revolution

4. 4. 1 Weakness in Total Factor Productivity and Bottlenecks in Industrial Upgrading

According to the IMF data, due to the weakening of total factor productivity in 2007-2017, the average annual growth rate of economic growth in developed countries and emerging market countries fell by about 5% and 12% respectively, and their negative impacts accounted for 47% and 85% respectively in the total loss of annual growth for the developed countries and emerging market countries. The short-term recovery driven by demand-side stimulus in BRICS countries is difficult to sustain for a long time, and it is thus imperative that supply-side reforms boost total factor productivity.

The BRICS countries in their transformation and development path, need to solve the following important issues: First, to maintain the sustainable development of high labor productivity industries; Second, high labor productivity industries should have abundant forward and backward linkages; Third, absorb as much labor force as possible; Fourth, promote the accumulation and innovation of the entire economy. From the distribution of the employment sector, the main population with employment in South Africa, India, Brazil, and China is in sectors where labor productivity is lower than the overall level, especially in India, where nearly 60% of the population is employed in the agriculture sector. This shows the great potential for increasing labor productivity through structural transformation and further promoting economic growth.

In addition, the economic transformation of the BRICS countries currently faces the following problems: First, most BRICS countries still exploit natural resources (such as mineral resources) to maintain trade and economic growth. This kind of development is not only affected by the resource endowments of a country, but also the price of the resource products. The limitation of its high labor productivity is also closely related to its capital-intensive industry characteristics. The labor resources absorbed are limited too. In addition, issues such as rent-seeking, corruption, unfair social distribution, and widening income gaps will also arise. Second, the financial, insurance, real estate, and business services industries have higher labor productivity, but the amount of labor absorbed here is relatively limited, and the labor quality requirements are relatively high. Since there is still much room for improvement in the quality of the workforce in the BRICS countries, it is thus difficult to surpass the development level of the secondary industry to realize leap-forward development. Thirdly, although labor-intensive service industries such as tourism in the BRICS countries are conducive to employment, they have the drawback that labor productivity is still at a relatively low level, and its pull on the rest of the economy, which is important for a sustainable economy, is insufficient. The accumulation of growth and the contribution of innovation are limited. At the same time, there is a clear pro-cyclicality with which is difficult to promote sustained and stable economic growth.

4.4.2 Industrial Planning not Fully Docked and Planning not Fully Designed for Promoting Economic Restructuring

Each of the BRICS countries has a clear plan for national economic and industrial development, but the degree of industrial development planning is limited and a more centralized economic development framework has not yet been established. In 2016, China promulgated *the 13th Five-Year Plan for China's National Economic and Social Development*, explaining the national strategic intentions, clarifying the priorities of the government, guiding the market entities, and making plans, goals and directions for major national construction projects, productivity distribution and important proportions of the national economy so as to make better national economic development prospects.

Russia has formulated t*he National Outline for Developing Industry and Enhancing Industrial Competitiveness* which aims at stimulating the development potential of the industrial sector and enhancing the competitiveness of industrial enterprises in the domestic and foreign markets. It hopes that re-industrialization will promote economic development. After Modi took office, he launched the *Made in India* plan, striving to increase the share of manufacturing in India's economy from 18% to 25%. Brazil issued *the Strategy for Industrial Power*. In May 2017, South Africa released the latest *IPAP* (*Industrial Policy Action Plan*), which seeks to establish an economic and manufacturing framework with a lower degree of concentration and higher competitiveness under the unstable global economic background.

However, while advancing the common sustainable development agenda of the BRICS countries, we have not yet established a comprehensive development plan or a single industrial development plan based on the development of each country. The focus of industrial development in each country has not achieved the internal interconnection of BRICS countries from the perspective of complementarity and interconnection, nor has it been possible for member countries to complement each other with resources and advantages. Also, seeking the best development path from the perspective of integration has not been achieved.

4. 4. 3   Insufficient Investment in R&D and Bottlenecks for the Investment and Financing Industrial Upgrading

Innovation and R&D are important driving forces for industrial upgrading. Scientific and technological innovation requires a steady stream of capital investment as a strong support. To embrace the fourth round of scientific and technological revolution, however, there is a large R&D investment gap for BRICS countries.

At present, the most recognized innovative countries in the world make their R&D investment generally more than 3% of the total GDP. For example, the R&D input of some developed countries in Northern Europe accounts for 3%-3. 5% of GDP while the R&D ratio of the BRICS countries is less than 3%. In 2016, R&D spending in India and South Africa accounted for a relatively low proportion of GDP, which were 0. 65% and 0. 8% respectively, followed by Russia and Brazil, which were approximately 1. 1%-1. 3%, both at a relatively low level. According to the statistics of the Ministry of Science and Technology of China, China's R&D expenditure accounted for about 2. 15% of the total GDP in 2017, ranking the first among the BRICS countries (Fig. 4. 5). Another benchmark index, the R&D personnel full-time equivalents are: 830000/year in Russia, 530000/year in India, 3. 88 million/year in China as the first, and 40000/year in South Africa (Fig. 4. 6).

In addition, taking China as an example, there are also gaps regarding other indicators between China and innovative countries, indicating that China's industrial upgrading and technological innovation still have a long way to go. First, China's technology contribution rate is about 50%, and that of the developed countries can be as high as 70%. The second case in point is the conversion rate of scientific and technological achievements. At present, the conversion rate of scientific and technological achievements in China is less than 30%, while developed countries usually stand between 60% and 70% in this measurement. Third, China's core/key technologies have an external dependence of 50%-60%, while advanced countries keep that See Chart as low as 30%.

(in percentage)

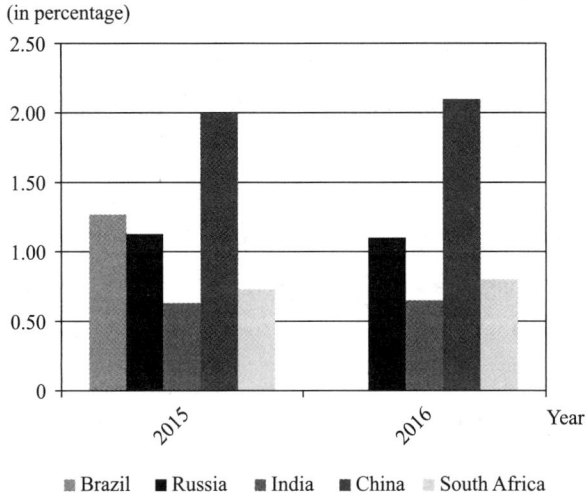

Figure 4. 5   R&D Expenditures and Their Share of GDP in the BRICS
Countries from 2015 to 2016（in percentage）

Source: Human Sciences Research Council, Eurostat, MCTIC, Department of Science and Technology, National Bureau of Statistics of China

(10000 People/Year)

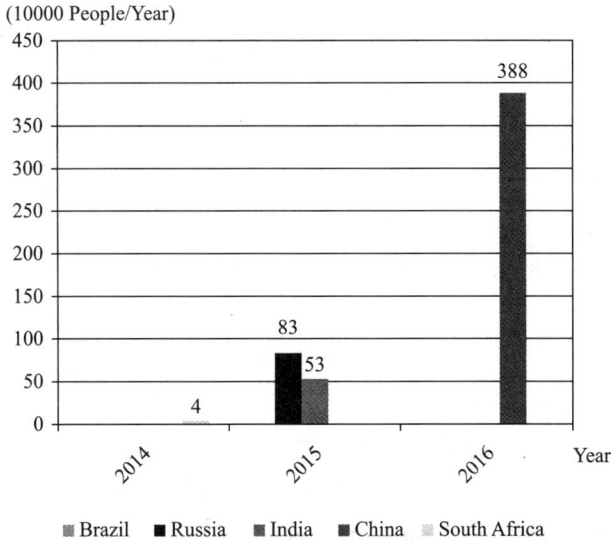

Figure 4. 6   Full-time Equivalent of R&D Personnel in BRICS Countries
（10000 People/Year）

Source: National Bureau of Statistics, BRICS Joint Statistical Manual 2017

In addition, structural reforms in technology are highly connected with investment and financing. Structural reform of technology is just like a race. Rapidly increasing R&D investment as well as timely and effective financial supply is conducive to the realization of supply-side goals. The speed of integration between financial innovation and technology revolution is critical, which directly affects the structural balance between the demand side and the supply side. In addition, financial innovations would stimulate social capital investment into the research and development industry, giving innovations and innovators higher market prices. However, the BRICS countries are still not investing enough in R&D, and there is still room for financial capital for R&D investment.

4.4.4   Imperfect Coordination of Industrial Chains and Production Standardization

The cooperation of complementary production capacities among the BRICS countries is an all-round one covering multiple aspects. Advantageous production capacity is the integration of R&D, manufacturing, marketing, service and other aspects of the industry. However, the BRICS countries lack uniform standards in raw materials, R&D design, professional talents, and system standards, which has become a shortcoming that restricts the development of manufacturing capabilities and industrial competitiveness.

In the production process, various aspects of production can be spatially separated and distributed in different countries to achieve global production. From the perspective of development, the most fundamental and crucial link in the formation of production cooperation among BRICS countries is the unification of standards. A country has an independent and complete manufacturing capacity and can achieve domestic product production. However, to form a division of labor among the BRICS countries, supporting production, forming technical synergy, and achieving economies of scale, it is necessary to establish a complete set of production standards and link them to make full use of the advantages of BRICS countries' internal production. Therefore, the production and manufacturing cooperation among BRICS countries is a comprehensive one, based on standard docking, covering multiple links, strengthening production supporting capabilities, linking production, supply and sales, and integrating technology R&D, product manufacturing and sales.

4.4.5 Weak Foundation of Industrial Cultivation in the Industrial Revolution

Among the BRICS countries, China and India have a good foundation for the industrial revolution. China and India have achieved success in the manufacturing industry and IT service industry, establishing their status as emerging powers. However, the gap of the nurturing foundation for the cultivation of technological industry in this region is relatively large, with no agreement reached on the development of it.

First, the BRICS countries have advantages such as abundant resources and large population, but if we want to set off a manufacturing revolution in the fields of aerospace and automobiles, we also need to introduce advanced technology and to create a good business environment that attracts foreign technology. However, the BRICS countries still maintain relatively conservative investment policies, intellectual property protection policies, etc., and fail to provide the best environment for attracting foreign direct investment as well as knowledge transfer.

Second, there isn't an industrial environment in which knowledge outcomes are rapidly transformed. The BRICS countries generally have a skilled workforce and gradually focus on education and training. For example, India has a strong high school and university education system. Students are recognized by multinational companies around the world. However, the reform of the education system and the transformation of knowledge products in the BRICS countries lack the industrial foundation. The high-tech skills possessed by highly educated students are difficult to be used in their work. In the short term, the BRICS government and the private sector need to establish training centers for vocational skills to improve employability. In the medium and long-term, solid foundations for industrial development and transformation are needed to connect the rapid transformation path of knowledge achievements in order to achieve the upgrading and optimization of the overall industrial structure of the BRICS countries through the industrial revolution.

Third, there is a lack of consensus on the application of emerging resources such as renewable energy. Compared with European and other developed countries, BRICS countries are relatively rich in natural minerals and energy but many countries are still in the stage of using resources and energy for development. Moreover, there is no consensus on the application of clean energy. Among the BRICS countries, China alone plans to allow the sale of renewable energy vehicles after 2020, and it is in a relatively leading position in pursuing a clean environment, other BRICS countries are not yet fast enough to reach long-term policy consensus on renewable energy.

[*Case: Naspers Holds Stock in Tencent's Project*]

In 2002, MIH of South Africa's newspaper giant Naspers owned Tencent's 46.3% stake and stayed as Tencent's largest shareholder. In March 2018, MIH, for the first time, sold 2% of Tencent's shares but still remained as the largest shareholder of Tencent with a 31.2% share. This case brings the following revelation:

The change in the way of thinking could lead to cooperative innovation. Since the digitization of paper media fails to fully meet the needs of today's world, the South African press industry has further started the process of all-media transformation. South Africa's newspaper industry has technological advantages, and more importantly, the transformation of thinking, the transformation of organizational structure, and the integration of media and society.

Investment and financing accelerate corporate transformation. South Africa's newspaper industry actively seeks overseas investment opportunities, and direct funds into companies that meet its own development philosophy through investors, providing cash flow for the invested companies and sharing the huge dividends generated by the Internet industry outbreak. ①

---

① See details in Appendix: *Case 6: Naspers Holds Stock in Tencent's Project.*

Chapter V Innovate the Investment and Financing Mechanism for BRICS Countries and Promote Pragmatic Cooperation and Mutual Benefits

5.1 Explore the Establishment of a Multilateral Credit Rating System for BRICS Countries

5.1.1 Flaws of the Current International Credit Rating Agencies

Credit rating agencies mark credit ratings for investors and financiers, which directly determines whether the debt could be successfully issued and how much the financing costs would be. At present, BRICS countries have relatively large capital requirements in terms of infrastructure construction, and the prerequisite for obtaining international credit and investment is a good credit rating. On the one hand, the BRICS countries can turn to the existing rating system and, on the other hand, create new credit rating system which is applicable to the BRICS countries. On the basis of this, the two sides can mutually recognize each other to reduce financing costs.

At present, there are three major institutions that provide credit ratings globally: Standard and Poor's, Moody's, and Fitch. At this stage, there are still flaws in the three major international rating agencies. First, most of the ratings tend to be stable, the information processing is slow, and the credit rating falls behind the fast-changing reality. Second, the system lacks accountability as the ratings are based on the subjective views and suggestions of analysts from various institutions of different countries. There is no accountability mechanism to ensure the authenticity of ratings. Third, the standard is single, since the rating agencies use the same rating system for both emerging countries and developed countries, and lack a whole set of financial indicators to illustrate the financial development of emerging economies and advanced economies respectively. Fourth, the rating lacks transparency and sometimes is biased. Fifth, sovereign rating services are difficult to obtain. These limitations cannot be changed within a short period of time. It is thus imperative that the BRICS countries establish our own credit rating agencies.

5.1.2   The Necessity and Feasible Approaches to Establish the Credit Mechanism of New Development Banks

The risk and return of a bond are the basic factors affecting the issuance of bonds. Therefore, the development of credit guarantee mechanisms for BRICS bonds and higher credit ratings of BRICS governments and corporate bonds are very important for the development of the local currency bond market. The credit rating of a bond is generally determined by the higher one among the bond issuer and guarantor. The guarantee mechanism can be strengthened from the following two aspects: First, the BRICS New Development Bank could provide guarantees for the issuance of local currency bonds; Second, the establishment of a BRICS bond guarantee fund which improves the credit ratings of the issuance of local currency bonds by the BRICS members.

First, the BRICS New Development Bank can provide guarantee services for the issuance of local currency bonds with its own high credit rating. The experience of the European Investment Bank (EIB) and its affiliated European Investment Fund (EIF) in this regard is worth learning. EIB and EIF support the financing of European SMEs through a wide range of traditional guarantee instruments. At the same time, EIF focuses on the innovation of guarantee instruments in the emerging asset securitization, and helps SMEs achieve a variety of funding sources by providing guarantees for the issuers of securitized products. By transferring credit risk, economic and regulatory costs are reduced. In recent years, EIB and EIF have become the leaders of European SME credit enhancement. As a multilateral development bank with 3A rating, they are able to persuade the financial institutions with which they cooperate to adopt 0% risk weights for their guaranteed assets.

Second, we can provide guarantees for the issuance of local currency bonds through the establishment of the BRICS National Credit Guarantee Fund. In addition to the experience of European investment funds, the Japan Federation of Credit Guarantee Corporation's experience in providing guarantees for domestic corporate finance and bond transactions is also worth learning. In 2004, Japan announced the establishment of *the Asian Bond Insurance System* to provide guarantees for foreign bonds issued by Japanese companies investing in East Asian countries and to help Japanese companies to raise funds in their host countries. This measure helps Japanese companies to issue bonds and raise funds in East Asian countries. The BRICS National Credit Guarantee Fund, established through joint ventures, can fully play the role of the Japan Federation of Credit Guarantee Corporations. The Fund can be built under the New Development Bank, so that the model of the European investment bank and the European investment fund can be adopted in practice.

5.1.3 Major Goals, Targets, Steps, and Defining Factors of the Establishment of the Credit Rating Agency of the BRICS Countries

5.1.3.1   The main goal of building a BRICS credit rating agency

The future BRICS credit rating agency will rate credit issuers in the emerging markets, allowing users to weigh the credit risk of ratings between the credit assessment conclusion and the issuer. The BRICS credit rating agency provides credit rating services that indicate the creditworthiness of the issuer in repaying foreign currency debt. The rating service used is neither a national system nor a global one, and the credit rating provided will focus on credit risk assessments of numerous issuers in the emerging markets.

5.1.3.2   Targets of the BRICS credit rating agency

The targets of the BRICS credit rating agency are: corporate debt, including bank loans, bonds, credit bonds, and other capital market instruments; public debt, mainly for state-owned enterprises and urban local institutions; structural financial transactions and financial institutions. The BRICS credit rating agency should develop internal sovereign risk assessments, which is important when rating the foreign currency debts by issuers across different countries. With the establishment and development of the BRICS credit rating agency, its rating services could be extended to other countries, and the BRICS credit rating agency can expand its business and do sovereign rating.

5. 1. 3. 3　Steps and defining factors of the BRICS credit rating agency

The establishment of the BRICS credit rating agency can be divided into three stages:

At the first stage, the BRICS credit rating agency should begin its business with the rating of foreign currency loans provided by the New Development Banks of the BRICS countries. It should also focus on credit ratings for foreign currency loans provided by multilateral agencies such as the International Monetary Fund, the World Bank and the Asian Development Bank, and also loans provided by development banks of specific member country under the internal banking cooperation mechanism of the BRICS countries. At this stage, BRICS credit rating agency needs to obtain the support of BRICS members. Member countries should therefore encourage multilateral institutions such as the New Development Bank, the Asian Infrastructure Investment Bank, and other domestic development banks of member countries to use the newly established BRICS credit rating agency when funding projects in their jurisdictions.

At the second stage, we should promote the popularity of the BRICS credit rating agency so that banks and financial institutions based on debts of BRICS members and emerging markets use the BRICS credit rating agency. Typical users will be the banks in the BRICS countries facing foreign exchange exposures in BRICS members or other emerging markets. The experience and credibility gained at the first stage should be used to encourage more groups to use BRICS credit rating services.

At the third stage, the BRICS credit rating agency should aim to expand its memberships and provide services to other emerging market countries such as Mexico, Philippines, Indonesia and Thailand. Once the BRICS credit rating agency has accumulated more experience in securities rating in various emerging markets, it will be able to achieve capitalization through national sovereign credit ratings for the emerging markets.

In the process of its establishment, there must be strong support from well-established rating agencies. Whether the BRICS credit rating agency will become a rating agency with good reputation in the emerging markets relies on the judgment of the market by its founding members. Each founding member needs to use its own professional expertise and establish a risk baseline based on an in-depth understanding of the national risk factors in the emerging markets. This is the basis for the development and growth of the BRICS credit rating agency. Therefore, at least in the initial years, the BRICS credit rating agency must have the support of a well-known credit rating agency with extensive experience in credit rating, especially in the emerging markets. Equity allocations should be evenly divided between multilateral institutions and development banks/ financial institutions of BRIC member countries to ensure the diversification and independence of the equity structure. The long-term goal of the BRICS credit rating agency should be to diversify the equity ownership so as to benefit other retail investors and institutional investors.

5.1.3.4 Shareholding structure, shareholding institutions and follow-up operations

First, ownership structure. Decentralized shareholdings are jointly held by development banks of BRICS member countries, financial institutions, and well-known credit rating agencies. In the founding phase, equity should include the following parts: first, the development banks of export credit guarantee agencies and other financial institutions in the BRIC member countries. Private financial institutions from these countries can also be invited to join the equity structure to ensure that the ownership structure is fully diversified. Second, a globally recognized and well-known credit rating agency should hold a certain amount of shares. This rating agency can use its widely-recognized credit rating experience to provide management expertise, experiences in rating methods, and employee training for the BRICS credit rating agency.

Second, we have to ensure that the rating is independent from the shareholding institution which issues the loan. BRICS countries have to ensure that there is a certain distance between the loan-issuing institutions that are the shareholders of this credit rating agency (such as banks and multilateral institutions) and the management team of the BRICS credit rating agency, as these shareholders themselves are the potential users of the ratings publicized by the BRICS credit rating agency. In short, shareholders and the management team of the BRICS credit rating agency should be independent from each other.

Third, the credit rating agency ought to get rid of political influence and conflict of interests. Since the credit rating agency will be featured by equity from the BRICS countries' financial institutions, development banks of BRICS members and multilateral institutions, the credit rating it publicizes might be regarded as a politically-inclined one to favor one or more BRICS countries, thereby undermining its independence and credibility. The credit rating agency mentioned above must have a diversified equity structure. BRICS countries may be indirect shareholders which obtain equity ownership through the New Development Bank, a development bank of BRICS member country, or a multilateral institution such as a financial institution. However, member countries cannot directly hold the equity of the credit rating agency. With the expansion of the credit rating agency, it must be ensured that the ownership of shares remains diversified, and that a single, individual country cannot control this institution alone.

Fourth, at the subsequent stage, a post-evaluation mechanism needs to be introduced to ensure that the quality of its rating continues to increase. Once the emerging market system of the BRICS credit rating agencies is determined, its popularity may lead to competition from globally renowned rating agencies who may adopt the system or develop their own emerging market systems to meet the requirements of this market segment. Although this may be seen as a potential competition and a threat to the commercial viability of the BRICS credit rating agency, their ultimate goal, the same as what the BRICS credit rating agency aims at, is to enable investors' funds to flow effectively to the core sectors of emerging economies. Therefore, at the subsequent stages, if other rating agencies choose to take the rating mechanism introduced by the BRICS credit rating agency when publishing their own rating, it will only increase the market acceptance of the BRICS system which enable investors make their investment based on evidence, and reduce financing risk and keep market stable in the emerging markets.

5.2 Promote the Development of the BRICS Bond Market

The bond market is the place where bonds are issued and traded. It is also an integral part of the financial system. For developing countries, in particular, the bond market plays a crucial role in improving the financing structure, reducing excessive reliance on banking, and enhancing the stability of the financial and economic system.

5.2.1 Prerequisites for Promoting the Development of the BRICS Bond Market

The development of the domestic bond market in the BRICS countries has become more and more mature. However, due to the limited resources in a single country, domestic financing alone is not enough to meet the funding demand. The international bond market can help institutions or companies to obtain funds from abroad, thereby greatly broadening the financing channel. On the other hand, thanks to the rapid development of emerging countries, the interest rates of BRICS countries' bonds are, in general, also higher than that of the developed countries, which is also an important factor in attracting international investment.

According to statistics, among the BRICS countries, China's unpaid international debt was comparatively high in the fourth quarter of 2017, reaching USD 190 million, while India and South Africa had relatively fewer debts, with USD 42 million and USD 35 million respectively (Fig. 5.1). Although the total foreign debt of the BRICS countries has generally risen, this number still falls far behind the total amount of USD 2.43 billion international debts of the United States within the same period of time. Therefore, the BRICS countries should strive to keep up with the developed countries and continue to promote the development of their own bond markets.

(in billion USD)

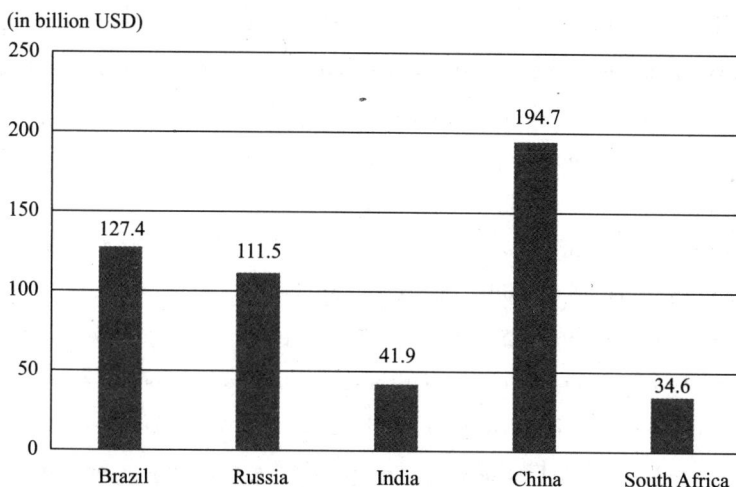

Figure 5. 1   Unpaid International Debt of the BRICS Member Countries in the
Fourth Quarter of 2017 (in billion USD)

Source of the statistics: Bank for International Settlements

5. 2. 1. 1   Increase the openness of the capital account

The openness in the capital account has a direct impact on the country's external financing. Only by liberalizing restrictions, more foreign capital can flow into the bond market and expand the scale of BRICS bonds. With the development of the globalization of financing, emerging market countries have gradually loosened their control of capital accounts. However, compared to developed countries, BRICS countries still retain a relatively high degree of capital control. Currently, the five BRICS countries, especially India and South Africa, still have very strict controls on capital flows. Admittedly, the opening of the capital account is not a one-step process. If it goes too fast, it will lead to increasing volatility of capital flows and bring risks to the stability of the financial system. The opening, therefore, should be a gradual process. We might begin with negotiation among the BRICS countries for reciprocal investment and openness to promote economic financing cooperation the five BRICS members. As we expand the channels for the use of foreign exchange reserves of the five countries, we thus reduce their dependence on the U. S. financial market. At the same time, we should further improve the local financial market regulations with appropriate regulatory measures such as additional taxes or other additional restrictions on the short-term flow of international capital.

5. 2. 1. 2 Vigorously promote the development of offshore financial markets and local currency bonds market.

The European currency market refers to the market where the currency is deposited and loaned outside the currency issuing country. It is commonly known as the *offshore financial market*. It originated in the 1960s and developed rapidly after the 1990s. Offshore financial markets are very attractive to countries because it is a completely free and open market with strong competitiveness. It is not subject to any country's government control and tax restrictions. The interest spreads between deposit and loan are relatively small while funds are highly flexible with simpler procedures. The business is done mainly based on credit. The development of local currency bonds can reduce the financing costs of a country and, at the same time, also promote the regionalization and even internationalization of a currency. On the other hand, some BRICS countries, such as China and Russia, have huge foreign exchange reserves but mainly invest in the markets of developed countries, which leads to excessive dependence on dollar assets. Promoting the transactions of local currency bonds among BRICS countries can greatly alleviate this problem.

According to statistics of unpaid international bonds (classified by the currency type of issuance) of the five BRICS countries in the fourth quarter of 2017 (Fig. 5. 2), BRICS countries' USD bonds account for more than 70% -90% of the total amount in each country while local currency bonds all stay less than 15% of the total amount. Among them, Brazil and Russia only have about 3%. Judging from the current situation, the local currency bond market still lags far behind the size of the U. S. dollar debt but, from another perspective, it also shows that there is still much room for improvement.

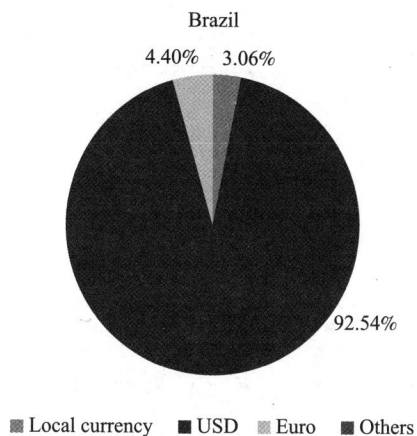

Brazil

Russia

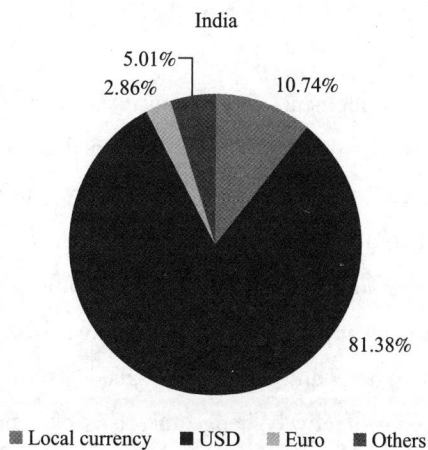

India

China

2.11%

9.09%   13.46%

75.35%

■ Local currency ■ USD ▓ Euro ■ Others

South Africa

4.62%   8.38%

6.94%

80.06%

■ Local currency ■ USD ▓ Euro ■ Others

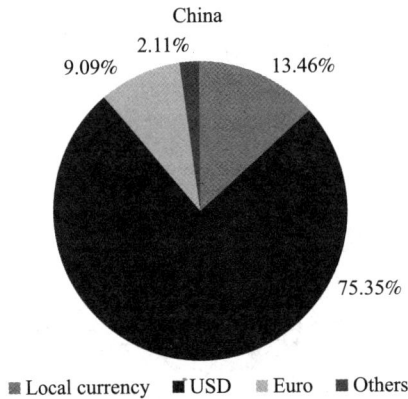

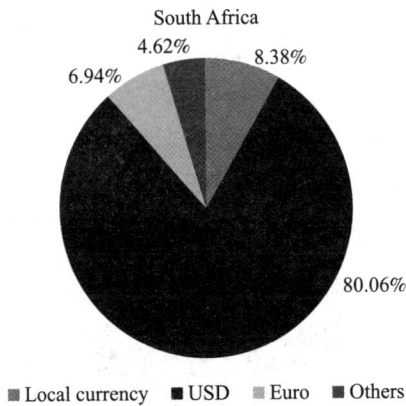

Figure 5. 2   Unpaid International Bonds of the Five BRICS Countries in the Fourth Quarter of 2017 (Classified by the Currency Type of Issuance)

As the financial development of emerging markets is still not perfect and the economic base is weaker than that of the developed countries, investors here face relatively higher risks. As a result, the value of the currency fluctuates greatly. Therefore, when a country issues foreign debt, foreign investors do not want to buy bonds in the domestic currency of developing countries because they are afraid of potential currency devaluation. Therefore, BRICS countries need to improve the financial system and establish a good risk-hedging mechanism. Financial derivatives can effectively hedge the risks of bonds. Along with bond transactions, BRICS countries could use forwards, options, currency swaps, etc. to somehow fix the forward rates. In doing so, BRICS countries can effectively help investors avoid exchange rate floating risks. With regard to the default risk of bonds themselves, investors can also purchase credit swap derivatives such as credit default swaps. Once a bond defaults, the swapping seller will compensate for the breach, thus greatly reducing the loss of default.

5.2.2   Measures to Promote the Development of the BRICS Bond Market

5.2.2.1   Strengthen mutual cooperation between BRICS countries and establish emergency insurance mechanism

The advantage of the BRICS countries lies in the rapid economic development and high profitability. However, investors are concerned particularly about the default risk of the bonds. Once a default risk occurs, the negative effect will be passed to other financial sectors and then even to other BRICS countries. Therefore, as the development of the bond market gradually advances, a cooperative emergency insurance mechanism should be established within the BRICS countries.

The role of the world's Lender of Last Resort is generally held by the IMF. However, since the IMF is not a central bank, the resources it can provide are limited. In addition, the voice of international financial institutions such as the IMF is mainly in the hands of developed countries. In the event of a financial crisis, the provisions of aid loans is highly political and limited. For example, in response to the European debt crisis in 2009, the Greek government must accept harsh financial rectification to get assistance from the IMF and the EU. To some extent, this worsened the local economy. Therefore, BRICS countries can jointly establish funds to cope with corresponding risks. For defaulted bonds (especially sovereign bonds), liquidity assistance can be provided under certain conditions to serve as a Lender of Last Resort, effectively reducing the risks and boosting the confidence of investors.

5.2.2.2   Strengthen the cooperation with international financial organizations and expand the scale of financing

Since overseas investors have limited understanding of bond issuers in the BRICS countries, it is difficult for ordinary companies to directly collect funds by issuing bonds in the international financial market. With an international financial organization as an intermediary, the credit rating of the bonds issued by those companies is generally higher so investors are more willing to buy. BRICS countries should strengthen cooperation with international financial organizations such as the International Finance Corporation and the Asian Development Bank to expand their business and provide more channels for the bond financing of other member countries so that more BRICS companies can have financing opportunities.

5.2.2.3   Promote inter-bank market cooperation among BRICS countries

The construction of the inter-bank market is one of the core elements in the development of a national bond market. At present, the inter-bank market of the BRICS countries is still much divided. There are apparent differences in the system and regulations, credit rating, auditing of conversion risks, clearing and settlement systems, etc. of inter-bank markets of BRICS countries. Our inter-bank markets still vary greatly in terms of developmental maturity. BRICS countries should strengthen the cooperation and communication in the inter-bank market and, through consultations, strengthen the accounting/auditing standards and improve compatibility among laws and regulations in different countries. We should also offer broader accessibility for investors among BRICS countries and enrich the investor structure so as to give full play to the complementary cooperation of BRICS country investors in capital, information, technology and other areas. Additionally, cross-border electronic trading platforms could be established in the inter-bank market of BRICS countries to further reduce the transaction costs.

5.2.2.4   Improve the regulation system and promote the transparency of information

The asymmetry of information has led investors to worry about the bonds of the BRICS countries, and the adverse selection has made high-risk bonds more buoyant in the market. As market managers, governments should formulate guidelines and supervise the implementation, increase the transparency of corporate information, and improve the legal regulations of debt contracts. From a political point of view, domestic audits and supervision may result in fraud.

Therefore, it is also necessary to strengthen the cooperation of information supervision among BRICS countries and establish mutual supervision mechanisms.

In short, advancing the development of the bond market can optimize the financial system of the BRICS countries, reduce and mitigate the risks of the financial system, and enable a more effective allocation of funds in the region. The opening of the capital account, the implementation of local currency bonds, the establishment of insurance mechanisms, the promotion of cooperation among international organizations and banks and the improvement of market supervision will all help to accelerate this progress. In the process of its implementation, BRICS countries should work together to actively explore and promote institutional innovation.

5.3   Build Stronger Local Currency Settlement and Currency Swap

The USD, Euro, GBP and Yen are the major currencies for the settlement of international trade. The currencies of the BRICS countries are basically non-convertible. Trade settlements need to be realized through the international hard currencies mentioned above, and the acquisition and accumulation of hard currencies are subject to the export capacity and net export surplus of these countries. Since the financial crisis of 2008, major currencies such as the U. S. dollar and the euro have undergone great fluctuations, and countries around the world are facing risks from the unpredictable exchange rate. As the trade volume of BRICS countries increases year by year, the cost of currency exchanges due to the use of non-local-currencies such as the USD is also increasing. The BRICS countries can promote cooperation in the settlement of trade, which can diversify currency allocation, facilitate trade, and stabilize the financial system. Besides, this measure can also help the BRICS countries to get rid of the over-reliance on the USD or other hard currencies.

5.3.1 Existing Problems in the Settlement in Local Currencies among BRICS Countries

First, BRICS countries have a weak foundation of cooperation for promoting the settlement in local currencies.

To a certain extent, the cooperation of the BRICS countries is a regional multilateral cooperation. The regional financial cooperation, however, depends on the economic integration of a region. Honestly, the BRICS countries are not as close in terms of geographic location and economic integration.

There are great differences in the economic development structure of the BRICS countries, and there is yet not enough sustainability of economic growth. In addition, the economic ties between BRICS countries are often far less close compared with their own economic ties with the developed countries. For example, China's economic and trade exchanges with the United States, Japan, the European Union and South Korea are more than those between China and other BRICS countries. Russia's trade volume with the EU is also higher than that with other BRICS members and Brazil's economic and trade relations with the United States have exceeded its relations of its BRICS partners. China has vigorously promoted the settlement in the local currency with countries all over the world, but it is still at the initial stage. BRICS countries need more mutual trust and willingness of cooperation to deepen the exchanges and discussions and seek official consensus on the common ground of our interests.

Second, trade products and methods among BRICS countries are relatively simple at the current stage.

For example, Russia and Brazil mainly export energy products while China and India have similar trade structures. Among the BRICS member countries, it is necessary to continue to expand the scale of mutual trade, optimize the trade structure, and increase the competitiveness and attractiveness of domestic exports. Both China and India are large consumers of raw materials while Russia and Brazil are large exporters of raw materials. This is conducive to the formation of demand-and-supply linkages among BRICS countries and the use of BRICS' currency settlement in commodity trading. Therefore, the promotion of local currency settlement can be started from bulk commodities transactions and gradually be promoted with the expansion of trade.

Third, the currency settlement system of banks in BRICS countries is not yet well-developed.

For example, commercial banks lack relevant systems to deal with local currency settlement risks. Since the head office of commercial bank does not have a special provision that is specifically designed to circumvent the risk of local currency settlement, it is only for each branch bank to bear the risk. In addition, bank local currency settlement services also needs to be further improved. The bilateral currency settlement methods are mainly in terms of remittances while the business of letters of credit (LC) and collection is still relatively small. While promoting the settlement in our own currencies, BRICS countries should also urge domestic commercial banks to improve their corresponding businesses in response to the growing needs of settlement.

Fourth, there are quite a number of restrictions on capital flows among BRICS countries.

For example, Russia imposes high tariffs on the cross-border transfer of cash/banknotes, which greatly increases the cost, affects the position of local currency in the bank, and restricts the development of the local currency settlement. BRICS countries should, in this regard, strengthen their communication and consultation, increase mutual trust and willingness of cooperation, and speed up the opening up of capital accounts.

Finally, after the outflow of sovereign currency, it is necessary to solve the problem of reflow.

BRICS countries should actively carry out cooperation in the capital market and permit the return of local currency funds to open accounts at home so as to invest in bonds or stocks. In the domestic bond market, countries could introduce cooperative investors and issue bilateral local currency bonds to diffuse the risks and promote the development of bilateral bond markets.

5.3.2 Current Problems in the Currency Swap among BRICS Countries

Compared with developed countries, emerging market countries have a weaker economic foundation and lower financial stability. To deal with the risk caused by the lack of liquidity, a series of cooperation should be established among the five member countries to promote the multilateral currency swap by our central banks. A currency swap is a transaction in which the two parties exchange different currencies, the same amount of principal and interest payments in accordance with rules agreed in advance, and return the principals when the swap contract expires. The prior agreement of both parties is called the currency swap agreement. According to different participants, currency swaps can be conducted between commercial institutions or between central banks too. The main purpose of currency swaps in commercial institutions is to reduce funding costs and avoid exchange rate risks; the central bank provides liquidity support through exchanges and reflects the willingness to strengthen cooperation and jointly respond to crises, thereby enhancing the market confidence and promoting regional financial stability. Compared with the liquidity rescue mechanism provided by the IMF, currency swaps have greater advantages: less prerequisites, more availability, and faster rescue.

On the other hand, the signing of a multilateral currency swap agreement will also help to promote the direct investment and growth among BRICS countries. The currency exchanged can also be directly allocated to the domestic commercial banks with related business and the bank can grant credit to trading companies so as to bring the swapped currency to specific trading activities such as trade financing, settlement and financing, and the opening of letters of credit (LC).

In practice, there are still some problems regarding currency swapping:

First, the swap is still based on the USD.

Since the currency used for foreign exchange intervention is mainly the USD, the exchange rate used for purchases and repurchases in currency swaps is based on the spot exchange rate of USD (for example, the 2000 *10 + 3 ASEAN* and *China-Japan-South Korea Chiang Mai Agreement* reached exchange agreements totaling USD 92 billion, most of which are done in dollars). Since De-Dollarization and trade settlements complement each other, countries need to gradually optimize their trade structure and bring trade out of the overdependence on the dollar so as to strengthen the status of the local currency as a reserve currency. Therefore, promoting the local currency settlement can also improve the mechanism of currency swap.

Second, the currency swap mechanism cannot avoid systemic risks.

The liquidity problem in a single BRICS country can be mitigated by the currency swaps with other member countries. However, when most of the member countries have such problems, the multilateral currency swaps among BRICS countries will encounter greater hardship, bring down the market's confidence in all emerging countries, and finally lead to systemic risks. As a result, the BRICS countries still need to cooperate with IMF and other international organizations to establish corresponding mechanisms to prevent systemic risks.

Third, to some extent, the pegging to the IMF brings restrictions on the multilateral currency swap mechanism.

Due to the lack of independent regional monitoring institutions, the current multilateral currency swap mechanism still prevents moral hazard with reference to the IMF's monitoring mechanism. It is thus defined as a supplement to the IMF and other international financial aid mechanisms. When pegged to the IMF's loan provisions, the swap will be constrained by the IMF financing system and will not fully play its due function, losing the necessary flexibility and immediacy. For example, in the Double I crisis in 2013, Indonesia's local currency exchange rate and capital markets underwent strong fluctuation, but it did not use the multilateral currency swap mechanism to buffer the impact; the Indian rupee fell by 20% against the USD in just 3 months. Although India did seek the intervention through foreign exchange from other emerging economies, it finally accepted financial aid from the Japanese government. Therefore, BRICS countries need to adjust and improve the agreement plan, properly relax the conditions for the use of reserves, and establish a more complete risk assessment system to determine the nature of the crisis, clearly identify 'capital income crisis', 'recurring balance crisis' or 'compound crisis' and, by doing so, make tailored plans to address specific problems in a country or a region.

Deepening the settlement in local currency and the currency swaps still requires close multilateral cooperation among countries. Although facing many challenges, promoting the development of these two would further perfect the investment and financing system of BRICS countries, help to improve national and regional welfare, and bring up the status of emerging market economies in the international economy.

[*Case: The Currency Exchange Fund*]

To address currency mismatches among countries in the emerging market, the Currency Exchange Fund (TCX) was established in 2007 by financial institutions for development, specialized microfinance investment institutions and other donors. Investors include the Dutch and German governments, and 22 multilateral and bilateral agencies. TCX's investors and customers provide financing to their borrowers in the local currency while using currency swaps and interest rate swaps to transfer currency risk to TCX, thereby protecting them from fluctuations of exchange rates and interest rates. Counterparties in the private sector also reduce their own risk through currency and interest rate swaps. TCX can hedge its own exchange rate and interest rate risk through hedging instruments, and can continue to provide customers with financial services of currency swap. BRICS countries may refer to this currency exchange fund and establish a wider range of currency swap mechanisms on the basis of local currency cooperation. ①

[*Case: Working Capital Loan Project of the Bank for Foreign Trade of Russia*]

In 2014-2015, the China Development Bank and the Bank for Foreign Trade of Russia (hereinafter referred to as the Russian Foreign Trade Bank) communicated and negotiated to jointly develop offshore RMB projects for financial institutions that support Sino-Russian trade projects as their financing purposes. The quota is 12 billion Yuan and the term is 3 years. As of now, 9.6 billion Yuan has been withdrawn. The project has a milestone significance for the

---

① See details in Appendix: *Case 7: The Currency Exchange Fund.*

development of large-scale overseas RMB cooperation of financial institutions by the CDB and other overseas financial institutions, for supporting the Belt and Road Initiative economic and trade cooperation, and for the internationalization strategy of RMB.

The project is of great significance for consolidating the strategic partnership between China and Russia as the largest single loan financing for overseas RMB cooperation between China and Russian financial institutions in recent years. It is also a major initiative of the China Development Bank in implementing the national 'Belt and Road Initiative' financial cooperation and promoting the internationalization of the RMB. It is thus a groundbreaking milestone event. This project takes the lead and sets up an example for future Chinese-funded banks and national financial institutions of countries along the 'Belt and Road' to carry out cooperation upon loans focusing on trade financing. The implementation of this project will speed up the promotion of the RMB as a currency for settlement of international market transactions, increase the purchasing power of the RMB in the international market, and realize the internationalization of the RMB. At the same time, the introduction of overseas RMB will help to promote the development of China's economic and trade relations with Russia and other regions and to maintain a steady growth of its foreign trade. ①

5. 4   Building a Multilateral Investment and Financing Model for the BRICS Countries and a ' Think Tank + Finance ' Cooperation Model

5. 4. 1   Establish a Multilateral Cooperation Model that Combines Development and Commercial Finance

Development finance is characterized by its support for businesses that are

---

① See details in Appendix: *Case 8: Working Capital Loan Project of the Bank for Foreign Trade of Russia.*

in line with national development strategies, and is more suitable for medium and long-term projects while commercial finance is market-oriented and has obvious advantages for medium and short-term business with more banking outlets and larger coverage. Development finance can play a *countercyclical* role while commercial finance is *progressive*. The development of financial cooperation in the BRICS countries should focus on development finance, gradually expanding the scope of cooperation, and pooling up all the resources available to diversify the cooperation among member countries.

5.4.1.1　Give full play to the role of different types of financial institutions

On the one hand, we should use development and policy-based finance as a lever to provide financial support for the incubation and start-up of key projects. For projects that have certain profitability but longer investment cycle and slower return, the financing guarantee would be provided by development finance; for the '*going out*' industry that needs supporting funds or subsidize, it would be covered mainly by policy-based finance with the financial affordability taken into consideration. On the other hand, for medium-and short-term overseas investments, commercial finance can provide market-oriented financing to lead commercial funds and resources of all parties to investment and construction, therefore forging a concerted effort to achieve better results. At the same time, for important overseas investment projects that are in line with the country's policy orientation, various funds can also enter at different stages of their life cycles and cooperate with each other to provide financial support.

Since the cost of policy-related funds is low and not profit-oriented, it may get involved in the starting stage or the no-profit-period of the project to provide financial subsidies or interest subsidies but also avoid excessive fiscal burden. The development funds can join when the profit of the project is low. On the one hand, it can provide lower-cost financial support for the project and, on the other hand, the project can thus be made bigger and better with more dividends to be shared. The commercial capital can come in when the project is mature and the return is stable. At this time, the project has already run for a period of time with a certain amount of credit accumulated. Even if it is now financed by the market, the cost will be relatively lower.

5. 4. 1. 2   Increase the application of public-private partnership projects (PPP) in the construction of infrastructure.

We have to fully mobilize social capital and private capital to participate in investment projects with higher yields. For projects with better returns, social capital and private capital should be jointly involved in the investment and construction. Financial infrastructures such as the Asian Infrastructure Investment Bank, the Silk Road Fund, and the China Development Bank could participate in investment projects with longer life circles, so it is necessary to establish an international public-private partnership business model to diversify the risks and improve the sustainability of financing. The BRICS countries need to improve the investment environment, optimize the risks of various stakeholders, and, with corresponding regulatory system, select suitable private partners to increase the probability of success. At the same time, BRICS countries can work with existing development financial institutions to make better use of global resources and establish mechanisms for information sharing.

5. 4. 2   Promote the Role of 'Think Tank + Finance' in the Sustainable Development of BRICS Countries

Through the cooperation of think tanks, we increase trust, clear doubts, and promote cultural exchange so as to lay a solid foundation for public opinion for expanding and deepen our cooperation. On the other hand, it promotes the influence and attractiveness by publicizing the achievements of cooperation among the BRICS countries. The continuous deepening of cooperation and exchanges among think tanks of BRICS countries has played a role as a 'propeller' and 'adhesive agent' for the comprehensive advancement of cooperation in security, economy and humanities, and has become an important link for mutual understanding and mutual trust among BRICS member countries, gathering resources and potential for the development of the BRICS countries. At the same time, all member countries of BRICS are faced with the important task of development and need to solve the structural problems of their economy and society. All countries should strengthen cooperation of think tanks and provide intellectual support for a new round of development of the BRICS countries.

The BRICS cooperation needs to take both capital and intellectual cooperation into account, which helps to deepen mutual understanding, increase mutual trust, diffuse misunderstandings internally among themselves, and enhance the overall influence of the BRICS in the world beyond. Specific measures include:

5. 4. 2. 1 Strengthen the establishment of think tanks and the communication and cooperation among international think tanks through uniting more organizations with higher diversity.

First, regular knowledge sharing and experience exchanges should be carried out so that the positive role of the 'Think Tank + Finance' model would be brought into full play. Regular exchanges among think tanks include mutual visits and joint academic events. On this basis, we should further establish a network of exchanges, and led by the leading think tanks in the BRICS countries so that exchanges and cooperation can be normalized and institutionalized. Exchanges among think tanks will play an even more important role in information-sharing and providing decision-making reference among BRICS countries.

Second, strengthen the cooperative research among the BRICS countries: Two or more think tanks of the BRICS countries jointly undertake research projects; the cooperation results are jointly issued by the participants and the voice of the BRICS think tanks spread on the international platform. BRICS countries should strengthen research cooperation in various ways and, with strong innovation, accelerate the development of BRICS think tanks. In the meantime, members should actively explore the organizational forms and management methods for a new model of think tanks in the BRICS countries.

Third, establish a joint research institute. Strengthen international exchanges among think tanks of the BRICS countries and establish joint research institutions to strengthen the international platform for think tanks. The BRICS think tank cooperation should combine both 'going out' and 'coming in' to vigorously carry out long-term or short-term international cooperation. Joint research organizations can be permanently based in one country or be run by all members in a rotating matter and, in either ways, be built into an international think-tank exchange platform with significant global influence.

Fourth, enhance the global awareness of the think tanks. Pay attention to research on major international issues such as energy supply, environmental protection, climate change, sustainable development, trade liberalization, public diplomacy, and global governance so as to improve its ability to handle international affairs. Broaden the channels for hiring BRICS experts to exchange their ideas and do collective research so as to better provide reference for the decision-making of BRICS. Cultivate a batch of think tank personnel with international influence, increase the openness of think tanks, formulate a unique vision of researchers, and bring up the research level.

5.4.2.2   Establish long-term planning through think tanks, promote institutional development

First, establish long-term plans through think tanks. Build a new think tank with distinctive characteristics of the BRICS countries to enhance the core competitiveness. Step out of the illusion of ' all-round players ' and define the focus of think tanks so as to conduct forward-looking study upon major, practical and hotly-discussed issues shared by BRICS countries. The think tanks ought to provide systematically constructive and operational policy recommendations. The construction of think tanks should be based on the overall economic and social development of the BRICS countries, with the aim of establishing plans and promoting mechanism building. Focus on intellectual products, improve the quality of research, and build high-end leading think tanks with strong competitiveness, high professional standards and ' hard plans ' (i. e. visionary, competitive and feasible plans).

The second is to promote the implementation of investment and financing projects through planning. Long-term comprehensive planning is of crucial importance for a country or a region to achieve leap-forward development. Development financial institutions can promote market construction, credit construction, and system construction through the cooperation among banks, governments and enterprises so as to make up for the market gaps and deficiencies. In addition, provide key infrastructure projects with investment and financing services. With the coordination of commercial finance, development financial institutions could ensure the implementation of the projects and, ultimately, achieve the national development goals.

[*Case*: *BRICS Interbank Cooperation Mechanism*]

On April 15, 2010, *China Development Bank*, *Brazilian Development Bank*, *Russian Development and Foreign Economic Activity Bank and India Export-Import Bank signed a Memorandum of Understanding on the BRICS Countries Bank Cooperation Mechanism in Brasilia*, *marking the formal establishment of the BRICS Interband Cooperation Mechanism. On April* 13, 2011, *the South African Development Bank joined the cooperation mechanism. Since the establishment of this cooperation mechanism*, *member countries have actively carried out multi-bilateral financial cooperation and played an important role in promoting the economic development and economic-trade cooperation among the BRICS countries. We have successively signed multilateral cooperation agreements such as the Inter-bank Local Currency Credit Agreement of the BRICS Cooperation Mechanism*, *The BRICS National Bank Cooperation Mechanism Credit Rating Conclusion Sharing Cooperation Memorandum*, *etc.*, *involving local currency credit*, *letter of credit confirmation services*, *sustainable development*, *infrastructure financing and other areas*, *effectively promoting financial cooperation and economic-trade investment facilitation in BRICS countries.* [1]

5.5 Establish a Sustainable Investment and Financing Model under the BRICS Framework

The BRICS cooperation should aim at common sustainable development. It is unique as it appeals BRICS member countries to take action together to eradicate poverty, promote economic growth, and meet social needs such as

---

[1] See details in Appendix: *Case* 9: *BRICS Interbank Cooperation Mechanism.*

education, health, social security and employment opportunities. With comprehensive social development, we thus lay a virtuous foundation of sustainable investment and financing. In the other way around, the positioning of investment and financing need to be in line with sustainable development. The investment and financing of BRICS countries will also concentrate on fields such as green development, people's livelihood, education and social security. We will shoulder the responsibility of development and solve the economic and social structural problems.

5.5.1   Give Full Play to the Unique Advantages of Development Finance and Take Development as the Primary Task

Specifically speaking, the primary goal of development includes: the elimination of extreme poverty and reduction of inequality; the establishment of safeguarding mechanisms for environmental and social security; the establishment of mechanisms for information exchange, accountability and post-crisis compensation; the demonstration of the leadership of the BRICS countries in sustainable development; the establishment of public consultation and discussion mechanisms; and the adoption of a true democratic governance structure. In the process of cooperation among BRICS countries, the sustainable development goals of regional economic cooperation can only be achieved through a more regionally-tailored cooperation mechanism for the development finance.

5.5.2   Further Tap the Convergence Points of Interests of All Parties Concerned in the Cooperation

As G20 gradually replaces G8 as the dominant force in global governance, BRICS countries should unite more closely together in global governance as participants in the institutional design of global governance. By balancing the economic and non-economic interests of all parties, we further tap the convergence points of interests among us. It is necessary to further focus on the reform of old, imperfect and inappropriate international regulations. Through multilateral dialogue mechanisms, BRICS countries ought to reach a consensus on the issue of global economic governance and seek a more just and fair international environment for the BRICS members, together with other developing countries, in international trade and investment.

In the process of cooperation, we will pay attention to the sustainable growth of national economies and combine the 'going out' and 'coming in' strategies to mobilize complementary economic advantages and thus achieve mutual promotion. For industries with strong competition, we will actively carry out international technical cooperation. In the fields of energy conservation and emission reduction technology, we should focus on project research and build an R&D team to promote technological breakthroughs. In the development of complementary industries, we will give full play to the advantages of all parties, strengthen economic and trade exchanges, form stable economic growth points, and establish an interaction between economic-trade and financial cooperation.

At the same time, we will further deepen mutual political trust among countries, strengthen cultural exchanges among the BRICS members, and promote the cooperation of countries in the fields of security, food, energy, climate, science and technology and education through dual-track exchanges between the government and the peoples.

5.5.3 Accelerate the Improvement of the Regional Financial Cooperation Mechanism

Accelerate the construction of financial regulatory mechanism. The globalization and regionalization of the financial industry must go hand in hand with regulatory measures. The establishment of the BRICS New Development Bank (NDB) has simplified the procedures for trade and financing among BRICS countries, facilitated financial services such as investment and financing among countries, and solved our financial shortages in the field of infrastructure construction, however, the lack of supervision will increase the systemic risk of the region.

With the establishment of the BRICS NDB and its emergency reserve arrangements, it is extremely urgent to establish a financial regulatory mechanism. In the process of building the regulatory mechanism, we should respect the financial sovereignty of all countries as the basic principle and achieve the fairness and efficiency of financial supervision in an open and transparent way. At the same time, establish mechanisms for capital flow monitoring and crisis warning. Secondly, accelerate the construction of the credit rating system and effectively evaluate the global and regional macroeconomics. In addition, the formulation of regulatory details for the NDB and emergency reserve arrangements of the BRICS countries should be accelerated to improve the management of the BRICS NDB. Drawing on the organizational structure, decision-making process and management system of the European Bank for Reconstruction and Development, the Inter-American Development Bank, the Asian Development Bank, etc. , BRICS members could establish a banking management system which is in line with the reality of emerging market countries. In doing so, we form the corporate culture of the BRICS New Development Bank and thus establish a good reputation of our cooperation.

5.5.4 Promote the Optimization and Upgrading of Industrial Structure and Appropriately Adjust the Economic Development Model

BRICS members have to meet the needs of financial cooperation and stabilize the external environment. In the process of optimizing and upgrading the industrial structure, the development of both traditional labor-intensive industries, technology and capital-intensive industries should be taken into consideration so as to improve the core competitiveness of the BRICS countries in the global industrial division of labor and seek a higher position in the global value chain.

Make full use of the investment and financing system of the BRICS countries with the New Development Bank as the core, increase infrastructure construction, and upgrade human capital. Members have to take the complementary advantages of market technology and energy of the BRICS countries to increase the utilization ratio of natural resources and form a new, open and mature industrial structure system. In the process of adjusting the economic development patterns, countries have to focus on stabilizing economic growth and make full use of comparative advantages, the broad market of BRIC countries and the existing cooperation results to reduce the negative effects brought by inadequate investment and infrastructure, the large income gap, poverty, and weak social foundations. In doing so, we adjust the economic structure and income distribution structure so as to enhance the overall national strength.

5.5.5 Encourage Multilateral Development Banks, the Green Climate Fund and Other Important Funds to Invest in the Green Growth of BRICS Countries

Give play to the leverage of international finance so as to steer funds to investment and financing of low-carbon infrastructure, which improves the quality of growth and helps to achieve sustainable development. The newly established AIIB and the NDB can expand their business and strengthen their international influence by investing in green infrastructures. In the investment process, it is necessary to strengthen the protection of the environment where the project is located, and integrate with the local urbanization process to promote local employment. Countries could, on the basis of infrastructure investment into climate change and sustainable growth, form its own unique international influence. In addition, 'sovereign wealth funds' should also be encouraged to invest in low-carbon sectors. As a special public investment fund with specific objectives, sovereign wealth funds can be used as a financing source for multilateral development banks, such as the AIIB, to invest in low-carbon sectors to expand their financing scale.

[*Case*: *ICBC's Acquires of South Africa's Standard Bank*]

In June 2007, *the Industrial and Commercial Bank of China and Standard Bank of South Africa reached a consensus of strategic cooperation based on equity. ICBC acquired* 20% *of the stakes in SASB with a consideration of approximately USD* 5.46 *billion. The equity transaction was completed in March* 2008 *after which ICBC became the largest shareholder of the South Africa Standard Bank Group. The SASB's first China-Africa Banking Center in the world was formally established in* 2017 *to further deepen the bilateral trade cooperation between China and Africa.*

The acquisition has become a typical example of inter-bank investment and financing cooperation among BRICS countries. Both ICBC and Standard Bank Group have increased the credit supply of projects involving Chinese companies in Africa. The amount of African loans approved by ICBC alone is up to USD 10 *billion in a single year, which strongly promoted the facilitation of China-Africa economic and trade cooperation. ICBC and SASB will continue to provide support for China-Africa industrial cooperation through integrated financial services and diversified financing channels, and actively respond to new financial needs such as inter-governmental currency swaps and the free trade zones to improve financial convenience and promote the deepening of non-economic and trade cooperation.* ①

5.6   Explore the Application of the Digital Economy (Block Chain etc.) in Investment and Financing

The BRICS countries will become typical carriers of industrial revolution and economic cooperation. They will take advantage of the opportunities from the industrial revolution to give full play to technological spillovers and learning-by-doing effects to promote financial innovation as well as the development of investment and financing. In the digital economy, block chain technology would help BRICS countries to achieve an *'overtaking on the curve'* in the competition of global value chain.

5.6.1   Significance of the Application of the Block Chain Regarding the Investment and Financing in the BRICS Countries

The establishment of a cross-border payment settlement system for BRICS countries through the use of block chain technology can not only greatly improve the efficiency of the cross-border settlement among BRICS countries but also break the financial privilege of the United States and put a fundamental impact on the international monetary and financial system. Under the current international monetary system, the USD is the dominant currency for cross-border payment and settlement. The US-controlled Society for Worldwide Inter-bank Financial Telecommunication (SWIFT) and the New York Clearing House Inter-Bank Payment System (CHIPS) are irreplaceable for USD-based

---

① See details in Appendix: *Case 10: ICBC's Acquisition of South Africa's Standard Bank.*

international settlement. The block chain, however, is one of the most influential technologies in the current global financial technology development, and it is possible to fundamentally change the current international monetary and financial system.

The block chain is essentially a huge decentralized distributed ledger database featuring decentralization, disintermediation, encryption security, etc. It may change the central-periphery model of the traditional international currency settlement system (i. e. a system centered on the US-controlled SWIFT and CHIPS with the rest of the system being peripheral). This approach, to a large extent, could break the financial privileges of the United States. Within the BRICS countries, cooperation based on block chain technology can be actively promoted while a cross-border payment and settlement system based on this technology can be attempted. This can be used as an opportunity to take an advantageous position in the reform of the international monetary and financial system.

First, the BRICS monetary authorities and financial institutions should work together to establish industry standards and guide the formulation of new international regulations of the block chain. At present, the block chain application in global banking is still in its initial stage of development, in which facing a series of technology and format alternatives and there are different possibilities for regulation and application. Three forces, including block chain fin-tech companies, large banks and regulatory agencies, will greatly influence the application and standards of the block chain in the future. Supervision, in particular, will become the dominant force in the application of block chain technology.

Secondly, after the implementation of block chain cooperation within the BRICS countries, the BRICS can exert greater influence while participating in the negotiation of international rules in the future. BRICS can establish industry supervision and corresponding technical standards through consultations among their regulatory agencies and, formulate game rules to grasp market opportunities.

Thirdly, establish a platform of block chain cooperation for BRICS countries, encourage financial institutions and financial technology companies to cooperate with the government, and strive to establish a cross-border payment system for BRICS countries based on block chain technology as soon as possible. This will completely break the USD monopoly on the international currency payment sector, which is of great significance for safeguarding the financial security of the BRICS countries.

5. 6. 2   The Characteristics of the Block Chain Itself and the Starting Point in the Investment and Financing of the BRICS Countries

Based on the decentralization, trustlessness, and traceability of itself, block technology can realize point-to-point value transfer. Through asset digitization and restructuring of financial infrastructure, it can achieve a significant increase of the efficiency of clearing and settlement after the trading of financial assets as well as a huge reduction of cost, both of which are the existing challenges faced by BRICS countries.

5. 6. 2. 1   Decentralization

In a centralized structural system, the central node controls the system and does the decision-making alone. In a decentralized structure, however, each node is equal and does not have the total control of the entire system. The decision-making is done by all participating nodes together based on the consensus mechanism. The market economy is a typical decentralized system where every economic entity conducts production and consumption under the influence of the invisible hand without external interference. Essentially, it is the decentralization of transactions between the two parties. In the BRICS cooperation, this method can be used to bypass the U. S. currency payment system and form an equal payment system among member countries.

5. 6. 2. 2   Trustlessness

Being trustless does not mean untrustworthiness or no requirement for credit. It refers to the use of technical rules to build up the credit and implement self-restraint through algorithm. Any malicious deception in the system will be rejected by all other nodes. Therefore, it does not rely on the credit endorsement of the central authority and can thus, in a certain degree and to a certain extent, replace the traditional way of establishing credits and complete the establishment of a trust relationship between peers. In the credit system built by block chain technology, participants do not need to rely on anyone for credit endorsements. As more participants join in, the difficulty of destroying the system goes higher too, which brings stronger system security. At the current stage, BRICS countries have not yet established a unified credit system. But through the application of block chain technology, we can complete irrevocable credit protection and promote the construction of credit systems through the application of block chain technology.

5.6.2.3 Traceability

A block chain keeps traceable data that cannot be tampered with. It therefore can be used to build a regulatory toolbox, required by the regulatory agency, which contains numerous tools to facilitate the implementation of accurate, timely, and multi-dimensional supervision. In the block chain, any block records all the information in the previous block and any transaction can be traced. The information of a complete block chain is maintained on each node. In BRICS countries, each transaction can save its details through the block chain, which facilitates the establishment of a complete information collection system in the region.

Block chain technology enables data to be transparent between parties of the transaction, bringing in a complete and streamlined flow of information across the supply chain which ensures that participants timely notice the problems emerging in the operation of the supply chain system. This advantage helps to find targeted solution to the problem and then improve the overall efficiency of the supply chain management. The block chain system is featured by data that cannot be tampered with and timestamp which proves the existence of data. These features make it very suitable for resolving disputes among the participating parties in the supply chain system and achieving easier proof and accountability. Finally, the combination between data irretrievability and transaction traceability can eradicate the problem of counterfeiting in the process of product circulation in the supply chain.

At this stage, the most feasible application in the BRICS is the block chain letter of credit and the issuance of LCs through agencies. At the current stage, most letters of credit are delivered in paper form after being issued. The security is thus low and the calibration is difficult. There is no electronic channel for the issuance of the inter-bank letter of credit. While the LC is modified or delivered, there is no channel of direct notification and information exchange, etc. Taking China as an example, the letter of credit uses Swift MT999, MT999, or the second-generation payment, whose message cannot be in Chinese and the message length cannot satisfy the user's needs.

Taking the application of block chain technology by the China Construction Bank through Runhe Software Company as an example, their cooperation has realized a simple application: the letter of credit applicants fill in an online electronic application form (on the block chain) and submit it to LC issuing bank A. The LC issuing bank A puts the information on the electronic LC information platform and passes it to the notifying bank B (the information is not modifiable and could not be repudiated). Subsequently the notifying bank B transmits the electronic notice of the LC to its beneficiary.

5.6.3   Possible Application Scenarios of Block Chain for BRICS Countries

5.6.3.1   The pain points regarding payment, settlement, and supply chain of the BRICS countries

In the area of payments, the cost of reconciliation (account checking), clearing, and settlement between cross-border financial institutions in the BRICS countries is relatively high with many manual processes involved. This not only results in the high cost of payment services by the back-end business terminals and the client terminals, but also makes it difficult to nurture the micro-payment business. In the field of asset management, assets such as equity, bonds, notes, income certificates, and warehouse receipts are escrowed by different intermediaries. This brings up the cost of asset transactions and can easily lead to document falsification.

In the area of clearing and settlement, the basic structures of equipment and business processes among different financial institutions are different from each other. At the same time, many manual processes are involved, which greatly increases the costs and the possibility of making errors. In the area of user identification, it is difficult to achieve efficient interaction among the user data of different financial institutions, which results in higher costs for duplicate authentication and, indirectly, the risk of the leakage of user identities by certain intermediaries.

In the supply chain area, the supply chain is a complex structure that consists of the flow of logistics, information and capital. It also connects suppliers, manufacturers, distributors, retailers, and users in the industry. Block chain technology, as a large-scale collaboration tool, is naturally suitable for the management of supply chains. The supply chain is composed of many participating entities who, of course, conduct a huge amount of interactions and collaborations among themselves. Information of all kinds generated during the operation of the entire supply chain is stored separately in each link respectively, making a low transparency of the information flow. This will bring two serious problems: first, since the information is not transparent or smoothly flowing, it is difficult for the participating parties in the chain to accurately understand the updates and problems of the related issues, thereby affecting the efficiency of the whole supply chain; secondly, when there are disputes among entities along the supply chain, the burden of proof and the accountability mechanism are both time-consuming, laborious and, in some cases, even not feasible at all.

5. 6. 3. 2   Specific application approaches and scenarios of the block chain technology among BRICS countries

The block chain technology can optimize the payment system regarding the construction of the credit system, the simplification of process, and the enhancement of transaction security. Specific applications are as follows:

First, the block chain technology is open-source and transparent. Transaction records and assets information on all blocks can be illustrated in the form of a distributed data system, which can easily verify the authenticity and integrity of the transaction and therefore improve the system's accountability. The combination of block chain, big data and other information technologies will effectively help to analyze the financial records, purchasing habits and business performance so as to give marks to all factors affecting the credit. This mechanism will help to build bilateral or multilateral trust to address problems related to credits in our financial interactions. In short, this approach is to reduce the cost of trust.

Second, through program design, block chain technology can achieve automation of the system. The program automatically processes the data on the block chain to simplify the settlement operation, which subsequently further reduces the probability of risk occurrence and improves the risk control as well as the competitiveness of financial institutions. At the same time, some of the manpower and material resources saved here can enter the productive industries to create real economic value.

Third, the traditional clearing settlement system is a centralized structure. If the center encounters technical failure or external attack, the whole network might be paralyzed. On the contrary, the block chain technology allows each node to save a copy of the data, which can effectively resolve systemic failures and resist external malicious attacks. The overall operation will not be affected by the failure of some part.

a. Application in Payment

In the area of payments, the application of block chain technology can help reduce the cost of reconciliation between financial institutions and the cost of dispute resolution, thereby significantly improving the speed and efficiency of payment services. This is especially true in cross-border payment. In addition, the lower-cost and higher-efficiency advantages brought by the block chain technology to the payment sector will enable the financial institutions to handle small-scale cross-border payments that were once deemed unrealistic due to cost factors, which is conducive to the implementation of inclusive finance.

b. Application in Asset Digitization

Various types of assets, such as equity, bonds, notes, income certificates, warehouse receipts, etc. , can be integrated into the block chain and become digital assets on the chain, enabling their owners to initiate transactions directly without the need for various intermediaries. The functions mentioned above can be carried out by infrastructure organizations in the industry who will act as custodians ensuring the authenticity and compliance of assets. Those organizations could also build a bridge between managed libraries and distributed ledgers to enable the latter one to have secure access to the trustworthy assets in former one. In addition, asset issuance can be carried out in either a confidential or a public manner as needed.

Specific business applications include:

- Application in asset securitization (ABS): First, shorten the issuance cycle and improve efficiency. Encourage multi-party participants to establish a multi-center management platform so as to improve business efficiency, Second, share the information and conduct cross-validation. With some of the information shared and transparency of information enhanced, cross-validation of information and mutual credit endorsement among multiple parties would be achieved. The third is to improve product liquidity and reduce financing costs. Provide participants with full-process management capabilities and form a positive multi-party securitization ecosystem.

- Application in letter of credit: First, forge a coalition chain involving trading companies, issuing banks, advising banks, logistics companies, taxation departments and enterprises. The second is that the information from different institutions stay synchronized through the consensus mechanism of block chain and the distributed ledger, reducing communication and collaboration costs and achieving mutual benefits in the industry. Third, once recorded on the block chain, the information of trade, letter of credit, logistics, and electronic invoice cannot be tampered with any more, which helps to improve the credibility of transactions and letters of credit as well as to reduce the risk of fraud. Fourth, the block chain completely records the process LCs, and the historical records can be tracked and queried, which enhances the transparency of business information so that users can keep updated with the progress of their business.

- Application in forfeiting: based on the authenticity and credibility of trade business and documents on the chain, expand the forfaiting business so as to reduce risks, help exporters to do financing with lower costs and optimize their financial situation.

- Application in bid bond and tender guarantee: First, establish a cross-system business collaboration connecting the out-of-office application system and in-line approval mechanism to achieve efficient and collaborative online processing of traditional businesses. The second is electronic storage of proof. The Hash value (document fingerprint) of the electronic contract is stored in the block chain, so that it is convenient to check and verify them at any time. When the block chain is connected with the notary office, judicial appraisal report and notarial certificate would be issued faster so as to strengthen the judicial effectiveness. The third is the whole process monitoring. By deploying the nodes, the supervisory authority can implement the entire process supervision of the bid bond service.

c. Application in Smart Securities

The transaction of financial assets is a contract based on certain rules between the relevant parties. The block chain can fully express these business logics with code, such as fixed income securities, repurchase agreements, various swap transactions, and syndicated loans. This in turn enables the automatic implementation of the contract and guarantees that the relevant contract is accessible only to the counterparty and kept confidential to unrelated third parties. Block chain-based smart securities can ensure that their operations comply with specific legal and regulatory frameworks through appropriate mechanisms.

d. Application of Supply Chain Finance

- Accounts Receivable Financing:
- Business process: The core enterprise confirms the accounts-payable and issues IOUs; the first-tier suppliers sign the receipt; the first-tier suppliers choose to transfer, finance or hold the maturity according to their own circumstances; the supplier can initiate financing application within the amount on the IOUs at any time online; and finally, the fund arrives in a timely manner.

- Business advantages: Realizes multi-level circulation of receivables vouchers (IOUs) based on core corporate credits in the supply chain; supports the split, transfer, and financing; effectively benefits multi-tier suppliers other than the first-tier ones; achieves multi-level transmission of core corporate credit; and, through the introduction of external financial institutions, provides low-cost financing rates for the accounts-receivable.

- Security Financing

- Business process: goods are put into storage, warehouse receipts are issued, and property rights are transferred to market makers; market makers pay IOUs to customers; customers choose to transfer, finance or hold it till due according to their own circumstances; suppliers can initiate financing applications within the limit of IOUs at any time online; and finally the fund arrives, almost instantly.

- Business advantages: the changes in circulation methods (from warehouse receipts to notes/IOUs) and payment of bills which is independent from the underlying contract bring better liquidity; IOUs can be divided and transferred to improve the financing capacity; IOUs and the commitments from core companies bring better liquidity of the bills; through factoring or banking, docking ABS and re-factoring, assets would have a higher degree of standardization.

e. Application in clearing and settlement

The crux of the block chain technology is the ability to achieve value transfer in a quasi-real-time manner without the involvement of a trustworthy third party. The transaction of financial assets involves two important aspects: payment and securities. Through the establishment of a statutory digital currency based on block chain technology or the creation of a specific 'settlement tool', the real-time peer-to-peer clearing and settlement can be completed by docking with the digital assets on the chain as described above, thereby significantly reduces the cost of value transfer and shortens the settlement time. In this process, all parties in the transaction have good privacy protection.

f. Application in customer identification (KYC)

Financial institutions around the world are strictly regulated. One of the most important rule is that financial institutions must fulfill customer identification responsibilities (Know Your Customer, KYC) when providing services to their customers. In the traditional way, KYC is a very time-consuming process which lacks the technology to automatically verify the identity of consumers, and therefore cannot work efficiently. In the traditional financial system, user's identity and transaction records among different agencies cannot be tracked consistently and efficiently, making it difficult for regulators to do their work. The block chain technology, however, can bring secure and reliable management of digital identity information and improve the efficiency of customer identification (KYC) so as to lower down the costs and protect the privacy of customers.

g. Application in logistics and trading

In the process of logistics, the use of digital signatures and public/private key encryption/decryption mechanisms can fully guarantee the security of information and the privacy of the senders and recipients. For example, the delivery needs to be signed by both parties' private keys. Each courier or delivery point has its own private key. People only need to check the block chain to see whether the delivery has been done or not. If the end-user has not received the delivery, there will be no signed receipt on the block chain, thus the courier cannot falsify the signature. Therefore, the mechanism prevents the couriers from evading assessment by forging the signature, reduces user's complaint, and prevents false claims of the goods. The real recipients do not need to display their real names on the delivery list. Since security and privacy are guaranteed, more people are willing to welcome the real-name system, thus promoting the implementation of the real-name logistics system of our country.

Appendix Cases of Investment and Financing Cooperation among the BRICS Countries

Case 1 : New Development Bank

1. General Information

The New Development Bank (hereinafter referred to as the 'NDB') is formerly known as the BRICS Development Bank. The BRICS leaders signed the Agreement establishing the NDB on July 15, 2014 in Fortaleza, Brazil. The NDB is a multilateral development bank established by the BRICS countries to 'mobilize resources for infrastructure and sustainable development projects in BRICS and other emerging economies'. The initial subscribed capital shall be USD 50 billion, equally shared among the five founding members. The Bank have an initial authorized capital of USD 100 million. The headquarters of the Bank is located in Shanghai. The NDB Africa Regional Center is established in South Africa concurrently with the headquarters. According to the Agreement of the NDB, the bank 'will support public or private projects through loans, guarantees, joint stock, and other financial instruments'. In addition, the NDB should also cooperate with international organizations and other financial institutions to provide technical assistance for World Bank-supported projects. The first president of the bank shall be from India. The first chair of the Board of Governors shall be from Russia. The first chair of the Board of Directors shall be from Brazil.

2. Opportunities and Challenges

As a developmental financial institution with developing country dominated, the fourdation of NDB is an important achievement of South-South cooperation. It emerges under the new world economic landscape and seeks to address the developmental problems of emerging economies that cannot be solved by the existing global governance system. As a development bank for the emerging market economies, the NDB is confronted with both opportunities and challenges since its inception.

Firstly, the foundation for cooperation should be further strengthened. The BRICS countries are cooperating under a relatively loose framework. There are still some conflicts among the member countries on international trade and other issues. The basis for cooperation is not solid enough, and there will be many difficulties ahead. Therefore, in the course of development, BRICS countries need to fully communicate their interests and concerns, seek common ground while reserving differences, and try to avoid and resolve conflicts and differences in a timely manner. When it comes to the cooperation between China and the BRICS countries, China should balance its overall national strategy and details, make necessary compromises when needed so as to promote the sound operation and steady development of the NDB.

Secondly, equal-footed decision-making model may bring about efficiency loss. As stated in the *Fortaleza Declaration*, 'The Bank shall have an initial authorized capital of USD 100 million and the initial subscribed capital shall be USD 50 billion, equally shared among the five founding members'.
Therefore, no member country of the NDB could be a dominant decision maker. Such an equal-footed decision-making model fully respects the wishes of all members. However, the downside is that efficiency in decision-making might be compromised, especially when there is a conflict of interests among member states. Therefore, with such a decision-making mechanism in place, efficiency should also be fully considered. With a well-defined governance structure and continuous optimization of the decision-making mechanism, we can ensure that the core mission of 'development' can be achieved.

3. Significance and Implications

Firstly, the New Development Bank will serve the BRICS countries and provide a model for 'South-South cooperation'. Since 2009, inequality in the financial system has been a major concern for the BRICS countries. How to carry out pragmatic reforms to deal with the complex and ever-changing international environment has been mentioned in various BRICS summits. The NDB offers important opportunities for South-South cooperation. Its initial subscribed capital is equally shared among the five founding members while the members of Board of Governors, the members of the Board of Directors and other executives are democratically elected and appointed. To some extent, the NDB has transformed the BRICS countries from capital and technology recipients to capital and technology providers. Such transformation of roles enables all countries to provide developmental financial services based on the principles of equal consultation, mutual benefit and win-win outcome. By actively participating in the decision-making and implementation of development-oriented financial affairs, the BRICS countries can enjoy equal access to opportunities and resources of infrastructure development and sustainable development.

Secondly, emerging economies will become more influential and have a greater say in international affairs. The 2008 financial crisis exposed the systemic risks of the global financial system, and emerging economies confront unprecedented challenges. However, the US-centered developed economies firmly grasp the top-level design and standards execution in the financial system, thus preventing emerging economies from gaining their foothold and discourse in the financial organizations, such as the International Monetary Fund and the World Bank. Any reforms implemented hereunder are based on the premise of not undermining the vested interests of the developed countries, and they have essentially hindered the rapid development and catching-up of emerging economies. The NDB is accomplished through years of negotiations and consultations among the BRICS countries. It aims at breaking developed countries' monopoly in international affairs. It is an important attempt for emerging economies to conduct strategic cooperation and participate in the rules formulation in the post-crisis era.

Thirdly, it will deepen multilateral cooperation among the BRICS countries and improve the global economic and financial structure. The NDB is confronted with important development opportunities. The economic situation of the BRICS countries during this period determines the resource contribution and support from the founding members to the NDB. In the face of complicated economic landscape, the Contingent Reserve Arrangement Agreement will supplement and reinforce the NDB. Through concerted efforts, it would become an effective way to promote cooperation within the BRICS framework. The New Development Bank is mainly responsible for providing infrastructure development loans when the economy is running smoothly, while the Contingent Reserve Arrangement Agreement relieves the short-term liquidity pressure of member countries when the economic climate deteriorates. The combination of the two is an important driver for deepening the inter-bank cooperation mechanism among BRIC countries and will profoundly change the global financial landscape.

Case 2: The BRICS Contingent Reserve Arrangement

1. Background

The mismatch between BRICS countries' foreign exchange risk exposure and the risk prevention and mitigation capacity of the current global financial system has led to the emergence of Contingent Reserve Arrangement. The BRICS countries hold a large amount of foreign exchange reserves. Given the frequent international capital flows, the scale of foreign exchange reserves of many member states is not sufficient to cope with the potential risks brought by such capital flows. The possibility of a 'financial crisis in the 21st century' still exists. At the bilateral level, no effective firewalls have been built by the BRICS countries. They have neither signed bilateral swap agreement as other western countries did, nor did they establish bilateral monetary security agreements with the Federal Reserve. Once large-scale capital flows and exchange rate fluctuations occur, it would be difficult for them to get timely assistance from the United States and other developed countries. Externally, the BRICS countries can turn to the IMF for help. However, Precautionary and Liquidity Line and other risk prevention and control resources provided by the IMF is not sufficient to meet the development needs of the BRICS countries. Under such circumstances, it is of great importance and urgency for the BRICS countries to establish their own risk prevention mechanisms.

2. Process and Progress

At the G20 Summit in June 2012, the leaders of the BRICS countries proposed the idea of establishing a Contingent Reserve Arrangement (CRA) for the 5th time. At the fifth BRICS Summit on March 27th, 2013, the BRICS countries formally decided to invest USD 100 billion to establish the BRICS CRA. At the G20 Summit on September 5th, 2013, BRICS leaders discussed in depth during the informal meetings and reached important consensus on key issues and details, such as reserve size, operational mechanism, and proportion of contribution from participating countries. On July 15th, 2014, Zhou Xiaochuan, the Governor of the People's Bank of China, represented the Chinese government and representatives of other BRICS countries in Brazil to sign the *Treaty for the Establishment of a BRICS Contingent Reserve Arrangement*. The parties agreed to establish self-managed financial reserves to deal with short-term international balance of payments pressures. The financial stability of the member states is further strengthened through mutual financial support. By then, the CRA has been initially established.

3. Content of the CRA Mechanism

The primary goal of the CRA is to provide a support framework through liquidity tools and preventative tools, which essentially is a currency swap agreement. All member states have made commitments to help with capital contributions in the event of a crisis. In non-crisis situations, no actual funding is required. Once a crisis occurs, countries in need of assistance can use their currencies at the agreed exchange rate to purchase the available credit from the Contingency Reserve Arrangement, and redeem the local currency as previously agreed at the end of maturity period. Through the signing of an inter central bank agreement, the five BRICS nations guide and regulate the operating procedures for the use of liquidity and preventive financial instruments.

The initial size of the BRICS CRA is USD 100 billion, and the contribution from the member states are shown as follows: USD 41 billion commitment from China; Russia, Brazil and India each promised to invest USD 18 billions, and South Africa would invest USD 5 billion. The maximum quota countries can request from the Arrangement is equal to their capital contributed (China, Russia, Brazil and India) or twice (South Africa).

To secure contributors' capital, the BRICS Contingent Reserve Arrangement refers to the *Chiang Mai Initiative Multilateralization*, with most of the funding linked to the IMF loans. The parties also agreed on the specific conditions for approval of the swap application and extension (such as the protection of creditor's rights etc.), and requested timely information sharing to avoid any default. The parties also agreed on the details of the obligations, legal compliance requirements, and fund payment guarantees for the implementation of the CRA. Detailed penalties and mitigation measures against possible breach of contract is formulated.

4. Significance and Implications

The Contingent Reserve Arrangement is an important achievement of the financial cooperation of the BRICS countries and has a profound strategic implication for future investment and financing cooperation under the BRICS mechanism.

First, prevent the crisis in advance. The significance of the CRA not only lies in the post-crisis mutual support, more importantly, it can boost market confidence before the crisis and prevent the crisis from happening in advance. Through currency swap commitments, the CRA can provide positive market expectations after the crisis, reduce future uncertainties, stabilize market sentiment, cushion the impact of external shocks on the member states, thus, reducing the likelihood and intensity of the crises.

Secondly, promote economic integration of the BRICS countries, boost South-South cooperation and facilitate global governance reform. Although the *Durban Declaration* did not mention the goal of promoting economic integration, the CRA and the NDB in essence play an important role in promoting practical cooperation among the BRIC countries and boosting economic integration. Counting on countries with vested interests to reform the old mechanism would be difficult. As a competitor to IMF and the World Bank and other international financial organizations dominated by developed countries, the CRA and the NDB promote global governance reforms through advancing self-reform of the original international financial organizations.

Thirdly, maintain the stability of the BRICS countries and the global economy. In the context of economic globalization, the world economy has become increasingly interconnected. Despite the geographical distance among the BRICS countries, the increasingly closer economic and financial exchanges together with similar levels of development make the crisis more contagious within the BRICS system. Once a country experiences a financial crisis, it would affect other economies. As a financial 'firewall', the CRA enhances the stability within the BRICS system, which in turn promotes the stability of the global economy and provides a good external environment for the development of BRICS countries.

Case 3: South Africa's Transnet SOC Ltd and China Development Bank's Joint Project

The Transnet SOC Ltd (hereinafter referred to as 'Transnet') is an important partner of the China Development Bank (hereinafter referred to as the 'CDB') in South Africa. Since the cooperation kicked off in 2013, the two sides have been in close contact. In March 2013, the CDB signed a USD 5 billion financial cooperation agreement with Transnet. In 2015, the two parties signed another loan agreement of 30 billion rand for upgrading the locomotives.

Currently, the cooperation between the China Development Bank and Transnet mainly adopts the direct financing model. This case briefs us on the project through the collaboration between CRRC Corporation Limited and Transnet SOC Ltd. on a locomotive procurement project.

1. Borrower's Profile

Founded in 1990, Transnet is a large monopolistic South African state-owned enterprise. Previously, it was known as the South African Transport

Services (SATS) which was established in 1980. In 1990, the South African government further restructured the South African transportation service system by following corporate-style management and renamed it as the Transnet SOC Ltd.

As the largest railway freight transport and logistics service provider in South Africa and Africa at large, Transnet is currently made up of the following operating divisions: Transnet Freight Rail, Transnet Engineering, Transnet National Ports Authority, Transnet Port Terminals and Transnet Pipelines. They are responsible for the railways, ports and other infrastructure construction, management and cargo transportation in South Africa. By the end of March 2017, the railway had an operating mileage of 30400 kilometers, 1064 in-service locomotives, and 3800 kilometers of transportation pipelines.

In 2010, the South African government promulgated the *National Transport Master Plan from 2005 to 2050*, South Africa will improve the efficiency of the existing railway network through large-scale transformation, vigorous development of the railway, gradual reduction of highway load of passenger and freight transportation. In this way, the strategic shift of transporting bulk cargo from the highway to the railway will be achieved. Additionally, the South African government will invest heavily to upgrade the existing freight transportation system, and the Transnet will be responsible for its execution.

On February 9th, 2012, South African President Jacob Zuma announced the Transnet Market Demand Strategy (MDS), which aims to promote economic growth and employment through Transnet's infrastructure development. With the MDS in place, Transnet will invest 300 billion Rand (approximately USD 25.343 billion) in seven years to expand existing infrastructure, including railways, ports and pipelines, making South Africa a transit hub for Sub-Saharan Africa, and strengthening its's position as a gateway to the African continent. As of the end of March 2017, the actual cumulative investment was 145 billion Rand (approximately USD 12.249 billion).

2. CRRC Corporation Limited and Transnet SOC Ltd. 's Locomotive Procurement Project

In March 2013, under the witness of President Xi Jinping and President Jacob Zuma, the President of the CDB, Zheng Zhijie signed the five-billion-dollar financial cooperation agreement with Transnet.

On March 17th, 2014, Transnet announced the bidding results for the locomotive procurement project. China South Locomotive & Rolling Stock Corporation Limited (hereinafter referred to as 'CSR') won the bid of 359 sets of electric locomotives and China Northern Locomotive & Rolling Stock Industry (Group) Corporation (hereinafter referred to as 'China CNR') won the bid of 232 sets of diesel locomotives. The Chinese bidder won over 50% of share with a total contract value of 32. 469 billion Rand, which is equivalent to USD 3. 032 billion (converted at Dollar to Rand exchange rate of 1:10. 71). This is the largest railway locomotive export order that China has ever had.

In September 2014, the CDB committed a loan of USD 2. 5 billion to Transnet for the payment of China CRRC and Transnet procurement contract with a project capital of USD 532 million. During the World Economic Forum on Africa held in Cape Town, South Africa on June 4th, 2015, the CDB and Transnet signed an advance portion of USD 2. 5 billion with a total loan contract of USD 1. 5 billion under the joint witness of the Minister of Public Enterprise (DPE) of South Africa and the Chinese Ambassador to South Africa. The term of the loan is 15 years with a construction period of 4. 5 years. By the end of April 2018, a total of USD 933 million was issued, with a loan balance of USD 933 million. Chinese railway equipment manufacturers have delivered 260 sets of railway locomotives to Transnet, and the contract is currently being executed smoothly.

3. Major Terms of Credit

3. 1   Amount of Credit

The amount of credit for this project is USD 2. 5 billion.

3. 2   Intended Use of the Loan

The loan is used to pay for the purchase of locomotives from CSR and China CNR. Transnet will purchase 459 sets of electric locomotives from CSR and 232 sets of diesel locomotives from China CNR respectively, with a total contract value of 32. 469 billion Rand, equivalent to around USD 3. 03 billion.

3. 3   Length of Maturity

The term of credit is 15 years with a construction period of 4. 5 years. It would be paid back with cash flow generated through the project.

4. Significance and Implications of the Project

First, as the largest railway locomotive export order that China has ever had, the project is a landmark achievement for CDB's 'going out' strategy as it leverages the advantages of development finance. It is of positive significance for CDB as it made business breakthroughs in Africa. In March 2013, jointly witnessed by President Xi Jinping and President Jacob Zuma, the project constitutes a major component of USD 5 billion financial cooperation agreement signed between President Zheng Zhijie of CDB and Transnet.

Secondly, given the weak financial capacity of African countries, less-developed investment climate, and imperfect laws and regulations, the CDB's business in Africa hasn't made major breakthroughs since the beginning of its international cooperation in Africa. South Africa, the country where the project is based, is the most developed and the most influential country in Africa. It enjoys an absolute leading position in Africa and is also an important point in China's diplomatic strategy of 'one point, one line and one piece' in Africa. The project will become a reference model for cooperation between the CDB and infrastructure SOEs in Africa and will pave the way for its future success in the African market.

Thirdly, South Africa, as an export-oriented and resource-based economy, railway plays a key role in South Africa's economic revitalization. This project will bring down the cost of transportation in South Africa and enhance its export competitiveness. It will link up Vele and Makhado and new mines with the transportation pipelines, enable ESKOM's shift from 'road-to-railway' for coal transportation. It is also conducive to South Africa's economic recovery. The partnership between SOEs in China and South Africa lays the foundation for growing South Africa's annual transportation capacity from 210 million tons to 350 million tons, marking a huge leap in its railway infrastructure development. Meanwhile, the project will also boost the export of China's locomotive equipment and other quality products, which has created about 8, 000 direct and indirect employment opportunities for South Africa. As a result, the production technology and industrialization level of locomotives in South Africa will be effectively boosted.

5. Summary of Experience and Implications

First, support Chinese companies going global with senior government officials' visits. As China-Africa relations enjoy sustained development, China's investment in South Africa is also growing. An increasing number of Chinese companies are going global while the CDB is also honoring its commitment by implementing projects agreed during senior government officials' visits to enable Chinese companies a plain sailing journey on their way to the global market. Secondly, focus on the bigger picture. Following the South Africa's practice, the CDB provides a dollar-denominated loan, and it is entitled to manage customer's funds and earn some profit. However, to better achieve strategic cooperation between the two parties, the CDB gives customers sufficient choice by allowing them to choose the bank for funds transactions. Thirdly, properly design the credit structure to better manage the credit risk. With the locomotive being the collateral, USD 1. 775 billion loan is granted, and the guarantee-free credit is USD 725 million.

The 'leading SOE + development banks' between China and South Africa serves as a good infrastructure cooperation model and can be shared and adopted among the BRICS countries, supporting their nuclear power, railways, highways and ports development as well as other infrastructure cooperation.

Case 4: Support China Three Gorges Corporation's Acquisition of Brazilian Hydropower Station Project with Investment and Loans

To help Chinese-funded enterprises further explore the Brazilian market, the China Development Bank, together with the China-Latin America Industrial Cooperation Investment Fund (hereinafter referred to as 'CLAICIF'), greatly supported China Three Gorges Corporation's successful bidding for the 30-year franchise rights of Brazil's Jupia and IlhaSolteria hydropower stations, making China Three Gorges Corporation the second largest private power generation company and the sixth largest power generation company in Brazil. The smooth operation of the project has become a successful case for the CDB to support Chinese-funded enterprises in infrastructure franchising investment in Brazil.

1. Borrower's Profile

China Three Gorges Group Brazil Co. , Ltd. (hereinafter referred to as 'CTG Brazil') was established in 2013 and is a wholly-owned subsidiary of the China Three Gorges Corporation. Its main business is the investment, development and operation of Brazilian hydropower and wind power projects. By the end of 2016, CTG Brazil has held shares in 17 hydropower stations and 11 wind farms, becoming the second largest private power generation enterprise and the sixth largest power generation enterprise in Brazil.

2. Project Background and Profile

To increase the fiscal revenue, in November 2015, 29 operating hydropower projects' franchising periods was due and the Brazilian government started a new round of bidding for 30-year franchising of around 6 million kilowatts started. Being the second largest hydropower market in the world, Brazil features a mature electricity market mechanism and embraces great potential for future development. The bidding offers strategic opportunities for foreign investors to invest in the Brazilian electricity market.

Brazil's Jupia and Ilha Solteria hydropower stations have a total installed capacity of 4. 995 million kilowatts, accounting for over 80% of the total installed capacity for bidding. The 30-year franchise period costs a total of 13. 804 billion Brazilian Real (equivalent to around USD 3. 68 billion, based on the exchange rate in November 2015). 70% of the generated electricity has a fixed annual electricity income (about 2. 381 billion Brazilian Real per year), while the remaining 30% needs to be consumed in the free market.

In December 2015, China Development Bank issued a loan in full amount, which finally led to the successful delivery of the franchise right from Jupia and IlhaSolteria hydropower stations to China Three Gorges Corporation on January 5th, 2016.

3. Significance and Implications

3.1   Leverage investment and loans to better support Chinese energy companies to 'going out'. In this project, the CDB provides favorable financing support through the combination of bank, fund investment and loans for China Three Gorges Corporation's acquisition of the Brazilian franchise project. By introducing the CLAICIF, it eases the company's immediate capital investment pressure and serves its 'going out' strategy.

3.2   Give full play to the advantages of integrated financial services and offer tailor-made financing solutions for the customers. Considering the credit capacity of the China Three Gorges Corporation and its overseas bond issuance in the future, the CDB designed a tailored and comprehensive financial service plans to satisfy customer's needs, which helps the customer to hedge against the risk of interest rate increase in the U.S. and reduce customer financial costs at the same time.

3.3   Strike a balance between economic and social benefits and create a model for Brazilian energy infrastructure cooperation. In this case, the innovative financing model not only helps the customer to accomplish its business strategy and promote the steady growth of its overseas business, but also stabilizes and consolidates the strategic partnership between the two parties. It provides important reference for other Chinese-funded enterprises when conducting infrastructure franchise projects in Brazil. In terms of social benefits, the bidding for franchising provides the government with a timely and effective source of funds when the going gets tough. To some extent, it also eases the problems of regional power supply and create employment opportunities.

Case 5: Innovative Local Currency Letter of Guarantee Supports State Grid's Successful Bidding for the Belo Monte Hydropower UHV Transmission Project in Brazil

1. Borrower's Profile

State Grid Brazil Holding Ltd. (hereinafter referred to as 'State Grid Brazil') was established in July 2010 and is mainly engaged in the planning, construction and operation of power transmission systems. It is the third largest power transmission company in Brazil and has won the 'Best Electric Utility Companies in Brazil' for three consecutive years. It features comprehensive competitive strength in the local power generation market.

In 2010, State Grid Brazil entered the Brazilian power transmission market by acquiring 7 Brazilian transmission franchise companies owned by a Spanish company. In 2011 and 2012, it partnered with Brazilian companies by establishing joint ventures to win the bids for 3 power transmission and transformation greenfield projects. And its assets scale quickly rose to the industry's top level in Brazil. In February 2014, the joint venture between State Grid Brazil and Brazilian Power Company with a 51% : 49% share ratio successfully won the bid for the first phase of the Belo Monte Hydropower Station Transmission Project in Brazil. In July 2015, State Grid Brazil itself won the bid for the second phase of Belo Monte Hydropower Station Transmission Project. Currently, State Grid Brazil has become one of the fastest-growing and best-developed Chinese-funded enterprises in Brazil.

2. Project Background and Profile

The first phase of the transmission project built for the Belo Monte Hydropower Station, which is the fourth largest hydropower station in the world. The project is the first ± 800kV transmission line and the two-terminal converter station in the Americas.

In February 2014, State Grid Brazil (proportion of share: 51%), together with 2 of Brazilian utilities' subsidiaries, Furnas (proportion of share: 24.5%) and Eletronorte (proportion of share: 24.5%) formed a joint venture, which had successfully won the bid for the project. The term of franchise of this project is 30 years. The construction period starts from June 2014 and is expected to end in February 2018.

In July 2014, under the witness of President Xi Jinping and President Dilma Rousseff, Chairman of the State Grid Corporation Liu Zhenya and CEO of Eletrobras Costa Carvalho Neto signed the Cooperation Agreement on Brazil's Belo Monte Hydropower UHV Transmission Project at the Brazilian presidential palace. In May 2015, Premier Li Keqiang and President Dilma Rousseff attended the groundbreaking ceremony of the project.

The total investment of the project exceeded R $ 5 billion, apart from the shareholder's capital and raising external debt, the Brazilian Development Bank offers a certain amount of direct loan. As one of the shareholders of the project, the State Grid Brazil applied for the Brazilian Development Bank's loan based on its proportion of shares, for which the CDB provided a financing guarantee. In April 2017, the Brazilian Development Bank issued the first round of loan for the project.

3. Significance and Implications

3.1 Serve the Brazilian real economy and realize the China-Brazil cooperation and win-win relationship. The Belo Monte Hydropower Station Transmission Project through the support by the State Grid Brazil has effectively improved the standard of Brazilian power transmission and transformation and stabilized the economic and social development. Moreover, the long-term investment and localized operation strategy has brought substantial benefits to the local societies and communities. The Rio city council awarded the president of the State Grid Brazil with the highest rank of decoration and honorary citizen, which showed the highly recognition to Chinese investment and financing by local societies.

3.2 Improve the Chinese enterprises investing environment in Brazil, lay foundation for the following cooperation. The first Phase of Belo Monte

Hydropower Station Transmission Project is of strategic significance to the exploration of the Latin American market. This project will strengthen the strategic cooperation between the CDB and the State Grid and lay a good foundation for future cooperation in Brazil and South America.

3. 3 Promote innovation in financing models to reduce the financing cost for enterprises in Brazil. The CDB issued a letter of guarantee for the State Grid Brazil to apply for a medium and long-term Brazilian local currency loan, which effectively reduces its medium and long-term financing costs and improves the bargaining power of the State Grid Corporation with the local banks.

Case 6: Naspers Holds Stock in Tencent's Project

1. Case Background

From 1995 to 2001, the proliferation of capital speculation and venture capital investment has caused a serious internet bubbles in several stock markets including Europe, America and Asia. After reaching its peak of 5048 on March 10th, 2000, the tech stock-dominated Nasdaq Composite Index plummeted to 4580 in just five days. As of 2001, the bubbles have subsided at full speed, and a large number of companies have exhausted their venture capital funds. Given their mounting debts, they have no choice but to sell assets or even to liquidate. Against this backdrop, international venture capital investors become increasingly cautious in the Internet industry investment.

Meanwhile, the Internet industry in China is undergoing drastic changes. With the overall network infrastructure been greatly improved, individuals and enterprises can have easier access to the Internet and their demand for Internet services has become more concrete and pragmatic. With a huge number of potential users and their growing appetite for the Internet services, the Internet sector in China embraces a promising future.

2. Profile of the Two Parties

2. 1   About Tencent

Founded in 1998, Tencent Holdings Co., Ltd. (hereinafter referred to as Tencent) is now one of the largest integrated Internet service providers in China. It offers a portfolio of services, including Internet value-added services, e-commerce and online advertising services. With the mission of 'becoming a one-stop online service provider' in mind, Tencent strives to meet the needs of users in communication, entertainment and information through its instant messaging tools QQ and its mobile social networking and communication service application WeChat.

As one of the largest patent holders among Chinese Internet companies, Tencent's patents cover 6 areas, including storage technology, distributed network and wireless technologies. In 2017, Tencent achieved steady growth in several core business units, such as online games, digital content, advertising and cloud services. It is dedicated to applying artificial intelligence technology to the existing products and services. As one of the leading Chinese Internet companies, Tencent has profoundly changed the way of life and communication of hundreds of millions of Internet users in China.

2. 2   About Naspers

Naspers was founded in 1915 as a media company in South Africa. Previously, it only had the newspaper business. In 1985, it founded M-NET to develop its business in electronic videos and entertainment, extending its business scope from printed media to broadcasting and film industry. In 1997, Koos Bekker became the CEO of Naspers, hence kicked off Naspers' remarkable development in the Internet sector. In terms of its business scale and growth prospect, the broadcasting, film and television businesses are far better than traditional newspaper business. Naspers has never been self-complacent in the printed media business and has been proactively exploring future possibilities and opportunities in the Internet business field. As early as 1997, Naspers' CEO, Koos Bekker had already invested in China's Internet business, but all those investment projects ended up in complete failure. With lessons learned, Naspers changed its global investment strategy. Instead of establishing and operating companies on its own, Naspers decided to invest in leading local companies. The following picture gives a snapshot of Naspers' main investment projects:

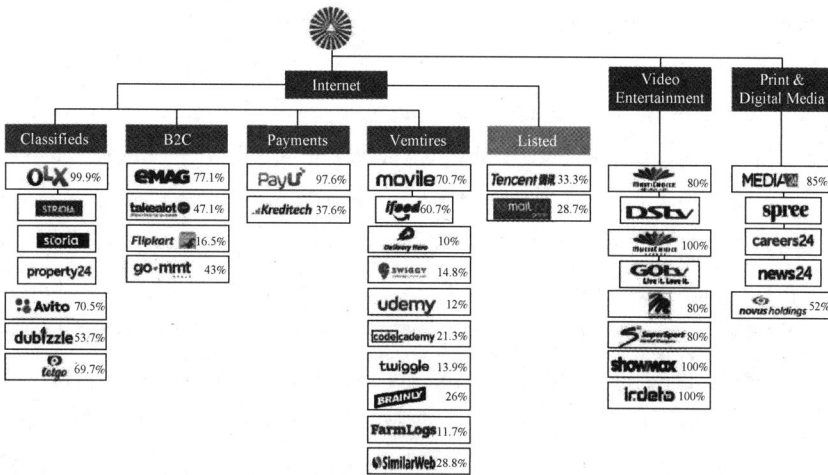

Figure 1　Major Investments Held by Naspers

Source: Publicly disclosed information

3. Process of Acquisition

In 2001, Tencent only had a single instant messaging product, QQ (formerly known as OICQ). The growing number of users pushed the company to continuously improve its technology and servers. On the one hand, Tencent's funds were being depleted, on the other hand, there wasn't a mature profit model to bring in additional funds. The initially raised USD 2. 2 million by Tencent would soon be exhausted and there was an urgent need for refinancing.

However, the crash of the NASDAQ stock market by then led to tightened capital supply. The two initial investors, IDG and HKT, intended to withdraw their investment from Tencent. They believed that Tencent's business model was no longer favored by the mainstream market. With the vast majority of Tencent's funding went into additional servers, it was unlikely to generate short-term profitability. Tencent had repeatedly negotiated with IDG and HKT in hopes of additional investment, but it also insisted on securing its founding team's control over the company. Finally, the two companies provided Tencent with a loan of USD 2 million, which was executed as convertible bonds. But they would not have any follow-up investment. By then, it has been 3 years since Naspers closed its Internet service company in China. In the meanwhile, it started to actively seek out Internet investment opportunities in China. Given its appetite for investment in the Internet industry, with a deep understanding of instant messaging tools, and a positive view of Tencent's future business development in China, the MIH (MIH Holdings Limited; its parent company is Naspers) which is responsible for the strategic presence, merger and acquisition, has reached out to Tencent, hoping to become its largest shareholder. MIH valued Tencent for USD 60 million, which was the highest valuation that Tencent could get in the market by then. In the end, HKT sold Tencent's 20% shares for USD 12.6 million, followed by IDG Capital's 12.8% share sale. MIH, a subsidiary of Naspers, bought 32.8% of the shares and became the second largest shareholder of Tencent. In 2002, MIH acquired another 13.5% stake from other Tencent's founders and became its largest shareholder. In the 17 years that followed, Naspers only got dividends and hasn't sold any share of Tencent. In March 2018, for the first time, MIH sold 2% of Tencent's shares, but it still ranks as the largest shareholder of Tencent with a 31.2% share.

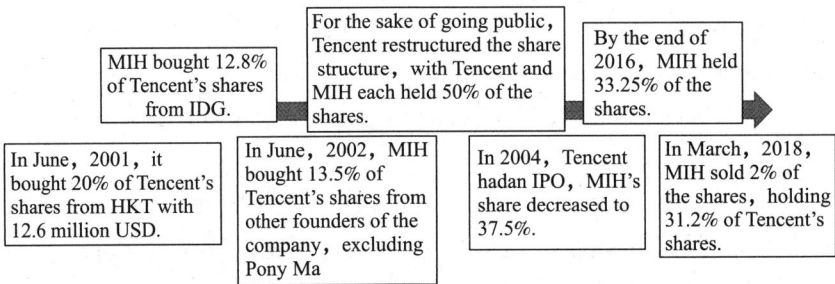

MIH bought 12.8% of Tencent's shares from IDG.	For the sake of going public, Tencent restructured the share structure, with Tencent and MIH each held 50% of the shares.	By the end of 2016, MIH held 33.25% of the shares.
In June, 2001, it bought 20% of Tencent's shares from HKT with 12.6 million USD.	In June, 2002, MIH bought 13.5% of Tencent's shares from other founders of the company, excluding Pony Ma	In 2004, Tencent hadan IPO, MIH's share decreased to 37.5%.	In March, 2018, MIH sold 2% of the shares, holding 31.2% of Tencent's shares.

Figure 2   Process of Share Acquisition

Source: Publicly disclosed information

4. Significance and Implications

The earlier failure of Naspers's business operation leads to its change of strategy. Instead of running the Internet company by itself, it searches for investment opportunities in excellent companies and entrepreneurs globally. Naspers is optimistic about the prospect of China's Internet sector. Tencent's exponential growth in its users captured Naspers' attention, resulting in the 'legend' of two world-class Internet giants and a 'miracle' in the equity investment community with a total return rate of 5, 000 times.

4. 1   Changing Mindset Leads to Cooperation and Innovation

This case highlights the importance of a changing mindset to cooperation and innovation. As a traditional printed media, Naspers faces a huge challenge posed by online media. It responded quickly by digitalizing the content of printed media, seeking business expansion and investment opportunities in the Internet sector. The challenge from the Internet has been turned into an opportunity for them, achieving what Joseph Schumpeter described as 'creative destruction'. When digitized printed media content failed to fully satisfy the needs of the times, Naspers embarked on an Omnimedia transformation journey. When it comes to the cooperation in investment and financing among the BRICS countries, we should be open-minded and change the way of thinking to build a creative cooperation model and framework so as to tackle the challenges in economic and financial development. In this way, we can achieve a win-win or all-win outcome.

4. 2   Investment and Financing Drives Faster Company's Transformation

Naspers' holding of Tencent's shares reflects the critical role of investment and financing in promoting organizational transformation. As the prospect of domestic pay TV and other services became clearer, Naspers stepped out of its comfort zone by actively seeking investment opportunities outside South Africa. Ultimately, with a huge consumer base, the emerging and booming Internet industry in China grabbed its attention. Learning the lessons from its earlier failure, Naspers decided not to act as an executor of the business, and quit the idea of establishing a company on its own. Instead, it opted to invest in companies with aligned development philosophy so as to share the huge dividends generated by the booming Internet industry. After the acquisition in 2001, Naspers did not stop its searching effort for the next Tencent globally by further exploring investment opportunities in the Internet sector with a particular focus on the emerging markets, such as countries in Asia, Africa and Latin America, and a member of the BRICS community, Russia. It can be predicted that investment and financing will continue to be an important driving force for organizational transformation under the wave of the fourth Industrial Revolution. It is also an important way for international financial cooperation in the new frontiers.

4.3   Hold on to the Right Strategic Trajectory

In the early days of Naspers' investment in the Internet sector, there were more failures than success, but its investment in the emerging markets' Internet industry has never been interrupted. After holding Tencent's shares, Naspers did experience several rounds of roller coaster in stock price. Although the founders of the Tencent reduced their holding of Tencent's stocks, this was never the case for Naspers as of 2017.

With a clear judgment about the market prospect and its own development strategy, short-term market fluctuations and irrational behavior would not disrupt its investment arrangement. Thanks to its early preparation, it gained abundant dividend after the market demand surged. When it comes to the cooperation among the BRICS countries, there are many uncertainties as well. Different countries have different interests and concerns, and they will for sure encounter difficulties and challenges in various aspects. In any case, cooperation among the BRICS countries is a strategic theme that should be consistently adhered to. Cooperation brings win-win outcome while confrontation leads to lose-lose outcome. In the face of adverse effects brought by international politics, financial markets, etc. We must stand firm to be a problem solver and a cooperator. Frequently reinventing the wheel should be avoided. Otherwise, it would be difficult for us to gain more benefits from investment and financing cooperation.

Case 7: The Currency Exchange Fund

1. Case Background

Most countries in emerging markets have varying degrees of currency mismatches, and the exchange rate of developing countries' currencies fluctuates greatly. Currency mismatch is defined as follows: when assets and liabilities of an equity entity (sovereign countries, banks, non-financial corporations or households, etc.) are denominated in different currencies such that net worth is sensitive to change in the exchange rate. (Goldstein & Turner, 2004) In addition, since the end of the Bretton Woods System in 1971, the currency of almost all developing countries has experienced a depreciation of at least 20% Funds for development financing are mainly provided and settled in U. S. dollars. In reality, financial institutions usually pass the risk of currency mismatching to the final borrower. As a result, exchange rate fluctuations lead to an increase in corporate credit default. For financial institutions with large foreign currency loans, currency-induced credit risks will then spread to other institutions in the financial system, and even lead to a financial crisis in that country.

To solve the above-mentioned problems, The Currency Exchange Fund (hereinafter referred to as TCX) emerged. TCX stakeholders (investors, financial institutions and borrowers) will prevent the risks, thus playing a crucial role in risk mitigation throughout the financial chain. For borrowers, currency mismatches no longer occur and the default rate of final borrower is reduced. For microfinance institutions (MFI), TCX provides tools for funds matching. The risk borne by the borrowers and MFIs is reduced. As a result, the credit problems of development financial institutions' and microfinance investment institutions' shareholders are effectively solved.

2. TCX's Profile

The Currency Exchange Fund was established in 2007 by Development Finance Institutions (DFI), Microfinance Investment Vehicles (MIV) and other donors to tackle currency risk issues. Currently, TCX's investors include the Dutch and German governments, as well as 22 multilateral and bilateral DFIs and MIVs. By hedging currency risks, TCX contributes to the sustainable development of emerging markets and frontier markets. It aims to develop local capital markets and protect TCX's customers and shareholders.

2. 1　Operation Model

TCX focuses on solving the problem of local currency financing difficulties for borrowers in developing countries. TCX's investors and clients provide financing to their borrowers in local currency, while using currency swaps and interest rate swaps to transfer currency risk to TCX, thereby staying immune to the exchange rate and interest rate fluctuations. Some private sector's counterparties also reduce their exposure through currency and interest rate swaps. TCX hedges its exchange rate and interest rate risk through hedging instruments, thereby continuing to provide customers with currency swap services.

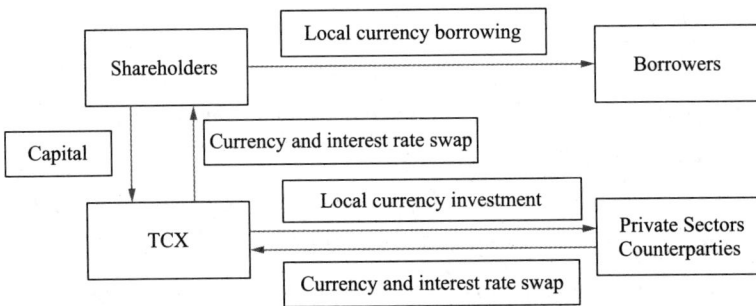

Figure 3　TCX's Operation Model

2. 2　Hedging Methods

TCX is priced according to the current market exchange rate and only hedges the actual potential risks of the real economy. For those currencies that have not been covered by commercial banks or other money providers, particularly, when there is no offshore hedging market, long-term hedging tools, or even no hedging markets, TCX plays a role as a market maker. This leaves TCX unable to hedge against the currency risks borne by itself and it must assume and manage its needed open positions.

TCX manages risk through diversified investment portfolios in multiple currencies around the world. By bringing together many actively traded currencies in the market, it can reach a level of diversification that no other financial institutions can achieve. Such diversification model is supported by the abundant capital of investors.

TCX's business is growing over the past decade and currently cover more than 70 currencies in sub-Saharan Africa, Eastern Europe, Central Asia, the Middle East and North Africa, Asia and Latin America, offering up to 30 years of hedge pricing. Its uniqueness lies in the use of currency hedging instruments: the transaction parties sign an agreement to exchange two currencies at a specific time in the future, and the exchange rate and interest rate are locked in advance through derivatives. TCX mainly uses two financial instruments, namely, forward and swap:

2.2.1 Forward contracts. It is an agreement to purchase or sell a certain amount of foreign currency at a designated price at a specified time in the future. Typically, the customer sells a fixed amount of a single local currency through TCX and obtains a fixed amount of USD from TCX on an agreed future date.

2.2.2 Currency swap. Swaps can be described as a series of bundled forwards. The two parties agree to exchange multiple fixed amounts (usually loan principal and interest) denominated in two different currencies. The client sells the local currency to TCX and TCX pays the USD for exchange. Interest on currency swaps can be fixed or floated around the benchmark interest rate.

2.3 Clients and Investors Profile

TCX's shareholders and counterparties are development financial institutions and privately managed microfinance investment institutions. The Dutch and German government provided financial support for TCX in the form of subordinate convertible bonds and a first-time loss loan. The institutional investors of TCX are shown as follows:

Figure 4   Current Institutional Investors

Currently, TCX's counterparties are mainly TCX investors, investors' clients and other customers (commercial banks, funds, and companies). Investors and clients can enjoy the priority to its hedging ability. By shifting local currency risk to a centrally managed and diversified cash pooling, TCX enables its investors to be more dedicated to providing long-term local currency lending to the clients.

3   Significance and Implications

3.1   Provide Currency Hedging Tools for Emerging Markets

As of 2018, TCX has been established for 11 years. *The 10-year Impact Assessment Report* released by TCX in 2017 analyzes its impact on local currency development in the past decade since TCX's inception. The results show that, as TCX's customers, there is no increase in credit defaults for microfinance institutions when the bank customers are affected by the depreciation and U.S. dollar borrowers are heavily delinquent in loans. Because TCX lends its clients international loans in local currency, the sharp depreciation of local currencies is absorbed by TCX and does not affect the final borrowers. TCX has provided currency hedging tools for investors and private institutions, greatly reducing the financial risks borne by borrowers and lending institutions in developing countries. Thus, it has greatly contributed to the financial system stability and the smooth development of the financing business.

3.2　Offer　Risk　Management　Models' Inspiration　for　Financial Institutions

TCX's risk exposure mainly comes from the market risk, and it has accumulated a lot of risk management experience during the past decade. Functionally, it separates executive and non-executive functions. In terms of organizational structure, the risk management committee directly reports to management team rather than the supervisory board, and a risk monitoring board is established at the board of supervisor's level. In addition, it also invites professional agencies to offer risk management services, helping TCX cope with global market risks. As the BRICS countries conduct investment and financing cooperation, they should also actively deal with exchange rates risk, interest rates risk and other market risks. Therefore, we can selectively use the TCX's functional design to highlight the importance of risk management from the cooperation mechanism and organizational structure's perspective. We can also consider inviting third-party professional risk management agencies and practitioners to enrich risk management experience and expertise. In this way, we can better serve BRICS cooperation and development financing services in a more professional way.

3.3　Provide Innovative Model for Multilateral Financial Cooperation

TCX's shareholders cover a large number of countries in Europe, Africa and Asia. In case of severe external shocks, it can receive financial assistance from multiple parties. Therefore, since the inception of TCX, it won the favor and support of international rating agencies, such as Standard & Poor's. As an independent financial entity, TCX can help to provide important public policy mandates to corporate shareholders and governments, support official developmental assistance with the help of the shareholders, and manage multiple risks in development financing through the establishment of special-purpose financial entities. As for the future multilateral financial cooperation among the BRICS countries, we can learn from past experience, establish cooperative relations based on common concerns, bring in more financial institutions with abundant capital, provide financial support and stronger risk management capabilities for BRICS financial cooperation and ensure greater financial security.

Case 8: Working Capital Loan Project of the Bank for Foreign Trade of Russia

From 2014 and 2015, after communication and consultation, the China Development Bank and the Bank for Foreign Trade of Russia (hereinafter referred to as 'BFTR') jointly developed offshore RMB projects for financial institutions so as to support and finance Sino-Russian trade projects. With a total amount of 12 billion yuan and a three-year term, 9.6 billion yuan has been drawn as of now. The project is a milestone event and lays the foundation for future large-scale offshore RMB cooperation between CDB and other overseas financial institutions. It will also support the economic and trade cooperation under the Belt and Road Initiative, and the internationalization strategy of RMB.

1. Project Background and Profile

In October 2014, the People's Bank of China and the Central Bank of the Russian Federation signed the *RMB/Ruble Currency Swap Agreement* between *the People's Bank of China and the Central Bank of the Russian Federation* with an amount of 150 billion yuan/815 billion rubles. Against this backdrop, to effectively bring into play the role and value of the RMB in the international market and better promote the development of good-neighborly and friendly relations between the two countries, the CDB went to Russia and held meetings with several Russian financial institutions. It was finally agreed that cross-border RMB loans will be used by the BFTR to jointly support two-way trade between China and Russia. The CDB will provide a bank loan of no more than RMB 12 billion to the BFTR to support the trade financing of Chinese and Russian enterprises with 'China content' for a period of three years.

2. Borrower/Actual Controller Profile

The Borrower, the Bank for Foreign Trade of Russia, was established in October 1990 and is the second largest commercial bank in Russia. In terms of market position, total assets and funds, financial performance and infrastructure scale, it is second only to Russia's largest commercial bank, the Sberbank of Russia. Its business network is widely distributed in Russia, it has 23 branches or Rep offices in CIS countries, Europe, Asia and Africa, and has a total of 100, 000 employees worldwide.

As of June 30th, 2017, 92. 2% of the shares of the BFTR are held by the Russian Federation government, where Federal Agency for State Property Management holds 12. 1% of common shares, State Cooperation Deposit Insurance Agency holds 32. 9% of Type A preferred stock, 47. 2% of Type B preferred stock, and 7. 8% of free-circulating common stock.

By the end of June 2017, the bank's total assets, total liabilities and owners' equity were approximately USD 212. 561 billion, USD 188. 415 billion and USD 24. 146 billion respectively. Its net profit was approximately USD 976 million, and its capital adequacy ratio was 14. 60% . The non-performing loan ratio was 6. 30% , the ROA was 0. 46% , and the ROE was 8. 20%.

As of the end of June 2017, the Bank for Foreign Trade of Russia took up 15. 6% of the corporate credit market, 20. 3% of the corporate deposit market, 14. 5% of the retail loan market, and 9. 7% of retail deposits market in Russia. Its retail loans increased by 21% compared to 2013. Currently, the BFTR (including VTB, its retail bank VTB24, and its acquired Bank of Moscow and ELTO Bank) has 1610 branches in 341 cities in 72 regions across Russia. Among them, VTB24 is the second largest retail bank in Russia with more than 12000 ATMs. Its international banking business spreads across Russia and other 22 countries, enjoying a highly competitive market position.

3. Project Progress and Update

Up to now, the RMB 8.5 billion loans issued by the CDB have been mainly used for the Sino-Russian enterprises' trade cooperation projects in metallurgy, mining, transportation, oil and gas, retail, wood pulp and food. 7 Russian financing companies and 31 Chinese trading enterprises were involved, among which, 18 projects were Russia's imports from China and 13 projects were Russia's exports to China. China's exports to Russia got a total financing of 6.8 billion yuan, accounting for 80% of the total funds used; while the China's imports from Russia got a total financing of 1.7 billion yuan, accounting for 20% of the total funds used.

4. Significance and Implications

In recent years, the Bank for Foreign Trade of Russia has been committed to supporting Sino-Russian trade and has accumulated a large customer base. By partnering with BFTR, a large number of Sino-Russian trade projects have enjoyed sound development and Sino-Russian economic and trade relations are also being promoted. The cooperation is conducive and significant to the diversification of Sino-Russian trade, and consolidation of the strategic partnership between the two countries.

This project features the largest single loan financing for offshore RMB cooperation between China and Russia financial institutions in recent years. It is also a major measure for the CDB to implement the 'Belt and Road' financial cooperation and promote the RMB internationalization strategy. This project will be a reference model for future Chinese-funded banks and overseas financial institutions along the 'Belt and Road' region to conduct loan cooperation with trade financing as its core component.

The project will accelerate the promotion of RMB as a currency for settlement in international market transactions, increase the purchasing power of RMB globally, and advance the internationalization of the RMB. Meanwhile, conducting offshore RMB cooperation will promote China's economic and trade relations with Russia and other regions and maintain the steady growth of its foreign trade.

Case 9: BRICS Interbank Cooperation Mechanism

1. General Information

To further boost economic cooperation and expand the fields of practical cooperation among the BRICS countries, under the framework of the BRICS leaders' meeting, with the joint witness of the former Chinese President Hu Jintao, Brazilian President Luis Inacio Lula da Silva, Russian President Dmitry Medvede and Indian Prime Minister Manmohan Singh, the China Development Bank (hereinafter referred to as the 'CDB') and the Brazilian Development Bank, the Bank for Development and Foreign Economic Affairs of Russia and the Export-Import Bank of India jointly signed the *Memorandum on BRICS Interbank Cooperation Mechanism* in Brasilia on April 15th, 2010. It aims to provide diversified financial services for the economy, technological cooperation and trade development among the BRICS countries. This marks the official establishment of the BRICS Interbank Cooperation Mechanism.

On April 13th, 2011, the CDB hosted the first annual meeting of BRICS Interbank Cooperation Mechanism—The first BRICS Financial Forum in Sanya. Member banks signed the *Protocol on Development Bank of Southern Africa's Accession to the Cooperation Mechanism*, making the Development Bank of Southern Africa an official member bank of the BRICS Interbank Cooperation Mechanism.

The BRICS Interbank Cooperation Mechanism will hold its annual meeting, the BRICS Financial Forum during each year's BRICS Summit and sign the outcome documents of the Financial Forum. Since its inception, the BRICS Interbank Cooperation Mechanism has signed 7 multilateral cooperation agreements under the witness of the leaders of the five countries, covering local currency credit line, confirmation of L/C services, sustainable development, infrastructure development and green financing. It has effectively promoted the financial cooperation and economic and trade investment facilitation among the BRICS countries. To prepare for the deliverables of the annual meeting and the financial forum, member banks of the BRICS Interbank Cooperation Mechanism would hold an annual technical group meeting (bureau level) and working group meeting (expert meeting) on an annual basis.

2. Updates on Cooperation

Since the inception of the BRICS Interbank Cooperation Mechanism in 2010, the CDB, as a member bank, has attached great importance to participating in the institutional building of the mechanism and has strengthened cooperation with various member banks within the mechanism's framework.

First, strengthen collaboration among the member banks and jointly implement the deliverables of multilateral cooperation. Since the first annual meeting of the BRICS Interbank Cooperation Mechanism and the first Financial Forum held in Sanya, China in 2011, member banks have signed 7 multilateral cooperation agreements under the witness of the leaders of the BRICS countries, covering various areas, including local currency credit line, confirmation of L/C services, support of sustainable development, innovation and cooperation. This cooperation was incorporated into the deliverables of the BRICS Summit, namely *Sanya Declaration*, *Declaration of Delhi*, *Durban Declaration*, *Fortaleza Declaration*, *Ufa Declaration* and *Goa Declaration*. These documents have played a positive role in facilitating the economic and trade investment and deepening financial cooperation of BRICS countries.

Secondly, deepen bilateral project cooperation and promote the sustainable development of BRICS countries. In terms of bilateral project cooperation, the BRICS countries are one of the key partners for CDB's international cooperation. In the past six years, following the principle of mutual benefit and win-win cooperation, the CDB leveraged the BRICS Interbank Cooperation Mechanism and actively conducted project cooperation with member banks and local companies. By of the end of 2017, the CDB has accumulatively committed loans of USD 134.6 billion and issued loans of USD 86.9 billion to the BRICS countries with a loan balance of USD 58 billion. The projects cover multiple fields, namely, energy, agriculture, electricity, infrastructure, processing and manufacturing, SMEs and finance, contributing to sustainable economic growth and socially inclusive development of the BRICS countries. From the perspective of bilateral inter-bank cooperation, it mainly includes:

The CDB signed a bilateral memorandum of cooperation with the New Development Bank, stipulating that they will carry out all-round cooperation in the areas of project co-financing, capital business, research cooperation, knowledge sharing, personnel and information exchange.

The CDB and Brazilian Development Bank signed the *Memorandum of Understanding for Deepening Comprehensive Strategic Cooperation* and the two parties will conduct project cooperation, covering transportation, electricity, municipalities, communications, science and technology, R&D centers, industrial parks, agriculture, and environmental protection, tourism, logistics and other fields.

CDB and Petrobras signed a *Comprehensive Strategic Cooperation Agreement*, and the two sides will further collaborate in financing and oil and gas sector to achieve comprehensive strategic cooperation.

In December 2010, the CDB and the Export-Import Bank of India signed a bilateral *Memorandum of Strategic Cooperation* to kick off their business cooperation.

Thirdly, strengthen personnel training and promote the cultural exchange among the BRIC countries. The CDB has trained 500 officials, leaders and experts from government institutions, financial institutions, and partner companies of the BRICS countries. The CDB also established a scholarship to fund 13 outstanding young talents from the BRICS countries to further their studies in China. The first financial innovation and joint development training for the BRIC countries was held in Beijing on June 29-30, 2017. The participating institutions not only enhanced their friendship, deepened their understanding, but also developed a better understanding of China's economic development model and developmental finance concept.

Fourthly, press ahead with institution (mechanism) building. In June 2017, five special working group seminars were held in Beijing, dealing with the topics of BRICS countries' local currency credit line, innovation and high-tech business, credit rating, emerging market economic framework research, personnel training and experience exchange. Experts discussed about the supporting models of innovative and high-tech businesses in emerging market countries, the path and mode of local currency credit line cooperation among member banks, the development path of national rating agencies in emerging markets, and the long-term cooperation mechanism and innovation experience for the study of emerging markets' economic and financial dynamics. Consensus was reached on further deepening cooperation.

Hosted the BRICS Think Tank Forum and the BRICS Financial and Business Dialogue, sharing development financial concepts, successful experiences and case studies so as to promote the 'soft power' exchanges and cooperation among the BRICS countries.

Participated in the BRICS Seminar on Governance and reached good results and earned positive feedback.

Hosted the 2017 BRICS Interbank Cooperation Mechanism Annual Meeting, the 7th BRICS Financial Forum, and several bilateral meetings with the Brazilian Development Bank, the Export-Import Bank of India, the Development Bank of Southern Africa, and ESKOM; jointly held a Brazilian Business and Investment Opportunity Seminar with the Brazilian government and signed several multilateral and bilateral cooperation outcome documents. Under the framework of multilateral cooperation, five member banks of the BRICS Interbank Cooperation Mechanism have jointly signed two multilateral agreements, *Interbank Local Currency Credit Line Agreement Under BRICS Interbank Cooperation Mechanism* and *Cooperation Memorandum Relating to Credit Ratings Under BRICS Interbank Cooperation Mechanism*. As the outcome documents of the annual meeting and the financial forum, they were included in the *BRICS Leaders Xiamen Declaration*.

3. Significance and Implications

3.1 The Interbank Cooperation Mechanism makes investment and international trade cooperation more convenient. The establishment of the BRICS Interbank Cooperation Mechanism has promoted local currency credit line, local currency settlement in international trade, expanded the scale of international loans, effectively hedged foreign exchange risks in trade and investment, thus, enabling a more convenient international trade and FDI flows among the BRICS countries. It lays a solid foundation for the further investment, economic and trade a cooperation among the BRICS countries.

3. 2   The establishment of Interbank Cooperation Mechanism allows the BRICS countries to timely communicate global financial market related information and boost financial sector dialogues within the BRICS. Think Tank sub-forums and senior-level dialogues will help member states to strengthen their dialogues in the fields of international trade, finance, and cooperation. They play a positive role in promoting coordination, consultation, and overcoming various challenges in the international financial cooperation, which are conducive to the establishment of a more equal and efficient interbank cooperation system.

3. 3   The Interbank Cooperation Mechanism will strengthen BRICS countries' investment and financing cooperation in the fields of high technology, resources and environmental protection. It serves as a bridge for project cooperation in key industries. Smoother investment and financing conditions would facilitate project cooperation in environmental protection and high-tech industries among the BRICS countries. Lastly, it enables financial cooperation helping BRICS members achieve mutually beneficial cooperation and win-win result in the real economy cooperation.

Case 10 : ICBC's Acquisition of South Africa's Standard Bank

1. Case Briefing

Global capital operation is an important feature of today's globalization. To stay competitive and enhance profitability through economies of scale, commercial banks extend their business presence to other countries via overseas mergers and acquisitions (M&A). As China deepens its financial market reform, overseas M&As have become an important way for Chinese commercial banks to implement their internationalization strategies. More specifically, the Industrial and Commercial Bank of China (ICBC) has long established its internationalization strategy and gradually expanded the scale of overseas institutions by means of M&As.

China invests heavily in South Africa and enjoys a promising development prospect there. Africa is China's third largest trading partner and boasts rich natural resources, such as oil and natural gas. South Africa bears great importance for China and it is a prioritized investment destination in Africa for China. South Africa is an important member of the BRICS and a major emerging economy. In 2007, China's investment in South Africa reached USD 454.41 million, and in 2008 it reached USD 4.81 billion. With a vision of 'strengthening business presence in Asia, consolidating market position in Europe, and making its way to the Americas', ICBC continues its internationalization by venturing into Africa.

South Africa is an important mineral resource country in the world, and its mineral types and reserves rank among the top globally. Compared to other African countries, its economic system is relatively open with sound investment climate. Therefore, it is an ideal investment destination for many Chinese companies. As of 2008, over 2000 Chinese companies have established production and sales offices in South Africa. Bilateral trade and foreign investment between China and Africa have driven the demand for financial services provided by Chinese-funded commercial banks. Prior to the Industrial and Commercial Bank of China's (hereinafter referred to as 'ICBC') acquisition of the Standard Bank in South Africa (hereinafter referred to as 'Standard Bank or SASB'), only Bank of China and the China Construction Bank had branches in Africa. The service scope of Chinese-funded banks in Africa was very limited. To get engaged in the African market business with the help of Standard Bank, and enhance shareholders' value through strategic investment, ICBC signed a *Strategic Cooperation Agreement* with Standard Bank to acquire 20% of its shares, achieving the strategic objectives of strategic shareholding of the Standard Bank's shares.

2. Case Background

Since China's access to the WTO in 2001, its trade liberalization and financial cooperation with other countries has been gradually improved. Chinese financial institutions are establishing overseas branches one after another to seek overseas development opportunities. Compared to local banks, it is difficult for Chinese banks to effectively obtain overseas market shares by establishing branches. Therefore, many Chinese banks choose to acquire local banks to gain access to the overseas markets. After the financial crisis in 2008, many local banks experienced operational difficulties. Chinese banks seized this opportunity by conducting overseas mergers and acquisitions. However, as they were less experienced, few of them succeeded. ICBC's acquisition of Standard Bank of South Africa is one of the most successful case and provides much food for thought for future interbank financial cooperation.

2.1   About ICBC

Prior to ICBC's inception in 1984, it mainly dealt with the industry and commercial credit services divested by the People's Bank of China. After more than 20 years of development, ICBC restructured to a joint-stock limited company in 2005. The Ministry of Finance and Central Huijin Corporation jointly established the Industrial and Commercial Bank of China Limited. In 2006, ICBC got listed in both Shanghai Stock Exchange and Stock Exchange of Hong Kong Limited. Central Huijin Investment, Ministry of Finance and Hong Kong Securities Clearing Company Ltd. (HKSCC) were the three controlling shareholders, holding 37%, 36% and 25% of the outstanding shares respectively.

After being listed in 2006, ICBC's net profit has maintained a relatively high growth rate, and its capital strength has been continuously improving. In the Tier-1 core capital-based ranking of banks, ICBC has been taking the top spots globally in recent years. Its internationalization process began with the establishment of the first representative office in Singapore in 1992. Following the principle of 'strengthening business presence in Asia, consolidating market position in Europe, and making its way to the Americas', ICBC has been extending itself overseas presence, and gradually establishing its international business network that covers important international financial centers and trade regions.

Over the past 30 years, ICBC seized the opportunity provided by the two financial crises and has rapidly established its overseas operations. After 2000, especially after the subprime mortgage crisis in 2007, the entry threshold for banking in some countries was lowered. ICBC seized the opportunities by conducting several overseas mergers and acquisitions and has achieved remarkable results in key target markets.

As of the end of 2017, ICBC has established 419 institutions in 45 countries and regions in the world. Through holding Standard Bank's shares, ICBC made its way to 20 African countries in the sub-Saharan region. It established correspondent banks with 1545 foreign institutions in 143 countries and regions. Its business covers six continents and important financial centers around the world. At present, under the overall framework of 'ONE ICBC', with unified strategy, unified system, unified culture, and well-coordinated bank, it's getting closer to the goal of 'one point of access, group-wide response, and global service'.

2.2　About South Africa's Standard Bank

Standard Bank was established in the United Kingdom in 1862. It was not until Standard Chartered Bank withdrew in 1987 that Standard Bank became a truly South African bank. After over a hundred years of development, it has become the largest bank in Africa, with branches in 18 countries in Africa. It has branches in Turkey, Argentina, the United Kingdom and Hong Kong SAR as well. With a strong distribution channel and comprehensive diversified businesses, Standard Bank has become a leader in the African banking industry.

Standard Bank is enjoying a plain sailing. With each financial indicator growing stably, it embraces a promising development prospect. As of the end of 2017, its overall revenue went up by 14% and reached 26.27 billion Rand. Its net asset value per share (NAV) was 9830 cents, registering an increase of 4% and its ROE increased from 15.3% to 17.1%.

3. Acquisition Process

3.1　Preparation Before Acquisition

Since 2005, senior executives of ICBC and Standard Bank has gradually discussed about business cooperation and equity cooperation. Given the two banks are highly similar in terms of their strategic layout, management style and market position, the two sides reached consensus on the strategic cooperation at the International Monetary Conference in June 2007. The concept of equity-based strategic cooperation was initially formed.

3. 2 Acquisition Process

On October 24th, 2007, ICBC's equity acquisition plan for Standard Bank was approved by the South African Reserve Bank. On October 25th, ICBC and Standard Bank jointly announced that the two parties have reached an agreement on equity transaction and strategic cooperation. The transaction amount is about USD 5. 5 billion. The detailed equity transaction method is shown as follows: (1) 50% of the shares acquired by ICBC were sold by the original shareholders, and ICBC purchased at the rate of 136 rand/share; (2) After its expansion of the capital stock, Standard Bank will have a private placement of 10% new shares to ICBC at the rate of 104. 58 Rand/share, and this would serve as the remaining 50% of the shares to be acquired by ICBC. The two types of equity trading methods are mutually premised. The combined premium for the acquisition of old stocks and private placements is about 15%.

After the completion of the equity delivery in March 2008, ICBC became the largest shareholder of the Standard Bank. ICBC sent two board members to the Standard Bank and established a strategic cooperation committee. The detailed timetable is shown in the following table:

Table 1 Timeline for ICBC's Acquisition of Standard Bank Timeline

Time	Steps taken
Oct. 24th, 2007	Acquisition plan approved by SARB
Oct. 25th, 2007	ICBC announced to buy 20% of Standard Bank's shares with USD 5. 5 billion
Dec. 3rd, 2007	Standard Bank's Shareholders Meeting approved the deal
Dec. 13th, 2007	ICBC's Shareholders Meeting approved the deal
Dec. 18th, 2007	The Court approved the deal
Jan. 23rd, 2008	CBRC approved the acquisition after its review
Mar. 3rd, 2008	Completed equity delivery

Source of Information: Announcement made by the 2 trading parties

After the completion of the acquisition, the two banks established strategic cooperation in accordance with the *Business Cooperation Agreement* in the following six areas: corporate banking, resource banking, global resource funds, investment banking, African and international businesses and global market operations. Cooperative teams were established accordingly to manage multiple investment and financing businesses, including direct investment, trusteeship, settlement and cash management. On the basis of equity cooperation, the two parties agreed that in the future, if only one of the two parties have established a business institution, the bank that has not established an institution will give priority to the established institution for business cooperation. In addition, the interbank cooperation team will also recommend key customers, such as large corporation groups to provide more comprehensive services.

3.3   Post-Acquisition Business Cooperation

Upon the completion of the acquisition, the two parties made great strides in business cooperation implementation. In just one year, the two banks have completed 9 out of the 65 joint projects, such as the financing of China Oilfield Services Limited' acquisition of Awilco Offshore ASA's equity, the debt underwriting of the Premium Group, and Alliance One International's export commodity financing project. The Botswana government also selected two banks as the lead for syndicated loans to jointly provide USD 825 million in export buyer's credit and USD 140 million in bridge loan services for the Morupule B coal-fired power plant project.

After becoming a major shareholder of Standard Bank, ICBC also acquired the Standard Bank Argentina, an affiliate of Standard Bank in August 2011. After becoming the first Chinese bank to acquire African financial institutions, ICBC became the first Chinese commercial bank to enter the Latin American market. In January 2014, ICBC announced the acquisition of a 60% stake in Standard Bank Plc. Through acquiring Standard Bank's London subsidiary, ICBC aims to participate in global financial business. After this acquisition, ICBC's shareholding in Standard Bank reached 20.1%.

4. Case Implications

4. 1   A   Reference   Model   for   Interbank   Investment   and   Financing
Cooperation

The acquisition of the SASB was the largest overseas investment made by
ICBC. It was also an overseas acquisition with the largest transaction amount
done by a Chinese commercial bank. As China's first commercial bank's M&A
of African financial institutions, this case is an important milestone in the
internationalization of Chinese banks. The two banks carried out equity based
strategic cooperation, and deepened mutual understanding and cooperation
through   personnel   exchanges,   which   pioneered   China-Africa   financial
cooperation. They complemented each other, shared resources, and established
a financial bridge for China-Africa cooperation, serving as an inter-bank
cooperation reference model.

4. 2   Enhance Business Capability through Complementing Each Other's
Advantages

With the help of the acquisition, ICBC proactively learns from and draws
on the experience and technology of the SASB and innovates its own products
and services so as to expand its overseas business resources. Prior to the
acquisition, ICBC's major business was corporate banking and personal
banking while the SASB's business mainly lied in personal and commercial
banking, corporate and investment banking, and wealth management, making
them mutually reinforcing to each other. By way of acquisition, ICBC learned
SASB's experience in commercial banking, investment banking and wealth
management, and implemented those practices in domestic and international
markets to enhance its business capabilities.

4. 3   Improve   International   Competitiveness   and   Boost   Its
Internationalization

The reason why ICBC chose SASB as partner is not only because of its
status as the largest commercial bank in Africa, but also because of the broad
strategic cooperation prospect of the two banks. Through the acquisition, ICBC
has expanded its customer channels in Africa and has been able to make its way
to several emerging businesses in the African market, marking an important

step in its internationalization strategy. During the ten years of holding SASB's shares, they have made remarkable achievements in trade financing, project financing, fund settlement, equity mergers and acquisitions, and information technology. In terms of financial service model innovation, the two banks launched a variety of products, including Sino-African cash management and cross-border direct remittance, providing Chinese companies and investors with multi-faceted financial services, such as fund management, credit financing, and investment banking for their operation in Africa.

5. Inspirations from the Case

5.1 The Acquisition Target and the Timing are Crucial to Interbank Investment and Financing Cooperation

According to the Market Power Theory, acquisitions allows acquirers to quickly enter a new market. Standard Bank is the largest bank in Africa. Before the acquisition, ICBC had established its own branches in Europe and the Americas, while the business in Africa remained unexplored. Through the acquisition of a bank, ICBC has opened up financial services in 18 countries in Africa, and gained abundant customers, business resources in Africa, and first-hand experience of offering local financial services. As the timing is properly selected, ICBC obtained substantial investment income to better support its overall performance.

5.2 Strategic Complementarity and Well-intentioned Acquisition are Effective Ways to Strengthen Inter-Bank Investment and Financing Cooperation

The key to the success of overseas acquisitions is the choice of target and post-acquisition integration. Since ICBC and SASB have strong strategic complementarity and cooperation intentions, the two sides have achieved a smoother post-acquisition integration. After 10 years of development, the two sides have achieved fruitful results and conducted comprehensive business cooperation in corporate banking, investment banking, global markets and funds. As Chinese banks are more likely to be affected by the 'China Threat Theory' in their overseas acquisitions, the good cooperation between the two sides is conducive to the pragmatic cooperation between China and foreign countries as it raised Chinese banks' international profile and laid a solid foundation for future cooperation.

5. 3   Investment in Emerging Market is an Important Area for Interbank Cooperation in Investment and Financing

The investment threshold in emerging markets is not as high as in developed regions. The higher economic growth in developing countries also brings more investment opportunities. Chinese banks' overseas cooperation shows that even paying a high cost, Chinese banks are still less influential in decision-making after entering the developed countries' markets . The effectiveness of cooperation is not satisfactory. In contrast, China has established good economic and trade cooperation with many developing countries, and it is more likely to succeed in emerging markets.

In this case, ICBC received a cash dividend of approximately 1. 21 billion Rand from SASB and a share dividend of 589 million Rand in the year when the acquisition was completed. The investment yield was around 7. 7% , which is much higher than the ROI of foreign bonds. Among ICBC's overseas institutions, the African region contributed the most to ICBC's pre-tax profits with the least relative investment assets. Compared with developed regions, where investment is high but the profits are not satisfactory. Therefore, in the future, Chinese financial institutions should pay more attention to emerging markets in their future cooperation.

References

[1] Mei Guanqun, "Research on the Cooperation Mechanism of BRICS Countries" [J]. *China Collective Economy*, 2017 (34): 20-22.

[2] Tian Feng, "Cooperation on the Economic Growth, Structural Transformation and Capacity among BRICS Countries" [J]. *Latin American Studies*, 2017 (08): 85-104.

[3] He Wei, "The Development Trend of the Global Value Chain and Our Corresponding Measures: In the Perspective of the Fourth Industrial Revolution" [J]. *Public Administration*, 2017 (06): 150-156.

[4] Yan Nan, "How to Change the Global Value Chain in the 'Industry 4.0' Era" [J]. *World Affairs*, 2015, (20).

[5] Zhong Yuan, "Big Data: Strategic Resources of the Fourth Industrial Revolution" [N]. *Economic Information Daily*, 2016-06-21.

[6] Chen Fengxian, "Emergency Foreign Exchange Reserve Arrangement in BRICS Countries: Cost-Benefit, Governance Defects and China's Choice" [J]. *South China Finance* 2014 (2): 4-13.

[7] Chen Jianyu, "The Background and Influence of the Establishment of the BRICS Development Bank" [J]. *Qinghai Finance* (Qinghai Jinrong). 2014 (11): 4-7.

[8] Dai Ming, Chen Jingxin, Jiang Han, "An Empirical Study of the Dual Equity Function in the Post-Industrial Economic Age, with Specific Examples" [J]. *Science and Technology Management Research*, 2016 (1): 196-201.

[9] Lin Songtian, Li He, "Making the BRICS Cooperation a New Platform for South-South Cooperation" [J]. *China Investment*, 2017 (18).

[10] Cheng Lian, "The BRICS New Development Bank: A New Model of

Win-Win Outcomes in the South-South Cooperation" [J]. *Ziguangge*, 2014 (9): 48-49.

[11] Li Yonggang, "Research on the Financial Cooperation Mechanism among BRICS Countries" [J]. *Journal of Jinan University* (Philosophy and Social Sciences), 2015 (12): 60-65.

[12] Pan Qingzhong, Li Daokui and Feng Ming, "What's New: The Background, Significance and Challenges of the Establishment of the BRICS New Development Bank" [J]. *International Economic Review*, 2015 (2): 134-147.

[13] Zhang Haibing, "The Development and Innovation of the BRICS New Development Bank" [J]. *World Outlook* 2015 (5), 20: 31.

[14] Lin Yueqin, "Research on the Local Currency Settlement (LCS) of in BRICS Countries" [J]. *Xue Hai* (Academia Bimestris), 2012 (4): 27-34.

[15] Liu Dongmin, Xiao Lizhen, Lu Ting, "Approaches for the Financial Cooperation of BRICS Countries" [J]. *China Finance*, 2017 (15): 84-86.

[16] Lu Dong, Wang Wei, "The Mode and Development of Bilateral Local Currency Settlement" [J]. *China Finance*, 2012 (4): 63-64.

[17] Lu Yue, "Research on the Relationship between the New Model of Internet Finance and the Financing of SMEs" [J]. *Modern Economic Information*, 2016: 268.

[18] Sun Dan, "'De-Dollarization' and Multilateral Currency Swap in the Perspective based on the BRICS Contingency Reserve Arrangement" [J]. *International Finance*, 2014 (9): 50-56.

[19] Tian Huifang, "Prior Issues and Policy Choices for Sustainable Development Cooperation in BRICS Countries" [J]. *International Economic Cooperation*, 2017 (8): 17-21.

[20] Wang Dan, Lu Fengling, "Practice of Currency Swap in the People's Bank of China" [J]. *China Finance*, 2012 (4): 61-62.

[21] Xu Deshun, "Bring New Ideas to Credit Cooperation among the BRICS Countries" [J]. *Theoretical Herald* (Jiangxi Li Lun Dao Bao), 2017

(9).

[22] Zhang Ming, "Global Currency Swap: Current Situation, Function and Potential Direction of the International Monetary System Reform" [J]. *International Economic Review*, 2012 (06): 65-88.

[23] Zhang Xiaomei, Liang Hong, Jiang Ruran, "Block Chain Financing and Credit Distribution of Small and Micro Enterprises" [J]. *Shanghai Finance*, 2016 (7): 35-40.

[24] Zhao Zhongxiu, Hu Xudong, "Development-Oriented Finance in the New Globalization, in the Perspective of BRICS Countries" [J]. *International Trade*, 2017 (12): 53-57.

[25] Preety Bhogal, "Re-Examining the Implications of Existing Credit Rating Agencies for the BRICS Countries" [J]. *Excerpted from the Report of the Indian Think Tank Observer Research Foundation*, May 2017.

[26] Li Wei, "The BRICS Mechanism and the Reform of International Financial Governance" [J]. *International Review*, 2013 (1): 6.

[27] Wang Houshuang, Guan Wei, Jin Yu, "The Impact of the BRICS Cooperation Mechanism on the Innovation of the Global Economic Governance System" [J]. *Asia-Pacific Economic Review*, 2015 (03): 3-8.

[28] Wang Xin, "The Impact of the rising International Financial Capacity of the BRICS Countries on International Finance and its Governance" [J]. *International Economic Review*, 2011 (01): 94-108, 5.

[29] Tang Lingxiao, Ouyang Yao, Huang Zexian, "BRICS Development Bank in the Perspective of International Financial Cooperation" [J]. *Large Country Economy Research*, 2014: 55-74.

[30] Sang Baichuan, Liu Yang, Zheng Wei, "Financial Cooperation among BRICS Countries: Status Quo, Problems and Prospects" [J]. *International Trade*, 2012 (12): 32-34.

[31] Han Yiyuan, "The History and Prospects of the BRICS Cooperation" [J]. *International Study Reference*, 2016 (11): 1-6.

[32] Cai Chunlin, Liu Meixiang, "Status Quo and Mechanism Innovation of the Trade and Investment Cooperation among BRICS Countries" [J].

Asia-Pacific Economic Review, 2017 (3): 33-39.

[33] Annual Report on the Development Strategy of the BRICS Mechanism (2016) [C], 2016: 76.

[34] Chen Deming et al. , *Economic Crisis and Reconstruction of Rules* [M]. The Commercial Press (Beijing), 2014.

[35] Ouyang Wei, Zhang Yabin, Yi Xianzhong, "The 'Shared' Growth of Foreign Trade between China and other BRICS Countries" [J]. *Chinese Social Sciences*, 2012 (10): 67-86.

[36] Zhu Jiejin, "The BRICS Bank, Competitive Multilateralism and the Reform of Global Economic Governance" [J]. *Journal of International Relations*, 2016 (05): 101-112, 155-156.

[37] Li Daokui, Xu Xiang, "The BRICS Cooperation Mechanism in the View of Global Governance" [J]. *Reform*, 2015 (10): 51-61.

[38] Zheng Wei, *"Expanding Economic and Trade Cooperation among BRICS Countries: Theoretical Foundation and Path Selection"* [D]. University of International Business and Economics, 2015.

[39] Zhang Haibing, "The Cooperation of BRICS Countries in the Adjustment of the World Economic Structure" [J]. *International Outlook*, 2014, 6 (05): 16-29, 150-151.

[40] Zhang Changlong, "The Dilemma and Way-Out for Developing Countries to Strive for a New International Economic and Financial Order—Taking the Formation of the BRICS Cooperation Mechanism as a Background" [J]. *Guizhou Social Sciences*, 2011 (07): 91-95.

[41] Lin Yueqin, "Deepening Financial Cooperation and the Common Development of Emerging Countries—In the Perspective of BRICS Countries" [J]. *Journal of Hohai University* (Philosophy and Social Sciences), 2016, 18 (2): 1-10.

[42] Cai Chunlin, Liu Meixiang, "Status Quo and Mechanism Innovation of the Trade and Investment Cooperation among BRICS Countries" [J]. *Asia-Pacific Economic Review*, 2017 (3): 33-39.

[43] Pu Gongying, "Analysis of People-to-People Exchange and Cooperation Mechanism in BRICS Countries" [J]. *Russian, Central Asian & East*

European Studies, 2017 (4).

[44] UNCTAD, "*World Investment Report* 2017: *Investment and The Digital Economy*" [R]. United Nations Publication, 2017.

[45] World Bank, "*Global Economic Prospects: Broad-Based Upturn, but for How Long?*" [R]. World Bank Group, 2018.

[46] World Bank, "*Russia Monthly Economic Developments*" [R]. 2018.

[47] IMF. World Economic Outlook: *Seeking Sustainable Growth-Short-Term Recovery, Long-Term Challenges* [R], 2017.

Postscript

In September 2017, the ninth meeting of BRICS Leaders was successfully held in Xiamen, China. During the meeting, China Development Bank Research Institute and China Council of BRICS Think-Tank jointly published *the BRICS Sustainable Development Report* (2017) (*Report* 2017), systematically analyzed the economic development of the BRICS countries and the major challenges they faced, and proposed advice on the economic and financial cooperation, etc.

In March 2018, China Development Bank (CDB) which was carrying out the national top-level Think-Tank construction work of *the BRICS Sustainable Development Report* (2018) (*Report* 2018) with the University of International Business and Economics (UIBE). *Report* 2018 is the continuation and renewal of *Report* 2017. At the end of March, CDB Research Institute organized the first discussion meeting of the joint writing group. After intense discussion on the outline and content of the research, it was determined that the entry point of *Report* 2018 is 'Innovating Investment & Financing Mechanism of BRICS Countries, Promoting Pragmatic Cooperation and Mutual Benefits'. Through a comprehensive review on the overall economic development and financial investment of the BRICS countries, the writing group elaborated the significance and objectives of deepening investment and financing cooperation, analyzed the key areas and industries, obstacles and problems of financial investment of the BRICS countries and proposed forward-looking policy recommendation.

In April, according to the editing plan in the meeting, CDB Research Institute and UIBE began to write intensively. Under the organizing of CDB Research Institute, the business experts from CDB's Research Institute, Planning Department, Legal Affairs Department, Capital Department, Risk

Management Department, International Finance Department, Global Cooperation Business Department, Information Technology Department, Henan Branch, Sichuan Branch, Rio de Janeiro Representative Office, Moscow Representative Office, India Working Group and South African Working Group participated in the data collection, collation, case studies and preparation of relevant chapters. Professors and experts from UIBE 'Belt and Road' PPP Development Research Center, Finance Academy, Regional and National Research Institute, World Trade Organization Institute participated in the preparation of relevant chapters of the report.

In terms of case selection, we have selected 10 typical investment and financing cases in BRICS countries and cooperation mechanism based on the principles of green, sustainable and far-reaching. Through institutional interviews and research and first-hand information and materials, we summarize the successful experience of the case, and provide guidance for the future development of investment and financing and pragmatic cooperation in the BRICS countries. The first draft of *Report* 2018 was completed in early May. CDB Research Institute held a meeting to discuss the first drafted version, and proposed amendments to the structure and content of the report, and refined the report to form an abstract Chinese version of *Report* 2018.

By the end of May, the English version of *Report* 2018 abstract was completed by Li Xiaomeng, Li Chenle, Wang Chun, Su Yurong. Li Lin, Li Xiao from UIBE, which is approximately 16000 words. With the help of Chinese council of the BRICS Think Tank, Zhao Zhongxiu, Vice President of UIBE, personally carried dozens of English version report to South Africa and president of UIEBE, personally carried dozens of English version report to South Africa and presented them at the BRICS seminar in Johannesburg for expert reference.

From June to July, based on full consultation with relevant experts, the Rio de Janeiro Representative Office, Moscow Representative Office, India Working Group and South Africa Working Group, the report was further revised and restructured, and finished the second draft of *Report 2018* (with Chinese, English, Russian, Portuguese versions). On July 25th, the chairman of CDB officially released the report at the annual meeting of the BRICS cooperation mechanism and Financial Forum held in Cape Town, South Africa. The report focused on the BRICS financial investment, highly aligned with the essence of the annual meeting of banks cooperation mechanism, in which connecting the industrial revolution, exploring the application of digital economy (such as blockchain) in the field of financial investment concerted the theme of the BRICS Leaders Summit in 2018. It contributes the 'Chinese wisdom' for the sustainable development of the BRICS economy and financial investment.

The leaders of CDB and UIBE attach great importance to this book. It is written under the direct guidance of Liu Yong, the Chief Economist of CDB and Direct General of CDB Research Institute. Zhu Wenbin, Deputy Director of CDB Research Institute, give specific guidance and repeatedly discuss with the writing team while participating in the wholeprocess and revising the final draft. Professor Wu Weixing from UIBE gives fully support to writing this book, and organize experts to join in the writing work. Li Yijun and Long Yan from CDB coordinate the theme design, outline drafting, case selection, writing, drafting, editing and publishing of the final version, etc.. A great number of experts from both institutions participated in th writing and editing work. In particular, many colleagues from the front-line of business department of CDB integrated their actual work experience into the report. Additionally, interns from CDB research institute including Mu Yaqi, Wu Haoxiang, Zhang Xinrui, Cai Yao, Zhou Jiaxi also participated in the writing and editing work of this book. The leading writers for the first and second version include but not limited: Long Yan, Mu Yaqi, Wu Haoxiang, Zhou Nianli for the First and Second Chapter; Mu Yaqi, Long Yan, Wu Haoxiang, Lan Qingxin for the Third Chapter; Mu Yaqi, Yin Yanfei, Zhang Xinrui, Long Yan, Li Yijun for the Forth Chapter; Yin Yanfei, Song Chen, Han Guoxin, Hu Yong, Shi Wenjuan, Li Yijun for the Fifth Chapter; Zhang Xinrui, Long Yan, Sun Yonghai, Zhou Zhenheng, Zhao Hongtao, Su Zhanping, Yang Guxin, Zhao Hao, Li Shengzhe for the 10 cases in appendix; Li Yijun, Wen Hao, Long Yan, Xia Guanzhong, Yin Yanfei, Mu Yaqi, Wu Haoxiang, Cai Yao, Zhou Jiaxi for the drafting, editing and publishing work of Chinese, English and Russian version of the book. At the same time, we would like to thank CDB General Office, Policy Rescarch

Office, International Finance Department and Accounting Department for supporting the translation, printing and publishing of the report. We would also appreciate publishing of this book at the BRICS Financial Forum with the coordination and help from the International Finance Bureau of CDB, and the organization and coordination help from Li Xiaomeng from International Office of UIBE and Wei Xiaoquan from "Belt and Road" PPP Center of UIBE.

In today's world, the economic and social development is changing with each passing day. The research in this book is still progressing and needs to be continuously tracked and updated in the future. We welcome and appreciate the readers' valuable suggestions.

Research Institute of China Development Bank

December 2018

Конспект

РАЗДЕЛ 1 Открыть второе золотое десятилетие БРИКС, углубить инвестиционное сотрудничество в формате БРИКС

1.1 Об экономическом развитии стран с формирующимися рынками

1.1.1 Страны БРИКС-драйвер экономического развития стран с новоформирующимися рынками

После того как наступил новый век, наблюдается необратимая тенденция подъема стран с формирующимися рынками. Доля стран с формирующимися рынками в мировом ВВП увеличилась до 34% в 2017 году против 23% в 2006 году (рис. 1.1). Страны БРИКС, как драйвер экономического развития стран с формирующимися рынками, добились впечатляющих успехов. За прошедшее 10 лет, вклад стран БРИКС в рост мировой экономики оценивался в размере 50%. В 2017-ом году, по экономическим параметрам наблюдаются позитивные тенденции в странах БРИКС, совокупный ВВП стран БРИКС составил 18.5574 трлн, что эквивалентно 68% совокупного ВВП всех стран с формирующимися рынками, ВВП на душу населения также сохранял растущую динамику в целом (рис. 1.2); совокупный внешнеторговый оборот стран БРИКС-3.239 трлн, на них приходилось 15% совокупной мировой торговли, в 2006-ом году эта цифра была 11% (рис. 1.3); объем внешних прямых иностранных инвестиций стран БРИКС повысился с 138.9 миллиардов долларов США в 2006-ом году до 278.1 миллиардов долларов США в

2017, приток инвестиций в страны БРИКС увеличился с 102. 8 миллиардов долларов США в 2006-ом году до 165. 4 миллиардов долларов США в 2017 (рис. 1. 4).

Рис. 1. 1   ВВП стран БРИКС, развивающихся рынков и общемировой ВВП в 2006 – 2017 гг.   (млрд долларов)

Источник: International Monetary Fund

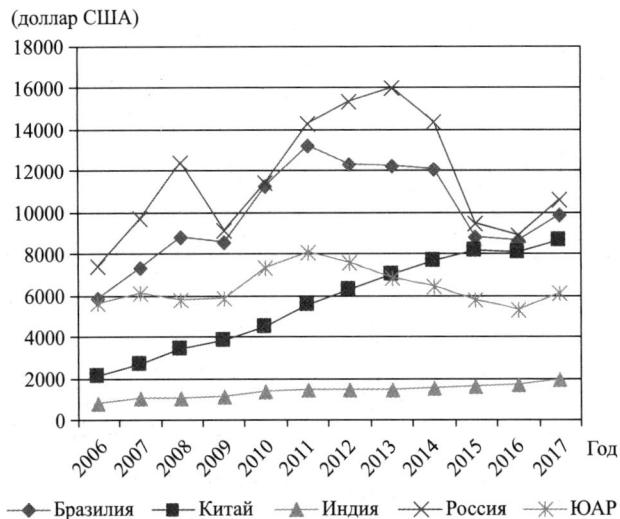

Рис. 1. 2   Среднедушевой ВВП стран БРИКС в 2006 – 2017 гг.   (доллар США)

Источник: International Monetary Fund

(млн долларов США)

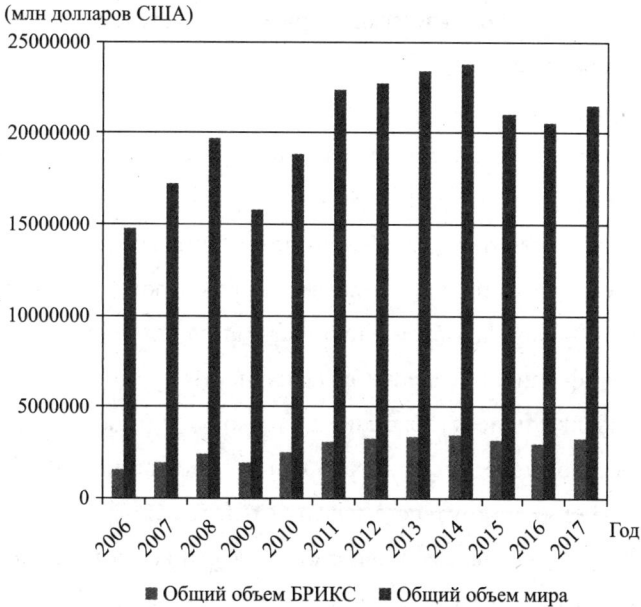

Рис. 1. 3 Суммарный товарооборот стран БРИКС и объем мировой торговли в 2006 – 2017 гг. (млн долларов США)

Источник: UNCTAD, International Monetary Fund

(млн долларов США)

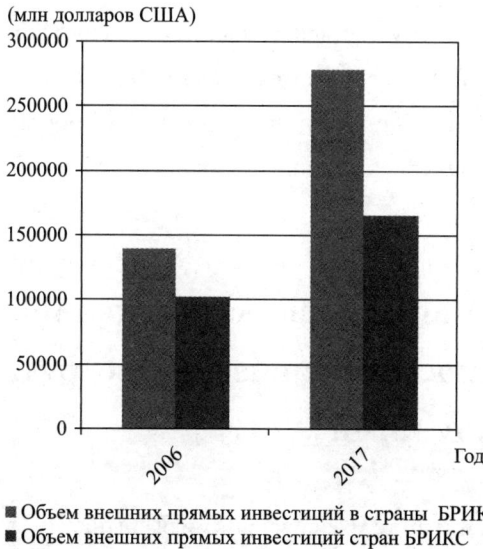

■ Объем внешних прямых инвестиций в страны БРИКС
■ Объем внешних прямых инвестиций стран БРИКС

Рис. 1. 4 Прямые иностранные инвестиции стран БРИКС и приток инвестиций в страны БРИКС в 2006 г. и в 2017 г. (млн долларов США)

Источник: CEIC

1. 1. 2 Обзор экономического развития других развивающихся рынков

В настоящее время наблюдается большой разрыв в уровнях экономического развития между развивающимися рынками, азиатские развивающиеся рынки занимают лидирующие позиции по экономическому развитию, за ним по пятам следуют страны на ближнем востоке и в северной Африке, а латиноамериканские страны чаще всего сталкиваются с рядом проблем, таких как высокий уровень бюджетного дефицита и инфляции, усиление волатильности курса валюты и др. Во-вторых, развивающиеся рынки в целом страдают от высокой безработицы, большое число безработных стало общей проблемой для всех стран. Третье, в контексте падения цен на продукты, ревальвации валюты в 2017 г., цены на развивающихся рынках в целом снизились, в связи с перенаправлением капиталов, внутренней экономической ситуацией, геополитической обстановкой и другими факторами, ситуация на развивающихся рынках, связанная с цен на товары сложилась по разному, инфляционное давление на некоторые экономики по-прежнему осталось высоким. Последнее, в 2007 г. развивающиеся рынки сталкиваются с рядом рисков в области притока прямых иностранных инвестиций, динамика роста гораздо хуже прогнозируемых, теперь ситуация в экономике у странах сложилась по разному.

1. 2 Общность развивающихся рынков и важность активизации сотрудничества между ними

Большинство стран с развивающимися рынками в начале 20-ого века были в колонии и полуколонии, были поставщиками сырья и рынками сбыт, их индустриальное развитие подчинялось игу метрополии. Хотя после второй мировой войны страны в Азии, Африке и Латинской Америке добились независимости и суверенитета, но исторические и другие факторы все время препятствовали их развитию. Именно потому, что страны с развивающимися рынками связаны схожей исторической судьбой, активизация экономического сотрудничества между ними является необходимой.

Первое, экономическое сотрудничество в рамках БРИКС способствует росту экономики развивающихся рынков. Сотрудничество в области экономики между странами БРИКС направлено на финансовую поддержку инфраструктуры, на восполнение недостатков развивающихся рынков в своем развитии и содействие модернизации производственной структуры и инновационному развитию экономики развивающихся рынков. Второе, экономическое сотрудничество в рамках БРИКС стимулирует реформирование финансовой системы и политическую инновацию на развивающихся рынках. Предпосылками для налаживания международного экономического сотрудничества является координация действий между его участниками в области функционирования экономики, системы контроля и экономической политики. Экономическое взаимодействие стимулирует реформирование экономической системы и усиление политической координации на развивающихся рынках. Третье, наращивание экономического сотрудничества в рамках БРИКС позволяет странам БРИКС получить доступ к финансовым ресурсам, технологиям и другим ресурсам друг у друга, более надлежащим образом быть интегрированы в глобальные цепочки стоимости. Например, Китай сегодня занимает центральное место в глобальных цепочках стоимости, импортирует сырье из развивающихся стран, привлекает финансовые ресурсы и внедряет технологии из развитых стран, на основе своей совершенной индустриальной системы теперь уже стал одной из крупнейших держав-производителей в мире. Четвертое, сотрудничество между странами БРИКС-эффективная защита от внешних политико-экономических рисков. В случае того, в условиях санкционного режима, развивающиеся рынки могут прилагать совместные усилия к усилению коллективной рыночной власти и укреплению позиции на переговорах, выступать единым фронтом в поддержку какого-либо развивающегося рынка, попавшего под несправедливые экономические санкции.

1.3 Перспективы практического сотрудничества БРИКС на следующее золотое десятилетие

Страны БРИКС, объединившиеся десятилетие назад, справились с мировым финансовым кризисом и другими серьезными испытаниями, показали всему миру яркий пример взаимовыгодного сотрудничества между странами с развивающимися рынками и развивающимися странами, достигли блестящих успехов.

В будущем, страны БРИКС должны и далее расширять торговое сотрудничество, создавать новую платформу для наращивания сотрудничества 《 Юг-юг 》, продвигать вперед модель взаимодействия 《 БРИКС ＋ 》, углублять финансовое сотрудничество, восполнять нехватку финансирования в совместных проектах БРИКС, повышать уровень взаимодействия в сфере инвестиции и финансирования, стимулировать культурный обмен и взаимопонимание между народами, наращивать партнерство БРИКС.

1.4 Инвестиционное сотрудничество-залог углубления сотрудничества в формате БРИКС

В настоящее время, постепенно расширяется инвестиционный масштаб внутри БРИКС, но сумма капиталовложения остается относительно маленькой, потенциал для будущего сотрудничества далеко не исчерпан. На фоне экономической и финансовой глобализации инвестиционное сотрудничество играет все более важную роль в содействии социально-экономическому росту. Наращивание инвестиционного сотрудничества в формате БРИКС-естественный выбор стран БРИКС для стимулирования собственного развития, и участия в международном финансово-экономическом сотрудничестве и финансово-экономической системе управления.

Новый банк развития БРИКС и Пул условных валютных резервов БРИКС представляют собой новую модель сотрудничества《 Юг-юг》, служит повсеместной гарантией и поддержкой экономического развития развивающихся стран, также совсем новой формой участия развивающихся стран в системе глобального управления, является полезным дополнением к существующей международной финансовой системе. Новый банк развития БРИКС и Пул условных валютных резервов БРИКС показали яркий пример межгосударственного взаимодействия в области инвестиции, заложили прочный фундамент для инвестиционного сотрудничества в формате БРИКС и по линии《Юг-юг》.

РАЗДЕЛ 2 Цели инвестиционного сотрудничества в формате БРИКС и его практика

2.1 Усовершенствовать систему глобального финансового управления

Глобальное финансовое управление-процесс участия правительств стран, международных организаций, неправительственных организаций, транснациональных корпораций и других субъектов в системе управления глобальными финансовыми делами, в целях уклонения от системных финансовых рисков и их профилактики, обеспечения финансово-экономической стабильности, установления здорового финансового порядка, путем координации действий, налаживания сотрудничества и достижения консенсусов. Одним словом, для выстраивания глобального финансового управления необходимо добиться《согласованности и скоординированности, стремления к выгоде и избежания потери》в сфере международных финансов. Существующий режим по системе глобального финансового управления уже показал свою ограниченность, в этом смысле примерами могут служить МВФ, Всемирный банк и ряд других международных финансовых институтов, они не полностью выполняют свою функцию регулирования мирового финансового рынка, либо не способны полностью выполнять такую функцию. К тому же, практика 《долларовый стандарт》 и непоследовательность макроэкономической политики США приведут к постоянному всплеску международных финансовых кризисово

Отношение стран к вопросам золотовалютных резервов во многом зависит от внутренней монетарной политики США, золотовалютные резервы стран легко подвергаются рисков девальвации. По той же причине в международной системе валютных курсов существуют многие факторы неопределенности, США передают валютно-курсовые риски странам-кредиторам путем печатания денег, но страны-кредиторы не могут делать то самое, чтобы передали подобные риски США. Очевидно, такая практика ущемляет интересы развивающихся рынков, прежде всего интересы стран БРИКС.

Благодаря Новому банку развития БРИКС и практике стран в сфере инвестиции и финансирования, теперь БРИКС уже стало важней движущей силой для стимулирования повышения институциональной возможности международного финансового сотрудничества и реорганизации международного финансового порядка. Как важные участницы структуры международной экономики, страны БРИКС принимают широкое участие в эффективном распределении финансового капитала во всем мире, усовершенствовании форм и инструментария финансового контроля. Постепенно расширяются географический охват инвестиций и вид активов, сферы влияния инвестиционной деятельности стран БРИКС, и она играет все более весомую роль в сохранении позитивных тенденции мирового экономического роста. По мере укрепления своей возможности, страны БРИКС видят в себе большую обязанность и ответственность за противодействие торговому протекционизму, обеспечение финансовой безопасности, защиту и развитие открытой мировой экономики, сохранение сбалансированности между регионального развития и многосторонней дипломатией. Вместе с этим, страны БРИКС-активные участницы существующей системы глобального финансового управления, приняли активное участие в переговорном процессе по 《Базель III》, по повестке дня ВТО, по всеобъемлющему и прогрессивному Соглашению о Транстихоокеанском партнёрстве, по реформе квот и прав голоса Всемирного банка и Международного валютного фонда, также в саммитах 《G20》, в целях усовершенствования   существующих   рамок   международных финансовых институтов.

2. 2　Содействовать структурным реформам в экономике стран

Проведение структурной реформы экономики внутри стран БРИКС остаётся тяжелой задачей, реформа в сфере предложения в Китае сталкивается с институциональными барьерами; ресурсная структура российской экономики нуждается в незамедлительной трансформации; проблемы индийской экономики, связанные с дуализмом, являются вкоренившимися; смена президента в Бразилии, также вялая национальная экономика приведут к бессилию реформы и экономической нагрузке; высокая зависимость Южной Африки от внешнеэкономических конъюнктурных факторов подрывает ее самостоятельность. В этой связи была поставлена задача перед объединением БРИКС наладить инвестиционное сотрудничество в поддержку структурных реформ в экономике стран.

Для того, чтобы выполнить данную задачу, в первую очередь страны БРИКС должны найти самую идеальную модель инвестиционного сотрудничества между собой путем эффективных контактов и координации действий, углубить отраслевое сотрудничество и инновационное сотрудничество, создать новые драйверы роста мировой экономики. Далее, наращивая инвестиционное сотрудничество, страны могут выявить относительное преимущество стран, координировать стратегии отраслевого развития, более активно принять участие в процессе международного разделения труда, по собственной инициативе быть интегрированы в глобальную систему экономического развития. Помимо этого, наращивая инвестиционное сотрудничество в формате БРИКС, страны могут укреплять многостороннюю торговую систему, противостоять торговому протекционизму в целях повышения уровня открытости и инклюзивности инвестиции и торговли стран БРИКС.

2.3 Способствовать развитию инфраструктуры стран БРИКС и отраслевому сотрудничеству между ними

За прошедшие 10 лет страны БРИКС направляли огромные усилия на наращивание инвестиционного сотрудничества, поиск новых моделей и механизмов для развертывания инвестиционного сотрудничества, улучшение инфраструктуры, повышение уровня либерализации торговли и взаимодействия в других отраслях. Государственный Банк развития Китая также принял участие в ряде крупных совместных проектов, внес свой вклад в содействие инфраструктурному строительству стран БРИКС. Например, ГБРК оказал поддержку финансирования компании Transnet ЮАР при ее приобретении тепловозов у китайских компаний CRRC, CSR и CNR; инвестировал и кредитовал проект по приобретению Китайской корпорации CTGC ГЭС Бразилии; выдал банковскую гарантию в национальной валюте Государственной электросетевой корпорации Китая для её участия в тендере на проект по строительству сверхвысоковольтных линий электропередачи от ГЭС《Бело Монте》в Бразилии. ГБРК совершил инновацию в инвестиционном сотрудничестве, снизил затрат по финансированию, стимулировал модернизацию инфраструктуры стран БРИКС, повысил социально-экономический эффект.

2.4 Активизировать товарооборот между странами БРИКС

Торгово-экономическое сотрудничество – один из важных драйверов интеграции развивающихся рынков в процессе экономической глобализации, ускорения экономического роста и процветания. Наращивание торгово-экономического сотрудничества между странами с новоформирующимися рынками стимулирует диверсификацию торговли, расширение ее масштаба, сокращает независимость новоформирующихся экономик от их традиционных торговых партнеров. Начиная с 2006 г. до сегодняшнего дня, товарооборот между странами БРИКС в целом растет, наблюдается пассивное сальдо в торговле услугами, но пока еще существуют проблемы, связанные с торговой структурой и торговой стабильностью между странами БРИКС, поскольку соответственные механизмы сотрудничества продвигаются слишком медленно.

В целях урегулирования этих проблем и содействия взаимодействию и контактам на самых разных уровнях, в рамках БРИКС был установлен механизм был установлен механизм заседания на министерском уровне, на постоянной основе были проведены деловой форум, также были установлены контактная группа по торгово-экономическим вопросам (CGETI), рабочая группа по электронной торговле, рабочая группа БРИКС по таможенным вопросам. По итогам Встречи министров экономики и торговли стран БРИКС в 2017 г. были приняты 7 документов, в том числе Программа сотрудничества в упрощении инвестиционной деятельности, экономико-технологическое сотрудничество впервые было включено в повестку дня торгово-экономического сотрудничества в формате БРИКС. По мере развития механизмов инвестиционного сотрудничества в формате БРИКС, в духе Сямэньского саммита страны БРИКС будут и далее укреплять взаимопонимание и взаимодоверие, продвигать финансовую интеграцию в интересах всестороннего процветания финансового сектора.

2.5 Играть лидирующую роль среди новоформирующихся стран в разработке правил и принципов международного инвестиционного сотрудничества

Принципы и правила международной инвестиционной деятельности пока фрагментизированы. В настоящее время отсутствует универсальный многосторонний режим в данной области, также отсутствует эффективные международные институты. Экономическая перестройка стран БРИКС в определенной степени подвергается ограничением существующих норм и принципов в области международного инвестиционного сотрудничества.

Страны БРИКС, как инициаторы усовершенствования международного финансового порядка, должны наращивать сотрудничество в области инвестиции, что способствует накоплению полезных опытов, задействованию лидирующей роли при разработке норм и принципов международной инвестиционной деятельности, стимулированию инвестиционной либерализации, поиску способа по усилению контроля за инвестиционной деятельностью, защите интересов реципиентов и инвесторов, и реализации экономических возможностей БРИКС.

РАЗДЕЛ 3 Ключевые области и отрасли стран БРИКС для инвестиционной и финансовой деятельности

3.1 Бразилия

После прихода к своей должности президент Темер принял Программу инвестиционного партнерства и проект《Умный город》, нацеленные на увеличение инвестиций в инфраструктуру страны. Бразилия имеет преимущество в сферах сельского хозяйства, лесоводства, животноводства, нефти и газа, автопроизводства, текстильной промышленности и услуг. В этой связи Бразилии можно продолжить усилить работу по привлечению иностранных инвестиций в сферу услуг и в такие отрасли, как торговля, финансовое и вспомогательное обслуживание, электричество и природный газ, добыча нефти и газа, горно-перерабатывающая промышленность, электромашины, прицеп, полуприцеп и соответствующие комплектующие, химикаты, машины и оборудование, одежда и аксессуары. Можно, с одной стороны, в полной мере использовать имеющийся задел иностранных капиталов, с другой, повысить конкурентоспособность Бразилии в тех сферах, где страна пока слаба по экспорту, чтобы оптимизировать отраслевую структуры в интересах экономического развития по всем направлениям.

3.2 Россия

После переизбрания на пост президента России В. В. Путин будет продолжать реализовать Концепцию долгосрочного социально-экономического развития Российской Федерации на период до 2020 года с акцентом на трансформацию отраслевой структуры, увеличение инвестиций, развитие инновационной экономики, ускорение модернизации традиционной промышленности, усовершенствование инфраструктуры, плавное продвижение процесса приватизации. В своем послании Федеральному Собранию Российской Федерации от 1 марта 2018 года президент В. В. Путин заявил, что в предстоящие шесть лет необходимо удвоить расходы на строительство и обустройство автомобильных дорог, направить на эти цели более 11 триллионов рублей (примерно 200 млрд долларов) и привлечь около 1,5 триллиона рублей (около 26 млрд долларов) частных инвестиций в обновление отечественной электроэнергетики. Что касается иностранных инвестиций, то России нужно всемерно привлечь инокапиталы в области финансов, страхования, оптовой и розничной торговли, обрабатывающей промышленности, строительства, специальности, научно-технической деятельности, текстиля, электроэнергетики, природного газа, административных и поддерживающих услуг, медицины и фармацевтики, чтобы оптимизировать отраслевую структуру и удовлетворить рыночный спрос.

3.3 Индия

В конце 2014-2015 финансовых гг. правительство Индии опубликовало политику внешней торговли на 2015-2020 гг., разработанную на основе выдвинутых премьер-министром Моди программ《Сделайте в Индии》и《Цифровая Индия》с тем, чтобы стимулировать экспорт товаров обрабатывающей промышленности и услуг из Индии, содействовать росту занятости в стране. Ключевая область, нуждающаяся в увеличении иностранных инвестиций-машиностроение и сервисная индустрия, а приоритетные отрасли-информация и коммуникация, финансы и страхование, продукты питания, машины и оборудование, оптовая и розничная торговля, автомобильная промышленность, электроэнергетика, угольный газ, химикаты и химические продукты. Это может способствовать ускорению индустриализации и модернизации, раскрывать потенциал в интересах устойчивого развития.

3.4 Китай

В 2013 году председатель Китая Си Цзиньпин выдвинул инициативу о строительстве《Экономического пояса Шелкового пути》и《Морского шелкового пути 21-ого века》(Один пояс и один путь), призванную объединить Азию, Европу, Африку и прилегающие к ним морские акватории, наладить и укрепить партнерство стран вдоль Пояса и Пути, задействовать потенциал региональных рынков, способствовать росту инвестиций и потребления, содействовать интегрированному развитию транспортировки, строительства ж/д, оборудостроения, строительной отрасли и других отраслей.《Сделано в Китае 2025》– стратегическая программа, разработанная китайским правительством на основе мировой тенденции развития промышленности с целью улучшения всех параметров качества и уровня производства Китая. Начиная с 2015 года Китай приложил и прилагает большие усилия к структурным реформам в отношении предложения. Акцент делается на ликвидации избыточных производственных мощностей и переизбытка рыночного предложения, сокращении чрезмерной долговой нагрузки, снижении себестоимости и восполнении недостаток. Ускоренными темами продвигается реформа научно-технической системы, чтобы придать импульс развитию зеленых низкоуглеродных отраслей. Важнейшими отраслями в Китае для привлечения прямых иностранных инвестиций являются производство, недвижимость, лизинг и бизнес-услуги, оптовая и розничная торговля, финансы, сельское хозяйство, лесное хозяйство, животноводство и рыболовство. Важно оптимизировать структуру экспорта, укрепить устойчивость развития, ускорить изменение отраслевой структуры, улучшить деловой климат и усовершенствовать модель экономического роста.

3.5 Южная Африка

В 2012 году в ЮАР опубликован Национальный план развития, где обозначены цели развития на период до 2030 г. К тому же была разработана программа строительства крупных инфраструктур в области автодорог, ж/д, электростанции и т. д., а также программа 《Пакиса》, нацеленная на развитие морской экономики и медицинской промышленности. По энергетике, горной и металлургической промышленности также составили соответствующие планы развития. Ключевыми областями, куда нужно привлечь иностранные капиталовложения, являются услуги и обрабатывающая промышленность, а приоритетными отраслями-переработка горных ресурсов, новая энергетика, переработка сельхозпродукций, электромашины, финансы, медицина, телекоммуникация, техники обработки металлов. Нужно полнее использовать богатые природные ресурсы и огромный потенциал рынка ЮАР, содействовать переходу экономики страны от потребительской модели, у которой не хватает потенциала устойчивого развития, к производственно-ориентированной, которая принимает больше рабочих сил. Необходимо постепенно изменить структуру 《двойственной экономики》 и обеспечить сбалансированность социально-экономического развития ЮАР.

РАЗДЕЛ 4 Аспекты инвестиционного сотрудничества между странами БРИКС, нуждающиеся в совершенствовании

4.1 Деловой климат

Чтобы углубить сотрудничество на основе взаимодополнения преимуществ, страны БРИКС прилагают активные усилия к улучшению делового климата. В рейтинге Всемирного банка Doing Business – 2017 все пять стран БРИКС разместились сравнительно низко и сильно отстали друг от друга, что говорит о наличии неигнорируемых проблем.

Сложная налоговая система и тяжелая налоговая нагрузка на предприятия. У почти всех стран БРИКС сложная налоговая система, а у некоторых из них даже имеет место двойное налогообложение. В Бразилии осуществляется порядок налогообложения на различных уровнях полномочий. Из-за обособления полномочий налогообложения и сильной разницы между регионами по ставке нужно затратить много времени для уплаты налогов. Центральное правительство Индии имеет право на законодательное регулирование налоговых вопросов и право на налогообложение, но власти штатов и местные администрации также обладают правом на взимание налогов, причем на региональных уровнях существуют весьма многообразные наименования налога и разные налоговые ставки. Что касается Китая, то согласно закону компания с зарубежным капиталом и иностранная компания облагаются подоходным налогом по ставке 33% , которая выше чем у других стран.

Устаревшие инфраструктуры, которые необходимо усовершенствовать. Инфраструктуры имеют важное значение для обеспечения устойчивости экономического роста и повышения международной конкурентоспособности страны по инвестиционной привлекательности. Однако инфраструктуры в странах БРИКС все еще нуждаются в совершенствовании. По железным и автомобильным дорогам Индия далеко отстала от других развивающихся государств, что серьезно препятствует развитию обрабатывающей промышленности страны. Например, хотя Индия числится в первых рядах в мире по масштабу железнодорожной сети, общая протяженность которой превышает 64 тысячи км. , но в стране не имеется высокоскоростная ж/д со скоростью свыше 200 км. У России огромная территория и многообразные географические условия. Автодорожный транспорт в стране сравнительно отсталый. Хотя для железнодорожного, воздушного и водного транспорта имеются инфраструктурные основы, но большинство из них построено еще во время СССР, поэтому уже устаревшее.

Повышение стоимости рабочих сил и снижение производительности труда. Страны БРИКС сталкиваются с разными вопросами по человеческим капиталам, но у всех проблема низкой производительности труда. В Бразилии снижение производительности труда продолжается уже много лет. Основная тому причина-низкий уровень образования рабочих сил в целом, дефицит квалифицированных специалистов, нехватка инновационных возможностей у предприятий, что затрудняет повышение производительности труда. Хотя в Китае производительность труда быстро повышается, но пока еще находится на низком уровне. Согласно докладу, опубликованному международным статистическим информационным центром Бюро статистики Китая, производительность труда в Китае составляет лишь 40% от среднего уровня в мире.

Раздутый государственный аппарат и низкая административная

эффективность. У стран БРИКС сложная структура государственного аппарата, иногда бывает дублирование функций административных органов. В результате, работы мало, но штат велик, а эффективность низкая. В рейтинге Всемирного банка Doing Business – 2017 среди 190 экономик мира пятерка БРИКС находится на низких позициях по индикаторам и《открытие предприятий》, и《получение разрешения на строительство》и《подключение к системе электроснабжения》.

Высокие пошлинные тарифы и неполноценная имплементация соответствующих законов и решений. В Индии отечественные компании уже в течение долгового времени находятся под сильной защитой, поскольку в стране поддерживается высокий уровень импортных пошлин, включая основные таможенные пошлины, налог на образование, налог, уравновешивающий льготное субсидирование, антидемпинговые пошлины, налог на безопасность и т. д.

4. 2　Законодательство

В БРИКС входят страны из 4 континента. Среди них у Индии и Южной Африки система общего права, а в России и Бразилии применяется континентальная система права, так что юридические культуры стран БРИКС весьма многообразны и сильно отличаются друг от друга. По правовой ситуации страны БРИКС в целом еще находятся на среднем уровне в мире либо ниже. Юридическая прозрачность и эффективность судебной системы там неудовлетворительны.

Правовые ограничения на покупки иностранными инвесторами земель. В общем приобретение земель остается камнем преткновения в привлечении иностранных инвестиций. Как предусмотрено законами Индии, чтобы купить землю, правительству или предприятиям необходимо получить разрешение у минимально 80% местных жителей. Премьер-министр Моди попытался выдвинуть Закон о приобретении государственных земель(National Land Acquisition Law), чтобы смягчить ограничение на земли, используемые для производства и инфраструктурного строительства. Законопроект был принят Народной палатой, но не нашел поддержку в Совете штатов и впоследствии был оставлен в стороне.

Наличие множества ограничений на найм иностранных рабочих сил. У пятерки БРИКС без исключения проблема высокого уровня безработицы, поэтому были введены ограничения на использование иностранных работников. Ограничительные меры правительства ЮАР в этом отношении весьма строгие. В принципе если можно найти подходящего работника из местного населения, то нельзя предлагать рабочее место иностранцам. С 2006 года правительство России ежегодно на 50% сокращает квоты на трудовые силы из стран, не входящих в состав СНГ, что негативно сказывается на приезде граждан других стран и регионов в Россию на работу.

Серьезная коррупция и неудовлетворительная квалификация правоохранительных органов. Правительства стран БРИКС предприняли целый пакет мер для борьбы с коррупцией, усиливая наказание коррупционеров. Но для искоренения коррупции предстоит еще много сделать. Согласно Докладу о качестве государственного управления, опубликованному Всемирным банком в 2016 году, у всех стран-участниц БРИКС оценки ситуации с верховенством закона неудовлетворяющие.

Существование множества ограничений и запретов на иностранное капиталовложение. В Бразилии иностранным инвесторам запрещается вложить капиталы в сферы атомной энергетики, здравоохранения, пенсионного фонда, морского промысела, почты и др. А в России запрещаются иностранные инвестиции в игорный бизнес и страхование жизни. В каталоге отраслевого ориентирования зарубежных инвестиций, опубликованном Министерством коммерции Китая в 2017 году, перечислен список сфер, в которые вложение инокапиталов ограничивается или запрещается. Среди этих сфер-производство автомобилей, изготовление спецавтомобилей, телекоммуникация, банковская деятельность, страхование, ценные бумаги, управление инвестиционным фондом на рынке ценных бумаг, фьючерс и т. д.

Строгость природоохранных законов и сложная процедура для получения экологического разрешения. Преследуя цель зеленого и устойчивого развития, страны БРИКС поставляют все более строгие экологические требования. В Бразилии в связи со строгими требованиями по окружающей среде часто долго затягивается выдача экологического разрешения. В зависимости от конкретных проектов иногда необходимо получить разрешение у различных уровней власти (штаты, округи, города). При реализации проектов, которые могли бы иметь воздействие на окружающую среду либо интересы местных жителей, без удовлетворения соответствующих экологических требований материнская и дочерняя компании могут быть привлечены к гражданской и административной даже уголовной ответственности.

4.3 Риски изменения курса

На фоне экономической глобализации монетарная политика США оказывает все более сильное влияние на другие страны мира. В последнее время в связи с очередным повышением процентной ставки Федеральной резервной системой США курс долларов вновь поднялся, в результате изменился поток передвижения капиталов во всем мире, огромное испытание выпало на долю новообразующихся экономик, из которых убегают краткосрочные трансграничные капиталы. Кроме того, из-за непрерывного укрепления американской валюты заметно увеличились стоимость продления срока облигаций и риски долларовых займов для новоформирующихся рынков. Все более частное повышение ФРС процентной ставки ударяет по ценам на крупные товары на мировом рынке, ущемляет интересы ресурсно-ориентированных новоформирующихся экономик, сдерживая развитие их торговли. В этой связи в интересах дальнейшего сотрудничества в рамках БРИКС важно решить тот вопрос, какую валютную и курсовую политику подобрать, чтобы противостоять различным рискам, в частности, негативному воздействию монетарной политики США.

Влияние изменения курса на прямые иностранные инвестиции. Девальвация валюты страны назначения позволяет снизить стоимость прямого зарубежного инвестирования, в особенности сократить затраты на рабочую силу, что помогает повысить прибыль от капиталовложения и содействует увеличению прямых иностранных инвестиций. А ревальвация валюты, наоборот, может привести к повышению относительной стоимости инвестирования, и поэтому не благоприятствует привлечению прямых зарубежных инвестиций.

Например, за период 2013 – 2016 гг. на фоне продолжительного обесценивания индийской рупии зафиксирована динамика роста прямых зарубежных инвестиций в Индию. А когда в 2017 году незначительно подорожала рупия, тут последовало сокращение объема прямых иностранных инвестиций.

Появление больших рисков и непредсказуемости для трансграничного инвестирования в связи с колебанием курса. Большая волатильность курса может донести прибыль от прямого капиталовложения до нуля даже наносить убытки зарубежным инвесторам. Колебание курса также увеличивает стоимость прямых иностранных инвестиций, поскольку даже если можно использовать инструменты хеджирования, это все равно приводит к повышению расходов трансграничных компаний. К тому же нарастающая непредсказуемость может сильно снизить заинтересованность зарубежных инвесторов в прямом капиталовложении. Предположение о возможном изменении курса тоже негативно влияет на решение иностранных инвесторов. Словом, рост волатильности курса не идет на пользу привлечению инвестиций в экономику и является фактором, препятствующим международному инвестиционному сотрудничеству.

Например, среди стран БРИКС волатильность обменного курса Китая относительно невелика, а общие прямые иностранные инвестиции относительно стабильны. С 2001 года ренминби оставался в пределах 6, 5%.

Только в 2008 и 2015 годах волатильность была немного больше-от 8% до 10% . По этой причине инвесторы, как правило, поддерживают оптимистические ожидания относительно колебаний обменного курса юаня. С точки зрения прямых иностранных инвестиций они в основном сохраняют устойчивый рост.

4.4 Вызовы для трансформации экономической структуры в контексте промышленной революции

Несопряжение национальных программ индустриального развития и отсутствие общего плана по содействию трансформации экономической структуры. В России разработана государственная программа《Развитие промышленности и повышение её конкурентоспособности》, Индия выдвинула проект《Сделайте в Индии》, а у Бразилии план по превращению страны в великую индустриальную державу, однако национальные программы этих стран не сопрягаются друг с другом. Не выработана общая программа развития, объединяющая все страны, чтобы сформировать более интегрированную рамку экономического развития.

Низкая общая факторная производительность и трудность модернизации производства. Как показали данные МВФ, общая факторная производительность за последние 10 лет оказалась весьма низкой. За 2007 – 2017 гг. темпы экономического роста развитых стран и новоформирующихся рынков ежегодно в среднем снизились на 5% и 12% соответственно, что привело к потери соответственно 47% и 85% объёма роста экономики в год. Восстановление экономики стран БРИКС, ориентированное на стимулирование спроса может быть только краткосрочным и неустойчивым. Актуальной задачей стало повышение общей факторной производительности путем реформ в отношении предложения.

Недостаточность вложений в исследования и разработки и сложность инвестиционно-финансовой поддержки индустриальной модернизации. В 2016 году среди стран-участниц БРИКС Бразилия и ЮАР заняли более низкие места по проценту расходов на НИОКР, который составил соответственно $0,65\%$ и $0,8\%$ от ВВП. У России и Бразилии показатель чуть выше-примерно в районе $1,1\% - 1,3\%$, но и она невысока. Согласно данным Министерства науки и технологий Китая за 2017 год Китай затратил примерно $2,15$ ВВП на НИОКР и по этому показателю лидировал в БРИКС. Для научно-технической инновации необходима непрекращающаяся финансовая поддержка, поэтому срочно нужны новые финансовые инструменты для привлечения социальных капиталов к инвестированию в исследования и разработки.

Неудовлетворительное состояние взаимодействия звеньев промышленной цепи и стандартизации производства. У стран БРИКС нет единых критериев в плане сырья, НИОКР, кадров, норм и стандартов. Низкий потенциал вспомогательного производства стал узким местом, препятствующим укреплению производственных мощностей и их международной конкурентоспособности. В этой связи странам БРИКС необходимо активизировать комплексное сотрудничество в конкурентоспособных отраслях, основываясь на производстве с охватом различных звеньев в целях укрепления потенциала вспомогательного производства.

РАЗДЕЛ 5 Обновление финансово-инвестиционной системы стран БРИКС, содействие взаимовыгодному практическому сотрудничеству

5.1 Поиск и создание многостороннего рейтингового механизма стран БРИКС

Существующие три крупнейших международных рейтинговых агентства имеют свои ограничения. Прежде всего, отмечается тенденция к устойчивости оценки уровней различных показателей. Долгое время международные рейтинговые агентства предпочитают сохранять устойчивость при оценке разных показателей. Затягивающийся процесс обработки данных приводит к несвоевременности кредитных рейтингов. Во-вторых, отсутствует механизма привлечения к ответственности. Для предварительной оценки кредитоспособности все страны мира применяют рейтинги указанных агентств, которые составляют их анализаторы, опираясь на личные мнения и рекомендацию. Отсутствие механизма привлечения к ответственности влечет за собой отсутствие гаранта подлинности сформированных рейтингов. В третьих, система оценки ограничивается своими единообразными критериями. В отношении растущих экономик и развитых стран применяется одна и та же оценочная система. Не имеется набора финансовых показателей, призванного различить уровень финансового развития между растущими экономиками и развитыми странами. В четвертых, имеющаяся рейтинговая система является не достаточно прозрачной и непредвзятой. В пятых, труднодоступны услуги по суверенному рейтингу. Немало рейтинговых агентств ограничивают публику в получении права по суверенный рейтинг.

Развитие механизма гарантирования размещения облигаций путем повышения качества кредитного портфеля, укрепление позиций ценных бумаг правительств и предприятий стран БРИКС в рейтингах имеют весьма важное значение для развития биржи облигаций в национальных валютах. Прежде всего, Новый банк развития БРИКС может за счет собственных позиций в рейтинге дать залог для размещения облигаций в национальных валютах. Во-вторых, путем создания фонда кредитного поручительства стран БРИКС гарантируется выпуск бонд в национальных валютах.

Основные цели создания рейтингового агентства стран БРИКС состоят в том, чтобы превратить растущие экономики БРИКС в независимое, доверительное рейтинговое агентство по оценке иностранных валют.

Создание рейтингового агентства может осуществляться по трем этапам. Во-первых, можно начать услуги рейтингового агентства стран БРИКС с предоставления Новым банком развития БРИКС кредитов в иностранных валютах для проектов стран БРИКС. Во-вторых, повышение популярности рейтингового агентства стран БРИКС с тем, чтобы банки и финансовые учреждения, занимающиеся облигациями стран БРИКС и растущих экономик, использовали рейтинги агентств стран БРИКС. В-третьих, рейтинговые агентства должны иметь своей целью расширение своих клиентов и предоставление больших услуг растущим экономикам, включая Мексику, Филиппины.

При организации рейтинговых агентств необходимо учитывать следующие факторы: первое, надзорные правила и правовые рамки. Второе, структура собственности, при дроблении акции должны держать их члены-банки развития, финансовые учреждения и известные рейтинговые агентства совместно, при концентрации акций у финансовых учреждении следует развивать техническое сотрудничество с известным рейтинговым агентством. Третье, обеспечение рейтинговых агентств независимыми от акционерских обществ, размещающих ценные бумаги. Четвертое, избежание влияния от конфликтов политики и интересов. Пятое, на последующей эксплуатационной стадии необходимо формировать систему по оценке работы в целях постоянного повышения уровня рейтинговой деятельности.

5. 2　Продвижение развития рынков облигаций БРИКС

Повысить открытость капитального счета. Считается целесообразным на начальной стадии провести взаимные консультации между странами БРИКС по паритетному открытию инвестиционных рынков, расширению каналов использования резервных валют, снижению зависимости от финансового рынка США.

Создать механизм гарантий и повышения качества кредитного портфеля, всемерно содействовать развитию оффшорных финансовых рынков и ценных бумаг в национальных валютах. Страны БРИКС должны совершенствовать финансовую систему, формировать благоприятный механизм противостояния рискам. При торгах ценных бумаг можно использовать форвард, опцион и валютный своп в целях фиксации форвардного валютного курса.

Укреплять сотрудничество между странами БРИКС, формировать механизм экстренного страхования. Страны БРИКС могут совместно создать фонд по противостоянию рискам. В отношении дефолтных бумаг оказать поддержку ликвидности и выступить в роли кредиторов последней инстанции.

Наращивать сотрудничество с международными финансовыми организациями, расширять масштаб финансирования и инвестирования.

В связи с тем, что внешние инвесторы не четко знают эмитенты облигаций стран БРИКС, так что для обыкновенных предприятий трудно собирать средства путем размещения ценных бумаг. Инвесторам было бы принять, если они имеют международного финансового посредника.

Активизировать сотрудничество между банками стран БРИКС на рынках. Стоит наращивать рыночное сотрудничество и контакты между банками стран БРИКС, наращивать совместимость норм и правил бухгалтерского учета между банками стран БРИКС и их нормативно-правовых актов. Облегчить взаимный допуск инвесторов друг к другу, и обогатить структуру инвесторов.

Совершенствовать надзорный институт, продвигать информационную транспарентность. Правительство, управляющее рынком, должно разработать его нормы и правила и контролировать их исполнение, повысить информационную открытость предприятий и совершенствовать законодательные нормативы по обязательствам и контрактам.

5.3 Углублять расчет в национальных валютах и своп

Страны БРИКС должны продвигать сотрудничество в области расчетов в национальных валютах, что позволяет субъектам хозяйственной деятельности самостоятельно обменивать национальные валюты для расчета и оплаты товаров и услуг. Тем не менее, предстоит немало проблем, требующих незамедлительного решения. Во-первых, фундамент сотрудничества по расширению расчетов в национальных валютах между странами БРИКС пока еще слабо стоит. Существует немалые разницы между странами БРИКС в географическом расположении, уровне экономической интеграции и структуре экономического развития. Во-вторых, недостаточно совершенным является механизм взаимных расчетов в нацвалюте между банками. К примеру, коммерческие банки не обладают соответствующими механизмами противостояния рискам, связанным с расчетами в нацвалюте. Требуют дальнейшего улучшения еще и банковские услуги по расчету в национальной валюте. Основной формой двусторонний расчет в нацвалюте являются денежные переводы, незначительными остаются услуги по аккредитивам и инкассо. В-третьих, существует немало ограничений, касающихся движения капиталов между странами БРИКС. Например, в России взимаются крупные налоги на трансграничную транспортировку наличных. В результате это заметно увеличивает себестоимость и ограничивает денежное обращение, тем самым ограничивает развития расчетов в национальной валюте.

В реальных операциях при валютном свопе имеются следующие основные вопросы: прежде всего, валютный своп осуществляется по-прежнему в американских долларах. Только постепенно освободить торговлю от зависимости от американских долларов, возможно укрепить позиции национальных валют как валютных резервов. Во-вторых, механизм валютного свопа не может избавиться от системных рисков. При возникновении проблем с ликвидностью государств-членов БРИКС их можно смягчить путем валютного свопа между государствами-членами БРИКС. В случае, если во многих странах БРИКС возникают подобные проблемы многосторонний механизм свопа не в состоянии им противостоять. Таким образом считается необходимым создание соответствующего механизма по противостоянию системным рискам в сотрудничестве с МВФ и другими международными организациями. В-третьих, увязка с МВФ в какой-то мере ограничивает многосторонний механизм валютного свопа. В этом случае страны БРИКС должны корректировать и улучшить соответствующее соглашение и планы, чтобы смягчить условия применения валютных резервов и создать совершенный механизм оценки рисков.

Пример-фонд валютного свопа

В целях решения проблем с валютным расхождением стран БРИКС

Фонд валютного свопа был создан в 2007 году финансовыми организациями развития, профильными организациями микрокредитования и инвестирования. Его инвесторами являются голландское и немецкое правительство, 22 многосторонних и двусторонних институтов. Инвесторы и клиенты Фонда валютного свопа предоставляют кредиты в национальных валютах, при этом перекладывают риски, связанные с валютно-процентными свопами на Фонд валютного свопа с тем, чтобы избегать последствий колебания процентной ставки и валютного курса. Контрагент частного сектора также снижает себе риски путем валютно-процентного свопа. Фонд валютного свопа в свою очередь с помощью хедж-инструментов хеджировать свои валютно-процентные риски, что позволяет им предоставлять финансовые услуги валютного свопа на постоянной основе. С учетом Фонда валютного свопа страны БРИКС могут создать более широкий механизм валютного свопа на основе сотрудничества между странами БРИКС в сфере национальной валюты.

5.4 Создание в рамках стран БРИКС моделей многостороннего инвестирования и финансирования, а также моделей сотрудничества《мозгового центра + финансирования》

Во-первых, необходимо создать модели многостороннего сотрудничества, координирующие финансовые институты развития с коммерческими финансовыми структурами. В первую очередь мы должны в соответствии с характеристиками проектов интегрировать различного рода финансовые институты и полностью раскрыть их потенциал. Используя рычаги финансирования развития и политики, мы оказываем финансовую поддержку зарождению и запуску ключевых проектов. Финансирование проектов с некоторой прибылью, но с большой длительностью инвестиционного цикла и медленной оплатой обеспечивают в основном финансовые институты развития. Что касается средне-и краткосрочного зарубежного инвестирования, то мы сможем привлечь и включить коммерческие средства и другие ресурсы в строительство при помощи коммерческих финансовых структур с рыночно-ориентированными финансовыми инструментами. Причем мы должны привлечь различного рода средства в соответствии с разными этапами развития проектов. Например, мы предлагаем субсидию и проценты во время разработки проектов или в бесприбыльный период, и только после формирования проектов и возникновения стабильной оплаты мы включаем коммерческие средства. Далее, необходимо увеличить роль государственно-частного партнерства (ГЧП) в строительстве инфраструктуры и мобилизовать социальный и частный капитал на инвестирование высокодоходных проектов. Для инвестирования и создания проектов с хорошей прибылью мы должны совмещать социальный и частный капитал. Необходимо создать модели международного ГЧП, чтобы смягчить риски и повысить устойчивость финансирования. В рамках стран БРИКС потребуется улучшить инвестиционную среду, оптимизировать риски заинтересованных сторон, отобрать подходящих частных партнеров, координируясь со соответственной системой контроля, чтобы увеличить вероятность успеха партнерских отношений.

Во-вторых, необходимо повысить роль 《 мозгового центра + финансирования 》 в устойчивом развитии стран БРИКС. Для сотрудничества в рамках стран БРИКС потребуется совмещение средств и знаний, которое не только углубляет взаимопонимание, укрепляет взаимодоверие и устраняет недоразумение между странами БРИКС, но и повышает их влияние на весь мир в целом. Мы должны предпринимать конкретные меры для совместной работы с различного рода финансовыми структурами, для укрепления создания международных мозговых центров, а также обмена и сотрудничества между ними. Кроме того, нам необходимо регулярно обмениваться знаниями и опытом, чтобы выявить положительную роль 《 мозгового центра +

финансирования》 в развитии стран БРИКС. Первое, мы сможем попытаться создать союз (институт) мозговых центров стран БРИКС, и тем самым полностью задействуем роль《 совмещения мозговых центров + финансирования》, сконцентрировав органы финансового управления, высокоуровневые мозговые центры и агентства по предоставлению финансовой информации этих стран, способствуем их интеграции и выявим их роль в сфере управления и принятия решения, интегрирования и распространения информации. Второе, нам следует укреплять международное сотрудничество, перенимать опыт западных развитых стран, например, опыт в строительстве и управлении Лондоном, обсуждать стратегическое взаимодействие финансовых центров СТЗ Шанхая и финансовых городов стран БРИКС, а также содействовать совмещению мозговых центров и финансированию в формате однорангового взаимодействия. Третье, необходимо разработать долгосрочные планы на создание мозговых центров, чтобы продвигать институциональное строительство. Финансовые институты развития смогут через сотрудничество банков, правительств и предприятий продвигать строительство рынков и кредитов, а также институциональное строительство, чтобы восполнить пробелы и нехватку на рынках. Они инвестируют и финансируют ключевые инфраструктурные проекты, продвигают запуск проектов с помощью коммерческих финансовых институтов, и тем самым осуществляют задачи развития страны.

Пример-механизм межбанковского сотрудничества стран БРИКС

15 апреля 2010 года Государственным банком развития Китая, Бразильским банком экономического и социального развития, Внешэкономбанком (Россия) и Экспортно-импортным банком Индии в городе Бразилии был подписан 《 Меморандум о создании механизма межбанковского сотрудничества стран БРИКС 》, что символизирует официальное основание механизма межбанковского сотрудничества стран БРИКС. 13 апреля 2011 года в данный механизм вступил Банк развития

Южной Африки. Со дня основания механизма все банки-участницы активно развивают финансовое сотрудничество на многосторонней и двусторонней основе и играют важную роль в экономическом развитии и торгово-экономическом сотрудничестве между странами БРИКС. Были поочередно подписаны 《Соглашение о кредитах в местных валютах》, 《Меморандум о сотрудничестве по взаимному принятию кредитных рейтингов》 и другие многосторонние соглашения о сотрудничестве, которые охватывают кредиты в местных валютах, подтверждение аккредитивов, устойчивое развитие, финансирование инфраструктуры и другие сферы, что значительно продвигает финансовое сотрудничество и упрощение торгово-экономического инвестирования в странах БРИКС.

5.5 Формирование модели устойчивых инвестиций и финансирования БРИКС

Сотрудничество в рамках БРИКС должно быть направлено на обеспечение совместного устойчивого развития. Его уникальность состоит в призыве в адрес всех государств-членов к совместным усилиям по ликвидации бедности, содействию экономическому развитию, удовлетворению требования в сфере образования, здравоохранения, социального обеспечения и трудоустройства. Заложить фундамент для создания благоприятного цикла устойчивого развития путем комплексного социального развития. С другой стороны, необходимо ориентировать конкретные сферы сотрудничества на устойчивое развития. Сферы инвестиций и финансирования стран БРИКС будут сконцентрированы на сферы зеленного развития, повышения благосостояния народа, образования и социального обеспечения. Страны БРИКС должны нести ответственность за развитие и преодолеть структурные проблемы социально-экономического развития. Ниже следуют конкретные меры:

Первое, исходить из статуса стран БРИКС как новых экономик,

задействовать преимущества финансовых организаций развития, ликвидировать крайнюю бедность и уменьшить неравноправность. Разработать меры по обеспечению благоприятной среды и социальной безопасности, создать механизм обмена данными, привлечения к ответственности и ликвидаций последствий ЧП.

Второе, опираться на характеристики работы БРИКС по разработке и развитию технологий, активно развивать международное технологическое сотрудничество, наращивать торгово-экономические контакты в взаимодополняемых сферах, осуществлять торгово-экономическое и финансовое взаимодействие

Третье, опираться на характеристики регионального финансового развития стран БРИКС, активизировать институциональное оформление финансового сотрудничество. Содействовать созданию механизма трансграничного финансового мониторинга, использовать механизм предупреждения и ликвидации рисков стран БРИКС в глобальном сотрудничестве. Параллельно продвигаются глобализация и локализация. Балансировать интересы стран БРИКС с ориентиром на открытость, транспарентность, равноправие и взаимную выгоду в интересах справедливости и эффективности финансового мониторинга.

Четвертое, исходить из потребностей стран БРИКС в оптимизации и модернизации структур производства, целесообразно корректировать форму развития в целях создания устойчивой финансовой внешней среды для финансового сотрудничества. Исходить из характеристики растущих экономик стран БРИКС, параллельно развивать традиционное трудоемкое производство, технико-емкое и капиталоемкое производства.

Пример-проект закупки Промышленным и коммерческим банком Китая (ICBC) Банка Стэндерт ЮАР.
В июне 2007 года между Промышленным и коммерческим банком Китая (ICBC) и Банком Стэндерт ЮАР достигнута договоренность о развитии стратегического сотрудничества в увязке с паями.

Промышленный и коммерческий банк Китая закупил 20 процентов акций Банка Стэндерт ЮАР за 5, 46 млрд американских долларов. Операция совершена в марте 2008 года. Таким образом, ICBC стал крупнейшим паедержателем Банка Стэндерт ЮАР. Китайский центр по банковским операциям в Африке при Банке Стэндерт ЮАР, основанный в 2017 году, призван в дальнейшем углублять двустороннее торговое сотрудничество между Китаем и Африкой. Данная закупка стала образцом межбанковского сотрудничества стран БРИКС в финансовой и инвестиционной сфере. ICBC и Банк Стэндерт ЮАР нарастили финансирование и инвестиции в проекты в африканском континенте, касающихся китайских компаний. Лишь объем кредитов в отношении африканских стран, одобренных ICBC, ежегодно достигает пример десятки миллиардов долларов, что позитивно продвигает упрощение торгово-экономического сотрудничества между Китаем и Африкой. ICBC и Банк Стэндерт ЮАР готовы продолжать оказывать поддержку китайско-африканскому индустриальному сотрудничеству путем предоставления комплексных финансовых услуг и развития диверсифицированных каналов финансирования, в ответ на требования правительства о развитии межправительственного обмена валютами и создании зон свободной торговли продвигать постоянное углубление китайско-африканского торгово-экономического сотрудничества

5. 6 Поиск путей внедрения цифровой экономики (блокчейна) в инвестиционной и финансовой сфере

Страны БРИКС стали бы ярким воплощением индустриального революционного регионального пространства и экономического сотрудничества. Используя возможности индустриальной революции в полной мере задействовать внешний эффект технологии и логики освоения при использовании, содействовать финансовой инновации, финансовому и инвестиционному развитию. В сфере цифровой экономики задействовать стимулирующую роль технологии блокчейна в опережении странами БРИКС других стран в глобальной стоимостной цепочке.

Страны БРИКС должны между собой активно развивать сотрудничество на основе технологии блокчейна, стараться создать трансграничную платежную систему на основе данной технологии, тем самым занять благоприятные позиции в реформировании международной валютной и финансовой системы.

В сфере платежа применение технологии блокчейна способствует снижению себестоимости сверки записей в бухгалтерской книге и урегулированию споров. В сфере цифровизации имущества активы разного рода, включая пай, бонды, ценные бумаги, накладную, могут быть интегрированы в технологию блокчейна, и стать цифровыми активами в цепи, что позволяет держателям инициировать транзакцию без посредников. В сфере интеллектуальных ценных бумаг торги финансовых активов осуществляются путем достижения торгующими сторонами контракта на основе определенных правил. Блокчейн позволяет полностью прояснить логику операций с помощью кодов, включая ценные бумаги с фиксированным доходом, сделку РЕПО, своп, синдицированный кредит, что обуславливает автоматическое исполнение соглашений. В сфере цепи поставок предоставляются такие конкретные услуги, как финансирование дебиторской задолженности, Стремимся к обороту расписки дебиторской задолженности (долговой расписки), основанной на кредитном рейтинге ключевых предприятий, на различных уровнях цепи поставок. Предоставлять низкую инвестиционную процентную ставку в отношении дебиторской задолженности за счет привлечения внешних финансовых организаций. В сфере клиринга и расчета торговля финансовыми активами осуществляется путём двух основных аспектов, а именно платежа и бонд. Посредством разработки легальной цифровой валюты на основе технологии блокчейна или какого-нибудь расчетного инструмента совершить операции по клирингу и расчету в режиме реального времени по протоколу P2P. В сфере идентификации клиентов технология блокчейна позволяет обеспечить безопасность цифровых индивидуальных данных и их надежного управления. При предпосылке обеспечения секретности клиентов повысить эффективность идентификации клиентов и снизить себестоимость.

Приложение – основные данные

Таблица 1 ВВП стран БРИКС, стран с растущими рынками и всего мира в 2006 – 2017 гг.

(млрд долларов)

Страна/год	2006	2007	2008	2009	2010	2011	2012	2013	2014	2015	2016	2017
Бразилия	1,106.37	1,396.10	1,694.86	1,667.66	2,207.53	2,613.86	2,464.18	2,471.17	2,455.71	1,799.71	1,793.07	2,054.97
Китай	2,774.29	3,571.45	4,604.29	5,121.68	6,066.35	7,522.10	8,570.35	9,635.03	10,534.53	11,226.19	11,221.84	12,014.61
Индия	949.118	1,238.70	1,224.10	1,365.37	1,708.46	1,823.05	1,827.64	1,856.72	2,039.13	2,102.39	2,273.56	2,611.01
Россия	1,063.64	1,396.48	1,784.51	1,313.68	1,638.46	2,051.66	2,210.26	2,297.13	2,063.66	1,368.40	1,281.29	1,527.47
ЮАР	271.812	299.033	287.095	297.221	375.304	416.879	396.332	366.821	350.901	317.698	295.678	349.299
Чили	154.788	173.477	179.52	172.528	218.311	252.115	267.083	278.388	260.574	244.021	250.008	277.042
Колумбия	162.766	207.465	244.302	233.893	286.954	335.437	369.43	380.17	378.323	291.53	279.987	309.197
Чехия	155.464	189.032	236.031	206.303	207.478	227.948	207.376	209.402	207.818	186.83	195.305	213.189
Египет	112.902	137.055	170.797	198.316	230.024	247.726	278.769	288.007	305.567	332.075	332.484	237.073
Греция	273.547	318.94	356.14	330.837	299.919	288.062	245.807	239.937	237.406	195.64	192.77	200.69
Венгрия	115.295	139.851	157.998	130.594	130.925	140.863	127.706	135.213	140.167	122.823	129.144	152.284
Индонезия	396.293	470.144	558.582	577.539	755.256	892.59	919.002	916.646	891.051	860.741	932.445	1,015.41

续表

Страны/год	2006	2007	2008	2009	2010	2011	2012	2013	2014	2015	2016	2017
Южная Корея	1,011.80	1,122.68	1,002.22	901.935	1,094.50	1,202.46	1,222.81	1,305.61	1,411.33	1,382.76	1,411.04	1,538.03
Малайзия	168.084	199.96	238.645	208.914	255.024	297.961	314.443	323.276	338.066	296.434	296.536	314.497
Мексика	975.383	1,052.70	1,109.99	900.047	1,057.80	1,180.49	1,201.09	1,274.44	1,314.39	1,169.63	1,076.91	1,149.24
Пакистан	137.236	152.369	170.853	167.875	177.166	213.588	224.384	231.218	244.361	270.556	278.913	303.993
Перу	87.887	102.187	121.591	121.019	148.013	168.76	189.001	197.867	203.075	192.353	195.432	215.224
Филиппины	122.211	149.36	173.603	168.485	199.591	224.143	250.092	271.836	284.585	292.774	304.906	313.419
Польша	344.759	429.473	533.8	440.14	479.161	528.571	500.846	524.399	545.074	477.347	471.216	524.886
Катар	60.882	79.712	115.27	97.798	125.122	167.775	186.834	198.728	206.225	164.641	152.469	166.326
Таиланд	221.759	262.943	291.383	281.71	341.105	370.818	397.558	420.334	407.339	401.384	411.847	455.378
Турция	550.796	675.01	764.643	644.47	772.29	832.497	873.696	950.328	934.075	859.449	863.39	849.48
ОАЭ	222.117	257.916	315.475	253.547	289.88	350.908	374.818	390.427	403.198	357.949	348.743	377.435
ВВП стран БРИКС	6,165.23	7,901.76	9,594.85	9,765.61	11,996.11	14,427.55	15,468.76	16,626.87	17,443.92	16,814.38	16,865.42	18,557.36
ВВП стран с растущими рынками	11439.20	14022.03	16335.69	15801.56	19064.63	22350.26	23619.50	25163.09	26156.55	24913.32	24988.97	27170.15
ВВП всего мира	51465.81	58059.69	63649.97	60280.21	65906.43	73119.33	74488.51	76551.27	78594.42	74311.46	75367.75	79280.94

(Другие страны с растущими рынками)

источник：International Monetary Fund

Таблица 2 Объём внешней торговли стран БРИКС и всего мира в 2006 – 2017 гг. (млн долларов США)

Страна/год	2006	2007	2008	2009	2010	2011	2012	2013	2014	2015	2016	2017
Бразилия	137,807	160,649	197,942	152,995	201,915	256,040	242,578	242,034	225,101	191,134	185,286	217,756
Китай	969,359	1,218,144	1,428,640	1,201,606	1,577,754	1,898,396	2,049,662	2,210,662	2,343,222	2,282,443	2,136,708	2,280,367
Индия	120,877	146,562	191,183	163,941	222,751	305,162	296,425	313,290	321,532	267,348	264,534	298,928
Россия	297,483	346,530	466,299	297,155	392,674	515,408	527,433	521,836	496,807	341,465	281,681	353,116
ЮАР	58,155	69,792	80,782	62,603	91,347	108,816	99,557	95,906	93,043	80,864	76,331	88,845
Общий объём БРИКС	1,583,681	1,941,676	2,364,847	1,878,300	2,486,441	3,083,822	3,215,654	3,383,728	3,479,705	3,163,255	2,944,541	3,239,012
Общий объём мира	14,768,822	17,229,775	19,751,940	15,810,662	18,828,212	22,362,639	22,736,067	23,420,837	23,801,744	21,074,575	20,581,287	21,466,282

Источник: UNCTAD, International Monetary Fund

Таблица 3 **Внешние прямые инвестиции в страны БРИКС в 2006 – 2017 гг.** (млн долларов США)

Страна/год	2006	2007	2008	2009	2010	2011	2012	2013	2014	2015	2016	2017
Бразилия	19,418	44,579	50,716	31,481	88,452	101,158	86,607	69,686	97,180	74,718	78,248	70,332
Россия	37,595	55,874	74,783	36,583	43,168	55,084	50,588	69,219	22,031	6,853	32,539	27,886
Индия	8,901	22,739	34,729	41,738	33,109	25,884	32,952	26,953	30,763	35,283	44,907	42,215
Китай	72,715	83,521	108,312	94,065	114,734	123,985	121,073	123,911	128,502	135,577	133,711	136,300
ЮАР	312	6,536	9,211	7,547	3,638	4,244	4,563	8,309	5,774	1,729	2,238	1,328
БРИКС	138,941	213,249	277,752	211,414	283,101	310,354	295,782	298,079	284,250	254,160	291,642	278,061

Источник: CEIC

Таблица 4 **Объем внешних прямых инвестиций стран БРИКС в 2006 – 2017 гг.** (млн долларов США)

Страна/год	2006	2007	2008	2009	2010	2011	2012	2013	2014	2015	2016	2017
Бразилия	28,798	17,061	26,115	-4,552	26,763	16,067	5,208	14,942	26,040	13,518	12,816	6,268
Россия	29,993	44,801	55,663	43,281	52,616	66,851	48,822	86,507	57,082	22,085	22,314	38,634
Индия	14,037	17,026	19,257	16,096	15,490	12,415	8,553	1,765	11,686	7,514	5,047	11,256
Китай	23,932	17,155	56,742	43,890	57,954	48,421	64,963	72,971	123,130	174,391	216,424	101,914
ЮАР	6,069	2,965	-3,134	1,158	-76	-257	2,990	6,656	7,674	5,744	4,480	7,377
БРИКС	102,830	99,008	154,642	99,873	152,747	143,497	130,537	182,841	225,611	223,252	261,082	165,449

Источник: CEIC

Таблица 5 Курс нацвалют стран БРИКС и объем внешних прямых инвестиций в страны БРИКС в 2006 – 2017 гг.

год	Бразилия курс (Реал в отношении доллара США)	Бразилия FDI (млн долларов США)	Россия курс (рубль в отношении доллара США)	Россия FDI (млн долларов США)	Индия курс (рупия в отношении доллара США)	Индия FDI (млн долларов США)	Китай курс (юань в отношении доллара США)	Китай FDI (млн долларов США)	ЮАР курс (рубль в отношении доллара США)	ЮАР FDI (млн долларов США)
2006	2.18	19418.1	27.2	37594.8	45.3	8,901.00	8	72,715.00	6.8	311.8
2007	1.95	44579.5	25.6	55873.7	41.3	22,739.00	7.6	83,521.00	7	6,535.60
2008	1.83	50716.4	24.9	74782.9	43.5	34,729.00	6.9	108,312.40	8.3	9,211.00
2009	2	31480.9	31.7	36583.1	48.4	41,737.60	6.8	94,065.00	8.5	7,546.90
2010	1.76	88452.1	30.4	43167.8	45.7	33,109.00	6.8	114,734.00	7.3	3,638.10
2011	1.67	101157.8	29.4	55083.6	46.7	25,883.70	6.5	123,985.00	7.3	4,243.70
2012	1.95	86606.5	30.8	50587.6	53.4	32,952.40	6.3	121,073.00	8.2	4,562.60
2013	2.16	69686.1	31.8	69218.9	58.6	26,953.10	6.2	123,911.00	9.7	8,309.50
2014	2.35	97179.6	38.4	22031.3	61	30,763.10	6.1	128,502.00	10.9	5,773.70
2015	3.33	74718	60.9	6853	64.2	35,282.70	6.2	135,577.00	12.8	1,729.50
2016	3.49	78248.4	67.1	32538.9	67.2	44,906.50	6.6	133,711.00	14.7	2,237.60
2017	3.19	70332.3	58.3	27886.3	65.1	42,214.90	6.8	136,300.00	13.3	1,327.80

Источник: CEIC, International Financial Statistics

RESUMO

I Abrir a Nova Página de Cooperação dos BRICS na Década de Ouro, Aprofundar a Cooperação em Investimento e Financiamento dos BRICS

1.1 Introdução do desenvolvimento econômico dos países emergentes em 2017

1.1.1 BRICS orienta o desenvolvimento económico dos mercados emergentes

Desde o inicio do novo século, os mercados emergentes creseram rapidamente e já se tornaram um motor de desenvolvimento insubstituível da época. A proporção do PIB deles no mundial aumentou de 23% em 2006 a 34% em 2017 (Quadro 1.1). Como o pioneiro dos mercados emergentes, os BRICS têm o desempenho mais extraordinário. A contribuição dos BRICS à economia mundial foi mais de 50% na última década. Em 2017, o desenvolvimento econômico dos BRICS mantêm uma boa tendência. Em termos do volume da economia, o PIB dos BRICS é de 185.057.400 milhões $, ocupando 68% do PIB das economias emergentes, com uma tendência crescente do PIB per capita dos países respectivos (Quadro 1.2). Em termos do comércio internacional, o valor total do comércio internacional dos BRICS é de 3,239 trilhões $, e a partiapação do valor total no comércio internacional cresceu em 11% em 2006 a 15% em 2017 (Quadro 1.3). Em termos do investimento, o valor dos investimentos estrangeiros aos BRICS aumentou de 138,9 bilhões $ em 2006 a 278,1 bilhões $ em 2017. Os investimentos diretos no exterior dos BRICS aumentaram de 102,8 bilhões $ em 2006 a 165,4 bilhões $ em 2017 (Quadro 1.4).

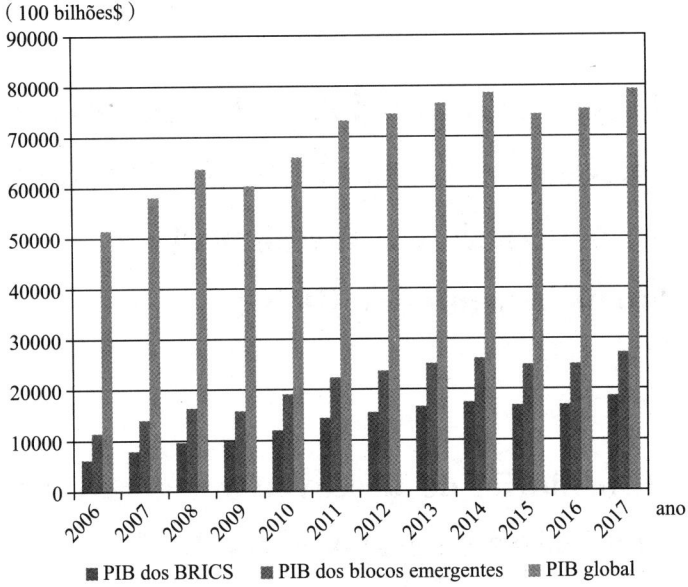

Quadro 1.1 PIB dos BRICS, dos países dos mercados emergentes e global de 2006 a 2017 (unidade: 100 bilhões $)

Fonte: Fundo Monetário Internacional

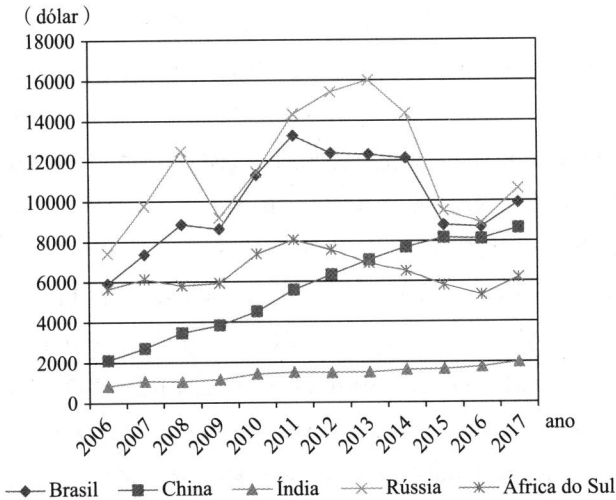

Quadro 1.2 PIB per capita dos BRICS de 2006 a 2017 (unidade: dólar)

Fonte: Fundo Monetário Internacional

(1 milhão$)

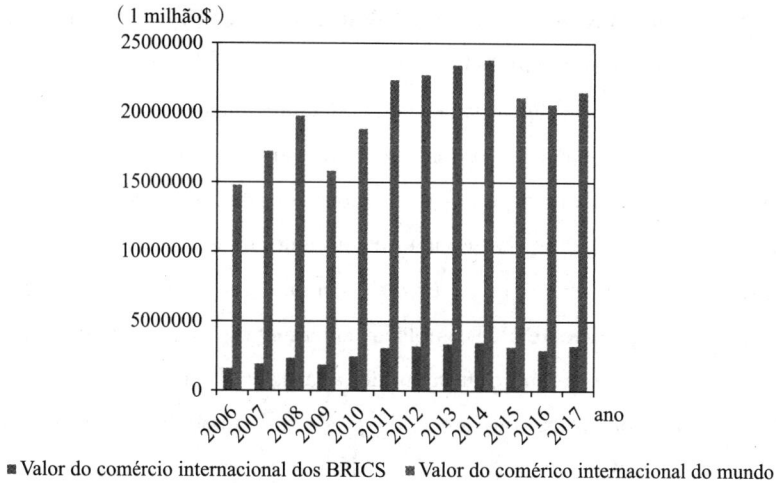

■ Valor do comércio internacional dos BRICS   ■ Valor do comérico internacional do mundo

Quadro 1. 3   Valor total do comércio internacional dos BRICS e
global de 2006 a 2017 (unidade: 1 milhão $)

Fonte: UNCTAD, Fundo Monetário Internacional

(1 milhão$)

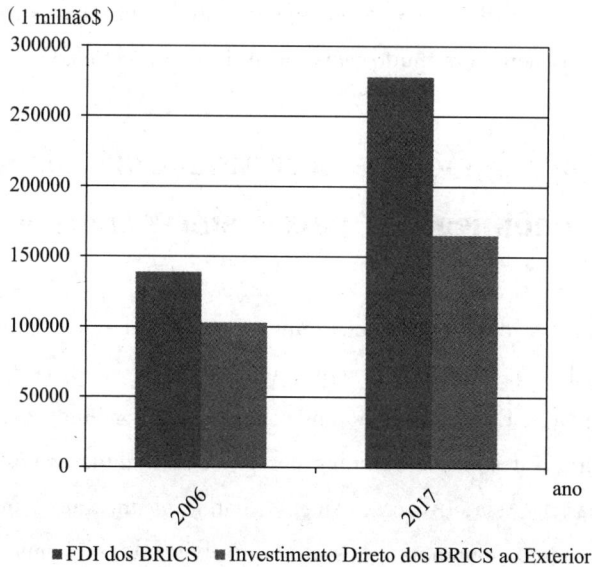

■ FDI dos BRICS   ■ Investimento Direto dos BRICS ao Exterior

Quadro 1. 4   Investimento direto estrangeiro (FDI) e Investimento direto ao
exterior dos BRICS de 2006 a 2017 (unidade: 1 milhão $)

Fonte: CEIC

1. 1. 2 Introdução do desenvolvimento econômico dos países emergentes em 2017

Primeiro, há uma diferenciação regional relativamente grande do nível de desenvolvimento económico dospaíses emergentes, os blocos asiáticos desenvolvem mais rápido, seguidos pelos blocos do Médio Oriente e do norte da Africa, porém, os países latino-americanos enfrentam os riscos de défice pública, inflação, turbulência da taxa de câmbio, etc. . Segundo, a taxa de desemprego está geralmente alta nos blocos emergentes, e quase todos os países no mundo também encaram o desafio de alta taxa de desemprego entre os jovens. Terceiro, por causa da queda do preço dos alimentos e da apreciação das moedas em 2017, o preço caiu nos blocos emergente, no entanto, por causa da mudança da fluência do capital internacional, da conjuntura económica e política regional dos países respectivos, existe alguma flutuação dos preços do mercado interno dos países emergentes, sendo gue uma parte dos países estão enfrentando uma grande pressão inflacionária. Quarto, em 2017, o desenvolvimento de FDI dos blocos emergentes ainda enfrentou vários desafios, dado gue o crescimento era muito mais baixo do que o estimado.

1. 2 Aproximação e necessidade de cooperação econômica dos países emergentes

A maioria dos blocos emergentes eram coloniais ou semicoloniais no início do Século X XI o, por isso, o desenvolvimento industrial deles foi restringido pelos colonizadores. Esses países foram considerados somente como origem da matéria primária e destino de dumping dos produtos manufaturados. Mesmo que as ex – colônias da Ãsia, Ãfrica e América Latina alcançaram a independência depois de 2 guerras mundiais, o sea desenvolvimento econômico ainda está relativamente devagar por algumas razões históricas e ourea. Com base da semelhança histórica, existe uma aproximação e necessidade da cooperação econômica entre esses blocos emergentes.

Primeiro, a cooperação econômica dos BRICS beneficia o desenvolvimento econômico dos blocos emergentes. Por via da cooperação econômica, os BRICS podem fortalecer a assistência do investimento na área de infraestrutura, que está carente nos países do mercado emergente, e também podem promover a otimização da estrutura industrial e a inovação da economia. Segundo, a cooperação econômica dos BRICS fomenta a reforma do sistema financeiro e inovação política dos blocos emergentes. A cooperação econômica precisa de coordenação de todos os lados em relação ao funcionamento econômico, sistema de supervisão, política econômica, etc.. A cooperação económica orienta a reforma do sistema econômico e a coordenação política. Terceiro, os BRICS podem integrar – se ainda maior na cadeia global de valor por via da cooperação econômica e da partilha dos recursos de capital e técnica Por exemplo, a China está na posição central da cadeia global de valor, importando as matérias primárias dos países em desenvolvimento, e ao mesmo tempo, introduzindo o capital e a técnica dos países desenvolvidos, e melhorando constantemente o sistema da indústria, para se tornar um grande país de produção do mundo. Quarto, a cooperação econômica dos BRICS pode ajudar a defender efetivamente os riscs político e económico exteriores. Por exemplo, perante as sanções económicas irrazoáveis, os blocos emergentes podem se unir para ganhar uma posição mais favorável durante a negociação, ou podem se dar mais ajuda quando algum bloco emergente sofre a sanção económica irrazoável.

1. 3 Perspectiva de cooperação pragmática dos BRICS na próxima década

O mecanismo da cooperação dos BRICS já data uma década, e os já venceu vários desafios duros como a crise financeiro. Durante essa década, BRICS já exploraram um novo caminho de união, cooperação, benefício recíproco e ganho partilhado dos blocos emergentes e países em desenvolvimento, tendo alcançado êxitos frutíferos e um grande potencial.

Perante o futuro, os BRICS devem promover ainda mais as cooperações comerciais, estabelecer umnova plataforma da cooperação Sul-Sul Devem.

fomentar o modelo de cooperação BRICS + , aprofundar a cooperação financeira, melhorar a cadeia de ualor da cooperação dos BRICS, elevar o nível em cooperação em investimento e financiamento, aprofundar os conhecimentos mútuos via interâmbio civil, com objectivo de consolidar as relações de parceaia entre os membros dos BRICS.

1. 4　Cooperação em investimento e financiamento como a base essencial de cooperação dos BRICS

Hoje em dia, o fluxo de investimento entre os membros de BRICS já tem um aumento óbvio, mas o valor é relativamente baixo, por isso, o potencial de cooperação é grande. Nessa época de globalização econômica e financeira, a cooperação em investimento e financiamento desempenha um papel de motorpara a economia e emsociedade, sendo gue a cooperação em investimento e financiamento dos BRICS é a opção mais efetia para incentivar o desenvolvimento económico, e aumentar a participação na governanca financeira global. ONovo Banco de Desenvolvimento dov BRICS e o Arranjamento das Reservas Contingentes são as novas formas de cooperação sul-sul, que não só oferecem a garantia e o suporte para a economia dos países em desenvolvimento, como também é uma nova forma de participação na governansa global, sendo um suplementoem relação ao sistema da finança internacional atual. O Novo Banco de Desenvolvimento dos BRICS e o Arranjamento das Reservas Contingentes são os modelos exemplares da cooperação em investimento e financiamento entre os estados, e também lançam uma base sólida para a cooperação em investimento e financiamento dos BRICS e para a cooperação Sul-Sul.

II Objetivos e Práticas de Cooperação em Investimento e Financiamento dos BRICS

2. 1 Aperfeiçoar o sistema da governança financeira global

A governança financeira global significa a participaeav dos governos dos países respetivos, as organizaçães internacionais, as organizaçães nåo-governamentais, as empresas transfronteiriças e outras entidade do mercado na administração da finança global, por via de coordenação, cooperação e ao consensos, de modo a evitar os riscos, manter a estabilidade econômica e financeira, estabelecer e defender a ordem das finanças internacionis. O sistema atual das finanças tem uma grande limitação em relação à Sua hierarguia, por exemplo, as organizaçães internacionais financairas, como O IMF, o Banco Mundial, etc. , não cumprem ou não são capazes de cunprir a tarefa de coordenar o mercado financeiro internacional. Além disso, por causa do sistema de *padrao – Dólar*, e da falta da coerência da política de macroeconomia dos Estados Unidos, é possível ocorrer crises financeiras de forma mais frequente. Os países também estão enfrentando o risco de depreciação das reservas da moeda estrangeira, por causa das políticas monetáruas dos Estados Unidos. Isto também cria mais fatores de incerteza no sistema internacional da taxa de câmbio, porque os Estados Unidos podem transferir o risco de fragilidade da taxa cambial aos seus credores, através da emissão de moeda, sendo gue, os seus credores não podem transferir o risco de taxa cambial aos Estados Unidos da mesma forma. É óbvio que essa contradição prejudica os interesses do comércio e investimento dos demais países, especialmente os BRICS.

Graças ao estabelecimento do Novo Banco de Desenvolvimento de BRICS e às práticas do investimento e financiamento dos países respectivos, o mecanismo de cooperação dos BRICS já é uma nova força de impulsionamento para neformar o mecanismo ds finanças internacionais e reestabelecer a ordem internacional das finanças. Como participantes importante na conjuntura da política e economia da comunidade internacional, OS BRICS atuam na disposição do capital e otimização dos métodos de supervisão financeira, e desempenham um papel cada vez mais essencial em relação à recuperação da economia mundial. Com o aumento da capacidade integral, OS BRICS encarregam cada vez mais responsabilidades pela comunidade internacional, designadamente nas áreas de combate ao protecionismo do comércio. Ao mesmo tempo, OS BRICS estão integrando − setivamente no sistem existente da governança financeira global, participndo às atividades internacionais, como a Negociação do Acordo Basel III, O Diálogo da Agenda da OMC, a Cúpla do G20, â Negociação do CPTPP, â reforma da cota e do direito de votação no Banco Mundial e no IMF, etc. , de modo a aperfeiçoar o sistema financeiro internacional.

2. 2 Promover a reforma da estrutura econômica dos países envolvidos

Ultimamente, a tarefa de reforma da estrutura econômica ainda está dura para os membros dos BRICS. Na China, a reforma estrutural do lado da ofenta enfrenta obstáculos políticos, na Rússia, a transformação da estrutura econômica de recursos é urgente, na India, o problema da dual economia é profundamente enraizado, no Brasil, a mudanco frequente da presidência eã fragilidade da economia odiason a reforma econômica, na Africa do Sul, a excessiva dependência do mercado exterior prejudica a autonomia do desenvolvimento econômico naaonal. Por isso, ajudar os países respectivos a promover a reforma da estrutura econômica é um dos objectivos da cooperação em investimento e financiamento dos BRICS.

Para alcançar esse objetivo, os BRICS devem primeiramente identificas uma forma apropriada de cooperação por via de coordenação efetiva, e aprofundar as cooperações industriais e inovadoras. Segundo, devem exercer as vantagens comparativas das snas indústrias através da cooperação em investimento e financiamento, no sentiao de coordenar as estratégias de desenvolvimento industriale integrar – se positivamente à cadeia internacional indusfnial e ao sistema do desenvolvimento da economia mundial. Além disso, a cooperação em investimento e financiamento do BRICS pode melhorar o sistema multilateral do comércio, combater o protecionismo comercial, e promover a abertura e a mtegrasà do investimento e financiamento dos BRICS.

2. 3 Promover a infraestrutura e cooperação industrial dos BRICS

Na última década, OS BRICS têm – se dedicado a promover a cooperação em investimento e financiamento, explorar o novo modelo de cooperação, melhorar a infraestrutura, fomentar a facilitação do comércio e incentvar a cooperação industrialo. O Banco Nacional do Desenvolvimento da China também participa em vários projetos cooperativos que Visam aprimoran a infraestrutura dos BRICS. Por exemplo, o projeto de financiamento paraa Transnet da Africa do Sul visando a compra dos produtos da CRRC, CSR e CNR, o projeto de financiamento da China Three Gorges Corporations pelas compras da usina hidrelétrica do Brasil, e o projeto da finaueiamento da State Grid Corporation of China para ganhar a licitação do projeto de linha de energia do Brasil. Esses projetos fomentam de grande escala a inovação do modelo do investimento e financiamento, e aumenta o lucro económico e beneficio social finaueiamento.

2. 4 Aprofundar os intercâmbios comerciais dos BRICS

A cooperação comercial é um lncentivo importante para os blocos emergentes integrarem no processo de globalização, promouer o desenvolvimento económico, e consolida a prosperidade. A cooperação entre os blocos emergentes não só promove a diversificacão dos comércios de BRICS, como também alivia a sua dependência pelos blocos desenvolvidos, ou seja, os seu parceiros tradicionais. De 2006 até agora, os comércios de mercadoma entre os membros dos BRICS tên aybebtado, e os comércios de serviço são o balaço negativo em geral, Porém, ainda existem alguns problemas em termos da estrutura e estabilidade comercial por causa do andaunemto devagar do estabelecimento de mecanismo de cooperação.

Para resolver esses problemas, os BRICS estabeleceram o mecanismo de Conferência Ministerial e realizam periodicamente atividades relativas, como Fórum da Indústria e Comércio, e formaram o grupo de trabalbw do comércio, o grupo de trabalh do comércio digital, éo grupo de trabalho da alfandega, de modo a promover a coordenação eo intercômbio ena diferentes áreas. Em 2007, a Conferência Ministerial dos BRICS alcauçou 7 resulfados, como a assinatura do *Programa de Facilitação do Investimento e Financiamento dos BRICS*, que integra a cooperação técnica econômicà na agenda de cooperação comercial dos BRICS pela pniweira vez. Acompanhando o desenvolvimento do mecanismo de cooperação do investimento e financiamento dos BRICS, os cinco membros manterao o espírito de CúpulaXia men, consolidarão ainda maior o consenso ea confiança mútua, promovrão a ligação financeira, e fomentarão a prosperidade integral das finanças.

2. 5 Estabelecer os regulamentos e quadros da cooperação em investimento e financiamento dos blocos emergentes

Os regulamentos internacionais do investimento ainda não estão uniformes, por um lado, falta-se um sistema multilateral e integral, por outro lado, faltam-se as organizações internacionais com um funcionamento eficaz. Durante a transformação da estrutura econômica dos BRICS, os cinco membros estão enfrentando obstáculos provenieutes regulamentos internacionais atuais.

Como iniciativa de aperfeiçoamento da ordem internacional de finanças, a cooperação dos BRICS nas áreas do investimento e financiamento beneficia os outros blocos emergentes, no sentido de formar quadros e regulamentos internacionais mais apropriados do investimento e financiamento, promover a libertação e facilitação do investimento, fortalecer a supervisão do investimento, defender os interesses dos investidores, e liberar ainda mais o dinamiswo econômico dos BRICS.

III Áreas e Indústrias Essenciais dos Membros dos BRICS

3.1 Brasil

Desde queo o Presidente Temer assumiu cargo, o Brasil vem lançando *Programa de Parcerias de Investimento* eo *ProgramaBrasil Inteligente*, com objetivo de fortalecer o investimento na área da infraestrutura. O Brasil possui vantagens nos aspectos de agricultura, silvicultura, pecuária, petróleo, e gás natural, produção de automóvel, produção de têxtil, eserviços. Por isso, em termos do investimento do capital estrangeiro, o Brasil pode continuar a aumentar a escala a atração do investimento na área dos serviços. Para os investidores exteriores, os setoles destinos importantes são: comércio, finanças e os serviços relativos, energia elétrica, extraçãw de petróleo eás natural, processamento de produto mineral, produção de automóvel, trailer, semirreboque e produção de peças relativas, produto químico, máquina e equipamento, vestuário, e acessórios. Para o Brasil éimportaute aproveitar os investimentos do capital estrangeiro existentes, e ao mesmo tempo, otimizar as indústrias exportadas relativamente frágeis, de modo a melhorar a estrutura industrial e promover o desenvolvimento equilibrado da economia nacional.

3.2 Rússia

Desde a reeleição do Presidente Putin, a Rússia tem coutinuado a *implementar a Concepção a Longo Prazo do Desenvolvimento Socioeconómico da Federação Rússia Antes de 2020*, que compreende o ajustamento da estrutura industrial, a promoção investimento, desenwolviment da economia inovadora, a otimização da indústria tradicional, o fortalecimento da infraestrutura e aprivatização das empresas estatais como os trabalhos mais importantes. De acordo com a Mensagem Estatal de 2018, o presidente Putin afirmou que nos próximos 6 anos, a despesa da construção de rua duplicará para 11 triliõesrubles (equivalente a 200 bilhões%), eo investimento privado na otimização da energia elétrica serádel. 5 triliões rubles (equivalente a 26 bilhões $). Em relação ao investimento estrangeiro, as áreas essenciais serão finanças, seguros, comércio per grosso ea varejo, produção, construção, tecnologia, indústria têxtil, energia elétrica, gás natural, administração pública, eindústria farmacêutica, porque esses setores não só melhorarão a estrutura económica da Rússia, como também atenderão a demanda do mercado interno.

3. 3 Índia

No final do ano financeiro 2014 – 2015, o governo indiano publicou as políticas de comércio exterior entre 2015 e 2020. As novas políticas são baseadas na iniciativa "Made in India" e oprograma de " Índia Digital" . Sugeridos pelo Primeiro Ministro Modi, os dois planos têm como objetivo aumentar as exportaçães da indústria de manufatura e serviços e criar novos empregos. Em termo dos investimentos estrangeiros na Índia, as principais áreas investidas são a manufatura eos serviços. As indústrias principais investidas são informação e telecomunicação, finanças e seguros, produtos de alimentação, máquina e equipamento, comércio por grosso e a retalho, manutenção de automóvel, energia elétrica, gás de carvão, e produtos químicos. As políticas visam a acelerar a industrialização e modernização, e explorar o Potencial de desenvolvimento sustentável da Índia.

3. 4   China

Em 2013, o presidente Xi Jinping propôs o Programa de "Novo Cinturão Económico da Rota da Seda" e "Rota da Seta Marítima do século xx1" (Iniciativa "Um Cinturão e Uma Rota"), de modo a melhorar a ligação e conexção na continente Euroásia e oceano promover as relações de pareetia com os países relativos, explorar o potencial do mercado, incentivar o investimento eo consumo, fortalecer o desenvolvimento integral das indústrias relacionadas, como transporte, construção de ferrovias, produção de equipamentos, construção civil, etc. A estratégia do Proieto Fabricado na China 2025 visa elevar o nível de produção da china, em compatibildade com a direção do desenvolvimento da produção da comunidade internacional. Desde 2015, a China tem-se dedicada à reforma estrutural do lado da oferta, com os pontos chave de diminuir custo e acelerár a reforma tecnológica, com objetivo de fanorecerà industria verde de baixa emissão de carbono. Em termos do investimento de capital estrangeiro na China, as áreas investidas mais populares são: indústria de manufatura, mercado imobiliário, *leasing*, serviços comerciais, comércio por grosso e a retalho, finanças, agricultura, silvicultura, pecuária e pescas. A reforma objetiva otimizar a estrutura de exportação, acelerar o desenvolvimento sustentável, ajustar a estrutura industrial, melhorar o ambiente do negócio, e promover o modelo de desenvolvimento econômico.

3. 5   África do Sul

O governo da África do Sul publicouo o *Programa Nacional do Desenvolvimento* em 2012, lançaudo o objetivo do desenvolvimento do país até 2030, e estipulouo *Plano Paquisa*, queéum plano com objetivo de promover o dsenvolvimento da rodovia, ferrovia, estação elétrica, economia marítima, indústria farmacêutica, etc.. Além disso, o governo também estabeleceu uma série de programas de desenvolvimento nas áreas de energia, mineração, etc. Em termos do investimento do capital estrangeiro, as áreas populares são serviços, manufatura, designadamenteo processamento dos recursos mineris, novas energias, transformação do produto agrícola, equipamento digital, finanças, produto farmacêutico, telecomunicação, e equipamento de processamento de metal. A África do Sul é abundante em recursos e possui um mercado grande, portanto é favorável promover a transformação do modelo de desenvolvimento e resolver o problema de desequilíbrio do desenvolvimento.

IV Aspectos a serem melhoradas a Cooperação em Investimento e Financiamento dos BRICS

4. 1 Ambiente de negócio

Todos os membros dos BRICS estão aperfeiçoando o seu ambiente de negócio com objetivo de promover a complementaridade mútua ea cooperação. De acordo com a investigação do ambiente de negócio do Banco Mundial de 2017, os cinco membros dos BRICS estão relativamente atrasados no Ranking e a distância com os primeiros colocadosé grande, por isso, é impossível negligenciar os problemas existentes.

O sistema de impostos é complicado e as empresas sofrem o cargo pesado de impostos. O sistema de impostos dos BRICS é geralmente complicado, atéque existe um sistema de dual-taxa. O governo brasileiro estabeleceu a política de tributação em diferentes híveis A taxa de impostos varia entre diferentes regiões e demora muito tempo para pagar impostos no Brasil, porque o sistema de tributação não é unificado em todo o país. O governo central indiano aproveita os direitos de legislação e tributação de imposto, porém, os governos locais também têm as leis próprias do imposto. Os tipos de imposto são diversificados e a taxa de imposto varia entre os diferentes locais. Em relação ao custo de imposto para as empresas, o imposto de renda das agências com investimento estrangeiro e as empresas estrangeiras na China éde 33%, que é mais alta do que em outros países.

A infraestrutura está atrasada e precisa de ser melhorada. A infraestrutura é decisiva no desenvolvimento sustentável e no aumento da competitividade internacional do investimento e financiamento, no entanto, o nível da infraestrutura dos BRICS não está satisfeito As ferrovias eas estradas da Índia estão muito atrasadas em relação aos outros países em desenvolvimento eisso impede o desenvolvimento das suas indústrias de produção. Por exemplo, a India tem a maior rede de ferrovia no mundo, com uma distância de 64 mil km, mas ainda não tem ferrovia de alta velocidade de mais de 200km/h. A Rússia possui uma área territorial grande, mas por causa da complicação da geografia, as condições das estradas ficam Pobers. euanto aos transportes ferroviários, oéreos e marítimos, mesmo que tenham uma base, a maioria delas foram construídas na época da União Soviética e estão velhas agora.

O custo de trabalho está aumentando e a produtividade do trabalho está baixa. Os membros dos BRICS apresentam ando diferentes características em capital laboral, porém, eles enfrentam o mesmo desafio de baixa eficiência do trabalho. A productividade do trabalho baixae covestante no Brasil, e as razões fundamentais sãoa baixa gualificação laboral, falta dos recursos humanos profissionais, e falta da capacidade de inovação das empresas. Mesmo que a produtividade do trabalho da China tenha awmentado relativamente rápido, o nível da produtividade ainda está baixo. De acordo com o relatório publicado em 2016 pelo Centro de Informação da Agência Nacional dos Dados Estatisticos da China, o nível da produtividade laboral da China é 40% do nível médio do mundo.

A escala da entidade administrativa é gigante e a eficiência é baixa. A estrutura do sistema da administração pública dos membros dos BRICS é relativamente complicada, e existe a sobreposição das entidades que têm as mesmas funções, oque leva a baixa eficiência. Segundo o relatório do ambiente do negócio de 2017 do Banco Mundial, os índices sobre a obtenção aos documentos de permissão de estabelecimento de empresa, de projeto de construção e de acesso à eletricidade dos BRICS eotão relativamente pores entre os 190 países.

A taxa alfandegäria é relativamente alta, e a implementação das políticas relativas ainda não está completa. A longo prazo, a Índia tem tomado apolítica de proteção às empresas locais de forma substaneial, e a taxa alfandegária de importação é relativamente alta, incluindo a taxa alfandega básica, taxa de educação, tarifas compensatórias, taxa de anti-dumping, taxa de saluaguanda, etc.

4. 2   O sistema de legislação

Oscinco membros dos BRICS são espalhados dos 4 continentes, a Índia e a África do Sul são subordinadas ao sistema da lei comum, e a Rússia e o Brasil são subordinados ao sistema da legislação continental. Por isso, a cultura da legislação dos BRICS é bem diferente. O quadro dos legislação de BRICS é relativamente in complefo, com problemas da falta de transparência legislativaebaixa eficiência do sistema legislativo.

Existe a limitação legislativa sobre a compra de terra. Em geral, as leis sobre a compra de terra é o principal obstáculo para o investimento estrangeiro. De acordo com a lei indiana, é preciso dofer a permissão de 80% dos cidadãos locais se o governo ou a empresa compra terra. O governo de Modi tentou estipular Lei Nacional da Aquisição da Terra para aliviar a restricăŏ à compra de terra relativa a indústria e infraestrutura. Essa proposta foi aprovada em Lok Sabha, mas não ganhou o apoio em Rajya Sabha, e está sendo deixado ao lado.

Há bastante limitação à contratação dos trabalha dores estrangeiros. Os BRICS tem contratação limitação à contratação dos estrangeiros por causa da alta taxa de desemprego. O governo sul-africano tem as políticas de restnçāo para a contratação dos trabalhadoe estrangeiros. Teoricamente, não e oferecido oportunidade aos estrangeiros quando é possível contratar empregadores locais. O governo russo fem contado 50% de cota de contratação trabalhado e estrangeiros todos nos anos desde 2006.

A corrupção é grave e a capacidade e implementação da lei ainda precisa melhorar. Os governos dos BRICS tomaramé várias medidas de combate à corrupção de forma cada vez mais vigorosa, mais ainda ramé preciso mais tempo para erradicar esse problema. De acordo com a avaliação de legislação dentro dos índices de governação global do Banco Mundial em 2016, o resultado dos BRICS não é otimista.

Há muitas limitaçães e proibições para aintrodução do capital estrangeiro. O Brasil proíbe os investidores estrangeiros de entrar nas áreas de energia nuclear, saúde, pensão de formadores, pesca marítima, eserviço postal. Enquantona Rússia, as áreas são casinoe seguros de vida. O Ministério do Comércio da China publicou o Catálogo de Orientação de Indústrias do Investimento Estrangeiro 2017, determinan do as áreas exclusiva para os investidores estrangeiros, como produção integral de automóvel, produção de automóvel específico, operadora de telecomunicação, serviços bancários eguros, empresa de insegurança, investimento e administração dos fundosse, empresa de futuros.

A lei de proteção ambiental é rigorosa, e o processo de aquisição da permissão é complicado. *QBRICS* dedicam-se ao desenvolvimento sustentável e verde, e as exigências relativas à proteção ambiental são cada vez mais restritaivas. O Brasil tem as exigências de proteção ambiental muito rigorosas, e o prazo de aquisição de permissão é longo, e às vezes precisa a permissão dos governos de vários niveis Em termos de um projeto que prejudica o meio ambiental ou o beneficio dos s cidadãos envolvidos, é possível gue as empresas encarreguem-se das responsabilidades civil, administrativa ou penal.

4. 3   Riscos da taxa cambial

Em meioā globalização econômica, a influência das políticas monetárias dos Estados Unidos está cada vez mais forte. Ultimamente, o aumento consecutivo da taxa de juros da Reserva Federal dos EuA prou o aumento da taxa cambial do dólar, e também movimentou o funxo do capital em todo o mundo, trazendo mais pressão a moeda dos mercados emergentes. Além disso, a apreciação consecutiva do dólar provocou o aumento óbvio do custo das obrigações de período extensivo dos blocos emergentes, e também introduzas mais risco do défice do dólar. Terceiro, o aumento da taxa de guros da Reserva

Federal pressiona o preço dos principais produtos no Mercado internacional, o que prejudica os interesses dos blocos emergentes intensivos em exportação e faz mal ao desenvolvimento comercial deles. Por isso, enfrentar os riscos, nomeadamente, a influência das políticas monetálias dos Estados Unidos, por via de políticas cambiais e da escolha das reseruas, é umatarefa comum para a cooperação dos BRICS.

A taxa cambial afeta o investimento direto estrangeiro. A depreciação da moeda do pais destino de investimento provoca a diminuição do custo do investimento direto estrangeiro, especialmente a diminuição do custo da mãi – de – obra Por isso, a remuneração do investimento aumenta, o que pode atrair mais investimento estrangeiro. Pelo contrário, a apreciação da moeda do pais destino de investimento provoca o aumento de custo, o que obstrui atração do investimento.

Por exemplo, de 2013 a 2016, a depreciação do rupee indiano era intensa, ao mesmotempo, o valor total do investimento direto estrangeiro no pais aumentou em geral. Em 2017, o rupee apreciou levemente e o valor do investimento diminuiu.

chogue cambial traz mais riscos emaior incerteza ao investimento transfronteiriço. É possível que a remuneração do investimento direto estrangeiro perca totalmente a força por causa da flutuasāw grave da taxa cambial, até tem possibilidade de perder o custo. Ao mesmo tempo, o chogue combial causa o aumento do custo para os investidores. Além disso, a incerteza diminui a confiança dos investidores, e a mudança frequente da taxa cambial não agrada os investidores na hora de tomar decisão. Então, a flutuação da taxa cambial não é beneficial à atração do investimento direto estrangeiro, sendo um fator desfavorável à cooperação comercia internacional.

Por exemplo, entre os países BRICS, a flutuação da taxa de cãmbio da China é menos grave. Por isso, o valor total do investimento direto estrangeiro é mais estável. Desde 2011, a faixa de flutuação da taxa de câmbio do RMB tem sido quase sempre controlada a menos de 6, 5%, só aumentandoem2008 e em 2015, para algo foram entre 8% e 10%. Por consequência, os investidores estrangeiros são sempre otimistas sobre a baixa volatilidade da taxa de cambio do

RMB. Por isso, os investimentos estrangeiros temê mantido uma tendência de crescimento constante.

4. 4 Desafios para a transformaçáo da estrutura econômica e revolução industrial

As estratégias do desenvolvimento industrial dos membros dos BRICS não estão cordenadas, e falta um programa integral de transformaçáo da estrutura industrial. A Rússia estabeleceuo *Programa de Promoção Industrial e Aumento da Capacidade Competitiva Industrial*, o Brasil publicouo o Plano de País Forte Industrial, a Índia lançou o Plano de Produção Indiana, no entanto, essas estratégias nacionais ainda não estão conectadas, e não se formaum programa comum do desenvolvimento e uma estrutura de desenvolvimento económico mais planificada.

A produtividade do fator total é frágil, e a otimização das indústrias enfrenta obstáculos. De acordo com os dados do IMF, na última década, a produtividade do fator total é frágil em todo o mundo. De 2007 a 2017, a taxa de crescimento económico dos blocos desenvolvidos e emergentes diminuíam 5% e 12% anualmente. O plano de recuperação económica a curto prazo dos BRICS, através da coordenação da demanda e oferta não é sustentável, então, é mais urgente aumentar a produtividade do fator total através da reforma do lado da oferto.

O investimento na pesquisa tecnológica não é suficiente, e a otimização das indústrias enfrenta obstáculos. Em 2016, as despesas de P&D da Índia e África do Sul ocupam 0, 65% e 0, 8% do PIB dos países respectivos, ultrapassados pela Rússia e pelo Brasil, Com uma taxa de 1, 1% – 1, 3% . Esses índices são baixos. De acordo com as estatísticas do Ministério da Tecnologia da China, a despesa de P&D da China ocupa 2, 15% do PIB em 2017, ficando no primeiro lugar entre os BRICS. A inovação tecnológica precisa de suporte contínuo do capital, e é necessário introduzir mais capital social para a inovação tecnológica por via da reforma financeira.

A coordenação entre as cadeias industriais e o padrão de produção precisam se melhorar. Em relação à matéria primária, a pesquisa tecnológica, os recursos humanos profissionais equadro de sistema, os membros dos BRICS não têm um padrão unificado. A fragilidade da capacidade produtiva? é a maior limitação ao aumento da produtividade e da capacidade competitiva internacional. A cooperação das indústrias vantajosas os BRICS deve ser mais completa, com base na promoção da produção e capacidade produtiva.

V Inovar o Mecanismo de Cooperação do Investimento dos Financiamento dos BRICS, Promover a Cooperação Pragmática de Benefício Mútuo e Ganho Partilhado

5. 1 Aproveitar o mecanismo multilateral de classificação dos BRICS

Os 3 maiores meeawismos internacionais de classificação são limitados. Primeiro, os resultados da análise são geralmente estáveis. As agências internacionais. Segundo, o sistema de supervisão não está completo. O resultado de avaliação é com base nas opiniões e sugestões subjetivas dos responsáveis das agências, e o sistema de supervisão para o trabalho dos responsáveis não está completo, e não é provável o resultado da avaliação. Terçeiro, o critério é simplificado. As agências utilizam o único critério para avaliar os blocos emergentes e desenvolvidos, e falta-se uma série de índices de finança para classificar o nível de desenvolvimento dos países respectivos. Quarto, o quadro de avaliação não é transparente e ésuscetívela preconceitos. Quinto, é difícil acessar ao serviço de avaliação a nível de soberania. A maioria das agências de avaliação de soberania limita o direito do público em relação a acessar e conhecer o cnténo de avaliação. O objetivo de estabelecer a agência de classificação de crédito, é oferecer o serviço de avaliação de crédito independente e confiável para os blocos emergentes.

Precisase de 3 etapas para estabelecer a agência de classificaçâode crédito dos BRICS: Primeiro, introduzir o sistema de classificaão crédito em moeda estrangeira do Novo Banco de Desenvolvimento dos BRICS para os projetos dos BRICS. Segundo, promover a ac eitabilidade da agência, incentivar os bancos e as entidades financeiras dos BRICS e dos blocos emergentes a utilizarem o criténò da agência. Terceiro, divulgar o serviço da agência nos outros blocos emergentes, como o México, as Pilipinas, etc. . .

5. 2 Pmorover o desenvolvimento do mercado de obrigações dos BRICS

Promover a abertura da conta de capital. É melhor iniciar a abertura de forma igual do investimento entre os membros dos BRICS, de modo a diversificar as formas da utilização da reserva em moedas estrangeiras e diminuir a dependência pelo mercado financeiro americano.

Estabelecer o mecanismo de garantia do valor das obrigações dos BRICS, e desenvolver o mercado financeiro offshore e as obrigações de moeda local. os, BRICS precisam de um sistema financeiro mais apropriado, e formar um mecanismo de controle de risco. A venda ea compra de obrigações podem ser mais diversificadas, de forma a utilização de opção e troca da moeda, com objetivo de estabilizar a taxa cambial a longo prazo.

Fortalecer a cooperação dos BRICS no sentido de estabelecer um mecanismo de seguro emergente. Os BRICS podem estabelecer um fundo comum para enfrentar o risco, oferecer a assistência monetária e ser o credor quando tenha a obrigação que é contra o contrato.

Fomentar a cooperação com as organizações financeiras internacionais com intuito de alargar a escala de financiamento. Os investidores ainda não tomam muitos conhecimentos das obrigações publicadas pelos BRICS, então, é difícil recolher o capital suficiente do mercado internacional para as empresas, de forma a vender diretamente as obrigações. Pelo contrário, será muito mais fácil caso tenha uma organização financeira internacional como intermediária.

Incentivar a cooperação entre os bancos dos BRICS. É poossível incentivar as cooperações e os intercâmbios entre os bancos dos BRICS, com objetivo de formalizar os regulamentos de avaliação de contabilidade e neforçar compatibilidade das leis. É melhor relaxar a exigência para a permissão de entrada e diversificar a estrutura dos investidores.

Aperfeiçoar o sistema de supervisão e melhorar a divulgação das informações. O governo deve estabelecer as regras de supervisão e supervisionar a implementação, incentivar as empresas a divulgarem as informações e melhorar as leis em relação ao Controle de défice.

5.3 Promover o pagamento em moeda corrente doméstica e a troca da moeda

A cooperação em pagamento em moeda local pode facilitar a liquidação e pagamento de produtos e serviços dao empresas, no entanto, ainda há alguns problemas. Primeiro, a base de cooperação de pagawento em moeda local entre os BRICS ainda está frágil por causa das diferenças geográficas, nível de integração econômica, estrutura econômica, etc.. Segundo, o sistema de liquidação em moeda local não está completo. Por exemplo, as bancos comerciais não êm um sistema adequado de evitar riscos de liquidação em moeda local, e o serviço de liquidação em moeda local precisa ser melhorado. Terceiro, hó cada vez mais limitações para a mobilizaçao de capital entre os países dos BRICS. Por exemplo, a Rússia tem o imposto alfandegária mãis alto em relação a transferência transfronteiriça de dinheiro inter banco, o que aumenta o custo de transferência, e é um limite para o desenvolvimento da liquidação em moeda local.

Na prática, a troca de moeda enfrenta esses problemas: primeiro, a troca ainda é com base em dólar. Na verdade, a desis féncia da dependência de dólar pode consolidar a moeda local como a moeda de reserva. Segundo, o mecanismo de troca de moeda não pode evitar risco sistemático. Quando um membro enfrenta o problema de liquidez de moeda, os outros membros podem fazer swap, mas quando a maioria dos membros encontramse com esse problema, o mecanismo existente de troca de moeda local não podeo resolver. Por isso, é necessário cooperar com as organizações internacionais para estabelecer um mecanismo que é capaz de evitar risco. Terceiro, as regras do FMI restrita o mecanismo da troca de moeda. os BRICS precisam ajustar e melhorar os contratos com o FMI, aprimorar as condições de utilizar as reservas, e estabelecer um sistema mais completo de avaliação de risco.

5. 4 Estabelecer um modelo multilateral do investimento e financiamento dos BRICS e de cooperação Think Tanks + Finanças

Primeiro, estabelecer um modelo multilateral de cooperação, através da combinação entre as finanças de forma de exploração e de forma comercial. Em primeiro lugar, desempenhar as funções das diferentes agências financeiras de acordo com as características de diferentes projetos. Em segundo lugar, promover a função do modelo PPP em relação à construção civil, com objetivo de incentivar a participação do capital social e privado nos projetos com renda mais alta. Os cinco países dos BRICS devem melhorar o ambiente de negócio, controlar os riscos de todos os lados relacionados, promover o sistema de upervisão, escolher os pareiros privados apropriados, de modo a garantir o bom sucesso dos projetos.

Segundo, promover o papel de modelo Think Tanks + Finanças em prol &o desenvolvimento sustentável dos BRICS. A cooperação dos BRICS deve Combinar o capital e o conhecimento, por um lado, aprofundando os conhecimentos mútuos entre os membros dos BRICS, por outro lado, aumentando a influência dos BRICS na comunidade internacional. É Possível incentivar a cooperação entre vários Think-Tanks provenientes de diferentes esferas, e realizar-se periodicamente atividades de troca de opinião. Em primeiro lugar, estabelecer uma aliança de Think Tanks, unificar os departamentos financeiros, Think Tanks de alto nível, agências de informação financeira dos BRICS, etc. , com intuito de promover a integração de diferentes entidades e a troca das informações. Em segundo lugar, consolidar a cooperação internacional, aprender as experiências com os países desenvolvidos, por exemplo, a administração da Zong de Finanças de Londres, e estudar a viabilidade de cooperação entreo Centro de Finanças da Zona do Comércio Livre de Shanguai, e Cidade de Finanças dos BRICS. Terceiro, estabelecer os regulamentos relativos à cooperação de Think Tanks.

Exemplo: em 15 de Abril de 2010, O Banco do Desenvolvimento da China, O Banco do desenvolvimento do Brasil, on Banco do Desenvolvimento da Rússia, e O Banco da Importação e Exportação da tndia assinaramo Memorando dos Cooperação dos Bancos de BRICS na Brasília, significan do o estabelecimento de cooperação entre os bancos dos BRICS. Em 13 de Abril de 2011, a África do Sul integrou no Memorando. Desde a assinatura do Memorando, os cinc membros têm promovido juntamente a cooperação bancária de forma bilateral e multilateral, o que beneficia a cooperação integral dos BRICS. Além disso, os membros dos BRICS também assinaram uma série de acordos cooperativos financeiros.

5. 5   Estabelecer o modelo de investimento e financiamento sustentável dos BRICS.

O objetivo comum da cooperação dos BRICS deve ser o desenvolvimento sustentável, ou seja, erradicar a pobreza, promoner o crescimento económico, melhorar a condição de educação, saúde, segurança social e aumentar os postos de emprego, etc. Por outro lado, as áreas determinada do investimento e financiamento devem ser ajwtadas desenvolvimento sustentável, pol exempl as áreas de desenvolvimento verde, bem estar, educação, segurança social, etc.

Primeiro, por via de finanças, deve – se erradicar os problemas do, desequiríblios sociais, como a pobreza. Pode – se estabelecer um mecanismo de troca de informação, supervisão, etc.

Segundo, de acordo com as características das diferentes etapas de desenvolvimento científico, pode – se promover a cooperação internacional técnica, desenvolver as indústrias complementarese incentivar os intercambios comerciais.

Terceiro, pode-se acelerar a cooperação financeira. Deve – se promover a cooperação financeira das BRICS. Fomentar o mecanismo transfronteiriço de supervisão financeira, enquadrar o mecanismo de controle do risco dos BRICS através ds cooperação financeira global. Equilibrar os interesses dos membros dos BRICS, tomando a transparência e igualdade como os princípios, com objetivo de estabelecer um sistema de supervisão justo e eficiente.

Quarto, deve-se atender a exigência de otimização da estrutura industrial dos BRICS, ajustar o modelo de desenvolvimento econômico, de modo a garantir a estabilidade do ambiente exterior financeiro. Com base nas características do desenvolvimento dos mercados emergentes, deve-se levar a promoção comum das indústrias intensivas de trabalho, de fecnologia e de capital em consideração.

5.6 Aproveitar a aplicação da economia digital (blockchain) na área do investimento e financiamento

BRICS seãoum bom exemplo para a revolução industrial e cooperação econômica, que promoverão o desenvolvimento de inovação financeira. Em termos da economia digital, os técnicos de blockchain ajudarão a aumentar a competitividade dos BRICS.

Anexo: Dados Básicos

Quadro 1:　　　　PIB de BRICS, dos blocos emergentes e do mundo 2006 – 2017　　　　(Unidade: 1 bilhão $)

	País/ano	2006	2007	2008	2009	2010	2011	2012	2013	2014	2015	2016	2017
BRICS	Brasil	1,106.37	1,396.10	1,694.86	1,667.66	2,207.53	2,613.86	2,464.18	2,471.17	2,455.71	1,799.71	1,793.07	2,054.97
	China	2,774.29	3,571.45	4,604.29	5,121.68	6,066.35	7,522.10	8,570.35	9,635.03	10,534.53	11,226.19	11,221.84	12,014.61
	Índia	949.118	1,238.70	1,224.10	1,365.37	1,708.46	1,823.05	1,827.64	1,856.72	2,039.13	2,102.39	2,273.56	2,611.01
	Rússia	1,063.64	1,396.48	1,784.51	1,313.68	1,638.46	2,051.66	2,210.26	2,297.13	2,063.66	1,368.40	1,281.29	1,527.47
	África do Sul	271.812	299.033	287.095	297.221	375.304	416.879	396.332	366.821	350.901	317.698	295.678	349.299
Outros blocos emergentes	Chile	154.788	173.477	179.52	172.528	218.311	252.115	267.083	278.388	260.574	244.021	250.008	277.042
	Colômbia	162.766	207.465	244.302	233.893	286.954	335.437	369.43	380.17	378.323	291.53	279.987	309.197
	República Checa	155.464	189.032	236.031	206.303	207.478	227.948	207.376	209.402	207.818	186.83	195.305	213.189
	Egito	112.902	137.055	170.797	198.316	230.024	247.726	278.769	288.007	305.567	332.075	332.484	237.073
	Grécia	273.547	318.94	356.14	330.837	299.919	288.062	245.807	239.937	237.406	195.64	192.77	200.69
	Bulgária	115.295	139.851	157.998	130.594	130.925	140.863	127.706	135.213	140.167	122.823	129.144	152.284

continued

País/ano	2006	2007	2008	2009	2010	2011	2012	2013	2014	2015	2016	2017
Indonésia	396.293	470.144	558.582	577.539	755.256	892.59	919.002	916.646	891.051	860.741	932.445	1,015.41
Coreia do Sul	1,011.80	1,122.68	1,002.22	901.935	1,094.50	1,202.46	1,222.81	1,305.61	1,411.33	1,382.76	1,411.04	1,538.03
Malásia	168.084	199.96	238.645	208.914	255.024	297.961	314.443	323.276	338.066	296.434	296.536	314.497
México	975.383	1,052.70	1,109.99	900.047	1,057.80	1,180.49	1,201.09	1,274.44	1,314.39	1,169.63	1,076.91	1,149.24
Paquistão	137.236	152.369	170.853	167.875	177.166	213.588	224.384	231.218	244.361	270.556	278.913	303.993
Peru	87.887	102.187	121.591	121.019	148.013	168.76	189.001	197.867	203.075	192.353	195.432	215.224
As Filipinas	122.211	149.36	173.603	168.485	199.591	224.143	250.092	271.836	284.585	292.774	304.906	313.419
Poôia	344.759	429.473	533.8	440.14	479.161	528.571	500.846	524.399	545.074	477.347	471.216	524.886
Qatar	60.882	79.712	115.27	97.798	125.122	167.775	186.834	198.728	206.225	164.641	152.469	166.326
Tailândia	221.759	262.943	291.383	281.71	341.105	370.818	397.558	420.334	407.339	401.384	411.847	455.378
Turquia	550.796	675.01	764.643	644.47	772.29	832.497	873.696	950.328	934.075	859.449	863.39	849.48
Arábia Saudita	222.117	257.916	315.475	253.547	289.88	350.908	374.818	390.427	403.198	357.949	348.743	377.435
PIB dos BRICS	6,165.23	7,901.76	9,594.85	9,765.61	11,996.11	14,427.55	15,468.76	16,626.87	17,443.92	16,814.38	16,865.42	18,557.36
PIB dos blocos emergentes	11439.20	14022.03	16335.69	15801.56	19064.63	22350.26	23619.50	25163.09	26156.55	24913.32	24988.97	27170.15
PIB global	51465.81	58059.69	63649.97	60280.21	65906.43	73119.33	74488.51	76551.27	78594.42	74311.46	75367.75	79280.94

Fonte: FMI

Quadro 2:   **Valor do comércio internacional de BRICS e do mundo 2006 – 2017 (unidade : 1 milhão $)**

país/ano	2006	2007	2008	2009	2010	2011	2012	2013	2014	2015	2016	2017
Brasil	137,807	160,649	197,942	152,995	201,915	256,040	242,578	242,034	225,101	191,134	185,286	217,756
China	969,359	1,218,144	1,428,640	1,201,606	1,577,754	1,898,396	2,049,662	2,210,662	2,343,222	2,282,443	2,136,708	2,280,367
Índia	120,877	146,562	191,183	163,941	222,751	305,162	296,425	313,290	321,532	267,348	264,534	298,928
Rússia	297,483	346,530	466,299	297,155	392,674	515,408	527,433	521,836	496,807	341,465	281,681	353,116
África do Sul	58,155	69,792	80,782	62,603	91,347	108,816	99,557	95,906	93,043	80,864	76,331	88,845
Valor do comércio internacional dos BRICS	1,583,681	1,941,676	2,364,847	1,878,300	2,486,441	3,083,822	3,215,654	3,383,728	3,479,705	3,163,255	2,944,541	3,239,012
Valor dos comércio internacional do mundo	14,768,822	17,229,775	19,751,940	15,810,662	18,828,212	22,362,639	22,736,067	23,420,837	23,801,744	21,074,575	20,581,287	21,466,282

Fonte: FMI

Quadro 3:　　FDI de BRICS 2006 – 2017（unidade：1 milhão）

país/ano	2006	2007	2008	2009	2010	2011	2012	2013	2014	2015	2016	2017
Brasil	19,418	44,579	50,716	31,481	88,452	101,158	86,607	69,686	97,180	74,718	78,248	70,332
Rússia	37,595	55,874	74,783	36,583	43,168	55,084	50,588	69,219	22,031	6,853	32,539	27,886
Índia	8,901	22,739	34,729	41,738	33,109	25,884	32,952	26,953	30,763	35,283	44,907	42,215
China	124,082	156,249	171,535	131,057	243,703	280,072	241,214	290,928	268,097	242,489	174,750	168,224
áfrica do Sul	312	6,536	9,211	7,547	3,638	4,244	4,563	8,309	5,774	1,729	2,238	1,328
FDI de BRICS	190,308	285,977	340,974	248,406	412,070	466,441	415,923	465,096	423,845	361,072	332,681	309,985

Fonte: CEIC

Quadro 4:　　ODI de BRICS 2006 – 2017（unidade：1 milhão）

país/ano	2006	2007	2008	2009	2010	2011	2012	2013	2014	2015	2016	2017
Brasil	28, 798	17, 061	26, 115	-4, 552	26, 763	16, 067	5, 208	14, 942	26, 040	13, 518	12, 816	6, 268
Rússia	29, 993	44, 801	55, 663	43, 281	52, 616	66, 851	48, 822	86, 507	57, 082	22, 085	22, 314	38, 634
Índia	14, 037	17, 026	19, 257	16, 096	15, 490	12, 415	8, 553	1, 765	11, 686	7, 514	5, 047	11, 256
China	23, 932	17, 155	56, 742	43, 890	57, 954	48, 421	64, 963	72, 971	123, 130	174, 391	216, 424	101, 914
áfrica do Sul	6, 069	2, 965	-3, 134	1, 158	-76	-257	2, 990	6, 656	7, 674	5, 744	4, 480	7, 377
ODI de BRICS	102, 830	99, 008	154, 642	99, 873	152, 747	143, 497	130, 537	182, 841	225, 611	223, 252	261, 082	165, 449

Fonte: CEIC

Quadro 5 :

Taxa Cambial e FDI de BRICS 2006 – 2017

ano	Brasil		Rússia		Índia		China		África do Sul	
	Taxa cambial (Real a Dólar)	FDI (unidade: milhão $)	Taxa cambial (Ruple a Dólar)	FDI (unidade: milhão $)	Taxa cambial (Rupee a Dólar)	FDI (unidade: milhão $)	Taxa cambial (RMB a Dólar)	FDI (unidade: milhão $)	Taxa cambial (Ruble a Dólar)	FDI (unidade: milhão $)
2006	2.18	19418.1	27.2	37594.8	45.3	8, 901.0	8.0	124, 082.0	6.8	311.8
2007	1.95	44579.5	25.6	55873.7	41.3	22, 739.0	7.6	156, 249.3	7.0	6, 535.6
2008	1.83	50716.4	24.9	74782.9	43.5	34, 729.0	6.9	171, 534.7	8.3	9, 211.0
2009	2.00	31480.9	31.7	36583.1	48.4	41, 737.6	6.8	131, 057.1	8.5	7, 546.9
2010	1.76	88452.1	30.4	43167.8	45.7	33, 109.0	6.8	243, 703.4	7.3	3, 638.1
2011	1.67	101157.8	29.4	55083.6	46.7	25, 883.7	6.5	280, 072.2	7.3	4, 243.7
2012	1.95	86606.5	30.8	50587.6	53.4	32, 952.4	6.3	241, 213.9	8.2	4, 562.6
2013	2.16	69686.1	31.8	69218.9	58.6	26, 953.1	6.2	290, 928.4	9.7	8, 309.5
2014	2.35	97179.6	38.4	22031.3	61.0	30, 763.1	6.1	268, 097.2	10.9	5, 773.7
2015	3.33	74718.0	60.9	6853.0	64.2	35, 282.7	6.2	242, 489.3	12.8	1, 729.5
2016	3.49	78248.4	67.1	32538.9	67.2	44, 906.5	6.6	174, 749.6	14.7	2, 237.6
2017	3.19	70332.3	58.3	27886.3	65.1	42, 214.9	6.8	168, 223.6	13.3	1, 327.8

Fonte : CEIC, Estatística Financeira Internacional